Congress, Progressive Reform, and the New American State

This study contributes to the ongoing attempt to trace the lineage of the modern American state. An understanding of the dynamics of state building requires attention to the progressive reform movements that influenced American politics during the early twentieth century and to the congressional decision-making process out of which the new governing institutions emerged. *Congress, Progressive Reform, and the New American State* provides detailed case studies of congressional legislation relating to railroad regulation, labor relations, and social policy and analyzes party and faction divisions in the House and Senate. It finds evidence of a fairly cohesive movement on the part of Congressmen from the South and Midwest to extend the regulatory powers of the federal government. However, many congressional progressives had serious reservations about the creation of powerful, partially autonomous regulatory agencies, and at key points their misgivings weakened the reforming impetus. Moreover, in rebelling against the disciplines of party government, the progressives themselves damaged the major source of central direction in congressional policymaking. Progressive reform undermined the system of party government without displacing it, ensuring that the modern American state would be a hybrid structure in which newer forms of governance coexisted with elements drawn from the older "state of courts and parties."

Robert Harrison is a Lecturer in History at the University of Wales, Aberystwyth, where he teaches history and American studies. His most recent book is *State and Society in Twentieth-Century America*, and he has published articles in several journals, including the *Journal of Urban History* and *American Nineteenth Century History*.

Congress, Progressive Reform, and the New American State

ROBERT HARRISON

University of Wales, Aberystwyth

CAMBRIDGE
UNIVERSITY PRESS

PUBLISHED BY THE PRESS SYNDICATE OF THE UNIVERSITY OF CAMBRIDGE
The Pitt Building, Trumpington Street, Cambridge, United Kingdom

CAMBRIDGE UNIVERSITY PRESS
The Edinburgh Building, Cambridge CB2 2RU, UK
40 West 20th Street, New York, NY 10011-4211, USA
477 Williamstown Road, Port Melbourne, VIC 3207, Australia
Ruiz de Alarcón 13, 28014 Madrid, Spain
Dock House, The Waterfront, Cape Town 8001, South Africa

http://www.cambridge.org

First published 2004

Printed in the United States of America

Typeface Sabon 10/12 pt.   *System* LATEX 2$_\varepsilon$ [TB]

A catalog record for this book is available from the British Library.

Library of Congress Cataloging in Publication Data

Harrison, Robert, 1944–
Congress, progressive reform, and the new American state / Robert Harrison.
   p.   cm.
Includes bibliographical references and index.
ISBN 0-521-82789-2
   1. United States. Congress – History – 20th century.   2. United States. Congress – Powers
and duties – History – 20th century.   3. Progressivism (United States politics) – History –
20th century.   4. Legislative power – United States – History – 20th century.   5. United
States – Politics and government – 1901–1953.   6. Legislation – United States – Cases.
I. Title.
JK1041.H37   2004
320′ .6′ 09730-041–dc21   2003055310

ISBN 0 521 82789 2 hardback

Contents

Tables

Preface

"Please send me a few of those publications that are printed by the Government," a constituent in search of free reading matter asked his Congressman. "I particularly want some of those eloquent eulogies that are delivered in Congress, because I dearly like to read about a dead Congressman."[1] It is to be hoped that the readers of this book will share at least some of that gentleman's fascination with the behavior of dead Congressmen. It may seem that another element in the title, progressive reform, is, as a historiographical quantity, hardly less moribund than the honorable gentlemen over whom valedictory addresses were read on the floor of the House of Representatives. What twenty or thirty years ago was a veritable historiographical boom area has become a kind of ghost town as the vein of scholarship dried up and historians moved on to other, seemingly more profitable, seams. But the territory is not deserted. Its abandonment by historians leaves it open to exploitation by historically minded political scientists interested in such questions as electoral realignment, congressional "modernization," the politics of regulation and the creation of the twentieth-century American state. While they do not always use the term, the subjects of their investigations are essentially aspects of what was once called "progressivism," albeit a rather spectral variety divorced from its corporeal historical context.

The thematic cement for *Congress, Progressive Reform, and the New American State* is formed by combining an older discussion of the character of twentieth-century American liberalism with a newer interest in the process of state making. By investigating critical episodes in the formation of the early twentieth-century American state it attempts to breathe new life into the hoary concept of progressivism. At the same time, through a close examination of progressivism in a national context it seeks to illuminate the conditions under which the foundations of the new American state were laid. This project is founded on the assumption that bringing together these two

[1] *New York Times*, 23 December 1905.

separate discourses is beneficial to both and that this objective can be best achieved through an investigation of progressive reform in the national Congress.

Many debts were incurred in the course of this project. Little could have been accomplished without the support of my colleagues in the Department of History and Welsh History at the University of Wales, Aberystwyth, who over many years have maintained a congenial and supportive atmosphere. In particular, I would like to thank successive Heads of Department, Rhys Davies, John Davidson, and Aled Jones, for their encouragement, sympathy, and sometimes patience. I am indebted for financial assistance for research trips and the purchase of microfilms to the Leverhume Foundation, the British Academy, and the Senate Research Fund of the University of Wales. Staff at numerous libraries and archives facilitated my access to research materials, including in particular the Manuscript Division of the Library of Congress; the State Historical Society of Wisconsin; the Historical Society of Minnesota; the Historical, Memorial and Art Department of Iowa; the Massachusetts Historical Society; the Sterling Library at Yale; and the Washingtoniana Room of the Martin Luther King Memorial Library, Washington, DC. I am grateful in particular to the Inter Library Loan staff at the University's Hugh Owen Library for helping me to overcome the locational disadvantages of living in Aberystwyth.

Most of all I owe a continuing debt to my family, to my wife Jean, and my sons Matthew and Stephen, who through their sometimes startling indifference to early twentieth-century American political development did their best to keep my feet on the ground.

Acknowledgments

Chapter 5 is a revised version of "The Ideal of a Model City: Congress and the District of Columbia, 1905–1909," *Journal of Urban History* 15 (1989): 435–463. I am grateful to Sage Publications Inc. for their kind permission to reproduce this article. Portions of this book draw on material published earlier in my *State and Society in Twentieth-Century America* published by Addison Wesley Longman Limited, 1997, and I am grateful to Pearson Education Limited for permission to make use of this work.

Abbreviations

BDAC	*Biographical Directory of the American Congress, 1789–1911* (Washington: Government Printing Office, 1913)
C.R., 59.1 (etc.)	*Congressional Record*, Fifty-ninth Congress, 1st Session
ANB	John A. Garraty and Mark C. Carnes, eds., *American National Biography* (24 vols., New York: Oxford University Press, 1999)
ISDHA	Iowa State Department of History and Archives
LC	Library of Congress
NA	National Archives
MasHS	Massachusetts Historical Society
METRP	Microfilm Edition of the Theodore Roosevelt Papers, Library of Congress
MinHS	Minnesota Historical Society
SGL	Samuel Gompers Letterbooks, American Federation of Labor Papers, Series 11: Files of the Office of the President, Library of Congress
SHSW	State Historical Society of Wisconsin
SLYU	Sterling Library, Yale University

Congress, Progressive Reform, and the
New American State

I

Introduction

The British novelist H. G. Wells visited Washington, "full of expectations and curiosities," in 1906, during the course of the lengthy Senate deliberations on the Hepburn rate bill. What appeared to confront him as he sat attentively in the visitors' gallery was a scene of unmitigated confusion. While one member spoke, his colleagues wrote letters, noisily rustled newspapers, stood around in "audibly conversational groups," walked carelessly between the speaker and the Chair, and occasionally summoned pages by loudly clapping their hands. The galleries were filled with "hundreds of intermittently talkative spectators." "The countless spectators, the boy messengers, the comings and goings kept up a perpetual confusing bafflement. . . . I have never seen a more distracted legislature." The disorderly scene that he witnessed in the Senate chamber seemed to reflect more fundamental defects in the American constitutional framework and in the organization of Congress itself: "The plain fact of the matter is that Congress, as it is constituted at present, is the feeblest, least accessible, and most inefficient central government of any civilized nation in the world west of Russia. Congress is entirely inadequate to the tasks of the present time."[1]

Wells's negative assessment was shared by other European commentators. Writing a few years earlier, the Russian political scientist Moisei Ostrogorski commented that Congress "does not initiate great measures, it does not solve the problems, the solution of which is demanded by the life of the nation." Likewise, James Bryce, in the 1910 edition of *The American Commonwealth*, noted that Congress made little effort to guide and illuminate its constituents. "It is amorphous, and has little initiative."[2] Frustration with the national legislature was expressed by many Americans, not least those that were

[1] H. G. Wells, *The Future in America* (new edn., London: Granville, 1987), 177 and 181–3.
[2] Moisei Ostrogorski, *Democracy and the Organization of Political Parties* (2 vols., London: Macmillan, 1902), 2:542–6; James Bryce, *The American Commonwealth* (2 vols., London: Macmillan, 1910), 1:304.

professionally obliged to deal with it, like Theodore Roosevelt, who at a White House dinner late in his presidency expressed a desire to turn sixteen lions loose on its members.[3]

Such dismissive comments came easily enough both to executive officers and scholarly observers. Yet they ignore a great deal of constructive legislation produced during this period. Roosevelt himself, a few years earlier, had gladly commended Congress for "the literarily phenomenal amount of good work" that it had performed.[4] The seemingly chaotic process which Wells witnessed in the Senate chamber eventuated in the passage of the Hepburn Act, which did more than almost any other statute to shape the pattern of federal supervision of the railroads and, indeed, the structure of the modern American regulatory state, as well as pure food and meat inspection legislation of comparable significance. That the resulting legislation, like the regulatory framework that it engendered, was seriously flawed can only partially be attributed to the institutional inadequacies of Congress itself; the outcome had a great deal to do with the difficulty of reconciling contesting interests and ideologies and the dynamics of party competition. Nonetheless, we cannot hope to understand the nature of the new American state that emerged from the Progressive Era without appreciating the role of Congress in creating it.

Progressivism and the New American State

As social scientists like Stephen Skowronek and Theda Skocpol have shown, the Progressive Era, which saw both government intervention on a mounting scale and a fundamental recasting of governing arrangements, was a critical moment in the development of a modern American state. The early years of the century saw a considerable enlargement of the regulatory powers of the federal government. Although the states retained jurisdiction over most aspects of governance, it came to be widely accepted that supervising the operations of an increasingly national economy was the responsibility of the national government. It came to be widely accepted also that the task could be most efficiently performed by bureaucratic agencies capable of performing the complex adjustments required in the management of a modern industrial society. Hence the United States began to acquire some of the administrative capacity required by a modern state.

This study contributes to the ongoing attempt to trace the lineages of the modern American state. Why precisely did it appear when it did? What social and political forces drove the process of state formation? How do we

[3] Lawrence F. Abbott, ed., *The Letters of Archie Butt* (Garden City, N.Y.: Page, 1924), 104.

[4] Theodore Roosevelt to James E. Watson, 18 August 1906, in Elting E. Morison et al., eds., *The Letters of Theodore Roosevelt* (8 vols., Cambridge, Mass.: Harvard University Press, 1951–4), 5:372–8.

account for its peculiar characteristics – its distinctive mixture of strength and weakness, purpose and incoherence? This study starts from the premise that it is impossible accurately to comprehend either the origins or the composition of the new American state without considering the time and place of its birth. This requires a close examination of the role of Congress. Capitol Hill, after all, was where the new regulatory agencies came into the world and where their form and functions were largely determined. Because of obvious continuities in its constitutional role and its identification with older patterns of governance, it is easy to forget how critical a role Congress played in the reconstitution of American governance.

A clear understanding of the dynamics of state building also requires some attention to the progressive reform movements that influenced American politics during the early twentieth century. The history of the American state in the last century was closely connected with the fate of liberalism.[5] In order properly to understand its constitution it is important to appreciate that it was a liberal state designed for liberal purposes; more specifically, in the early twentieth century it was a progressive state designed for progressive purposes (leaving aside for the moment precisely what the terms "liberal" and "progressive" signify). We need to identify precisely who were its architects, what were their intentions, and under what circumstances those intentions could be at least partially realized. As Eldon Eisenach suggests, we would be incapable of reaching a full understanding of twentieth-century American political institutions and practices without employing the discourse and doctrines that brought them into being.[6] Hence we need to locate the state-building process in the historical context framed by the Progressive Era.

As Sidney Milkis notes, "interest in the meaning of progressivism has intensified as we have approached a new century." Contemporary Americans regard the Progressive Era as "a historical period that can teach us something important about ourselves and the possibilities of our own political time."[7] Yet, in large measure, progressivism eludes our understanding. It has been many years since historians have felt able to write with confidence about the character and composition of the "progressive movement." Their collective endeavors to define progressivism have produced so confused and contradictory a picture that any attempt to categorize it as a coherent social movement has been more or less abandoned. In the historical imagination, progressivism has shattered into a kaleidoscopic pattern of unconnected fragments,

[5] See Robert Harrison, *State and Society in Twentieth-Century America* (Harlow, Essex: Longman, 1997).
[6] Eldon J. Eisenach, *The Lost Promise of Progressivism* (Lawrence: University Press of Kansas, 1994), 18–19.
[7] Sidney M. Milkis, "Introduction: Progressivism, Then and Now," in Sidney M. Milkis and Jerome M. Mileur, eds., *Progressivism and the New Democracy* (Amherst: University of Massachusetts Press, 1999), 1, 11.

continually changing with the angle of vision.[8] Since historians lost confidence in the concept of a unitary and cohesive "progressive movement" they have found it difficult to relate the various reform impulses to one another. One way of bringing some measure of cohesion to what has become a highly disjointed subject is to examine their treatment at the hands of the national legislature. The proliferation of studies of local progressive movements and campaigns for particular progressive reforms tends inevitably to point up their heterogeneous nature, while playing down what they had in common. A national study makes it easier to plot the linkages and shared resonances. It makes it easier to determine which pieces of the puzzle fit together and which do not, to distinguish those issues that were related and those individuals and groups whose ideas and interests were broadly the same. Then, perhaps, we shall be in a better position to make sense of the complex political world of the "Age of Reform" and to appreciate the context in which the twentieth-century American state came into being.

A "New Political Order"

The Progressive Era saw a major transformation in the style and practice of governance. Both the scale of government intervention and the manner in which policy was formulated and executed changed beyond recognition. Nineteenth-century American politics was infused with the spirit of "localism." The general mode of government intervention was essentially "distributive," involving the allocation of resources and privileges, such as tariff protection, subsidies, land grants and corporate franchises, to private individuals and groups. The chief institutional forum for this kind of "pork barrel politics" was the legislature. The main coordinating agencies, in what Richard L. McCormick calls the "party period" of American politics, were the political parties, which carried out essentially constituent and integrative, rather than policy-making, functions.[9] The development of a complex and integrated national economy around the turn of the century gave rise to various conflicts of interest that were difficult to resolve within the framework of the nineteenth-century polity: between, for instance, railroads and shippers,

---

[8] Peter Filene, "An Obituary for the 'Progressive Movement'," *American Quarterly* 22 (1970): 20–34; John D. Buenker, "Essay," in John D. Bunker, John C. Burnham, and Robert M. Crunden, *Progressivism* (Cambridge, Mass.: Schenkman, 1977), 31–69. For a review of the literature, see Richard L. McCormick, "Progressivism: A Contemporary Reassessment," in McCormick, *The Party Period and Public Policy: American Politics from the Age of Jackson to the Progressive Era* (New York: Oxford University Press, 1986), 263–88; Daniel T. Rodgers, "In Search of Progressivism," *Reviews in American History* 10 (1982): 113–32.

[9] Richard L. McCormick, "The Party Period and Public Policy: An Exploratory Hypothesis," *Journal of American History* 66 (1979): 279–98; James Willard Hurst, *Law and the Condition of Freedom in the Nineteenth-Century United States* (Madison: University of Wisconsin Press, 1956), 3–70.

labor unions and employers' associations, dairymen and oleomargarine manufacturers, petroleum producers and refiners. Many of these groups turned to government to redress their grievances, forcing it, in McCormick's words, "to take explicit account of clashing interests and to assume the responsibility for adjusting them through regulation, administration and planning."[10]

The shift to regulatory policies required, says Stephen Skowronek, a fundamental recasting of the institutions of government; "it entailed building a qualitatively different kind of state."[11] Its main features were the appearance of administrative agencies entrusted with wide discretionary power and a consequent diminution of the role of both legislatures and courts in the conduct of economic policy. The "bureaucratic remedy" recommended itself as a means of resolving conflicts in society by referring them to panels of specialists who would decide on the basis of an impartial investigation of the facts, thereby, it was hoped, "transforming ideological conflicts into matters of expertise and efficiency." The complex problems presenting themselves to modern government called upon various kinds of technical expertise for their solution. Perhaps the best illustration is Samuel P. Hays's study of the conservation movement, in which professional and scientific elites, imbued with the spirit of rational planning, worked to promote a system of decision making more conducive to the rational management of resources than was possible in the haphazard arena of legislative politics. More generally, says Skowronek, members of "an emergent intelligentsia rooted in a revitalized professional sector and a burgeoning university sector" worked to replace the traditional modes of governance with "the discipline of cosmopolitan bureaucratic routines," in order to expand the administrative capacity of the federal government and to institutionalize the influence of the new professionals in the affairs of state.[12]

Many progressive reformers developed a preference for bureaucratic procedures over the vagaries of legislative "log-rolling," which was all too susceptible to constituency and partisan pressures. They regarded the traditional practices of party politics as antipathetic to rational decision making. Reform would therefore take key decisions "out of politics." The growing

[10] Richard L. McCormick, *From Realignment to Reform: Political Change in New York State, 1890–1910* (Ithaca, N.Y.: Cornell University Press, 1981), 255; Samuel P. Hays, *American Political History as Social Analysis* (Knoxville: University of Tennessee Press, 1980), 250–5, 308–24.

[11] Stephen Skowronek, *Building a New American State: The Expansion of National Administrative Capacities, 1877–1920* (Cambridge, 1982), 4, 163–284. See also Arthur S. Link and Richard L. McCormick, *Progressivism* (Arlington Heights, Ill.: Harlan Davidson, 1983), 58–66; McCormick, *Realignment and Reform*.

[12] Robert H. Wiebe, *The Search for Order, 1877–1920* (New York: Hill and Wang, 1967), 159–63, 185; Skowronek, *Building a New American State*, 42–5, 165–6; Samuel P. Hays, *Conservation and the Gospel of Efficiency: The Progressive Conservation Movement, 1890–1920* (paperback edition, New York: Atheneum, 1969).

importance of regulatory issues created in time "a new political order" in which the force of localism and the influence of political parties were substantially diminished.[13]

Thus the political history of progressivism has been substantially redefined. It has been rewritten as a story of the formation of a new set of governing arrangements, of a new American state. The plot includes an enlargement of the scope of government regulation; an accentuation of national, as against local, authority; a preference for bureaucratic over judicial modes of decision making; the development of a new "administrative class"; and the displacement of political parties from their central role in the process of government. However, the new narrative is complicated by discordant themes. In Skowronek's judgment, "modern American state building...yielded a hapless confusion of institutional purposes, authoritative controls, and governmental boundaries."[14] The administrative capacity of the United States government was extended in an uneven, piecemeal fashion. Its components were constituted in different ways and given different, sometimes inconsistent, tasks to perform. At the same time, the courts, the principal forums for resolving differences and formulating rules of conduct in nineteenth-century America, gave up little of their aggregate power, losing some of their functions to newly established executive agencies but tightening their hold on others. Although there is no doubt that parties were losing some of their grip on the levers of action, party still framed the context in which most political decisions were made.[15] The force of localism, the authority of the courts and the influence of political parties were not displaced by the new governing arrangements but maintained a more than residual presence within the structures of the new American state.

Theories of the State

It is fairly evident that the processes of state formation and political change were connected with the fundamental transformation of American society that occurred around the turn of the century: the climactic stages of industrialization, the rise of the big business corporation and other forms of

---

[13] McCormick, *From Realignment to Reform*, 251–72; Link and McCormick, *Progressivism*, 43–58; Martin Shefter, *Political Parties and the State: The American Historical Experience* (Princeton: Princeton University Press, 1994), 72–81; Sidney M. Milkis, *Political Parties and Constitutional Government: Remaking American Democracy* (Baltimore: Johns Hopkins University Press, 1999), 42–71; Hays, *American Political History*, 293–8, 318–24.

[14] Skowronek, *Building a New American State*, 287. See also Ellis W. Hawley, "Social Policy and the Liberal State in the Twentieth Century," in Donald T. Critchlow and Ellis W. Hawley, eds., *Federal Social Policy: The Historical Dimension* (University Park: Pennsylvania State University Press, 1988), 125–9.

[15] See, for example, Thomas J. Pegram, *Partisans and Progressives: Private Interests and Public Policy in Illinois, 1870–1922* (Urbana: University of Illinois Press, 1992).

specialized, hierarchically structured organization, and the intensification of conflicts between interest groups. It is less clear precisely how.

The oldest explanation, and that accepted by many progressives themselves, attributed the reforms that resulted in the growth of the new American state to the impact of a wide-ranging popular movement, supported by millions of ordinary Americans, to place restraints on the economic and political power of big business. To Benjamin P. De Witt, writing in 1915 what was probably the first comprehensive study of the phenomenon, progressivism "began as a well-designed and well-intentioned attempt to prevent special interests from continuing to use the national government for their own selfish purposes." Such a movement attracted support from all sections of the community, except those who were associated with the malign influences that supposedly perverted government power to their ends. As Arthur Mann explains, De Witt, like most progressives, envisaged "an undifferentiated majority oppressed by a minority of corrupt politicians and monopolists."[16] Such an interpretation did not stand up to the evidence that later historians have produced of the complex array of interest groups that supported regulatory legislation. That "undifferentiated majority" disintegrated on closer examination into a kaleidoscope of warring fragments. Nevertheless, it would be a serious error to decline on those grounds to listen to the language of moral outrage in terms of which contemporaries themselves sought to make sense of their situation and which informed the political choices that they made. Nor would it be wise to ignore the background of popular agitation against which the process of state building was carried on.

To proponents of the "organizational synthesis," like Robert H. Wiebe and Louis Galambos, the growth of the state was a necessary part of a broader organizing impulse in American society at that time. However, the "technological determinism" at the heart of the "organizational synthesis" has proved ultimately unconvincing as a source of genuinely historical explanations, while what Daniel T. Rodgers has called the "peculiar bloodlessness" of some of its products does not encourage emulation.[17] There is little reason, on historical grounds, to question that the social and economic forces that have shaped the modern world do, among other things, create conditions which require government intervention on a growing scale. However, the "organizational synthesis" does not say much about the historical

---

[16] Benjamin P. De Witt, *The Progressive Movement* (Arthur Mann, ed., Seattle: University of Washington Press, 1968), xix, 4–5, 26.

[17] Rodgers, "In Search of Progressivism," 119; Gerald Berk, *Alternative Tracks: The Construction of American Industrial Order, 1865–1917* (Baltimore: Johns Hopkins University Press, 1994), 6–8. For characteristic expositions, see Robert H. Wiebe, "The Progressive Years, 1900–1917," in William H. Cartwright and Richard L. Watson, eds., *The Reinterpretation of American History and Culture* (Washington, D.C.: National Council for the Social Studies, 1973); Louis Galambos, "The Emerging Organizational Synthesis in Modern American History," *Business History Review* 44 (1970): 279–90; Hays, *American Political History*.

processes by which such intervention occurs. Nor does it specify the human agents of change, an essential component of any satisfying historical explanation.

The so-called "corporate liberal" interpretation, on the other hand, sees progressive reform as driven, in the last analysis, by the efforts of corporate leaders and their political and intellectual spokesmen to assimilate governing arrangements and political culture to the requirements of a newly established corporate capitalism. The Progressive Era, it is argued, was the period in which Americans learned to live with the business corporation. While the work of scholars like James Weinstein, Martin J. Sklar and James Livingston has greatly enlarged our understanding of the ideologies and interests that underlay the movements for business regulation and banking reform, "corporate liberal" perspectives do not provide a sufficient explanation for progressive state building as a whole. Although the outcome of regulation in some cases may have served the interests of corporate capitalism, the evidence for corporate influence on decision making, particularly on congressional deliberations, is, to say the least, ambiguous, and, where located, that influence is often found to be arrayed against, rather than in support of, the enlargement of federal regulatory power. Then, as since, the majority of American corporate executives displayed a profound mistrust of the state.[18]

Scholars have more often been impressed with the diversity of interest groups seeking to apply pressure on government. A bewildering variety of trade associations, professional bodies, labor federations, farmers' organizations, and "public interest" lobbies competed with one another for leverage in the political marketplace. Groups of what might be called "ordinary people," like farmers, workers and women, through organizing, developed increased capacity to influence government.[19] Elizabeth Sanders attributes key regulatory legislation in the late nineteenth and early twentieth centuries to the demands of social movements and "'producer' coalitions" located in the economic "periphery" of the South and West. It is her contention "that agrarian movements constituted the most important political force driving

---

[18] See, for example, James Weinstein, *The Corporate Ideal of the Liberal State, 1900–1918* (Boston: Beacon, 1968); James Livingston, *Origins of the Federal Reserve System: Money, Class and Corporate Capitalism, 1890–1913* (Ithaca, N.Y.: Cornell University Press, 1986); Martin J. Sklar, *The Corporate Reconstruction of American Capitalism, 1890–1916: The Market, the Law and Politics* (Cambridge: Cambridge University Press, 1988). For a critique, see Ellis W. Hawley, "The Discovery and Study of a 'Corporate Liberalism,'" *Business History Review* 52 (1978): 309–20; Gerald Berk, "Corporate Liberalism Reconsidered: A Review Essay," *Journal of Policy History* 3 (1991): 70–84.

[19] Elisabeth S. Clemens, *The People's Lobby: Organizational Innovation and the Rise of Interest-Group Politics in the United States, 1890–1925* (Chicago: Chicago University Press, 1998); Julie Greene, *Pure and Simple Politics: The American Federation of Labor and Political Activism, 1881–1917* (Cambridge: Cambridge University Press, 1998); Skocpol, *Protecting Soldiers and Mothers*.

the development of the American national state in the half century before World War I."[20] The growth of the state is therefore attributed to the demands of social groups which were too numerous or too well organized for government officials to ignore.

The development of the American state was not determined by technological change or organizational process, by the hegemony of the corporation, by social pressures, or by the dynamics of class struggle; it was, to some extent at least, autonomous. It was shaped by the actions of key administrators and political entrepreneurs who exploited the space created by interest-group conflict and the balance of economic forces. It was, at the same time, constrained by the character of existing institutions, such as political parties, the judiciary, and the civil service, the distribution of constitutional authority, and the legacy of past policies. It emerged, in other words, from a distinctive historical process. A number of contemporary political scientists and historical sociologists have therefore turned from the analysis of extended longitudinal time series and the construction of elaborate causal models to an effort to trace in detail the precise linkages between economic and social change and the building of political institutions. The outcome of their conversion to a "state-centered" approach has been a renewed interest in political history.[21] It is in the same spirit that this study sets out to trace the lineages of the modern American state through a detailed examination of key episodes in American political development during the early twentieth century.

Congress and Progressive Reform

Most studies of state making have bypassed Congress. Their protagonists are enterprising and innovative administrators, not legislators, who are seen to represent the older politics of "courts and parties." Because of its identification with older patterns of governance and because of the evident continuity of its role within the constitutional framework, Congress has been treated as a constant, as a neutral marketplace in which contending parties negotiated

[20] Elizabeth Sanders, *Roots of Reform: Farmers, Workers, and the American State, 1877–1917* (Chicago: Chicago University Press, 1999), 1.

[21] Examples are Skowronek, *Building a New American State*; Theda Skocpol, *Social Policy in the United States* (Princeton: Princeton University Press, 1995); Barry D. Karl, *The Uneasy State: The United States from 1915 to 1945* (Chicago: Chicago University Press, 1983). See also David Brian Robertson, "The Return to History and the New Institutionalism in American Political Science," *Social Science History* 17 (Spring 1993): 1–36; David B. Robertson and Dennis R. Judd, *The Development of Public Policy: The Structure of Policy Restraint* (Glenview, Ill.: Scott, Foresman, 1989); Karen Orren and Stephen Skowronek, "Editors' Preface," *Studies in American Political Development* 1 (1986): 1–2; Peter B. Evans *et al.*, eds., *Bringing the State Back In* (Cambridge: Cambridge University Press, 1985); Ira Katznelson, "The State to the Rescue? Political Science and History Reconnect," *Social Research* 59 (1992): 719–37.

the terms upon which the institutions of the new American state were to be constructed. Its role is seen as reactive, residual, maybe even epiphenomenal. Yet Congress was ultimately responsible for passing the laws which gave these institutions their being. In an important sense the new American state was a congressional creation.

Congress is an arena in which we can evaluate the forces that drove the process of state making. What outside pressures were brought to bear on Congress, and to which was it most responsive? We shall attempt, as far as is possible from the available evidence, to evaluate the influence of public opinion, reform lobbies and economic pressure groups, and to determine how far Congress was responsive to policy suggestions emanating from inside the federal government itself, and particularly from the presidency. What role did political parties play in the process of progressive state building? Was it in any real sense a partisan creation reflecting the programmatic purposes of political organizations, or did it constitute a negation of the spirit of party, a displacement of the nineteenth-century "state of courts and parties" by a nonpartisan administrative state? A final object of this study is to investigate how Congress as an institution adjusted to the demands placed upon it, the extent to which habits and procedures formed in the nineteenth century were adapted to meet the more complex demands of governance in the twentieth century.

There have been few systematic studies of progressive reform in Congress. But, if political historians in recent years have neglected the study of Congress, political scientists have not. Since Nelson Polsby's pioneering study of "The Institutionalization of the U.S. House of Representatives," they have set out to investigate historical trends in recruitment, rates of turnover, voting patterns, seniority norms, and leadership. Others, like David W. Brady, have sought to examine the influence of electoral realignment on congressional behavior.[22] It is notable how many of these studies point out the pivotal significance of the Progressive Era, yet they do so with little appreciation of its special character. With their interest in establishing long-term trends or in drawing broad contrasts between the world of contemporary politics and that of the nineteenth century, such studies are sometimes marred by an insensitivity to historical context. Their conclusions, as E. P. Thompson

---

[22] See, for example, Nelson Polsby, "The Institutionalization of the U.S. House of Representatives," *American Political Science Review* 62 (1968): 144–68; Ronald M. Peters, Jr., *The American Speakership: The Office in Historical Perspective* (Baltimore: Johns Hopkins University Press, 1990); H. Douglas Price, "Careers and Committees in the American Congress: The Problem of Structural Change," in William O. Aydelotte, ed., *The History of Parliamentary Behavior* (Princeton: Princeton University Press, 1977), 28–62; Norman Ornstein, ed., *Congress in Change* (New York, 1975); David W. Brady, *Critical Elections and Congressional Policy Making* (Stanford, Cal.: Stanford University Press, 1988); Joseph Cooper and David W. Brady, "Toward a Diachronic Analysis of Congress," *American Political Science Review* 75 (1981): 988–1006.

would have said, need to be "thrust back into the ensemble of meanings of a specific historical context once again."[23] It is for that purpose, among others, that this study has been written.

During the period covered Congress enacted several measures commonly regarded as triumphs of progressive reform, as well as critical stages in the construction of the legal framework and institutional apparatus of the new American state. The Hepburn Act of 1906 and the Mann-Elkins Act of 1910 greatly augmented the power of the Interstate Commerce Commission over the nation's railroads. The Pure Food and Drug Act of 1906 required more accurate and informative labeling of processed foods and patent medicines, while a parallel statute provided for more rigorous federal inspection of meat products. Controls were imposed on the hours worked by employees of interstate railroads, and a more generous employers' liability law was enacted. The federal government finally took steps to regulate child labor in the District of Columbia. In 1909 a comprehensive, but damagingly inconsequential, revision of tariff duties was undertaken, and the following year a system of postal savings banks was created. Besides the reforms enacted during these years, Congress considered aspects of federal antitrust policy, the conservation of natural resources, and the direct election of Senators.

Analysis of congressional action on these issues can tell us something about the nature of progressivism, at least in so far as it found expression at a national level. Which elements in Congress supported progressive reform? What social forces did they respond to? What partisan, sectional or other characteristics did they share? Did congressional supporters of reform regard the various pieces of reform legislation as part of a common political project, and in what terms did they conceptualize that project? How, for example, did progressives in Congress envisage the proper relationship between private advantage and the "public interest"? What was their attitude to political parties? These are among the questions to which we shall seek answers in our analysis of congressional proceedings during the early years of the twentieth century, in the hope of clarifying our understanding of progressivism, and with it the historical context in which the modern American state was formed.

I do not approach this analysis in the expectation of gluing back together the fragments of the conceptual entity that used to be called the "progressive movement." All the king's horses and all the king's men will never put that particular Humpty-Dumpty together again. There is, in fact, substantial evidence of a fairly cohesive progressive coalition in Congress that held together over a wide range of issues. Examination of members' voting behavior and the political language in which they expressed themselves offers a salutary reminder of certain central features of progressivism that have

[23] E. P. Thompson, "Anthropology and the Discipline of Historical Context," *Midland History* (1972): 46.

been largely forgotten. However, I agree with Eisenach that "From an institutional and regime-change perspective . . . the issue of whether there 'really was' a Progressive movement and whether that movement had coherence is really misplaced."[24] Much more important is to place progressivism in the framework of the broader changes in political culture and political institutions and, by identifying the principal actors and exploring the roots of their actions, to add definition and meaning to our understanding of American political development.

[24] Eisenach, *Lost Promise of Progressivism*, 18.

2

Congress and the Nation

To set the scene for the accounts of substantive policy making that follow, this chapter examines in some detail the composition and organization of Congress in the Progressive Era. It describes the characteristics of the membership, the composition of congressional business, the nature of the legislative process, and the influence of party organizations on parliamentary decision making, which led in both chambers to a concentration of authority virtually without historical parallel. It looks also at the relationship between Congress and the wider political environment, considering in particular the implications of the electoral changes that followed the so-called "critical realignment" of the 1890s and the ambitious state-building project initiated by President Theodore Roosevelt.

Men and Measures

At noon on 4 December 1905 members of the Fifty-ninth Congress were called to order by the Clerk of the House. Once the Chaplain had offered up a suitable prayer for the eighty million persons who had been entrusted to their care, the Clerk proceeded to call the roll. The Representatives who answered to their names conformed very much to a type. They were typically large, well-built men, imposing in manner and physical presence. They sported cutaway jackets, somewhat shiny and not too well pressed, lest they acquire a reputation as "dudes" among the folks back home, and wore their hair somewhat longer than current fashion prescribed. The battered felt hat, rumpled black jacket, sagging trousers and carefully cultivated untidiness of Speaker "Uncle Joe" Cannon, regularly the target of sardonic ridicule from metropolitan journalists, lay well within the sartorial norms of the House. The few who dressed fashionably and expensively, like Nicholas Longworth

TABLE 2.1. *Characteristics of Members of the House of Representatives, 59th Congress*

Membership	386	Previous government office:	
Average age	49.0	local or county	197
Highest educational level attained:		state legislature	152
college or university	223	other state	26
secondary school	80	federal	28
other	83	none	91
Occupation:		Average prior service (terms)	2.4
law	262	Members serving first term	87
business	78	second term	100
farming	15	third term	47
journalism	15	fourth term	41
other	16	beyond fourth term	111

Source: Biographical Directory of the American Congress, 1789–1911 (Washington, D.C., 1913).

of Ohio, the future son-in-law of President Roosevelt, stood out almost as exotic creatures.[1]

They were in most respects a typical body of Congressmen (see Table 2.1). Two out of three were in their forties and fifties, with an average age of just under forty-nine. The oldest, at seventy-eight, was Nehemiah D. Sperry of Connecticut, who cast his first presidential vote in 1848, the youngest the twenty-seven-year-old Anthony Michalek from Chicago, the first native of Bohemia to be elected to Congress. They were, for their generation, unusually well-educated: 223 (59.3 percent) could boast of having attended a university or college, a privilege enjoyed in 1870 by only 1.7 percent of the relevant age group.[2] Their occupational distribution was similarly distorted. As in every Congress since the early Republic, lawyers formed a large majority, in this case 69.1 percent. Law, as Champ Clark observed, was a profession which trained a man in public speaking and debate, kept him in the public eye and widened his circle of acquaintances. Just over 20 percent recorded some kind of business activity as their principal means of subsistence, but only fifteen were farmers and only one, John Hunt of Missouri, described himself as a manual worker.[3]

[1] C.R., 59.1:38–9; *New York Times*, 5 December 1905, 8 December 1907.
[2] Biographical data, unless otherwise indicated, are derived from ANB and BDAC. Age-group participation in higher education in 1870 from U.S. Bureau of the Census, *Historical Statistics of the United States, Colonial Times to 1957* (Washington: Government Printing Office, 1960), 211.
[3] Champ Clark, *My Quarter Century of American Politics* (2 vols., New York: Harper, 1920), 2:35; George B. Galloway, *History of the House of Representatives* (New York: Crowell, 1961), 34–6. Cf. Howard W. Allen and Robert Slagter, "Congress in Crisis: Changes in Personnel and the Legislative Agenda in the U.S. Congress in the 1890s," *Social Science History* 16 (1992): 405–8.

James Bryce described the majority of Representatives as "second-rate lawyers or farmers, less often merchants or manufacturers."[4] Such an assessment is hard to refute. Early twentieth-century Congressmen were men of considerable standing within their own communities – but rarely beyond. Apart from the lumberman Joseph W. Fordney of Michigan, the Illinois traction magnate William B. McKinley, John W. Weeks of Massachusetts, who had amassed a fortune in banking and brokerage, and the newspaper magnate William Randolph Hearst, whose appearances on Capitol Hill were rare and fleeting, few had substantial business interests, and few could be described as rich. A handful had attained higher office at state level, including two former governors, or filled major federal posts below the cabinet level. Only the New York Congressman Charles A. Towne had served in the upper chamber, but that was by appointment to an uncompleted term lasting no more than two months. Altogether members of Congress were men who had yet to make a wider reputation and who sought to make one in the House.

The House of Representatives was a difficult arena for those who aspired to political fame. A new Congressman discovered himself to be a person of little importance in the Washington scheme of things. As Woodrow Wilson noted, "He finds his station insignificant, and his identity indistinct." Only after a service of two terms could he hope to master the complexities of congressional procedure and gain the respect of his seniors; only after four terms was he likely to acquire real influence.[5] In 1905, 87 members (22.5 percent) stood on the threshold of their congressional careers, 100 (25.9 percent) were commencing a second term; only 111 (28.7 percent) had four or more terms behind them. The tribulations of the freshman are a recurrent theme in congressional history, but the species was becoming rarer. The Fifty-ninth Congress contained the smallest infusion of new blood to date. As Table 2.2 reveals, this formed part of a continuous downward trend in the turnover of House membership. During the 1870s, 49.1 percent of members were serving for the first time, while the average Congressman had no more than 2.08 terms behind him. By the 1900s the equivalent figures were 23.8 percent and 3.43 terms respectively.[6] Differentiation from its environment, as "the

[4] James Bryce, *The American Commonwealth* (2 vols., New York: Macmillan, 1910), 1:150.
[5] Woodrow Wilson, *Congressional Government* (New York, 1956), 59; Robert L. O'Brien, "The Troubles of the New Congressman," *Outlook* 81 (2 December 1905): 818–22; David W. Brady, *Congressional Voting in a Partisan Era* (Lawrence: University Press of Kansas, 1973), 149–52.
[6] Nelson Polsby, "The Institutionalization of the U.S. House of Representatives," *American Political Science Review* 62 (1968): 146–7; H. Douglas Price, "Careers and Committees in the American Congress: The Problem of Structural Change," in William O. Aydelotte, ed., *The History of Parliamentary Behavior* (Princeton, N.J.: Princeton University Press, 1977), 36–9; Price, "Congress and the Evolution of Legislative 'Professionalism,'" in Norman W. Ornstein, ed., *Congress in Change* (New York: Praeger, 1975), 4–12; Price, "The Congressional Career Then and Now," in Nelson Polsby, ed., *Congressional Behavior* (New York: Random House, 1971), 14–27; Morris Fiorina et al., "Historical Change in House Turnover," in Ornstein, ed., *Congress in Change*, 24–57.

TABLE 2.2. *Trends in the Turnover of House Membership, 1861–1921*

Congresses	Years	Average terms	Percentage first-term
37th–41st	1861–71	1.97	50.3
42nd–46th	1871–81	2.08	49.1
47th–51st	1881–91	2.47	39.0
52nd–56th	1891–1901	2.54	39.7
57th–61st	1901–11	3.43	23.8
59th	1905–7	3.48	21.0
60th	1907–9	3.61	22.5
61st	1909–11	3.84	19.9
62nd–66th	1911–21	3.55	26.2

Source: Nelson Polsby, "The Institutionalization of the U.S. House of Representatives," *American Political Science Review* 62 (1968): 146–7.

organization establishes and 'hardens' its outer boundaries," constitutes one of the most significant aspects of what Nelson Polsby calls the "institutionalization" of the House. Whatever the reason, the decline in turnover denotes a profound shift in the relationship between Congress and the nation which it represents.[7]

As soon as the House had organized itself for business, members stood up in turn to present bills and resolutions. By the end of the first day they had introduced 3012 separate legislative proposals. Over the life of the Congress the number swelled to 25,897 bills and 189 joint resolutions, while 8627 bills and 98 joint resolutions originated in the upper chamber. Although most of this tide of legislation got no further than a shelf in a committee room, the Fifty-ninth Congress contrived to pass 775 public and 6249 private acts and resolutions – more than any of its predecessors.[8] Much of this business was private in character, addressed to the concerns of private individuals over such matters as pensions and claims against the government, rather than those of the general public. Many public bills also served the interests of particular localities, while such omnibus measures as civil appropriation, river and harbor, and public building bills contained a multitude of appropriations for local projects all over the United States.

---

[7] Polsby, "Institutionalization," 146. For alternative explanations see Price, "Congressional Career"; Brady, *Congressional Voting*, 107–8; Fiorina, "Historical Change in House Turnover," 31–4; Robert G. Brookshire and Dean F. Duncan III, "Congressional Career Patterns and Party Systems," *Legislative Studies Quarterly* 8 (1983): 65–78; Samuel Kernell, "Toward Understanding 19th Century Congressional Careers: Ambition, Competition, and Rotation," *American Journal of Political Science* 21 (1977): 669–93; Robert Struble, Jr., "House Turnover and the Principle of Rotation," *Political Science Quarterly* 94 (1980): 669–93.

[8] C.R., 59.1:38–42; *New York Times*, 3, 5, 26 December 1905.

Congressmen's commitment to such business was notorious. Assuming that they would be judged on their ability to bring home immediate and tangible rewards, they devoted themselves wholeheartedly to that end. As a freshman, Joseph M. Dixon of Montana had the simple objective of putting "my hand into the bag as often as it was passed around my way." His special project was to open up the Crow and Flathead Reservations to settlement, something which, after persistent importuning of the Speaker, he managed to achieve. George Norris, who represented a highly marginal district in Nebraska, set out to persuade Cannon that "the appropriation by Congress of money for the building of a public building at Grand Island would make my re-election secure." Each and every member shepherded a host of pensions and other claims on their troubled way through the legislative wilderness. Champ Clark, who was as assiduous about such matters as any junior member, introduced over six hundred pension and relief bills in the space of ten years.[9]

Constituency duties did not end there. "Strange to say," observed Richard Bartholdt of Missouri, "the task of legislation is actually the least part of the work." The papers of contemporary Congressmen are full of letters about appointments and other routine matters, such as pension claims or requests to help young men into or out of the army. It was not surprising that the floor of the House was often nearly deserted; when general debate began members rushed off to deal with correspondence and constituency business. Besides running around the departments, Congressmen were expected to be liberal with copies of government publications, such as committee reports, Department of Agriculture reports on such esoteric topics as "Diseases of the Horse" and "The Usefulness of the American Toad," and the florid encomia on deceased statesmen in which the age delighted. Most ridiculous of all perhaps was the jealously guarded tradition by which the Department of Agriculture, through the medium of Congressmen, distributed free seeds, ostensibly for the improvement of agriculture but more often for the beautification of someone's garden. The very triviality of such requests made them difficult to refuse for fear of betraying an Olympian indifference.[10]

Not surprisingly, some members found these chores tiresome. Senator John C. Spooner of Wisconsin claimed to be "so engrossed with the routine work, and errands and pensions and the like" that he could "find little time

[9] Jules A. Karlin, *Joseph M. Dixon of Montana: Senator and Bull Moose Manager, 1867–1917* (2 vols., Missoula: University of Montana Press, 1974), 1:54–6; Richard Lowitt, *George W. Norris: The Making of a Progressive, 1861–1912* (Syracuse, N.Y.: Syracuse University Press, 1963), 84–5; Geoffrey T. Morrison, "A Political Biography of Champ Clark" (Ph.D. diss., St. Louis University, 1971), 96–9.

[10] Richard Bartholdt, *From Steerage to Congress* (Philadelphia: Dorrance, 1930), 191–3; Clark, *My Quarter Century*, 1:212–18; Peter T. Harstad and Bonnie Lindemann, *Gilbert T. Haugen: Norwegian-American Farm Politician* (Iowa City: State Historical Society of Iowa, 1992), 73–81. On seeds, see *Outlook*, 79 (8 April 1905), 863–4.

to read or study great questions." At the close of his senatorial career he continued to find such distractions "multitudinous, irksome and annoying."[11] But the prominence of such business in the working lives of Congressmen is a clear indication of the role which they believed that they were expected to play. Reform of the system, argued Senator Jonathan Bourne, would "be difficult to work out until members of Congress and their constituents take a broad National view of all matters of legislation, and are not willing to sacrifice National good for their own local popularity and advantage." In this respect early twentieth-century Congressmen differed little from their nineteenth-century predecessors.[12]

In the House of the "Czar"

In a campaign speech Victor Murdock of Kansas recounted the experience of an imaginary new member who eagerly comes forward with a measure close to the hearts of his constituents. But soon he learns "that the introduction of a bill of a public nature has become merely an expression of opinion rather than the initiation of a serious legislative purpose; and that the few great public bills which pass are known to the speaker and approved by him before they are introduced." Eventually he is forced to wait upon the Speaker to beg permission for his constituents' case to be heard. Similar rites of initiation were undergone by all new members, although insurgents like Murdock liked to exaggerate, for dramatic effect, their prior innocence. George Norris recalled with similar disingenuousness his surprise on discovering as a freshman member of the Committee on Public Buildings that "it seemed to be taken for granted" that the decision on whether there should be a public buildings bill that session "was to be made by the Speaker."[13]

The powers of the Speaker, which had been augmented by successive occupants of the Chair in the late nineteenth century, particularly Thomas B. Reed in the 1890s, reached their apogee during the tenure of Joseph G. Cannon (1903–11). The Speaker, believed Senator Albert Beveridge, was now "almost absolutely powerful" in the House. Taking this sentiment to its logical conclusion, one Congressman responded to a constituent's request for a copy of the House rules by forwarding a photograph of Cannon.[14]

---

[11] Dorothy G. Fowler, *John Coit Spooner: Defender of Presidents* (New York: New York University Publishers, 1961), 101–2; John C. Spooner to J. B. Gilfillan, 11 June 1906, Spooner Letterbooks, LC.

[12] Jonathon Bourne, Jr., "How to Spend a Billion Dollars," *Outlook* 93 (9 October 1909): 297–302.

[13] Draft of speech, Box 110, Victor Murdock MSS, LC; George Norris, *Fighting Liberal: The Autobiography of George W. Norris* (New York: Macmillan, 1945), 95–7. Cf. Mark Sullivan, "The People's One Chance in Two Years," *Collier's* 24, no. 5 (6 March 1909): 15.

[14] Albert J. Beveridge to L. C. Hughes, 24 November 1906, Beveridge MSS, LC; Blair Bolles, *Tyrant from Illinois: Uncle Joe Cannon's Experiment with Personal Power* (New York: Norton,

The sheer weight of business necessitated some means of preliminary evaluation and selection. This task was entrusted to the House's fifty-nine standing committees. Theirs was the responsibility for evaluating the merits of legislative proposals, many of them arcane or complex in nature, requiring close examination of the testimony of numerous expert witnesses and interested parties. It was there that effective scrutiny of a bill's provisions was carried out and legislation was shaped and drafted. Effectively, the House delegated a large part of its deliberative function to its committees. Except in the case of highly controversial measures, members tended to accept without question the judgment of the responsible committee. The committee in charge of a bill could choose to alter its content, substitute another of its own choosing, report it adversely or, more often, simply decline to report it, or even to consider it at all. Most bills never reemerged from the committee room to which they had been consigned; it was, in practice, virtually impossible to secure the release of a measure so imprisoned.[15] Within each field of legislation considerable discretionary power resided in the hands of the appropriate committee, and especially its chairman, who called meetings, set the agenda and decided the order in which bills should be considered. He determined which members should draft particular pieces of legislation, which should report them and take charge of them on the floor of the House. "The leaders of the House," said Woodrow Wilson in 1885, "are the chairmen of the principal Standing Committees."[16]

Committee chairmen, like other committee members, were chosen by the Speaker. This was a power of profound importance. Though constrained by the demands of seniority, geographical balance and the need in some cases for special expertise, Cannon used it to advance legislation of which he approved and to obstruct legislation of which he disapproved. For example, he

1951), 95. On the growth of the Speaker's power, see Ronald M. Peters, Jr., *The American Speakership: The Office in Historical Perspective* (Baltimore: Johns Hopkins University Press, 1990), 52–91; DeAlva S. Alexander, *History and Procedure of the House of Representatives* (Boston: Houghton, Mifflin, 1916), 165–72, 196–222; Randall B. Ripley, *Party Leaders in the House of Representatives* (Washington, D.C.: Brookings Institution, 1967), 88–91; Charles R. Atkinson, *The Committee on Rules and the Overthrow of Speaker Cannon* (New York: Columbia University Press, 1911). On Cannon and "Cannonism," see also William R. Gwinn, *Uncle Joe Cannon: Archfoe of Insurgency* (New York: Brookman, 1957); George R. Mayhill, "Speaker Cannon under the Roosevelt Administration" (Ph.D. diss., University of Illinois, 1942); Joseph Cooper and David W. Brady, "Institutional Context and Leadership Style: The House from Cannon to Rayburn," *American Political Science Review* 75 (1981): 411–25; Scott William Rager, "The Fall of the House of Cannon: Uncle Joe and His Enemies" (Ph.D. diss., University of Illinois, 1991).

15 Wilson, *Congressional Government*, 57–98; Galloway, *History of the House of Representatives*, 64–96; Ch'ang-Wei Ch'iu, *The Speaker of the House of Representatives since 1896* (New York: Columbia University Press, 1928), 87–92, 115–16, 252–5; Paul D. Hasbrouck, *Party Government in the House of Representatives* (New York: Macmillan, 1927), 67–8, 72–5; Clark, *My Quarter Century*, 1:202–5.

16 Wilson, *Congressional Government*, 58.

gave preference to staunch protectionists among the Republican members
of the Ways and Means Committee by appointing James T. McCleary of
Minnesota and William Alden Smith of Michigan in 1905 and removing the
ranking member, James Tawney, who, being suspected of revisionist leanings
on the tariff, was shifted sideways to chair the Appropriations Committee,
on which he had never served. As he all but admitted, Cannon shaped the
composition of the Judiciary and Labor Committees so as to thwart the
legislative demands of the American Federation of Labor. In 1907 the Committee on Agriculture was almost wholly reconstituted in reaction to the
meat inspection controversy of the previous summer.[17]

Overall, Cannon did not offend against the principle of seniority any
more than other Speakers of the period. Polsby and his associates found that
Cannon violated seniority in the selection of committee chairmen in only 45
out of 231 instances, only 20 of which were not compensated for by place-
ment at the head of committees of equivalent or higher rank.[18] However,
such instances were given added weight by the growing expectation that
seniority should normally prevail. Although it had yet to acquire the adamantine force that it was later to hold in determining the allocation of positions
of power in the House, and was certainly not regarded as an absolute norm,
the principle was routinely adduced by ranking members in support of their
claims. On the basis of a statistical analysis of longitudinal trends in committee appointments, Walter Dean Burnham found a marked increase in
the application of seniority around the turn of the century. As James Robert
Mann, a close confidant of Cannon, explained, "it was generally understood
that long and faithful service counted as a man worked up on a Committee
and that men were encouraged to work with the idea that in turn they might
become chairman," an understanding which, he implied, was shared by the
Speaker. But it did not yet constitute a prescriptive right.[19]

In any case, while seniority largely marked out the places of established
members, where freshmen started out was wholly within the gift of the
Speaker. Thus in 1905 the Chicago Representative Martin B. Madden was
set on a fast track to congressional influence by being placed on the Ways and
Means Committee, while two years later George R. Malby of New York was

[17] *New York Times*, 12 December 1905; "Government by Oligarchy," *Outlook* 89 (2 May
1908): 12–14; Alexander, *History and Procedure*, 67–70; Mayhill, "Speaker Cannon," 118–
26; Hasbrouck, *Party Government*, 48–50; Ch'iu, *Speaker*, 65–8, 255–7.

[18] Nelson Polsby *et al.*, "The Growth of the Seniority System in the U.S. House of Representatives," *American Political Science Review* 63 (1969): 791–802; Ch'iu, *Speaker*, 68–71; Michael
Abram and Joseph Cooper, "The Rise of Seniority in the House of Representatives," *Polity*
1 (1969): 53–85.

[19] Mann quoted in James H. Davidson to John Jacob Esch, 28 September 1907, Esch MSS,
SHSW; Abram and Cooper, "Rise of Seniority," 68–9; Walter Dean Burnham, *Critical Elections and the Mainsprings of American Politics* (New York, 1970), 100–6. But cf. Price, "Careers
and Committees," 45–57.

picked out from the ranks for a place on Judiciary. Most new members had to be content with service on such committees as Claims, Patents, and Invalid Pensions. Vacancies on major committees offered similar opportunities for intervention. Committee assignments determined more than anything else the career prospects of individual Congressmen. The power of appointment therefore was a valuable source of patronage which greatly strengthened the Speaker's hand in his dealings with members.[20]

Even after the committee system had weeded out a majority of bills, hundreds remained to be disposed of. To some extent, the order in which they were taken up was determined by the rules. Certain kinds of business, like that dealing with the District of Columbia, were in order at specified times. Appropriations bills were "privileged" and took precedence over other business, as well as consuming immense amounts of parliamentary time. Certain committees had the right to report at any, while conference reports and special orders from the Committee on Rules were also privileged. The enormous volume of bills before the House and the claims of various categories of privileged business made it virtually impossible for ordinary legislation to reach the floor except by unanimous consent or under suspension of the rules. Much of the business of the House was transacted in this way. Thus 416 pension bills were passed by unanimous consent in sixty minutes during one not untypical session of the Fifty-ninth Congress.[21] No such legislation could be introduced without the consent of the Speaker, who used his "absolute and uncontrolled power of recognition" to recognize members on matters which he thought ought to be considered and decline to recognize them where he did not. This gave Cannon substantial control over the order of business and over the relative prospects of competing measures.[22]

Important business that lacked privileged status relied on special orders from the Committee on Rules, a committee appointed and chaired by the Speaker, to clear a path through the parliamentary undergrowth. These special rules, which required only a simple majority for adoption, set out the period allowed for debate and the time when a vote should be taken and in some cases restricted the possibility of amendment from the floor. The Hepburn railroad bill and the pure food bill were among the measures which benefited from such privileged treatment in the Fifty-ninth Congress, as the Vreeland emergency currency and Payne tariff bills did later.[23] Public bills which were not so favored stood scant chance of consideration. The Republican whip James Sherman told Henry C. Adams of Wisconsin, who was anxious to secure passage of a bill increasing the appropriation for

[20] See the comments by George Norris in *C.R.*, 60.2:1056.
[21] *C.R.*, 60.1:1649; 60.2:2652; Alexander, *History and Procedure*, 213–25.
[22] Ibid., 56–61; Mayhill, "Speaker Cannon," 60–4; Ch'iu, *Speaker*, 166–72.
[23] Atkinson, *Committee on Rules*, 51–60; Ch'iu, *Speaker*, 115–36; Alexander, *History and Procedure*, 205–21; Mayhill, "Speaker Cannon," 175–9; Hasbrouck, *Party Government*, 207–9.

agricultural experiment stations, that "no similar bill had been brought in under the rules in opposition to the Speaker more than five times in sixteen years."[24]

Speaking during the opening session of the Fifty-ninth Congress on the customary motion to adopt the rules of the preceding House, John Sharp Williams, the Democratic floor leader, pleaded in vain with members on the other side to seize their one opportunity to assert their independence of the party leaders by voting it down. They were, he chided, like "blanket Indians" too timid to come off the reservation.[25] It may seem surprising that rank-and-file members should consent to so severe a restriction on their freedom of action. Yet all the evidence suggests that the leadership had the support of most Republican Congressmen. As Daniel Anthony of Kansas pointed out, "the Republican majority in Congress is entirely responsible for the powers possessed by the Speaker of the House." Republican Congressmen accepted Cannon's leadership and the prevailing way of doing business, out of ignorance or confusion, fear or personal ambition, or merely as a *pis aller*, but all but a few dozen accepted them.[26]

During the course of a bitter altercation with the party leaders over a proposal to admit New Mexico and Arizona as one state, Henry C. Adams complained that "an appalling percentage" of his Republican colleagues were "unmitigated political cowards when it [came] to entering into a contest with the powers that be in their own party." Their reluctance was not altogether surprising considering the costs of disloyalty. Adams himself described how party leaders were "taking men into their private offices and threatening them with the loss of appropriation bills, public buildings and all sorts of disfavor, bulldozing and scaring some of the timid and using patronage to get some of the others."[27] Not only did the Speaker, through his control of the distribution of committee places, influence the career prospects of individual members, but, equally importantly, through his control of the order of business, he decided the fate of the many private and local bills which their constituents desired. It was natural, observed Norris, that a member

---

[24] Quoted in Henry C. Adams to Ben Adams, 14 February 1906, Adams MSS, SHSW. See also *C.R.*, 60.2, 601–5; *New York Times*, 28 May 1906.

[25] *C.R.*, 59.1:42.

[26] Daniel R. Anthony, Jr. to William Allen White, 18 April 1908, White MSS, LC. See also James E. Watson, *As I Knew Them: Memoirs of James E. Watson* (Indianapolis: Bobbs, Merrill, 1943), 120; Theodore Roosevelt to William Howard Taft, 10 November 1908, in Elting E. Morison et al., eds., *The Letters of Theodore Roosevelt* (8 vols., Cambridge, Mass.: Harvard University Press, 1951–4), 6:1340–1; Taft to William Allen White, 12 March 1909, White MSS, LC; Elisha M. Keyes to Henry C. Adams, 22 January 1906, Adams MSS, SHSW.

[27] Henry C. Adams to Robert M. La Follette, 6 December 1905; to A.S. Mitchell, 14 January 1906, Adams MSS, SHSW. See also Henry C. Adams to Grant Thomas, 15 January 1906; to William D. Hoard, 17 January, 8 February 1906, Adams MSS, SHSW; John Jacob Esch to G. W. Fargo, Jr., 12 January 1906, Esch Letterbooks, SHSW; *New York Times*, 14, 25 January, 15 March 1906.

"should strive to please the man who has the power to advance or ruin his political prospects." For, as the veteran Wisconsin Republican John Jenkins put it, a show of independence was all very well in a campaign, "but how many harbor improvements will it secure and how many federal buildings will it get you?"[28]

Republican leaders countered contemporary charges of "bossism" by arguing that responsible party government required loyalty and discipline. James Tawney, who had flirted with insurgency on the statehood issue, explained to the House why he had finally resolved to toe the line: "the Government of this country is government by party, and as a member of the party now controlling I bow to the judgment of the majority." John Dalzell, a member of the Rules Committee, insisted that the majority was "charged with the responsibility for legislation" and, consequently, had the right to prescribe rules under which legislation could be had. Party government required a set of rules and procedures that would enable the majority to govern.[29] Perhaps the clearest statement came from Cannon himself:

This is a government by the people acting through the representatives of a majority of the people. Results cannot be had except by a majority, and in the House of Representatives a majority, being responsible, should have full power and should exercise that power; otherwise the majority is inefficient and does not perform its function.

The Speaker has always believed in and bowed to the will of the majority in convention, in caucus, and in the legislative hall, and today profoundly believes that to act otherwise is to disorganize parties, is to prevent coherent action in any legislative body, is to make impossible the reflection of the wishes of the American people in statutes and in laws.[30]

Such statements were not just special pleading. Senior Republicans considered party discipline and effective organization essential to coherent government. This conviction had been formed and hardened in the course of the legislative struggles of the last century. A rigorous set of parliamentary rules was required, they believed, to avoid a return to the chaotic, even anarchic, procedures which had preceded the adoption of the Reed Rules in 1890.[31]

Many ordinary members harbored similar convictions. In the statehood debate Charles E. Fuller of Illinois, a Representative of only one term's service, proclaimed that "By organization and concerted action alone can any

[28] C.R., 60.2:1056; Jenkins quoted in Robert Griffith, "Prelude to Insurgency: Irvine L. Lenroot and the Republican Primary of 1908," *Wisconsin Magazine of History* 49 (1965): 17.

[29] C.R., 59.1:1503 (Tawney); 60.2:8 (Dalzell). See also C.R., 59.1:963, 1500–1, 7433 (Grosvenor).

[30] C.R., 61.2:3436–7. See also L. White Busbey, ed., *Uncle Joe Cannon: The Story of a Pioneer American* (New York: Holt, 1927), 139–40.

[31] See, for example, the remarks of Marlin E. Olmsted in C.R., 60.2:579–82. President Roosevelt also welcomed the fact that in the House "the majority as a whole stands by the responsible leaders." Roosevelt to George von Lengerke Meyer, 1 February 1906, *Letters*, 5:145.

party hope to achieve results." He had not been sent to Washington as a "free lance" to set his own "individual judgement" up against the "combined wisdom of the Republican party," but "to carry out the principles and decrees of the party whose representatives we are."[32] There is every reason to believe that such views were typical of rank-and-file Republicans. This was an era of intense party loyalties, which were reflected in what were, by historical standards, exceptionally regular patterns of party voting.[33] George Norris, for example, entered Congress in 1903 as "a bitter Republican partisan.... I believed that all the virtues of government were wrapped up in the party of which I was a member." The bitter struggles of the Civil War era left a legacy of intense partisan feeling, and Congressmen of the Progressive Era had grown up in a political culture in which party identification played a central role.[34]

The acceptability of the methods employed to secure the passage of a program of legislation ultimately depended on the degree of consensus regarding its merits.[35] Republican party unity at the turn of the century drew strength from the acceptance of a common program, at the core of which was a commitment to the use of federal power to promote economic development: through river and harbor improvements, subsidies to shipping, land reclamation projects, the financing of agricultural education and research, and, above all, tariff protection. The Republican party in this period elected Congressmen from a wide variety of sections and types of constituency, from almost everywhere but the South and certain inner-city districts. It was not that they shared identical interests, but that their constituents' needs could be accommodated within a common program which distributed protection and aid to a variety of economic groups. These were what Theodore J. Lowi calls "distributive" policies. As Richard L. McCormick has pointed out, the political viability of such policies rested on the assumption that "distributive policies were almost infinitely divisible"; government favor to one locality or group did not preclude assistance to others. As Lewis L. Gould observes,

---

[32] *C.R.*, 59.1:1582.

[33] The unusual influence of party on congressional voting in this period is shown by David W. Brady and Philip Althoff, "Party Voting in the U.S. House of Representatives, 1890–1910," *Journal of Politics* 36 (1974): 753–75; David W. Brady, Joseph Cooper, and Patricia A. Hurley, "The Decline of Party in the U.S. House of Representatives, 1887–1968," *Legislative Studies Quarterly* 4 (1979): 381–407; Jerome M. Clubb and Santa Traugott, "Partisan Cleavage and Cohesion in the House of Representatives, 1861–1974," *Journal of Interdisciplinary History* 7 (1977): 375–401.

[34] Norris, *Fighting Liberal*, 89. On partisanship in Gilded Age politics, see Morton Keller, *Affairs of State: Public Life in Late Nineteenth-Century America* (Cambridge, Mass.: Harvard University Press, 1977), esp. 239–49.

[35] Cf. David W. Brady and David Epstein, "Intraparty Preferences, Heterogeneity, and the Origins of the Modern Congress: Progressive Reformers in the House and Senate, 1890–1920," *Journal of Law, Economics, & Organization* 13 (1997): 26–49; Peters, *American Speakership*, 87–91.

"Republicans depicted society as a web of interconnected producers" who all benefited from policies which promoted prosperity and employment. This notion of a potential "harmony of interests" among the various elements in society conferred a symbolic unity upon the disparate elements of the Republican legislative program, a unity which became increasingly hard to maintain in a world rent by growing sectional and class divisions.[36]

The Speaker's authority owed much to his personal qualities. Cannon was an affable politician of the old school who affected, with his colorful language, disheveled clothes, and persistent tobacco chewing, a bucolic manner which belied a considerable political finesse. Despite his almost ostentatious vulgarity, an amiable manner and a droll sense of humor made him good company. He cultivated close relations with the "boys," treating junior members with genuine kindness and making himself readily available for advice and consultation. As befitted the original "standpatter," Cannon was highly conservative in his politics, although his record on occasions betrayed an unexpected flexibility.[37] Cannon, it might be said, epitomized the virtues that his followers admired. When in 1908 *Collier's* canvassed Republican Congressmen for their views on whether Cannon should remain in the Chair, his supporters in nearly every case laid emphasis on his personal virtues of competence and, above all, honesty and integrity, rather than his political ideas. In a phrase reminiscent of Roscoe Conkling's brusque dismissal of the "man-milliners" of politics, Richard Bartholdt declared that he loved Cannon for the enemies that he had made: "namely, the short-haired women and long-haired men who have attacked him most unjustly." Cannon, in such terms, was made to stand for a robust normality in political and other matters.[38]

Cannon benefited, of course, from the support and advice of a coterie of senior Republican Congressmen. The paramount power of the Speaker did not alter the essentially collegial nature of leadership in the House.[39] Those

[36] Theodore J. Lowi, "American Business, Public Policy, Case Studies, and Political Theory," *World Politics* 16 (1964): 677–715; Richard L. McCormick, "The Party Period and Public Policy: An Exploratory Hypothesis," *Journal of American History* 66 (1979): 279–98; Lewis L. Gould, *Reform and Regulation: American Politics, 1900–1916* (New York, 1978), 12. See also Charles W. Calhoun, "Political Economy in the Gilded Age: The Republican Party's Industrial Policy," *Journal of Policy History* 8 (1996): 291–309; John Gerring, *Party Ideologies in America, 1828–1996* (Cambridge: Cambridge University Press, 1998), 57–116; Richard Franklin Bensel, *The Political Economy of American Industrialization, 1877–1900* (Cambridge: Cambridge University Press, 2001).

[37] Charles W. Thompson, *Party Leaders of Our Times* (New York: G. W. Dillingham, 1906), 173–83; Gwinn, *Uncle Joe Cannon*, 4–10; Rager, "Fall of the House of Cannon," 43–4; Bolles, *Tyrant from Illinois*, 3–8, 11–12, 19–24; Mark Sullivan, *Our Times* (6 vols., New York: Scribner's, 1926–35), 4:374–7; Mark Sullivan, *The Education of an American* (New York: Doubleday, Doran, 1938), 244–8.

[38] "For and Against Cannon," *Collier's*, 5 December 1908. Cf. Keller, *Affairs of State*, 245–9.

[39] Ripley, *Party Leaders*, 81–6; Ch'iu, *Speaker*, 313–17.

TABLE 2.3. *Chairmen of Major House Committees, 59th Congress*

Rules	Joseph G. Cannon, Ill., Speaker (6/15)
Ways and Means	Sereno E. Payne, N.Y. (8/10)
Appropriations	James A. Tawney, Minn. (6)
Judiciary	John Jenkins. Wis. (5)
Banking and Currency	Charles Fowler, N.J. (5)
Interstate and Foreign Commerce	William P. Hepburn, Iowa, Caucus Chair (6/9)
Rivers and Harbors	Theodore E. Burton, Ohio, (5/6)
Merchant Marine	Charles Grosvenor, Ohio (7/10)
Agriculture	Wadsworth, N.Y. (7/9)
Foreign Affairs	Hitt, Ill. (12)
Military Affairs	Hull, Iowa (7)
Naval Affairs	Foss, Ill. (5)
Post Office and Post Roads	Overstreet, Ind. (5)
Public Lands	Lacey, Iowa (8)
Indian Affairs	James Sherman, N.Y. (9)

Notes: Figures in brackets refer to the number of terms of continuous and, where appropriate, total prior service.
Source: C.R., 59.1, 297–9.

who took strategic decisions were, besides the Speaker, the majority members of the Rules Committee, John Dalzell and Charles Grosvenor, and the floor leader Sereno E. Payne, who was also chairman of the Ways and Means Committee. To these may be added James Tawney, who chaired the other top-ranking committee, Appropriations; James E. Watson of Indiana, whose good humor and talent for peacemaking especially fitted him for the recently-created post of Republican whip; and the Chicago Representative James Robert Mann, whose thorough knowledge of parliamentary procedure and sharp attention to detail enabled him to take on many of the day-to-day tasks of floor leadership.[40] The chairmen of the major committees (listed in Table 2.3) were potent political chieftains in their own right, but their influence did not extend far beyond their area of expertise. By its nature, the committee system turned members' activity into narrow channels. Men were urged to specialize, to learn one subject thoroughly, in order to command the attention and respect of their colleagues. But such specialization, together with the time-consuming nature of committee business, tended to divert their attention from questions of general strategy.

With a few exceptions, younger men like Mann who thrust themselves forward by their ability or by catching the Speaker's eye, the Republican

---

[40] Rager, "Fall of the House of Cannon," 22–30; Bolles, *Tyrant from Illinois*, 52–8; *ANB*, 6:45–6; 9:661–3; 17:175–6; 21:349–50; 22:794–5; Thompson, *Party Leaders*, 157–64 and 194–204; Herbert F. Margulies, *Reconciliation and Revival: James R. Mann and the House Republicans in the Wilson Era* (Westport, Conn.: Greenwood, 1996).

leaders were senior in both years and congressional service. Most had entered the House after the 1892 election, when the Republican party recovered ground lost in the debacle of 1890. Only Hitt, Payne, Dalzell, Wadsworth, and Hull had a record of continuous service that went back beyond that great divide. Cannon, Grosvenor, Hepburn, Lacey, and Sherman were numbered among the fallen in 1890. Tawney entered for the first time in 1893; Burton, Fowler, Foss, Jenkins, Overstreet, and Watson in 1895. In other words, they constituted a cohort of individuals who had laid the foundations of their congressional careers in the intense and shifting party struggles of the 1890s, culminating in the "Battle of the Standards" and the election of McKinley, a cohort which had been initiated into the congressional brotherhood by Reed and Cannon. As the turnover in membership dropped after 1896 the proportion of senior members increased and the leadership acquired a fixity that it had not possessed before. What bound these men together was not just a community of belief, though that existed, or a common interest in the "pork barrel," though that existed too, but strong ties of personal acquaintance and common experience.[41]

The House Democrats

A journalist in 1906 described the Democratic party in the House as a "disorganized, undisciplined mob.... Chaos is its best word of description.... A ploughing, snorting herd of Texas steers, suddenly released from all restraint, is its nearest analogue."[42] Certainly, divisions existed over the leadership claims of William Jennings Bryan and William Randolph Hearst. The Northern minority, representing the tenement districts of the inner city, shared little common experience with the Southern majority. But in 1905 that minority was small. Only 21 out of 136 Democratic Congressmen represented what had been free territory in 1860, along with 11 from Maryland, West Virginia, and Missouri. Its dismal electoral performance in the North lent the Democratic party in the House an unusual degree of homogeneity. More importantly, perhaps, after a decade of defeat, Democrats in the House, like Democrats elsewhere, were ready to shelve personal differences in pursuit of victory.[43]

Under the leadership of John Sharp Williams, what had been a "chaotic, irresponsible, feather-headed crew," as the *New York Times* put it, became

[41] Brady notes that many committee chairmen during the late 1890s were recent arrivals (*Congressional Voting*, 149–52). Most were still in place in 1905.
[42] Thompson, *Party Leaders*, 184–5.
[43] David A. Sarasohn, "The Democratic Surge, 1905–1912: Forging a Democratic Majority" (Ph.D. diss., University of California, Los Angeles, 1976), 9–11; Claude E. Barfield, "The Democratic Party in Congress, 1909–1913" (Ph.D. diss., Northwestern University, 1965), 6–11.

a much more effective political force which pursued an agreed policy and usually voted as a unit. Indeed, the level of party cohesion exhibited by the House Democrats during this period surpassed even that of the Republicans under Cannon.[44] Williams was a Mississippi planter's son, educated, like many Southern statesmen, at the University of Virginia and, more unusually, at Heidelberg. Though described by George E. Mowry as "the essence of cotton-planting traditionalism," he had long advocated a variety of progressive reforms. Williams was recognized as one of the finest debaters in the House, adept at extempore rejoinders and a fluent speaker.[45] As party leader he relied on persuasion and consultation, employing a mixture of flattery and tact to secure the acquiescence of his colleagues. A "kitchen cabinet" met weekly to formulate strategy, and party caucuses were called to commit the party to a united policy. Instead of the practice in earlier days, when "every man was his own leader," of regularly contradicting each other, Democratic spokesmen agreed on a common line of attack in order to probe weak points in the majority's position. According to the *Outlook*, Williams "supplied what his party has for years sorely lacked – sane, competent direction."[46] Opposition to his leadership never rose above "personal grudges and offended pride, with a seasoning of Hearst influence," as the *New York Times* put it, and soon dissolved. Williams easily won reelection as minority leader until he resigned in 1909 to take up a seat in the Senate.[47]

Williams's second-in-command was Champ Clark, an able and quick-witted speaker who frequently led the party in debate on the floor of the House. He was nominated by his party for the Speakership, and hence the minority leadership, at the beginning of the Sixty-first Congress.[48] As a Missourian, Clark was better placed to bridge the gap between the party's two sectional wings than other leading Democrats, most of whom were Southerners. The Southern delegations threw up their usual crop of elderly and distinguished statesmen, but few who stood out as effective parliamentary leaders. Williams found it easier to work with some of the more industrious younger members like Albert S. Burleson of Texas, Oscar Underwood of Alabama, and Henry D. Clayton of Alabama, who became chairman of the Democratic caucus in 1907. Many of the "boys" whose careers were

[44] *New York Times*, 25 February 1907; Brady, Cooper, and Hurley, "Decline of Party," 384.

[45] George E. Mowry, *The Era of Theodore Roosevelt, 1900–1912* (New York: Harper, 1958), 119; George C. Osborn, *John Sharp Williams: Planter Statesman of the Deep South* (Baton Rouge: Louisiana State University Press, 1943), 2–26, 120–3, 139–42; Thompson, *Party Leaders*, 184–93.

[46] Osborn, *Williams*, 108–10, 112–14; Barfield, "Democratic Party," 9–10; *New-York Times*, 12 January 1907.

[47] Ibid., 12 January and 24–25 February 1907; John Sharp Williams to Albert S. Burleson, 17 May, 17, 27 July 1905, Burleson MSS, LC.

[48] Morrison, "Champ Clark," 118–19, 169–71.

TABLE 2.4. *Characteristics of U.S. Senators, 59th Congress*

Average age	61.3	Previous offices held:	
Median age	58	Member of Congress	35
Educational attainment:		governor	21
college or univ.	48	state legislator	35
secondary	22	other state	23
other	12	municipal or county	31
Occupation:		United States	11
law	62	Service in Senate:	
business	19	1 term or less	44
farm	4	over 1 term	44
other	3	over 2 terms	11
		average service	1.1 terms
			(6.7 years)

Source: *Biographical Directory of the American Congress, 1789–1911* (Washington, D.C., 1913).

advanced by Williams went on to take up positions of leadership when the party regained power in 1913.[49]

"The Millionaires' Club"

"It seems to have become fashionable lately to criticize harshly the United States Senate," complained Senator George C. Perkins of California in April 1906.[50] The gentlemanly ease of the Senate was most seriously disturbed by a series of articles from the pen of the muckraking journalist David Graham Phillips which were collectively entitled "The Treason of the Senate." But Phillips's was only one of a number of attacks on "The Senate of Special Interests" during the opening decade of the new century.[51]

In composition the upper chamber differed markedly from the House (see Table 2.4). The average Senator at the beginning of the Fifty-ninth Congress had been in the world for 61.3 years and was more than a full decade older

[49] John Sharp Williams to Albert S. Burleson, 17 July 1905, Burleson MSS, LC; Evans C. Johnson, *Oscar W. Underwood: A Political Biographer* (Baton Rouge, La., 1980); Clark, *My Quarter Century*, 2:341–2; Barfield, "Democratic Party," 10–11.

[50] George C. Perkins, "The United States Senate and the People," *Independent* 60 (12 April 1906): 839.

[51] David Graham Phillips, *The Treason of the Senate* (ed. George E. Mowry and Judson Grenier, Chicago: Quadrangle, 1968), 22–7, 30–6; Henry B. Needham, "The Senate of Special Interests," *World's Work* 11 (February 1906): 7206–11; Louis Filler, *The Muckrakers: Crusaders for American Liberalism* (new edn., State College, Pa.: Pennsylvania State University Press, 1976), 252–5; David J. Rothman, *Politics and Power: The United States Senate, 1869–1901* (Cambridge, Mass.: Harvard University Press, 1966), 256–65; C. H. Hoebecke, *The Road to Mass Democracy: Original Intent and the Seventeenth Amendment* (New York: Transactions, 1995), 89–124.

than the average Representative. Most venerable were the Alabama Senators John T. Morgan and Edward W. Pettus, who had served as brigadiers in the Army of the Confederacy. Senators remained in their seats longer. The average member had already served just over six years. Twenty-one had completed a full senatorial term and seven more than three, that is eighteen years or more. Senior in terms of continuous service were William Boyd Allison of Iowa (who entered the chamber in 1873), Morgan (1877), Eugene Hale and William P. Frye of Maine, and Nelson W. Aldrich of Rhode Island (1881). Their educational attainment almost exactly matched that of the House. So did their occupational distribution, with lawyers once more constituting the overwhelming majority. Nineteen members were engaged in some form of business activity, most commonly in banking or insurance. Three of the Southern members described themselves as planters, while Francis E. Warren of Wyoming was a cattle and sheep rancher on a grand scale whom Jonathan Dolliver characterized as "the greatest shepherd since Abraham."[52]

The chief difference lay in the greater eminence of Senators in their chosen field. The upper house contained several distinguished lawyers who, like most talented practitioners, had served corporate clients. Allison of Iowa, Chester I. Long of Kansas, Frank P. Flint of California and John C. Spooner of Wisconsin were among the many who had represented leading railroad companies. Philander C. Knox of Pennsylvania was involved in the formation of the Carnegie Steel Company, while Joseph B. Foraker of Ohio and Joseph W. Bailey of Texas found it difficult to shake off allegations concerning their relationship with Standard Oil.[53] Whether they continued to perform such services in the Senate is harder to prove. Spooner for one denied retaining "any corporate connections": "No man or corporation has had any right to demand of me any service as a Senator. I have kept free from every possible complication which could affect my duty as a public man."[54] What cannot be ascertained is the extent to which the assumptions and habits of mind acquired in corporate boardrooms continued to influence Senators' actions. Whereas businessmen in the lower house tended to operate on a local scale, several Senators had more extensive interests: Nelson Aldrich was a wholesale grocer who had invested wisely in local traction companies and later acquired large holdings in rubber; Morgan G. Bulkeley of Connecticut and John F. Dryden of New Jersey were involved respectively in the creation of the Aetna and Prudential Insurance Companies; Redfield

---

[52] Sullivan, *Our Times*, 4:366. Biographical information gathered from *BDAC* and *ANB*.

[53] On Bailey, see Sam H. Acheson, *Joe Bailey: The Last Democrat* (New York: Macmillan, 1932), 139–51, 215–18, 224–7; *New York Times*, 28 June 1906. On Foraker, see Everett Walters, *Joseph Benson Foraker: An Uncompromising Republican* (Columbus: Ohio State University Press, 1948), 273–82; Theodore Roosevelt to William H. Taft, 19 September 1908, *Letters*, 6:1243–4.

[54] John C. Spooner to J. W. McCormick, 5 June 1906; to A. J. Aikens, 14 June 1906, Spooner Letterbooks, LC.

Proctor of Vermont presided benevolently over the world's biggest marble company; Stephen B. Elkins possessed extensive coalmining interests in West Virginia; and William A. Clark of Montana was one of the more notorious of the Western mining kings.

It is difficult to determine precisely how much wealth resided in the chamber. Phillips estimated that the Senate contained twenty-five millionaires. Perkins, on the other hand, claimed that there were no more than ten and that his colleagues' wealth did not "exceed the average accumulation of the business man, farmer or professional man of the New England or Middle States." A *New York Times* writer listed twenty-nine wealthy Senators but did not claim that they were all millionaires. Richest was Clark of Montana with a fortune of about $200 million, with Elkins and Alger at around $20 million and Aldrich at around $10 million following some way behind. Others described as millionaires were Murray Crane of Massachusetts, who had inherited his father's papermaking company but also had a presence on Wall Street as director of both General Electric and Bell Telephone; Eugene Hale, who had married into money; Thomas S. Martin of Virginia, a lawyer and manufacturer; and James P. Taliaferro, a banker in Jacksonville, Florida. A list compiled in 1910 by an aide of the Wisconsin progressive Robert M. La Follette included the names of twenty-nine Senators who were believed to own a million dollars or more, eight who were close to that figure, and eight who were "fairly rich." Although this last estimate almost certainly overstates the riches accumulated in the upper house, it is evident that the Senate was far from the congregation of average citizens described by Perkins.[55]

Whereas few Representatives had developed political careers beyond the local level, Senators had accumulated a much more impressive record of office holding before entering the chamber. Thirty-five had served in the House of Representatives, 21 in the governor's mansion and 13 in some other statewide office. Several had been appointed to high federal office: Alger, Elkins and Proctor as Secretary of War, Henry M. Teller as Secretary of the Interior, Knox as Attorney General. Senators were men who had moved beyond local contacts and support to build up a wider reputation and a wider following.[56] Many now in the Senate had carefully established commanding positions within their state party organizations. Boies Penrose, despite his Harvard education and "Proper Philadelphia" background, was first lieutenant, then successor, to Matthew S. Quay as the manager of the Pennsylvania Republican organization. Spooner was one of a triumvirate which for many years had dominated Wisconsin Republican politics. Several Southern Senators, like Benjamin R. Tillman of South Carolina and

[55] Phillips, *Treason of the Senate*; Perkins, "U.S. Senate and the People," 840; *New York Times*, 27 May 1906; A. O. Barton to Paul L. Benedict, 4 March 1910, Robert M. La Follette MSS, LC.

[56] Cf. Rothman, *Politics and Power*, 126–31.

Furnifold M. Simmons of North Carolina, had attained a similar statewide influence before securing election to the Senate.[57]

Those who did not command the organization had to command its support. Until the ratification of the Seventeenth Amendment in 1913, Senators were chosen by state legislatures which were, on occasions, subject to bribery, more often to the influence of powerful political machines and their business allies. In the West the railroads exerted a considerable influence in state politics and often, therefore, in the selection of Senators. Long "was known as a railroad Senator," William Allen White recalled, who owed his election to the support of the Santa Fe and Missouri Pacific Railroads. The "Regency" which dominated Iowa Republican politics at the turn of the century and which supported Allison's continuance in the Senate included representatives of the Burlington and the Chicago and Northwestern Railroads. Frank P. Flint was allegedly indebted for his election to the Southern Pacific "organization" in California. As Winston Churchill described in fictional terms, railroad influence, in this case that of the Boston and Maine, also weighed heavily in New Hampshire politics, contributing to the election of Senators Gallinger and Burnham.[58] The suspicion that party bosses and corporate magnates played an undue role in the selection of Senators, along with serious allegations of bribery and malpractice in several state legislatures, constituted the major reason for the rising demand for popular election of Senators which culminated in the ratification of the Seventeenth Amendment.[59]

It is hard to substantiate the widespread charges that corruption tarnished the senatorial ermine. A *Collier's* series on "Senate Undesirables" published during 1908 cited little hard evidence of malpractice beyond accusing Charles W. Fulton of Oregon and Levi Ankeny of Washington of bribing legislators to secure their election. Albert J. Hopkins of Illinois was accused of building up

---

[57] Walter Davenport, *Power and Glory: The Life of Boies Penrose* (New York: Putnam's, 1931); Fowler, *Spooner*; Francis B. Simkins, *Pitchfork Ben Tillman: South Carolinian* (Baton Rouge: Louisiana State University Press, 1944); Richard L. Watson, Jr., "Furnifold M. Simmons," *North Carolina Historical Review* 44 (1967): 166–87; Rothman, *Politics and Power*, 159–87.

[58] William Allen White, *The Autobiography of William Allen White* (New York: Macmillan, 1946), 350–4, 366–7; Joseph R. Burton to Victor Murdock, 19 December 1906, Murdock MSS, LC; Robert S. La Forte, *Leaders of Reform: Progressive Republicans in Kansas, 1900–1916* (Lawrence: University Press of Kansas, 1974), 26–8, 70; J. M. Oskison, "Long of Kansas," *Collier's* 41 (18 July 1908): 8–9; Leland L. Sage, *William Boyd Allison: A Study in Practical Politics* (Iowa City: State Historical Society of Iowa, 1956); George E. Mowry, *The California Progressives* (Berkeley: University of California Press, 1951); James Wright, *Progressive Yankees: Republican Reformers in New Hampshire, 1906–1916* (Hanover, N. H., 1987), 56–61.

[59] *Outlook* 79 (14 January 1905): 98–9; C. P. Connolly, "Senate Undesirables: III. Fulton of Oregon," *Collier's* 41 (4 April 1908): 13–14; C. P. Connolly, "Ankeny of Washington," *Collier's* 41 (22 August 1908): 15–16; George H. Haynes, *The Senate of the United States: Its History and Practice* (2 vols., Boston: Houghton, Mifflin, 1938),1: 86–115, 126–35; Phillips, *Treason of the Senate*, 41–4.

a political machine through the systematic use of federal patronage, which most Senators tried to achieve, and Long of close relations with the railroads, which most Senators tried to cultivate.[60] The corruption that Phillips had in mind was that of Senators working directly to advance their own and their friends' business interests by influencing legislation. The "treason" of which they stood accused was that they had betrayed the people of the United States by "giving aid and comfort" to their "enemies," the mercenary "special interests." He offered no fresh evidence to support these charges, seeking instead to demonstrate, by comparing "interests" with legislative outcomes, that his subjects had secured the specified outcomes with the deliberate intention of advancing the specified interests.[61] Phillips's cynical assumptions regarding human motivation ruled out the possibility that conservative Senators acted as they did because they genuinely believed that policies designed to promote particular business interests also served the public welfare. Their political beliefs naturally reflected the social milieu in which they moved, one of corporate wealth and high-level political management. They reflected also the tradition of "promotional governance" that permeated government-business relations during the Gilded Age.[62] It was not easy for Senators who had forged their careers in that late nineteenth-century world to question the political values or the standards of conduct by which they had operated so long and so successfully.

Party Organization in the Senate

Moisei Ostrogorski, writing in 1902, lamented that the Senate no longer bore "any resemblance to that august assembly which provoked the admiration of the Tocquevilles." The "iron discipline" of the party caucus had throttled individual judgment and responsibility. A body of men who traditionally prided themselves on their independence of spirit had cravenly submitted to the dictates of the "machine."[63] As in the House, the concentration of authority and the development of a responsible party leadership, in place of the freer but less productive practices of the past, had occurred quite abruptly around 1890 and was complete by the turn of the century, when Ostrogorski wrote.[64]

---

[60] The series included A. S. Henning, "Senate Undesirables-Albert J. Hopkins," *Colliers's* 40 (7 March 1908): 11–12; (14 March 1908): 13–14; Connolly, "Fulton of Oregon"; Oskison, "Long of Kansas"; Connolly, "Ankeny of Washington."

[61] Phillips, *Treason of the Senate*, 27–30, 58–60, 97–8.

[62] On "promotional governance," see Alan Lessoff, *The Nation and Its City: Politics, "Corruption," and Progress in Washington, D.C., 1861–1902* (Baltimore: Johns Hopkins University Press, 1994).

[63] Moisei Ostrogorski, *Democracy and the Organization of Political Parties* (2 vols., London: Macmillan, 1902), 2:542.

[64] The best account of the change is Rothman, *Politics and Power*, 11–72.

The root problem was the same in both chambers. Both suffered under the overwhelming pressure of legislative business. Unlike the House, the Senate had few rules to expedite its business. Traditionally, it spurned use of the previous question to curtail debate. Senators claimed the right to speak as long as they chose and could not be compelled to yield the floor without their consent.[65] What coherence of purpose there was in the chamber was provided by party organization. Remembering the frustrations of previous decades, members were prepared to combine to execute a party program. "Whatever their defects," said Henry Cabot Lodge, "party organizations cause responsibility in government. If you wipe out the organization you wipe out the responsibility, and with it a great conservative force." For this to be effective, members of the party must submerge their differences and accept the will of the majority. The Democratic leader Joseph W. Bailey was no less certain that a "divided party" deserved contempt: "The unity of a party is of incomparably more importance than the personal fortunes of an individual Senator."[66]

The institutional expression of party unity was the caucus. Senators of each party met at the beginning of the session to select a party leader and at various times thereafter to consider questions of strategy. Republican leaders preferred not to use the caucus "to bind any Senator," relying on less blatant, but more effective, means to command consent.[67] Senate Republicans left the day-to-day management of business to a steering committee chosen by the caucus chairman at the beginning of the session. In practice, its membership acquired a degree of permanence over time. Since 1897 its chairman, who was also chairman of the caucus, had been William Boyd Allison, one of the leading figures in the consolidation of the party organization in the 1880s and 1890s. As his growing frailty revealed itself, Eugene Hale took on more responsibility for managing the order of business, and it was he who succeeded Allison as chairman on his death in 1908. This committee arranged the daily order of business, choosing which measures reported from committee should be defined as the "unfinished business" to be taken up each day after the close of the morning hour. Controversial and divisive issues could be referred to the full caucus, but members preferred, where possible, to leave such decisions to the steering committee.[68]

The caucus also elected majority members of the standing committees. This task was delegated to a committee on committees, nominated by the chairman, whose slate was invariably ratified by the caucus as a whole.

---

[65] Haynes, *Senate*, 1:377–8, 385–401; Lindsay Rogers, *The American Senate* (New York: F. S. Crofts, 1926), 184–90; Rothman, *Politics and Power*, 39–41.

[66] Henry Cabot Lodge to R. L. O'Brien, 28 January 1909, Lodge MSS, MasHS; *C.R.*, 61.1, 4314; *New York Times*, 8 February 1906. See also Rothman, *Politics and Power*, 43–9, 221–31.

[67] *C.R.*, 59.1:2212; *New York Times*, 1–4, 6–8 February 1906. On the development of the caucus, see Rothman, *Politics and Power*, 17–19, 59–61.

[68] Ibid., 59–60, 74; Haynes, *Senate*, 1:483–8.

La Follette commented on the casual manner in which so crucial a decision was made: "Nobody said anything. . . . Then and there the fate of all the legislation of this session was decided."[69] Seniority governed committee rankings, more decisively than in the House, and was rarely transgressed. However, the assignment of new members and the movement of older members to vacancies on more prestigious committees enabled the leadership, over time, to exert considerable influence over their composition.[70] The committee on committees was at the start of each Congress flooded with requests for favorable assignments. The capacity of party leaders to grant or refuse such requests represented a powerful source of patronage.

Choice committee assignments were most unevenly distributed. The Committees on Appropriations and Finance, which had a hand on the federal purse strings, Foreign Relations, which held jurisdiction over a cherished area of senatorial authority, Interstate Commerce, which considered matters relating to railroads and other aspects of national economic policy, Judiciary, which considered significant constitutional and legal questions, and Rules were drawn almost exclusively from the senior members of the chamber. The average Senate service of the Republicans serving on Finance and Appropriations was seventeen years, on Rules thirteen, on Foreign Relations twelve, on Interstate Commerce ten, and on Judiciary seven.[71] The personnel of the top committees bore something of the character of an interlocking directorate. The six committees mentioned had forty-four places for Republicans. Twenty-eight individuals, half of the total, held all these seats, with five Senators holding three and five more holding two places apiece. These ten men, who included the most influential party leaders, held 59 percent of the majority places on the six most important Senate committees.[72] Allison was, of course, chairman of the party caucus. Hale, Aldrich, Cullom, Clark, Spooner, and Kean were also members of its committee on committees, along with Perkins, Nelson, and Beveridge. They monopolized places on important conference committees. It was they who offered motions, on behalf of the steering committee, concerning the order of business. Hale and Lodge, along with Allison when fit, were also prominent as party managers on the floor of the Senate.[73]

The senior Republicans were not equal in influence. It was widely believed that a small group, comprising Aldrich, Allison, Spooner, and Hale, made

---

[69] Ibid., 1:273–7, 284–5; Rothman, *Politics and Power*, 49–50.

[70] H. Douglas Price dates the systematic application of seniority to the 1870s and 1880s. "Congressional Career," 12–14. See also Rothman, *Politics and Power*, 50–8; Randall B. Ripley, *Power in the Senate* (New York: St. Martin's Press, 1969), 42–7; Haynes, *Senate*, 1:292–301.

[71] Committees are listed in *C.R.*, 59.1:573–8.

[72] Cf. Brady and Epstein, "Intraparty Preferences," 35–7.

[73] The committee on committees is listed in William B. Allison to John C. Spooner, 7 December 1905, Spooner MSS, LC.

most of the key strategic decisions.[74] Among these, Aldrich was acknowledged to be *primus inter pares*. Nelson Aldrich was a successful Rhode Island
merchant who had made a fortune through the consolidation of Providence
street railroads and enlarged it by shrewd investments on Wall Street, where
he developed close relations with J. P. Morgan and other financial magnates.
In many ways he came to express the Wall Street view in government, adher-
ing consistently to the Hamiltonian position that it was the responsibility of
government to promote the prosperity of industrial and commercial interests, which would then percolate downwards to other citizens. Representing
what amounted to a "rotten borough" in Rhode Island, Aldrich had less
incentive than other Senators to monitor public opinion, which he mostly
disregarded as unthinking and unstable. A large and dignified man, he cut a
commanding figure on the Senate floor, but he preferred to work behind the
scenes, in committee or in private discussion with other Senators. Aldrich
was "a chess player with men" who deployed his personal charm, shrewd
judgment of human nature, knowledge of legislative business, influence over
the selection of committees, and access to campaign funds to win consent.[75]

Allison was, in contrast, an adept politician, highly responsive to the shifting currents of opinion in the Midwestern state which he had the sometimes
troublesome honor to represent. Long associated both professionally and politically with the dominant railroads in the state, he contrived by a mixture of
clever compromise, bland rhetoric and exquisite tact to maintain a durable
popularity with Republican voters. His popularity with fellow Senators and
his careful discretion in dealing with their tender egos qualified him especially
for the delicate task of attaining and institutionalizing party unity during the
last two decades of the previous century. A caucus or a steering committee
chaired by Allison appeared less forbidding and less threatening to senatorial independence than one chaired by Aldrich might have been. However,
by 1905 he was well into his seventies, and his health was failing.[76] Allison's
junior both in years and service, John C. Spooner was a highly respected
constitutional lawyer, an expert legislative draftsman, and a formidable or-
ator. He was a high-ranking member of the Republican machine which had
long dominated Wisconsin politics but which was now disintegrating under
the assault of La Follette's insurgent faction.[77]

With Aldrich preferring to work behind the scenes and Allison frequently
indisposed, Eugene Hale took on more and more of the visible tasks of
floor leadership. Other prominent Republicans were Hale's colleague Frye,

[74] Thompson, *Party Leaders*, 25–32; Horace S. and Marion G. Merrill, *The Republican Command, 1897–1913* (Lexington: University Press of Kentucky, 1971), 17–21.
[75] Thompson, *Party Leaders*, 32; Stephenson, *Aldrich*, 132–7, 177–204, 218–25; Merrill, *Republican Command*, 21–7. For a more critical view of Aldrich's career, see Phillips, *Treason of the
Senate*, ch. 2; Lincoln Steffens, *The Struggle for Self-Government* (New York, 1906), 79–119.
[76] Sage, *Allison*; Merrill, *Republican Command*, 29–32; Thompson, *Party Leaders*, 32–3.
[77] Fowler, *Spooner*; Thompson, *Party Leaders of Our Time*, 34–5, 47–56; Shelby Cullom, *Fifty
Years of Public Service* (Chicago: McClurg, 1911), 357–60.

a popular and respected Senator who was repeatedly elected to the office of president *pro tempore*; Henry Cabot Lodge, a scholarly New Englander who sustained a close personal friendship with Roosevelt; Stephen B. Elkins, who chaired the Interstate Commerce Committee; and Murray Crane, a relatively junior Senator who rapidly endeared himself to the leadership by his dependability and capacity for hard work.[78]

The most prominent Republican dissident was the newly elected Robert M. La Follette, whose arrival was awaited with anxious anticipation after his angry struggle with the party machine in Wisconsin. Although the Senate was used to taming wild men, La Follette persistently declined to abide by its unwritten rules. His attitude to the Old Guard in the Senate matched his attitude to the Old Guard in Wisconsin: he regarded them as subservient spokesmen of corporate wealth and enemies of reform in the public interest; he regarded himself as fighting a lonely battle for the right similar to that which he had fought for years at home. Although, in fact, he practiced the arts of the politician with great skill, he perceived himself rather differently: as engaged in a crusading mission. La Follette, says John Milton Cooper, Jr., "came to view public life as a morality play defined mainly in terms drawn from the Bible and himself as a prophet, also along biblical lines." According to David Thelen, La Follette entered the Senate like a wild boar in a china shop, refusing to accept the tissue of compromise and adjustment that held the party together. Not surprisingly, many colleagues despised La Follette, who admitted to being the most unpopular Senator since Charles Sumner. La Follette worked hard to achieve concrete legislation, but his larger aim was to use the Senate as a platform from which he could speak to the general public, challenging fellow Senators to go on record in opposition to popular reform measures, so that he could then "read the roll call" to their constituents and either shame them into changing their ways or bring about their replacement by more progressive individuals.[79]

---

[78] *New York Times*, 2, 8 January 1907; Thompson, *Party Leaders*, 35–6, 38–46; Cullom, *Fifty Years*, 219–20; *ANB*, 9:821–2; John A. Garraty, *Henry Cabot Lodge* (New York: Knopf, 1953); Richard M. Abrams, *Conservatism in a Progressive Era: Massachusetts Politics, 1900–1912* (Cambridge, Mass.: Harvard University Press, 1964), 31–43; Oscar D. Lambert, *Stephen Benton Elkins* (Pittsburgh: University of Pittsburgh Press, 1955); Johnson, *Crane*, 33–45.

[79] Robert M. La Follette, *La Follette's Autobiography* (Allan Nevins ed., Madison, Wis.: University of Wisconsin Press, 1960), 159–82; John M. Cooper, Jr., "Robert M. La Follette: Political Prophet," *Wisconsin Magazine of History* 69 (1986): 91; David P. Thelen, *Robert M. La Follette and the Insurgent Spirit* (Boston: Little, Brown, 1975), 51–4; Bernard A. Weisberger, *The La Follettes of Wisconsin: Love and Politics in Progressive America* (Madison, Wis., 1994), chs. 1–2; Nancy Unger, *Fighting Bob La Follette: The Righteous Reformer* (Chapel Hill: University of North Carolina Press, 2000); Carl R. Burgchardt, *Robert M. La Follette, Sr.: The Voice of Conscience* (Westport, Conn.: Greenwood, 1992); *New-York Times*, 11 February 1907; Robert M. La Follette to A. M. Lewis, 14 January 1906, La Follette MSS, SHSW; La Follette to Belle C. La Follette, 4, 5, 8 December 1906, La Follette MSS, LC. On the "roll call," see La Follette to Levi Ankeny, 16 April 1907, La Follette MSS, LC; Belle C. and Fola La Follette, *Robert M. La Follette* (2 vols., New York: Macmillan, 1953), 1:211–13, 218–20, 230–4.

In its formal structure the Democratic party organization closely resembled the Republican. The steering committee and the committee on committees had some years earlier been merged into one body which combined the functions of its Republican equivalents, though less effectively. Deprived of power for so long, the Democratic leadership lacked the means to enforce compliance to its wishes. This was one reason why it depended so heavily on caucus resolutions as a means of compulsion. It was declared that a member who refused to abide by a decision supported by a two-thirds majority would be debarred from future caucuses and refused assignment to committees as a Democrat. Such threats had little force as long as the party remained a minority. An attempt in 1906 to use the caucus as a means of disciplining four "White House Democrats" for voting to ratify the President's treaty with Santo Domingo gave rise to an embarrassing public wrangle which dissuaded the party from similar exercises in the future, and the caucus became, by all accounts, "little more than a debating society." The affair demonstrated how fragile was its nominal authority to overcome serious internal divisions.[80]

Unlike their counterparts in the House, the Senate Democrats lacked effective leadership. Arthur P. Gorman of Maryland, caucus chairman and minority leader until his death in 1906, was ill and feeble. Bailey, his successor, though an able debater, was erratic in behavior and violent in temper, lacking the tact or discretion required to unite so motley a band. Moreover, his reputation was clouded by allegations that he had acted as attorney for the Waters-Pierce Oil Company, a subsidiary of Standard Oil. Charles Culberson of Texas, who reluctantly succeeded Bailey, was too reserved and uncommunicative to make an effective leader. The choice of Hernando D. Money of Mississippi, who was partially blind, suffering from ill health and on the verge of retirement, to replace Culberson as minority leader in 1909 apparently indicated a preference for having no leader at all.[81]

The Legislative Process

Woodrow Wilson's *Congressional Government* told important truths about the Congress of the late nineteenth century, many of which remained valid in the early twentieth. He recognized that proceedings on the floor of the House

La Follette was also extremely ambitious, with his eyes firmly fixed on the White House. Herbert Margulies, "Robert M. La Follette as Presidential Aspirant: The First Campaign," *Wisconsin Magazine of History* 80 (1997): 258–79.

[80] Rothman, *Politics and Power*, 61–9; Haynes, *Senate*, 1:475–88; Barfield, "Democratic Party," 12; *New York Times*, 1–8 February 1906.

[81] Ibid., 20 November, 23 December 1905, 3, 29 January 1906, 30 January, 4 March 1907; Albert S. Burleson to Jefferson Johnson, 18 April 1908, Burleson MSS, LC; Barfield, "Democratic Party," 11–14; Thompson, *Party Leaders*, 109–18; Acheson, *Bailey*, 139–51, 215–18, 224–7, 254–5; James W. Madden, *Charles Allen Culberson* (Austin: University of Texas Press, 1929); *ANB*, 1:888–90, 5:833–4, 15:671–2.

of Representatives were largely a stage play. They were acted out in an atmosphere of tumultuous distraction – "The raising and dropping of desk lids, the scratching of pens, the clapping of hands to call the pages,... the pattering of many feet, the hum of talking on the floor and in the galleries" – which prevented more than a handful of adjacent members from following what was being said.[82] Debate was largely perfunctory, confined as it was by special orders, motions to suspend the rules and ruthless application of the previous question. The function of speech making was less to influence the decision of the House than to create a record for consumption by the folks back home. Indeed, many of the carefully constructed arguments, the diligently marshaled facts and figures, and the ornate passages of rhetoric that fill the pages of the *Congressional Record* were not delivered on the floor but inserted later (for which leave was readily granted by colleagues, in anticipation of reciprocal indulgence towards their own unspoken flights of oratory).[83] Rather than carefully weighing the arguments, Representatives, many of them arriving in haste from lobbies or committee rooms, customarily followed the guidance of party leaders or members of the responsible committee in deciding how to vote. Other than appropriations and revenue measures, which were exhaustively scrutinized, legislation once reported from committee was rarely altered significantly on the floor of the House. As H. G. Wells discovered, conditions in the Senate were ostensibly similar, although real debate was still possible there. Bills reported from committee commonly underwent substantial revision, like, for example, the Hepburn rate bill, which emerged noisily debated but unscathed from the floor of the House but was substantially modified on the floor of the Senate.

As in the late nineteenth-century Congress, as, indeed, the late twentieth-century Congress, the real work of legislating was carried out in committee. The standing committees of both House and Senate played an important gatekeeping role, turning aside the overwhelming majority of legislative proposals, modifying others to meet their tastes and ideological preferences. It was there that the merits of legislation were given their fullest consideration, where arguments from interested parties were heard, and where the content of most measures was effectively determined. Committee members guided bills through to passage on the floor, and committee members staffed the conference committees which played the often critical role of resolving differences between the two houses. They blew the initial breath of life into legislation and crafted its final shape. Such was the influence wielded by the committees within their respective substantive domains that Wilson

---

[82] Bryce, *American Commonwealth*, 1:145; Wilson, *Congressional Government*, 73–4.

[83] The *Record* therefore does not provide an accurate transcript of what was said on the floor of the House, but it is usually possible, with the assistance of newspaper reports, to distinguish between what was actually spoken and what was not.

concluded that it was "no great departure from the fact to describe ours as a government by the Standing Committees of Congress."[84]

The major departure from the institution that Wilson described, and, indeed, that described by more recent analysts, was the dominating role of party organizations. Never before nor since has their influence been so pronounced. The Speaker of the House not only prospectively shaped legislation through his power to appoint the standing committees but also, through his power of recognition and his leadership of the Rules Committee, determined which of the measures reported would be considered by the House. He also selected the House representatives on conference committees. In the Senate the leadership of the majority party exerted a comparable, though less commanding, influence. A small group of senior Republicans, through their control of the party's steering committee, but also through their personal influence and prestige, largely directed the affairs of the Senate. Hence the committee system operated within a framework determined by party organization.

So intensified a form of party government required certain ambient conditions. It depended on a desire for greater efficiency in dealing with the increased volume of legislation generated by a growing economy and a more active government. It depended also on the fear of legislative anarchy felt by many senior Republicans, in reaction to their experiences in the 1880s and 1890s. They shared an image of their Democratic opponents as obstructionists, prone to irresponsible and destructive filibustering unless held in check by a disciplined Republican party armed with a set of rules that enabled the majority to govern. It depended, above all, on a degree of party unity that has rarely been matched. Republicans representing a variety of sections and economic interests responded to a program of economic development and a set of distributive policies, especially protective tariff duties. The result was, perhaps, the closest equivalent to "responsible" party government that has been achieved in the United States. But these were rarefied conditions, and they did not last. The progressive reforms that resulted in the establishment of the new American state divided Republicans and fractured the consensus on which the authority of the "partisan speakership" and the "Senate Four" was ultimately founded. The result was a less centralized, more diffuse pattern of congressional decision making which was not always conducive to systematic and cumulative policy formation.[85]

Congress and the Electorate

The roll of the House in the Fifty-ninth Congress contained 250 Republicans and 136 Democrats, the most overwhelming Republican majority since

---

[84] Wilson, *Congressional Government*, 55–6.
[85] Peters, *American Speakership*, 87–91; Brady and Epstein, "Intraparty Preferences."

Reconstruction. Every Congress between 1895 and 1911 was securely in Republican hands, though not by so wide a margin. This protracted hegemony stands in sharp contrast to the close contest between the major parties that characterized national politics during the last quarter of the nineteenth century. The congressional election of 1894, in the wake of the economic downturn of the previous year, and the presidential election of 1896, the famous "Battle of the Standards," initiated a long period of Republican domination in national politics, and generally in state politics outside the South, which endured, with relatively brief interruptions, until the 1930s.[86]

For some decades political scientists have investigated the seemingly regular shifts in the aggregate partisan preference of the electorate which separate one period of electoral stability from another. One such "critical realignment," they believe, occurred in the 1890s.[87] However, critical realignment theory presents a number of conceptual and methodological problems that have never been wholly resolved.[88] In particular, the crucial linkage between electoral change and governance, without which the identification of electoral cycles is of little more than aesthetic interest, has been difficult to establish empirically, especially for the "System of 1896." At a national level the outcome of realignment was control of the federal government by a Republican party committed to traditional Republican policies and led by traditional Republican politicians of the old school. The major changes associated with progressivism came a decade later.[89] Indeed, it could be argued that progressive reform emerged, not as a direct consequence of electoral realignment,

---

[86] Paul Kleppner, *Continuity and Change in Electoral Politics, 1893–1928* (Westport, Conn.: Greenwood, 1987), 66–115; Walter Dean Burnham, "The System of 1896: An Analysis," in Paul Kleppner, ed., *The Evolution of American Electoral Systems* (Westport, Conn.: Greenwood, 1981), 147–202.

[87] See, for example, Burnham, *Critical Elections*; Jerome Clubb, et al., *Partisan Realignment* (Beverly Hills, Cal.: Sage, 1979).

[88] Allan J. Lichtman, "The End of Realignment Theory? Toward a New Research Program for American Political History," *Historical Methods Newsletter* 15 (1982): 170–88; Lichtman, "Political Realignment and 'Ethnocultural Voting' in Late Nineteenth-Century America," *Journal of Social History* 16 (1983): 55–82; Richard L. McCormick, "Walter Dean Burnham and 'The System of 1896,'" *Social Science History* 10 (1986): 245–62; McCormick, "The Realignment Synthesis in American History," *Journal of Interdisciplinary History* 13 (1982): 85–105; Joel Silbey, "Beyond Realignment and Realignment Theory: American Political Eras, 1789–1989," in Byron Shafer, ed., *The End of Realignment? Interpreting American Electoral History* (Madison: University of Wisconsin Press, 1991), 3–23. For a defense, see Kleppner, *Continuity and Change*, 1–18, 239–47; Burnham, "Periodization Schemes and 'Party Systems'"; Burnham, "Critical Realignment: Dead or Alive?" in Shafer, ed., *End of Realignment*, 101–31.

[89] See, for example, Clubb, *Partisan Realignment*; David W. Brady, *Critical Elections and Congressional Policy Making* (Stanford, Cal.: Stanford University Press, 1988). The limited impact of the 1890s realignment is emphasized by McCormick, *From Realignment to Reform: Political Change in New York State, 1893–1910* (Ithaca, N.Y.: Cornell University Press, 1981); McCormick, "Walter Dean Burnham," 253–8; Allen and Slagter, "Congress in Crisis."

but as a reaction to the pattern of one-party rule that followed from it, in state capitals as well as in Washington.[90]

It is important to recognize that the electoral events of the 1890s did not have a determining influence on those of the following decades; the realignment of the 1890s, such as it was, did not decisively set the mold for the politics of the Progressive Era. The "System of 1896" was a dynamic system, in which the partisan distribution of the vote fluctuated erratically.[91] One of the most significant features of the era's electoral politics was a swing to the Democrats, which can be traced back to 1908, and in some states to 1904. Outside the Midwestern heartland of Republican insurgency, popular support for reform manifested itself in a growing preference for the candidates of a Democratic party which, at both state and national levels, offered more progressive policies and more progressive candidates. The trend was to some extent obscured by the public prominence of Republican progressives like Cummins, La Follette and, above all, Roosevelt. It was Roosevelt's immense popularity and his personal identification with reform that prevented his party from suffering the hemorrhage of votes in national elections that was already apparent by 1904 in states like Massachusetts and Minnesota. As David A. Sarasohn has convincingly argued, it was only Roosevelt's presence on the ballot as an independent Progressive candidate that prevented a still greater leakage of Republican votes to the Democrats in 1912. It may be possible to describe the Democratic gains in the period 1904–1916 as an incipient Progressive Era realignment, which was then reversed in the postwar repudiation of the Wilson Administration.[92]

In congressional elections, which are our chief concern, the steady pro-Democratic trend is evident. While the Democratic vote rose from 24.5 percent of the total electorate in 1904 to 28.2 percent in 1908, and from 22.2 percent in the off-year of 1906 to 24.3 percent in 1910, the Republican vote fell from 36.8 percent in 1904 to 33.8 percent in 1908, and from 27.1 to 24.7 percent in the off-years. With each biennial election after 1904 the Democratic share of the popular vote rose until the party secured a majority in 1910. The gains were most pronounced in the urban areas of southern New England, the Mid-Atlantic states, and the Midwestern states of Ohio, Indiana and Illinois. In 1904 only 23 Democratic Congressmen were elected outside the former slave states, 10 of whom represented New York City. By 1910 the number had risen to 101, including 40 from Illinois, Indiana, and Ohio, and 41 from New York, New Jersey, and Pennsylvania.[93]

---

[90] Martin Shefter, *Political Parties and the State: The American Historical Experience* (Princeton, N.J.: Princeton University Press, 1994), 75–81;

[91] Electoral fluctuations after 1896 are examined in Burnham, "System of 1896"; Kleppner, *Continuity and Change*, 37–42 and passim.

[92] Sarasohn, "Democratic Surge," 273–93. For a contrary view, see Kleppner, *Continuity and Change*, 125–46.

[93] Ibid., 128; *Guide to U.S. Elections* (Washington: Congressional Quarterly, 1975), 697–716.

Politicians, of course, listened carefully for signs of public opinion, and from about 1905 they detected an increasing popular sentiment in favor of reform. "The Frisco Quake was only a zephyr compared to the earthquake that is now shaking our nation," declared a correspondent of Allison in June 1906, somewhat mixing his metaphors. The cumulative effects of local reform movements all over the country and the exposure by muckraking journalists of political corruption and business malpractice combined to produce what Theodore Roosevelt called "a very unhealthy condition of excitement and irritation in the popular mind."[94]

Congressmen were naturally alert to what Beveridge called "the present popular unrest." "It appears to me," he observed in August 1906, "and appears very clearly that we have entered upon a new era in American politics." A great "moral movement" was "sweeping the country."[95] Conservative ears were no less sensitive. "I have never known a time when there was such an unsettled condition in the public mind in this part of the country as there is today," Tawney reported to Cannon from his Minnesota district. What was welcome to a progressive like Beveridge was, of course, profoundly disturbing to a Stalwart Republican like Tawney. The same disquiet is evident in the private writings of Spooner, who in June 1906 commented sadly on "the wave of accusation and distrust" and the "tendency to hysteria" abroad in the land. When, in the winter of 1906, Lincoln Steffens visited Washington in order to "muckrake" Congress he found its members deeply worried about the "unsettled" political climate and anxious to learn how soon, in his opinion, the "reform wave" would "blow over."[96] Four years later political conditions were no more settled. The "progressive sentiment," Beveridge noted in April 1910, was "now almost universal among the people." The Democratic Senator Francis G. Newlands agreed that "the majority of the people are insurgent against existing conditions."[97] Though most pronounced in the Midwest, signs of popular agitation could also be read further east. "We are having troubled times here," observed Henry Cabot Lodge. The people, he told Roosevelt, were "in a discontented frame of mind."[98]

---

94 William B. Allen to William B. Allison, 1 June 1906, Allison MSS, ISDHA; Theodore Roosevelt to William Howard Taft, 15 March 1906, *Letters*, 5:183.

95 Albert S. Beveridge to Lyman Abbott, 17 August 1906; to Albert Shaw, 19 August 1906; to Clarence A. Kenyon, 22 August 1906; to Frank E. Munsey, 10 November 1906, Beveridge MSS, LC.

96 Tawney quoted in Bolles, *Tyrant from Illinois*, 143; John C. Spooner to J. B. Gilfillans, 11 June 1906; to A. J. Aikens, 14 June 1906, Spooner Letterbooks, LC; Lincoln Steffens, "The Senate as It Sees Itself," proof of article dated 28 January 1906, Robert M. La Follette MSS, LC.

97 Albert S. Beveridge to Walter Bradfute, 11 April 1910; to Joseph L. Bristow, 16 July 1910, Beveridge MSS, LC; Beveridge to Robert M. La Follette, 26 September 1910, La Follette MSS, LC; Francis G. Newlands, "Interview," n.d. 1910, Newlands MSS, SLYU.

98 Henry Cabot Lodge to William S. Bigelow, 5 March 1910; to Theodore Roosevelt, 19 April 1910, Lodge MSS, MasHS.

While progressivism was both more and less than a simple expression of the will of the American people, it is clear that a pronounced upsurge of public feeling was an important element in the politics of the period. No one can read far into the written records of the period without becoming aware of it. By 1900, wrote the journalist Mark Sullivan, the average American, the "forgotten man," had come to feel " that his freedom of action, his opportunity to do as he pleased, was being frustrated in ways mysterious in their origin and operation." The "purpose of the average man to make himself heard was part of a mood which determined much of the political and social history of this quarter-century."[99] Echoing Sullivan, historians like Irwin and Debi Unger and Otis L. Graham have noted the "vulnerability" felt by ordinary Americans when confronted with the great concentrations of political and economic power which had emerged so suddenly around the turn of the century. The persistent rise in the cost of living that began around 1897, modest by recent standards but alarming to a generation accustomed to stable or falling prices, pointed to a link between the rise of big business and the general welfare. Magazine articles on the rising cost of living became more numerous after 1905. According to George H. Lorimer, editor of the *Saturday Evening Post*, "the pay envelope, the meat bill, the coal bill, and the gas bill are the people's text books of political economy." A "consumer consciousness" in the face of rising prices and unsatisfactory goods and services was, according to Thelen, a major ingredient of the contemporary discontent.[100]

"Muckraking" journalism played a crucial role in alerting the public to these problems. Beveridge maintained that "the great volume of the cheaper magazines which are circulating among the people and which have become the people's literature have wrought almost a mental and moral revolution among the people."[101] The dominant theme to emerge from the great body of investigative journalism was the corrupt linkage between businessmen and politicians – as Richard L. McCormick puts it, "The Discovery That Business Corrupts Politics." According to McCormick, the impact of the muckrakers was decisively reinforced between 1904 and 1906 by a series of alarming disclosures of corruption and business influence in almost every state of the Union. In New York State, for example, the critical event was the revelation of the political activities of the life insurance companies that emerged during the Armstrong investigations of 1905–6; in the Midwestern states the political influence of the railroads was the focus of resentment;

---

[99] Sullivan, *Our Times*, 1:70, 137.
[100] George H. Lorimer to Theodore Roosevelt, 28 May 1906, METRP, Reel 65; Irwin Unger and Debi Unger, *The Vulnerable Years: The United States, 1896–1917* (New York: New York University Press, 1977); Otis L. Graham, Jr., *The Great Campaigns: Reform and War in America, 1900–1928* (Englewood Cliffs, N.J.: Prentice-Hall, 1971); Thelen, *La Follette*.
[101] Albert J. Beveridge to Joseph L. Bristow, 16 July 1910, Beveridge MSS, LC; Filler, *Muckrakers*.

in New Hampshire an apparently insignificant racetrack gambling bill generated a surprising level of public outrage. Such revelations spurred local reform movements across the land whose chief objective was to break the corrupt links between business and government. McCormick believes that this "Discovery That Business Corrupts Politics" served as a catalyst, drawing together a number of political trends and providing a specific object for public anxieties to work upon. In that sense it was a key moment in the development of progressivism as a national phenomenon.[102]

The Man in the White House

Congressmen during the first decade of the century not only confronted a more volatile electorate than their predecessors but also a more volatile Chief Executive. Unlike the amiable William McKinley, who for all his political skill conformed in most respects to the normal expectations of a late nineteenth-century president, Theodore Roosevelt presented them with a series of more or less unwelcome challenges.

As his biographers have demonstrated, Roosevelt, when he entered the White House in 1901, was essentially a conservative in his political views, not far removed from the Republican mainstream. Nor did he ever wholly renounce his conservative views while in office. Animated by a deeply rooted fear of violence and social conflict, he regularly censured "extremists" of the right and left, whom he accused of a dangerously selfish indifference to the public interest. Moved by a patrician's distaste for materialism and the pursuit of narrow private or class interests, Roosevelt aspired to transcend class politics in the name of higher national ideals. However, this required the firm intervention of an active federal government which, by offering a "Square Deal" to all citizens, would arbitrate between conflicting class interests and hold individuals to a higher standard of conduct. It seemed axiomatic to Roosevelt that the growing complexity of an urban-industrial society required the guiding hand of government, and, unlike most Americans of his generation, he had little fear of its exercise.[103]

---

[102] Richard L. McCormick, "The Discovery that Business Corrupts Politics: A Reappraisal of the Origins of Progressivism," *American Historical Review* 86 (1981): 247–74.

[103] See John M. Blum, *The Republican Roosevelt* (Cambridge, Mass.: Harvard University Press, 1954); Blum, *The Progressive Presidents: Roosevelt, Wilson, Roosevelt, Johnson* (New York: Norton, 1980), 23–60; John M. Cooper, *The Warrior and the Priest: Theodore Roosevelt and Woodrow Wilson* (Cambridge, Mass.: Harvard University Press, 1983), 79–86, 113–17; William Henry Harbaugh, *The Life and Times of Theodore Roosevelt* (2nd ed., New York: Oxford University Press, 1975), especially 251–9; Mowry, *Era of Theodore Roosevelt*, 106–15; Stephen Skowronek, *The Politics Presidents Make: Leadership from John Adams to George Bush* (Cambridge, Mass.: Harvard University Press, 1993), 228–59; William B. Gatewood, Jr., *Theodore Roosevelt and the Art of Controversy* (Baton Rouge: Louisiana State University Press, 1970).

Roosevelt regarded himself as the "steward of the people," holding a primary responsibility for the public welfare. Rather than restricting himself to the powers explicitly conferred by the Constitution, he pushed the authority of the executive to its limits. As John M. Blum and Stephen Skowronek have shown, Roosevelt offered "creative leadership" in the reconstitution of institutional power, seeking to forge administrative mechanisms capable of meeting the challenges of the new century. To that end he worked persistently for bureaucratic reorganization and civil service reform. Administrative efficiency lay close to the heart of his conception of government. Administrative process rather than rigid statutes was the way to resolve the complex technical problems of governance in the modern era and to elevate public interest above private power. Where possible, as in his antitrust and conservation policies, Roosevelt sought to achieve his goals through the elaboration of existing executive authority.[104] Where that authority did not exist he was compelled to turn to Congress.

As befits a creator of the modern presidency, Roosevelt was conscious of the importance of public opinion and consciously set out to cultivate it. He was the first president systematically to court the press, displaying a sensitive understanding of what constituted a news story and how it was produced. By manipulating the media he was able to manage the development of a political controversy, maintaining a barrage of headlines to stir up public interest and undermine his adversaries. Roosevelt's colorful personality, effervescent manner and ebullient energy – the "fun of him" – communicated themselves through the medium of the press to the American people, making him, in the modern sense of the word, very much a "celebrity."[105] His popularity flowed as much from the public's perception of what he was as from its response to his policies. He deliberately cultivated a legend of his career as that of an indomitable "Henty hero," a personification of rugged manliness and individual self-reliance at a time when such virtues appeared to be undermined in an increasingly urban society.[106] Above all, Roosevelt inspired contemporaries by appealing to their deeper moral sensibilities. His

---

[104] Stephen Skowronek, *Building a New American State: The Expansion of National Administrative Capacities, 1877–1920* (Cambridge: Cambridge University Press, 1982), 170–3; Blum, *Republican Roosevelt*, 17–21, 73–105, 109–10; Roosevelt, *Autobiography*, 362–5, 464; Samuel F. Hays, *Conservation and the Gospel of Efficiency: the Progressive Conservation Movement, 1890–1920* (Cambridge, Mass., 1959); Harold T. Pinkett, "The Keep Commission, 1905–1909: A Rooseveltian Effort for Administrative Reform," *Journal of American History* 52 (1965): 297–312; Gould, *Presidency of Theodore Roosevelt*, 197–223.

[105] George Juergens, *News from the White House: The Presidential-Press Relationship in the Progressive Era* (Chicago: University of Chicago Press, 1983); Sullivan, *Our Times*, 3:72–80; Butt, *Taft and Roosevelt*, 1:29–31; Cooper, *Warrior and Priest*, 69–70; Gould, *Presidency of Theodore Roosevelt*, 19–20.

[106] Kathleen Dala, "Why America Loved TR," *Psychohistory Review* 8 (1979): 16–26; Arnoldo Testi, "The Gender of Reform Politics: Theodore Roosevelt and the Culture of Masculinity," *Journal of American History* 81 (1995): 1509–33.

public rhetoric, if not his political actions, conjured up, for many, a trans-forming vision of a common purpose that related the moral uncertainties of individuals to a set of political symbols.[107]

There is ample evidence of the fond public regard for Roosevelt and the public support for the "Roosevelt policies." When in 1906 a newly elected Brooklyn Congressman asked his constituents what course of action he should take, the great majority of the fourteen hundred replies urged him to follow the President's lead. Two years later, when a New York magazine conducted a poll of its subscribers, ninety percent of the respondents favored a third term for Roosevelt, even though he had publicly declined to run, and a canvass of Midwestern newspaper editors and local politicians taken by the Chicago *Tribune* showed overwhelming support for his policies.[108] Congressmen like Henry C. Adams did not need reminding "how universal is the popular regard for the president and how dangerous it is politically for a member of congress to disagree with him upon any subject whatever." That popularity was an important asset for the President in his dealings with Congress.[109]

More than any of his predecessors, Roosevelt formulated a legislative program and set out to secure its enactment. He summoned Congressmen to the White House, bombarded Congress with special messages and for-warded bills drafted in the executive departments.[110] In practice, having ex-pended most of his patronage resources in securing renomination, Roosevelt depended for his success upon negotiation and compromise with congres-sional leaders. For some years he consulted Cannon on a regular basis. "I think Mister Roosevelt talked over with me virtually every serious recom-mendation to Congress before he made it, and requested me to sound out the leaders in the House," recalled Cannon in the rosy glow of hindsight, although his recollections more accurately describe events before than after 1906. Both, as Jim Watson pointed out, were "party men" who "knew that it was necessary to stand together." "This administration has no stouter friend

---

[107] See, for example, William Allen White, "Roosevelt: A Force for Righteousness," *McClure's* 28 (February 1907): 386–94; Lyman Abbott, "A Review of President Roosevelt's Administration: IV–Its Influence on Patriotism and Public Service," *Outlook* 91 (27 Febru-ary 1909): 430–4.

[108] *New York Times*, 7 February 1906, 27 January, 2 March 1908; *Outlook* 87 (7 September 1907): 3–4.

[109] Henry C. Adams to L. C. Nieman, 5 March 1906, Adams MSS, SHSW. Cf. Albert S. Beveridge to Theodore Roosevelt, 16 October 1906, Beveridge MSS, LC; Francis G. Newlands to E. L. Bingham, 6 January 1906, Newlands MSS, SLYU; George Norris to H. L. Hilyard, 24 January 1906, Norris MSS, LC; Henry C. Adams to editor of Milwaukee *State Journal*, 12 April 1906, Adams MSS, SHSW.

[110] See, for example, Steffens, "The President is President"; Steffens, "The President as a Boss"; or, for a less sympathetic view, Augustus O. Bacon, "The President and Congress," *Indepen-dent* 60 (8 March 1906): 546–9; Samuel W. McCall, "The Fifty-Ninth Congress," *Atlantic Monthly* 98 (November 1906): 585–6.

than the Speaker of the House," Roosevelt told a friendly labor leader in September 1906. "We could not have done in the past the things you and I believe in, and we shall not continue to do them in the future without the kind of backing that he has given us."[111] His overtures to the "Senate Four" are well documented. Aldrich's biographer believes that "at some time early in his administration he and the Four agreed that he should have his head in all things outside economics and finance, and that they should govern his policy in the reserved subjects." This discounts such initiatives that Roosevelt did take in antitrust policy and probably would not apply to the second term. It is more likely that the presidential self-abnegation, such as it was, applied only to tariff revision and perhaps currency reform. However, it was clear to Roosevelt that he could only with very great difficulty secure action from the Senate without their support.[112]

As his performance in the long session of the Fifty-ninth Congress shows, Roosevelt was capable of great skill in negotiation and compromise, displaying an acute sense of timing and a clear grasp of the possible. By playing off the various factions in the Senate against each other he contributed to the passage of a railroad bill that met most of his initial demands. Beveridge believed that his meat inspection amendment would never have passed Congress "if Roosevelt had not picked up his big stick and smashed the packers over the head with it and their agents in the House and Senate." In summing up the session in June 1906, the *New York Times*, never free with praise of Roosevelt, recognized his success in articulating public demands and forcing congressional action.[113]

After 1906 Roosevelt was, in effect, a lame-duck president; like other holders of the office he found it increasingly difficult to influence Congress. Once they had secured reelection in the congressional election of that year, with the assistance of a "blanket endorsement" from the President, Republican Congressmen were effectively free of his influence.[114] They knew that in 1908 their reelection would inevitably be linked to that of a presidential candidate whose prospects Roosevelt would not wish to jeopardize by conducting public rows with recalcitrant legislators. Hence they could ignore his

---

[111] Busbey, *Uncle Joe Cannon*, 219; Watson, *As I Knew Them*, 56–7; Theodore Roosevelt to Edgar E. Clark, 5 September 1906, *Letters*, 5:397–8; to George Van L. Meyer, 1 February 1906, *Letters*, 5:145; Rager, "Fall of the House of Cannon," 34–49; Gwinn, *Uncle Joe Cannon*, 74–80, 85–7.

[112] Stephenson, *Aldrich*, 197–204 and 218–25; Fowler, *Spooner*, 261–3, 268–72; Mowry, *Era of Theodore Roosevelt*, 129–30; Sage, *Allison*, 285–8, 295–7.

[113] Albert S. Beveridge to Francis E. Baker, 1 August 1906; to Albert S. Shaw, 20 May 1906, Beveridge MSS, LC; C.R., 59.1:8766; *New York Times*, 19 May, 25, 30 June 1906; Lyman Abbott to Theodore Roosevelt, 8 May 1906, METRP; Francis G. Newlands to Norman Hapgood, 8 February 1907, Newlands MSS, SLYU; Blum, *Republican Roosevelt*, 73–105.

[114] Theodore Roosevelt to James E. Watson, 18 August 1906, *Letters*, 5:372–8; James E. Watson to John F. Lacey, 20 August 1906, Lacey MSS, ISDHA; Merrill, *Republican Command*, 222–35.

legislative proposals with relative impunity. Conservative Republican leaders in both houses blocked consideration of his legislative agenda and, despite the considerable rank-and-file support for the President's program, reverted to their determination to "stand pat."[115] Besides blocking his legislative proposals, congressional leaders entered into a series of public controversies with the President: over his dismissal of a company of black troops following a riot at Brownsville, Texas, over his forestry policy, over his plans for naval expansion, over his employment of Secret Service agents in the prosecution of land frauds, and over his appointment of commissions of inquiry without congressional permission.[116]

In important respects Roosevelt's presidential project had failed. Although he had made creditable progress in forging the institutional instruments appropriate to the task of governing a modern society, he had signally failed in his efforts to reposition the Republican party. He had come to believe that, in rebutting what he saw as the "destructive" radicalism of Populism and the Bryan Democracy, his party had become dangerously "fossilized" into a rigid "standpat" conservatism. It ran the risk of alienating in the future the public support that it enjoyed at present. A staunch Republican, he sought to vindicate the party's hegemonic position by drawing from it a "constructive" response to the challenges of the new society, so that it might retain the political initiative. Yet, in the end, Roosevelt's strategy of conciliation did nothing to shift the party leadership towards a more reformist stance. In particular, his reluctance to undertake the thorny task of tariff revision left a dangerously divisive issue for his successor to deal with. For all his achievements, Roosevelt as president failed either to move the center of gravity of the Republican party or to heal the divisions that were opening within it as it confronted the issues of progressive reform.[117]

[115] *New York Times*, 4, 31 December 1907, 16, 21, 29 April, 2, 5, 12, 31 May 1908; *Outlook* 89 (16 May 1908): 89–90; Gould, *Reform and Regulation*, 68–73; Mowry, *Era of Theodore Roosevelt*, 220–3; Bolles, *Tyrant from Illinois*, 88–105; Cooper, *Warrior and Priest*, 109–14.

[116] Gould, *Presidency of Theodore Roosevelt*, 230–94; Merrill, *Republican Command*, 235–43; Harbaugh, *Life and Times of Theodore Roosevelt*, 290–4, 312–18, 344–5; Busbey, *Uncle Joe Cannon*, 230–42; Gatewood, *Theodore Roosevelt and the Politics of Controversy*, 236–83.

[117] Skowronek, *The Politics Presidents Make*, 229–32, 235–43.

3

The Troubled Subject of Railroad Regulation in the Progressive Era

"The federal regulation of the railroads," suggests Gabriel Kolko, was "the first example of national Progressivism, and possibly its most important single illustration." Railroad companies, dependent for their very existence on privileges and sometimes subsidies conferred by government, had long been recognized as "affected with a public interest" and therefore liable to government supervision to a degree that other forms of business enterprise were not.[1] For a generation state and federal governments had struggled with the economic and legal problems of railroad regulation. During the Progressive Era, in the shape of federal rate making by an independent commission, a solution was found that was wholly characteristic of government-business relations in the early twentieth century. The political struggles that brought it into being exemplify the processes that created the new American state.

Most early studies of railroad regulation identified advancement of the "public interest" as the primary, if not the sole, objective. The most obvious variety of "public interest" was that of consumers in low fares and freight rates, but the interest of the "people," in relation to the railroads, was more commonly identified with that of their immediate customers, the farmers, merchants and manufacturers that shipped their goods by rail, who were characteristically depicted as small producers at the mercy of powerful corporations. The purpose of regulation was to protect the "unorganized" against the "organized."[2] Most recent scholarship gives pride of place to private, rather than public, interest in the politics of regulation. Lee Benson, Gerald D. Nash, and Robert Wiebe trace the involvement of shippers'

---

[1] Gabriel Kolko, *Railroads and Regulation, 1877–1916* (Princeton: Princeton University Press, 1965), 6; Herbert Hovenkamp, *Enterprise and American Law, 1836–1937* (Cambridge, Mass.: Harvard University Press, 1991), 126–30.

[2] See, for example, Benjamin P. De Witt, *The Progressive Movement* (New York: Macmillan, 1915), 36–7; I. L. Sharfman, *The Interstate Commerce Commission*, (4 vols., New York: Commonwealth Fund, 1931–7). An updated version is Elizabeth Sanders, *Roots of Reform: Farmers, Workers, and the American State, 1877–1917* (Chicago: University of Chicago Press, 1999).

organizations in campaigns for the passage and amendment of the Interstate Commerce Act. In contrast, Kolko contends that the railroads themselves "were the most important single advocates of federal regulation from 1877 to 1916," since only through the exercise of government power "could the destabilizing, costly effects of cutthroat competition, predatory speculators and greedy shippers be overcome." In each case the demand for regulation is traced back to organized interest groups whose object, whatever might be the language in which it was expressed, was essentially to protect or advance their economic welfare.[3]

Regulation, as James Q. Wilson reminds us, is essentially a "political art."[4] At every stage it involves the attainment of consent and the building of coalitions of interested parties, but also of those who are not directly or primarily involved. No economic theory of regulation can do justice to its complexity. This realization directs attention to the creative role of political leaders in assembling coalitions and seeking a resolution of conflicts of interest. As John M. Blum and Stephen Skowronek have described with reference to Theodore Roosevelt, federal officials exploited the political opportunities available to them to forge new regulatory mechanisms, as part of a broader reconstitution of institutional power relationships.[5] What is missing from most recent discussions of railroad regulation is a detailed examination of the role of Congress. Kolko is largely silent on congressional politics, presumably regarding it as merely reflecting the distribution of economic power. Skowronek's protagonists are enterprising and innovative administrators, not legislators, who represented the older politics of "courts and parties." Only Elizabeth Sanders of recent historians pays due attention to the deliberations of Congress. Since two landmarks in the extension of federal control of the railroads, the Hepburn Act of 1906 and the Mann-Elkins Act of 1910, fall within the period of this study, the object of this chapter is both to fill this gap in the historical study of regulation and to investigate the role of Congress in the construction of the twentieth-century regulatory state. In order to do so it is necessary to investigate which elements in Congress

[3] Historical studies emphasizing the influence of private interest on railroad regulation include Kolko, *Railroads and Regulation*; Lee Benson, *Merchants, Farmers and Railroads: Railroad Regulation and New York Politics, 1850–1887* (Cambridge, Mass.: Harvard University Press, 1957); George H. Miller, *Railroads and the Granger Laws* (Madison, Wis.: University of Wisconsin Press, 1971); Edward A. Purcell, Jr., "Ideas and Interests: Businessmen and the Interstate Commerce Act," *Journal of American History*: 54 (1967): 561–78; Robert H. Wiebe, *Businessmen and Reform: A Study of the Progressive Movement* (Cambridge, Mass.: Harvard University Press, 1962).

[4] James Q. Wilson, "The Politics of Regulation," in Wilson, ed., *The Politics of Regulation* (New York: Basic Books, 1980), 357–94; Thomas K. McCraw, *Prophets of Regulation* (Cambridge, Mass.: Harvard University Press, 1984), 63.

[5] John M. Blum, *The Republican Roosevelt* (Cambridge, Mass.: Harvard University Press, 1954), 73–105; Stephen Skowronek, *Building a New American State: The Expansion of National Administrative Capacities, 1877–1920* (Cambridge: Cambridge University Press, 1982), 248–84.

supported railroad regulation, and under what pressures, what compromises were embodied in the resulting legislation, and how effectively and coherently it met the requirements of creating an efficient and equitable regulatory framework.

Demands for Regulation

The movement for railroad regulation in the Progressive Era flowed from the deficiencies of earlier federal ventures in the field. Emerging from a variety of political pressures and a succession of legislative compromises, the original Interstate Commerce Act of 1887 reflected in its inconsistencies the manner of its making. It required that rates be "just and reasonable" and prohibited various forms of discrimination, especially by charging more for a short haul than for a longer haul which included the same route "under substantially similar circumstances and conditions." The question of what constituted "substantially similar circumstances and conditions" bedeviled interpretation of the clause well into the next century. While Congress struggled to remedy the evils of discrimination, it also prohibited pooling agreements between railroads which might have mitigated the cutthroat competition that lay behind it. The commission established to administer the law was authorized to condemn a rate as "unreasonable" but not explicitly empowered to determine what rate might be "reasonable" in its place. Nevertheless, in its early years, the Interstate Commerce Commission (ICC) assumed a broad discretion, prescribing rules for the adjudication of long and short haul cases, permitting certain forms of collusive rate agreement and assuming the power to set rates. But its authority and influence were severely curtailed by a series of Supreme Court decisions which laid down a permissive definition of "substantially similar circumstances and conditions" in the long and short haul section, confirmed the illegality of pooling agreements and denied the existence of a rate-making power under the Act. As Justice John Marshall Harlan observed in a dissenting opinion, the Commission had been left "with power to make reports and to issue protests" but had "been shorn, by judicial interpretation, of authority to do anything of an effective character."[6]

By 1900 the impotence of the ICC was manifest. Yet many of the original problems remained, and new ones had appeared. Hence there developed a powerful movement to enlarge its powers, which ultimately bore fruit in the shape of the Hepburn and Mann-Elkins Acts.

---

[6] Ari and Olive Hoogenboom, *A Short History of the ICC* (New York: Norton, 1976), 1–38; Skowronek, *Building a New American State*, 121–62; William Z. Ripley, *Railroads: Rates and Regulation* (New York: Macmillan, 1912), 441–86; Kolko, *Railroads and Regulation*, 7–83; Albro Martin, "The Troubled Subject of Railroad Regulation in the Gilded Age: A Reappraisal," *Journal of American History* 61 (1974): 339–71; Gerald Berk, *Alternative Tracks: The Construction of American Industrial Order, 1865–1917* (Baltimore: Johns Hopkins University Press, 1994), 75–115.

Although the structure of the railroad industry had changed substantially since 1887, most demands for legislation focused on essentially the same issue. Leading supporters and opponents of railroad regulation agreed that the major issue was not the overall level of rates but discrimination between localities and shippers.[7] "The great evil to be reached and dealt with is discrimination," proclaimed the conservative Senator Joseph B. Foraker, quoting his arch-enemy Theodore Roosevelt in corroboration. The economist, and later Interstate Commerce Commissioner, Balthasar Meyer concurred: "Generally speaking, it is probably true that the relation of rates is more important than the absolute level of rates." What primarily occupied the minds of those addressing the problem of railroad regulation in 1905–6 was not disputes over aggregate rates but complaints of unreasonable discrimination between persons and places, which, if less extensive and more localized than a generation before, was still irksome enough to those who suffered from it.[8]

The most striking instances of local discrimination were to be found in the West and South. Low through rates on transcontinental routes penalized intermediate points like Denver, Spokane and Wichita, whose citizens protested that railroad rating policies laid them "under tribute principally to Kansas City." A discriminatory rate structure encouraged jobbers to take their business elsewhere and manufacturers to relocate their operations. According to Meyer, "The man who has control over the rate can say where another man can buy or sell or ship."[9] Broadly similar conditions prevailed in the South, where the "basing point" system left local rates substantially higher than long-distance rates. The pronounced differentials gave rise to especially aggravated cases of local discrimination, such as that of Danville,

---

[7] For an alternative view, see Albro Martin, *Enterprise Denied: Origins of the Decline of American Railroads, 1897–1917* (New York: Columbia University Press, 1971); Martin, "Troubled Subject of Railroad Regulation"; Berk, *Alternative Tracks*, 130, 153–8.

[8] Statement submitted to Senate Committee on Interstate Commerce, in Joseph B. Foraker, *Notes of a Busy Life* (2 vols., Cincinnati: Stewart and Kidd, 1916), 2:215–16 (Roosevelt had earlier given a similar assurance to a delegation of railroad workers. *New York Times*, 15 November 1905); Balthasar Meyer to Robert M. La Follette, 23 March 1906, La Follette Papers, SHSW; Ray Stannard Baker, "The Railroad Rate: A Study in Commercial Autocracy," *McClure's* 26 (November 1905): 47–59; Ray Baker to Theodore Roosevelt, 11 and 17 November 1905, Baker MSS, LC; William Z. Ripley, "President Roosevelt's Railroad Policy: I. The Problem," *Atlantic Monthly* 97 (September 1905): 377–85; Paul Morton, "Railway Rate Regulation," *Outlook* 79 (14 January 1905): 119–21. It was, in any case, hard to demonstrate that aggregate rates had increased unduly. The ICC economist Henry Carter Adams calculated that rates rose by an average of 7.73 percent between 1900 and 1905, significantly less than the rate of inflation. Ripley, *Railroads*, 411–31; W. Morton Grinnell, "Railway Rates," *North American Review* 180 (February 1905): 235–42.

[9] Balthasar Meyer to Robert M. La Follette, 23 March 1906, La Follette Papers, SHSW; Robert S. La Forte, *Leaders of Reform: Progressive Republicans in Kansas, 1900–1916* (Lawrence: University Press of Kansas, 1974), 56. See also Baker, "Railroad Rate"; Ripley, *Railroads*, 118–46, 215–95, 395–400; Richard H. K. Vietor, "Businessmen and the Political Economy: The Railroad Rate Controversy of 1905," *Journal of American History* 64 (1977): 61–3.

Virginia, which also displayed the incapacity of the ICC to furnish relief. Citizens of Danville appearing before the Commission accused the Southern Railroad of setting rates which discriminated in favor of the neighboring city of Lynchburg. The Commission found the rates in question to be "unreasonable" but admitted that, since it could not "determine definitely for the future the relationship in rates that should exist between Danville and Lynchburg," it could do little to redress their grievances.[10]

It was quite natural that those who suffered from the prevailing rate structure should prefer some other means of deciding a matter so crucial to their economic welfare. As Ray Baker explained, "They believe that such great power is better in the hands of the government than in the hands of individuals."[11] Richard Vietor has shown a close correlation between the impact of discrimination and support for ICC rate regulation. Many shippers' organizations and civic groups which had earlier complained to the Commission about adverse discrimination, almost invariably unsuccessfully as the law then stood, made representations before the Senate Committee on Interstate Commerce during the summer of 1905 in favor of empowering the ICC to set rates. On the other hand, many of those favored shippers whose competitive advantages were the subject of complaint testified in opposition to such a proposal.[12] Congressmen received numerous telegrams and letters from merchants and manufacturers warning how dangerous it would be to disturb the pattern of rates established by "competitive forces" or to incite "sectional strife" by government rate making.[13] Hence, attempts to create an inclusive shippers' association were ultimately abortive.[14]

There is ample evidence to support Kolko's assertion that the railroads wished to see the powers of the Interstate Commerce Commission enlarged. That they abominated rebates to powerful shippers is not in doubt. Nor is their desire to bring private car lines, the "mileage charge" on which amounted to a substantial rebate, under ICC supervision. Most of all, the railroads wished to be permitted to enter into binding traffic agreements, alleviating the damaging and disruptive competition which still characterized much of the railroad network.[15] That in 1906, as in 1887, they were unable to

[10] Ripley, *Railroads*, 215–55, 380–92; Ray Baker, "The Way of a Railroad with a Town," *McClure's* 27 (June 1906): 131–45; C.R., 59.1:6949–51; Vietor, "Businessmen and the Political Economy," 63–5; Dewey Grantham, *Southern Progressivism* (Knoxville: University of Tennessee, 1983), 147–55.

[11] Baker, "Railroad Rate," 64.

[12] Vietor, "Businessmen and the Political Economy."

[13] See, for example, David M. Parry to Albert J. Beveridge, 12 November 1905, Beveridge MSS, LC; Grand Rapids Lumber Co. to Robert M. La Follette, 13 February 1906, La Follette MSS, LC; Van Brunt Manufacturing Co. to John C. Spooner, 12 February 1905 Spooner MSS, LC; J. H. Beek to Knute Nelson, 1 November 1905, Nelson MSS, MinHS.

[14] Kolko, *Railroads and Regulation*, 92–4, 102–7; Wiebe, *Businessmen and Reform*, 51–5.

[15] See, for example, Lucius F. Tuttle to Henry Cabot Lodge, 11 November 1905, Lodge MSS, MasHS; J. W. Midgley to John C. Spooner, 7 December 1905, 4, 25 January, 3, 6 March,

attain this, their most heartfelt, desire is testimony to their failure to control the actions of Congress. There is, on the other hand, precious little evidence of railroad support for the central principle of government rate making. Declarations to the contrary resound through the magazine articles written by railroad presidents and their testimony before the Senate Committee on Interstate Commerce. In the autumn of 1905 they orchestrated a massive publicity campaign in a vain attempt to turn public opinion against it.[16] When some railroad men, like Alexander J. Cassatt of the Pennsylvania, did finally accept the principle of government rate making it was out of a realization that continued opposition would be futile.[17]

Thus railroads were arrayed against shippers, and shippers against shippers. But an interpretation of the politics of railroad regulation which restricted itself to a classification of interest groups would be hopelessly wide of the mark. Public opinion was evidently a factor in the equation. Although a few writers pointed to the interest of the public, as consumers, in lower rates, public perception of the railroad question was determined by more than pecuniary considerations. The wave of mergers, the exposure of communities of interest and the activities of infamous figures like Edward P. Harriman and J. J. Hill combined to inflame popular apprehension of the monopoly power of the great railroad corporations. "It is charged," said the publisher S. S. McClure, "that ten men today control practically the entire transportation system of the nation."[18] The railroads brought down upon

---

26 May 1906, Spooner MSS, LC; "Railway Rebates and Preferences," *Outlook* 80 (1 July 1905): 577–9; Paul Morton, "Railway Rate Legislation," *Outlook* 79 (14 January 1905): 119–21; Ripley, *Railroads*, 185–214; Kolko, *Railroads and Regulation*, 117–26.

[16] Baker, "How Railroads Make Public Opinion"; Ray Baker to Theodore Roosevelt, 14 October 1905, Baker MSS, LC; Ripley, *Railroads*, 496–8. For examples of railroad opposition, see Samuel Spencer, "Railway Rates and Industrial Progress," *Century* 71 (1906): 381; Lucius Tuttle, "Railway Rates and Government Regulation," *Outlook* 79 (11 February 1906): 375–80; David Wilcox, "Government Rate-Making Is Unnecessary and Would Be Very Dangerous," *North American Review* 180 (March 1905): 410–29. For contemporary comments, see Theodore Roosevelt to Henry Cabot Lodge, 24 May 1905, Elting E. Morison et al., eds., *Letters of Theodore Roosevelt* (8 vols., Cambridge, Mass.: Harvard University Press, 1951–4), 4:1191–3; Grenville M. Dodge to William B. Allison, 12 May 1905, Allison MSS, ISDHA; J.W. Midgley to John C. Spooner, 27 November 1905, 25 January 1906, Spooner MSS, LC; J. J. Esch to S. R. Van Sant, 2 October 1905, Esch Letterbooks, SHSW. Kolko's claim that the railroads favored government rate-making (*Railroads and Regulation*, 127–54) is rebutted by Albro Martin, *Enterprise Denied: Origins of the Decline of American Railroads, 1897–1917* (New York: Columbia University Press, 1971), 111–13; Vietor, "Businessmen and the Political Economy," 50–3 and 65–6; William R. Doezema, "Railroad Management and the Interplay of Federal and State Regulation, 1885–1916," *Business History Review* 50 (1976): 162–6.

[17] *New York Times*, 6 December 1905; Kolko, *Railroads and Regulation*, 146–7.

[18] "The Railroads on Trial," *McClure's* 25 (October 1905): 673. Cf. Ripley, *Railroads*, 490–2; Charles A. Prouty, "The President and the Railroads," *Century* 71 (1906): 644–53; "Railroad Rate Regulation," *Outlook* 80 (1 July 1905): 563; "The Oil Trust and the Railroads," *Independent* 60 (10 May 1906): 1116–17.

themselves a great measure of the contumely under which they labored by their own involvement in state politics, including the maintenance of permanent lobbies in state capitals, the cultivation of close relations with influential political leaders and the distribution of free passes to state officials, politicians and newspapermen. As the Kansas editor William Allen White told Roosevelt,

There is a definite anti-railroad feeling in the various middle western states, but it has become bitter, not so much because of poor service nor because of excessive rates, but because the local attorneys of Mr. Harriman and Mr. Gould and Mr. Morawetz insist on interfering in local politics, in matters like the primary and pass laws, which are clearly none of their business.

The people would be more friendly to the railroads if they would "stop trying to name our Senators and Governors, and let us govern ourselves." Public concern about the corrupting influence of business corporations on the nation's political life naturally picked out the railroads as a prime target. As vast arterial systems, reaching into every corner of the land and wielding immense economic and political power, they "summoned powerfully negative symbols" that went to the heart of a republican political culture. They thereby raised important "constitutive issues" about the relationship between private power and public welfare. Thus antirailroad feeling fed upon many of the sources that nourished progressivism as a whole.[19]

There can be no doubt that much of the impetus behind the movement for regulation came from government officials, including in particular leading members of the Interstate Commerce Commission. The Commissioners, believing that the agency's capacity to contribute to a solution of the railroad problem, and indeed its very survival, required an extension of its authority, had been pressing for reform ever since the adverse court decisions of the 1890s. As public servants they naturally longed for powers that would enable them to carry out their duties more effectively; as bureaucrats they looked kindly on measures that would enhance the size, status and authority of the agency which they directed. Their experience in office caused them to be "regulation-minded." Indeed, the Commissioners' persistence led hostile critics like the *New York Times* to accuse them of whipping up the demand for railroad reform by their own efforts.[20]

---

[19] William Allen White to Theodore Roosevelt, 15 March 1907, METRP, Reel 72; Jeffrey K. Tulis, *The Rhetorical Presidency* (Princeton, N.J.: Princeton University Press, 1988), 102–6; Mark Sullivan, *Our Times* (6 vols., New York: Scribner's, 1926–35), 3:203–13; La Forte, *Leaders of Reform*, 60–4.

[20] *New York Times*, 6 December 1905; Thomas K. McCraw, "Regulation in America: A Review Article," *Business History Review* 49 (1975): 182; Skowronek, *Building the New American State*, 252–3; Thomas S. Ulen, "The Market for Regulation: The ICC from 1887–1920," *American Economic Review* 70 (1980): 306–10.

Roosevelt himself showed little interest in the issue before 1904. When he did it was not on the basis of any detailed understanding of railroad economics. He was motivated by an acute sense of political priorities combined with a strong, if not clearly articulated, moral conviction. Morality for Roosevelt usually entailed a balancing of opposing forces. This theme, central to his conception of the "square deal," recurs repeatedly in his statements on the issue. It would be "as gross a wrong," he insisted, for the government to fail "to protect a railroad that was in the right" as to render "an improper service to the railroad at the expense of the public." He was more concerned with imposing higher standards of conduct on individual railroad managers than with reordering the structure of ownership and control.[21] Such considerations led him to the conclusion that railroad regulation was essentially an administrative task. Only an impartial administrative agency would possess the expertise to identify the solutions which best met the requirements of justice and to harmonize the competing interests of railroads, shippers and the general public. To Roosevelt, the deliberations of impartial administrative experts were more likely to achieve these ends than the adversarial procedures of the courts or the particularistic concerns of legislators. Only a permanent commission could develop policy in an affirmative and systematic, rather than a reactive and intermittent, fashion.[22] It became apparent as the Hepburn bill wound its way through the congressional thicket during the first six months of 1906 that what mattered to Roosevelt was less its substantive provisions than the administrative instruments through which they were to be enforced.

There was, then, more than one definition of the "railroad problem." To many shippers, especially in the West and South, the problem was one of blatant and harmful discrimination in rates and services. To the railroads themselves the prime desideratum was a more orderly rate structure and a curtailment of destructive competition. Members of the public were troubled by the disproportionate economic and political power apparently wielded by a small and cohesive group of individuals. To the Administration the problem was one of devising institutional mechanisms that would best contribute to defusing conflict and meet the complex demands of an industrial society. Regulation meant very different things to different people. As Thomas K.

---

[21] Kolko, *Railroads and Regulation*, 112; Roosevelt to Lyman Abbott, 11 January 1905, *Letters*, 4:1099–1100; to Ray S. Baker, 20, 28 November 1905, *Letters*, 5:83–5, 100–1; to Chester I. Long, 31 January 1906, *Letters*, 5:142–3; Blum, *Republican Roosevelt*, 85–6, 90–1; Lewis L. Gould, *The Presidency of Theodore Roosevelt* (Lawrence: University Press of Kansas, 1990), 149–50; Tulis, *Rhetorical Presidency*, 108–10; Leroy G. Dorsey, "Theodore Roosevelt and Corporate America, 1901–1909: A Reexamination," *Presidential Studies Quarterly* 25 (1995): 732–6.

[22] Fourth Annual Message, in Theodore Roosevelt, *The Works of Theodore Roosevelt*, (National Edition, 20 vols., New York: Scribner's, 1926), 15:226; Blum, *Republican Roosevelt*, 87–105; Skowronek, *Building a New American State*, 254–5.

McCraw says of the late nineteenth century, there was not one "railroad problem" but several.[23]

The Hepburn Bill

The Hepburn bill formed part of a sequence of attempts to amend the Interstate Commerce Act. The Elkins Act of 1903, an antirebating measure which required only that railroads should not depart from their published rates but established no way of determining whether those published rates were reasonable in themselves, tackled only part of the problem of discrimination. Hence the pressure for a more comprehensive revision continued to gather strength.[24] From 1904 the movement enjoyed the support of Roosevelt, whose Annual Message to Congress in that year included a brief but unequivocal demand for rate regulation. While he considered it undesirable, if not impracticable, "finally to clothe the commission with general authority to fix railroad rates," he urged that it "should be vested with the power, where a given rate has been challenged and after a full hearing found to be unreasonable, to decide, subject to judicial review, what shall be a reasonable rate to take its place."[25]

Within a few weeks of receiving the President's message, acting with remarkable dispatch, the House of Representatives, though not the Senate, passed a rate bill, the Esch-Townsend bill.[26] The reason why the House moved so expeditiously, Blum has explained, is because Roosevelt disarmed opposition to railroad regulation by raising the prospect of tariff revision. The issues tended to produce a similar sectional alignment within the party: Standpatters on the tariff were usually also standpatters on the railroad issue, but less adamantly so. Blum believes that an agreement was reached with congressional leaders, especially Speaker Cannon, trading inaction on the tariff against action on railroad regulation.[27] The existence of some such understanding was a matter of widespread contemporary comment. Governor Albert J. Cummins of Iowa claimed to have seen a section relating to tariff reform in the 1904 Message which had to be removed, Roosevelt explained, because "Aldrich and Cannon had told him very forcibly that they could not allow the President' interstate commerce program to get before

---

[23] Thomas K. McCraw, *Prophets of Regulation* (Cambridge, Mass.: Harvard University Press, 1984), 61.

[24] Hoogenboom, *Short History of the ICC*, 43–6; Kolko, *Railroads and Regulation*, 85, 94–101; Ripley, *Railroads*, 492–4.

[25] Fourth Annual Message, *Works*, 15:226.

[26] Kolko, *Railroads and Regulation*, 102–3; *Outlook* 79 (28 January 1905): 208; (11 February 1905): 354–5.

[27] Blum, *Republican Roosevelt*, 75–87; Blum, "Theodore Roosevelt and the Legislative Process: Tariff Revision and Railroad Regulation, 1904–1906," in *Letters of Theodore Roosevelt*, 4:1333–42. The existence of such an agreement is questioned by Hoogenboom, *Short History of the ICC*, 48; Gould, *Presidency of Theodore Roosevelt*, 152.

Congress unless he would abandon tariff revision." Many Congressmen, like Henry C. Adams of Wisconsin, believed it "perfectly evident" that the President had made a deal with Cannon: "The President is to keep his mouth shut about tariff revision and Mr. Cannon is to carry through the railroad rate legislation and the joint statehood schemes, which are pet projects of the President." Champ Clark alluded to a "modus vivendi" on the floor of the House.[28] Whether or not an explicit bargain was struck, it is probable that congressional leaders gave ground on the railroad issue for fear that Roosevelt might disinter the tariff, and, although congressional leaders maybe could not have held back railroad regulation, it was likely to pass more expeditiously, and in a more satisfactory form, with their cooperation than without it.

The Esch-Townsend bill went further than Roosevelt had desired by authorizing the Commission to set definite, rather than merely maximum, rates.[29] During 1905 Roosevelt became more insistent on his own, more modest, proposal. When Ray Baker pointed out that it would not meet cases of discrimination caused by unreasonably low rates to favored shippers or localities, he argued that the power to set a maximum rate would "meet the immense majority of evils." It would be an adequate first step on the road to effective railroad regulation. Maximum rates might not cover cases of place discrimination so effectively as cases of personal discrimination, but it was "much more difficult to say what ought to be done in any given case as regards localities" in view of the many complicating factors. Political pressures, the "pulling and hauling by rival communities to influence the Commission," might lead to "improper decisions." Roosevelt, clearly influenced by railroad thinking on the causes of local discrimination, was by no means confident of finding a cure. Hence he preferred to focus on the more blatant evil of personal discrimination.[30]

The Annual Message with which Roosevelt greeted the new Congress in December 1905 deviated only in that respect from the principles enunciated twelve months earlier but spelled them out in more detail:

In my judgment the most important provision which such law should contain is that conferring upon some competent administrative body the power to decide, upon

[28] Note on interview with Albert J. Cummins, 9, 19 March 1925, in Biographer's Notes, Aldrich MSS, LC; Henry C. Adams to Ben Adams, 18 December 1905, Adams MSS, SHSW; remarks by Champ Clark, *C.R.*, 59.1:728. See also *New York Times*, 17 November 1905; *Washington Post*, 29 November 1905, 1, 8 June 1906; Scott William Rager, "The Fall of the House of Cannon: Uncle Joe and His Enemies" (Ph.D. diss., University of Illinois, 1991), 38–42.

[29] On the Esch-Townsend bill, see *New York Times*, 5, 7 December 1905; *Outlook*, 81 (14 October 1905), 343–4; J. J. Esch to John A. Troutman, 20 September 1905, Esch Letterbooks, SHSW; Charles E. Townsend to J. J. Esch, 30 October and 4 November 1905, Esch MSS, SHSW.

[30] Roosevelt to Ray S. Baker, 13, 28 November 1905, *Letters*, 5:76–7, 100–1. See also Roosevelt to Baker, 20, 22 November 1905, *Letters*, 5:83–5, 88–9; Baker to Roosevelt, 11, 17, 21, 25 November 1905, Baker MSS, LC; *New York Times*, 8 November 1905.

the case being brought before it, whether a given rate prescribed by a railroad is reasonable and just, and if it is found to be unreasonable and unjust... to prescribe the limit of rate beyond which it shall not be lawful to go... this decision to go into effect within a reasonable time and to obtain from thence onward, subject to review by the courts.

The power to establish a maximum rate was "essential to any scheme of real reform in the matter of railroad regulation." Roosevelt also recommended the prohibition of all forms of rebating, such as "midnight tariffs," fictitious claims for damages, brokerage payments or elevator allowances, as well as preferential rates for the use of private cars, which should be brought under ICC supervision. Roosevelt also indicated his support for legalized pooling: "The best possible regulation of rates would, of course, be that regulation secured by an honest agreement among the railroads themselves to carry out the law." Such agreements, if carefully supervised and "clearly in the interest of the public," should be permitted. The use of the subjunctive mood betrayed his awareness of the unlikelihood of this proposal's being acted upon.[31]

A bill drawn up at a White House conference and consistent with the ideas expressed in the President's Message was presented to the House Interstate and Foreign Commerce Committee at the beginning of the 59th Congress by the committee's chairman, William P. Hepburn, who had previously shown little enthusiasm for railroad regulation. This Republican members of the committee agreed to accept as the "ground work for action."[32] John Jacob Esch and Charles E. Townsend naturally resented "that the chairman at the eleventh hour... should come in and steal our thunder." More significantly, they regarded the Hepburn bill as markedly weaker than their own. It provided only for the setting of maximum rates. It allowed more scope for judicial review by including the requirement that rates set by the ICC should be "fairly remunerative," with the result that "the whole thing is to be fought over again in the courts," where its findings of fact would be regarded as "only prima facie." Esch believed that the courts should only pass judgment on the "unlawfulness" of the Commission's rates. Otherwise it "would degenerate into a body with functions little more than clerical" – the status quo, in fact. Moreover, its orders were to be suspended pending review. "I believe," said Esch, "that in allowing the current rate to stand pending proceedings in the courts all hope of speedy adjudication must be given up."[33] The Hepburn bill was more conservative than earlier House bills, but, for all its deficiencies, it entrusted the ICC with a substantial, if

---

[31] Roosevelt, Fifth Annual Message, *Works*, 15:275–8.

[32] *New York Times*, 30 November 1905, 5 January 1906; Briggs, *Hepburn*, 231–4, 249–62, 264–8.

[33] Edward A. Moseley to J. J. Esch, 10 January 1906, Esch MSS, SHSW; Esch to C. F. Baldwin, 10 February 1906, Esch Letterbooks, SHSW. See also Esch to W. B. Tscharner, 16 January

limited, authority to set rates. So Esch and Townsend concurred in a motion to report the bill favorably. The minority members having agreed to sign a unanimous report in return for certain amendments, the bill emerged from committee with bipartisan support.[34]

Debate on the floor of the House was characterized by a good-natured tone and a high degree of consensus. It was agreed that the government must act to protect shippers against extortionate charges. According to James Robert Mann, "There should be a power over and beyond the railway to which the merchant may appeal for judgment when he believes that his interests are unduly prejudiced by his transportation charges." And this had to be an administrative agency. The courts, recourse to which was expensive and fraught with delay, offered a "futile remedy." The government's constitutional responsibility to protect the public against "unreasonable" transportation charges had been vested in the Interstate Commerce Commission. But the Commission could not declare a rate unreasonable unless it was able to fix a substitute: "I never knew how a man could determine what was unreasonable unless he first knew what was reasonable," said Townsend. Republicans in particular were at pains to affirm how modest the proposal was and how little disruption it would cause to railroad operations or the flow of commerce. Only maximum, not absolute, rates would be set. "The power to fix generally absolute rates is the power to destroy competitive forces, to paralyze industries, to injure railroads, to interfere with all of the principles and methods of modern business life," declared Mann, but that power the bill did not confer.[35]

Every Democrat who spoke on the bill spoke in its favor. Several took the occasion to regret that it was not stricter and to present amendments to remedy what they saw as its deficiencies: by making railroad officials criminally liable for granting rebates, by authorizing the Commission to set rates on its own initiative, by bringing sleeping car and express companies under the terms of the bill, and by strengthening the long and short haul clause of the Interstate Commerce Act.[36] As a result of a bipartisan agreement

1906; to Baldwin, 13, 25 January 1906; to William E. Chandler, 23 January 1906, Esch Letterbooks, SHSW.

[34] *New York Times*, 14 November, 4, 14 December 1905, 31 January 1906; John Sharp Williams, "The Democratic Party and the Railroad Question," *Independent* 60 (1 March 1906): 485–8; David A. Sarasohn, *Party of Reform: Democrats in the Progressive Era* (Jackson, Miss.: University of Mississippi Press, 1989), 3–10.

[35] *C.R.*, 59.1:1763–70 (Townsend), 2242–8 (Mann), 2001–8 (Esch), 2252–6 (Hepburn); *New York Times*, 31 January, 2, 4, 6 February 1906; Chicago *Inter-Ocean*, 7 June 1905, J. R. Mann Scrapbooks, Vol. 29, LC.

[36] See, for example, *C.R.*, 59.1:1770–8 (William C. Adamson), 1977–88 (Gordon Russell), 1993–6 (Henry Clayton), 2248–52 (Williams). Democrats critical of the bill's limitations include Thomas Heflin (1904–8), Robert L. Henry (1996–2001), John W. Gaines (2095–2100), Thomas W. Hardwick (2100–2), Oscar W. Gillespie (2156–7) and William Sulzer (2181–91).

not to encumber the bill with amendments, none of these were adopted, and, after several days of talking, the bill went through unamended.[37]

Only a handful of Republicans spoke against the bill, while only seven voted against it.[38] It is probable that many others shared some of their negative feelings. Critical speeches, by all accounts, received admiring applause from the majority benches, and it was estimated that a secret ballot would find only twenty Republicans votes in favor.[39] This was certainly a wild understatement, but it is unlikely that everyone who voted for the bill did so out of conviction. A number of factors contributed to the positive result. One was the influence of Cannon, who, many believed, forced the bill through the House. The authority and prestige of a popular President no doubt persuaded others. Some Republicans, especially Midwesterners like Hepburn, found it inexpedient to ignore the intense public demand for regulation. A final consideration which might, as in earlier sessions, have influenced some conservative Republicans was the expectation, expressed by a New Hampshire Congressman, that "the objectionable features would be eliminated or greatly modified in the Senate." Those who did go on record against the bill were probably marked less by their beliefs or an unusual configuration of sectional interests, distinguishing them from other New Englanders or New Yorkers, than by a peculiarly strong measure of ideological rigidity and intestinal fortitude.[40]

The Senate and Judicial Review

"I think it is of the utmost importance to the republicans of the Senate that Mr. Elkins' Committee shall bring in a report that will unite our friends upon this important subject," William B. Allison wrote to Nelson Aldrich before the session commenced. The Committee on Interstate Commerce, therefore, should take its time to secure "general agreement." If an acceptable compromise were reached in committee it would probably be adopted in the Senate, "but a divided report, I think, would be very unfortunate."[41] As it turned

---

[37] C.R., 59.1:2256–70; J. J. Esch to S. B. Kebber, 9 January 1906, Esch Letterbooks, SHSW; *New York Times*, 8 February 1906.

[38] The fullest critique came from Samuel W. McCall of Massachusetts. C.R., 59.1:1969–76; *Outlook* 79 (18 February 1905): 406–8; Samuel W. McCall, "The Fifty-ninth Congress," *Atlantic Monthly* 98 (November 1906): 582–5; Lawrence B. Evans, *Samuel W. McCall: Governor of Massachusetts* (Boston: Houghton, Mifflin, 1916), 73–6. See also the speeches by Charles Littlefield (2970–9) and Joseph Sibley (1897–1904); *New York Times*, 4, 6, 7 February 1906.

[39] Sarasohn, "Democratic Surge," 17–19.

[40] Lincoln Steffens, "The Reign of Public Opinion," proof of article dated 18 February 1906, Robert M. La Follette MSS, LC; Frank D. Currier to J. O. Lyford, 8 February 1906, Biographer's Notes, Nelson W. Aldrich MSS, LC. See also McCall, "Fifty-ninth Congress," 583; *New York Times*, 24 February 1906; Briggs, *Hepburn*, 231–4, 258–62.

[41] William B. Allison to Nelson W. Aldrich, 19 October 1905, Aldrich MSS, LC. See also Henry Cabot Lodge to Winthrop M. Crane, undated (probably December 1905), Lodge MSS, MasHS; *New York Times*, 31 January, 3 February 1906.

out, an "acceptable compromise" could not be reached. Four Republican members of the committee, led by Aldrich, believed the Hepburn bill to be defective in its wording and, above all, objectionable in its failure to provide for judicial review. However, Aldrich's efforts to unite his party behind a broad review amendment were frustrated by the Midwestern Republicans Dolliver, Clapp and Cullom, who supported the President's program.[42] Together with the minority members, they forced through a motion to report the House bill without amendment. The failure of the Republicans on the committee to arrive at a compromise meant that a resolution had to be found under much less favorable conditions in open Senate.[43]

Unlike its predecessors, the Hepburn bill deliberately left open the question of review. It required merely that a rate ordered by the ICC should be effective within a "reasonable time" unless it were "suspended or set aside by a court of competent jurisdiction." This was no more than to state the obvious.[44] Conservative Republicans in the Senate turned their attention upon this area of uncertainty, demanding that the form and extent of judicial review be made explicit. The issue was essentially twofold. First, the ICC was empowered, on complaint, to determine the limit beyond which a "just and reasonable and fairly remunerative" rate might go. Might a federal court, in considering an appeal against an ICC order, review the facts and pass once more upon the "reasonableness" of its decision, effectively retrying a case already determined by the Commission? Second, pending a review of the case, could the court grant an injunction delaying the imposition of the rate ordered by the ICC and keeping in force the rate complained of during the course of judicial proceedings which, on the basis of past experience, could go on for years?[45]

"I have no hesitation in saying that a bill drawn upon the theory that the orders of the commission shall be final and unassailable in the courts would be unconstitutional," said Philander C. Knox, until recently Roosevelt's Attorney-General. Knox and Spooner acknowledged that investigation of the "reasonableness" of a rate was "a nonjudicial power" which might properly be entrusted to an administrative body. But this, like any agency of government, was subject to the restraining power of the courts.

[42] On the distribution of opinion within the committee, see *New York Times*, 14, 23–25 November 1905; Winthrop M. Crane to Henry Cabot Lodge, 11 August 1905, Lodge MSS, MasHS; Thomas R. Ross, *Jonathan Prentiss Dolliver* (Iowa City: State Historical Society of Iowa, 1958), 195–204; Oscar D. Lambert, *Stephen Benton Elkins* (Pittsburgh: University of Pittsburgh Press, 1955), 270–6.

[43] *New York Times*, 10, 17, 19, 20, 22–25 February 1906; Edward P. Bacon to Robert M. La Follette, 12 January 1906, La Follette Papers, SHSW; Stephenson, *Aldrich*, 291–6; Ross, *Dolliver*, 199–205; James W. Neilson, *Shelby M. Cullom: Prairie State Republican* (Urbana: University of Illinois Press, 1962), 223–5.

[44] Briggs, *Hepburn*, 254–5.

[45] See *Independent* 60 (8 March 1906): 533; Blum, *Republican Roosevelt*, 96–8; Stephenson, *Aldrich*, 287–90.

The railroads were entitled to receive "just compensation" for their services and to appeal against government orders which infringed that entitlement. If the Commission was to be given the power to set rates the courts must have the authority to determine whether they were "just and reasonable," and, in doing so, should have authority to examine any aspect of the case which it considered necessary.[46] The broad review Senators were profoundly unhappy with the rate bill as it had emerged from the House. On 22 February Knox introduced an amendment, which permitted the courts to pass on the "lawfulness" of ICC orders, inviting a wide-ranging review of the evidence and arguments heard by the Commission; they could issue restraining orders on appeal and determine for themselves "what practices shall be pursued pending the litigation." Knox's proposal raised the standard around which the broad review Senators rallied.[47]

The defenders of narrow review, in contrast, maintained that the Commission was the proper body to determine whether or not a rate was reasonable. "The power to fix rates is a power of Congress," claimed the Iowa Senator Jonathan P. Dolliver, "and the rate fixed by the commission is a rate fixed by Congress." It was constitutionally anomalous to subject its decisions to review by the courts. Further,

The chief reason for creating a commission to determine these questions is because the questions require the skill of experts. They are not questions of law; they are questions of business policy which require in their settlement the experience and practical knowledge which is a small part of the education and habits of our courts. We know as well as we can learn anything from experience that the enforcement of law regulating commerce becomes ineffective if it is left in the hands of the courts.[48]

The right to appeal was not denied. But judicial review should not go beyond an investigation of whether the ICC had overstepped the limits of the power delegated to it by law or whether the rate imposed entailed in effect a "confiscation" of railroad property. There was a wide margin between a rate that was "confiscatory" and one that was "fairly remunerative" within which the Commission's discretionary authority should apply.[49] This was Roosevelt's position also. He told Allison that he wished review to be "limited strictly to the question of the Commission's acting within its authority

---

[46] *C.R.*, 59.1:4115–22 and 4156–66 (Spooner), 4376–84 (Knox); *New York Times*, 12, 20, 23 February, 23, 29 March, 4 April 1906; Philander C. Knox to Theodore Roosevelt, 19 December 1904, Knox MSS, LC; John C. Spooner to W. A. Jones, 6 June 1906; to Horace Baker, 14 June 1906, Spooner Letterbooks, LC.

[47] *New York Times*, 12, 20, 23 February, 29 March 1906; Stephenson, *Aldrich*, 294.

[48] Dolliver, "Railroad Rate Legislation," 837; Dolliver to A. J. Earling, 12 January 1906, William B. Allison MSS, ISDHA.

[49] *C.R.*, 59.1:6691, 4643. Cf. Samuel H. Cowan to Roosevelt, 28 February 1906, METRP, Reel 63.

and to each man having his constitutional rights secured."[50] What he and Dolliver wished to avoid was the adoption of a formula which would invite the courts to go over all the evidence and retry the case afresh, substituting its own judgment for that of the Commission.

Dolliver believed that a court review amendment was unnecessary, because the right of access to the courts existed independently of any congressional enactment, and dangerous, because it would invite the courts to test the reasonableness of the Commission's actions. Roosevelt, too, thought the bill already provided the right to appeal, "which no legislation can deny."[51] To avoid any risk of the law's being declared unconstitutional and to meet the objections of broad review Senators, Roosevelt and Dolliver were willing to incorporate a statement which would affirm the jurisdiction that they believed the courts already possessed but which would not, as Dolliver put it, be so framed "as to enlarge the jurisdiction of the circuit court and make it practically an appellate Interstate Commerce Commission."[52]

It was feared, secondly, that the courts would, by issuing injunctions which denied, and at best delayed, the execution of ICC orders, frustrate the law's regulatory intent. As Henry M. Teller of Colorado explained, it was "well known that in nine times out of ten when a carrier finds fault with an order of the Commission and complains to a judge, he will find a judge who will issue a temporary injunction for him . . . which will tie up the case from that time on until the expiration of the period fixed in the bill." It was, said Joseph W. Bailey, a "monstrous proposition" to permit "inferior judges" to suspend "a careful opinion rendered by a government tribunal . . . without a full and complete inquiry."[53] Such views were embodied in an amendment offered by Bailey which curtailed the courts' power to issue temporary injunctions suspending the orders of the Commission without allowing for a full hearing. Thus the Commission's rate would be in force "unless and until set aside by the courts."[54]

Whether or not Congress had the power to determine the procedures of the inferior courts formed one of the principal technical issues during the long weeks of debate. The leading Republican lawyers, like Knox and Spooner, insisted on the independence of the judiciary from legislative control, especially in equity cases, where the courts' power to deliver judgment could

---

[50] Roosevelt to William B. Allison, 12 April 1906, *Letters*, 5:210–11. See also Roosevelt to Philander C. Knox, 22 April 1906, *Letters*, 5:215.

[51] Dolliver, "Railroad Rate Legislation," 838; Roosevelt to Joseph G. Cannon, 19 February 1906, *Letters*, 5:157–8.

[52] Ross, *Dolliver*, 209; Roosevelt to Edmund H. Hinshaw, 20 February 1906, *Letters*, 5:158–9.

[53] *C.R.*, 59.1:6677, 6671–8; New York *Tribune*, 20 March 1906.

[54] *C.R.*, 59.1:3449–50, 3953–9, 4977–90; *New York Times*, 7, 9, 16, 20 March, 11, 14 April 1906; "Analysis of Senator Bailey's Speech of April 10, 1906," Knox MSS, LC; J. J. Esch to William P. Welch, 19 April 1906, Esch Letterbooks, SHSW; Sam H. Acheson, *Joe Bailey: The Last Democrat* (New York: Macmillan, 1932), 198–200.

not be inhibited by legislation, and they eventually succeeded in convincing Roosevelt that the Bailey amendment was unconstitutional.[55] Roosevelt had at first regarded prompt application of ICC decisions as a "vital feature" of the bill, but by April 1906 he had concluded that the scope of review was much more significant than the risk of suspension by court orders.[56] Bailey, on the other hand, while anxious to regulate the terms under which the courts might issue injunctions, did not necessarily wish to limit their scope. His amendment did not restrict the right of appeal against a rate set by the Commission and permitted its suspension should the court "find that such rate ... will not afford just compensation ... or that the regulation ... is unjust and unreasonable." Asked by Aldrich whether he was willing to have "a full and fair judicial determination finally of the question whether the rates furnish just compensation or not," Bailey agreed at once that he was. He wished to restrict the issuance of restraining orders but not to deny the railroads full access to the courts.[57] In other words, those who wished to restrict court review did so in different ways and for different reasons.

Some observers, like David Graham Phillips, regarded the struggle over court review as a "sham battle."[58] Although it is probably true that the lawyers in the Senate contrived to spin a more elaborate web out of the legal and constitutional issues involved than was strictly necessary, they were engaged in more than an exercise in legalistic hairsplitting. Practical railroad men saw the issue as crucially important. Cassatt expressed deep concern that, in the absence of effective review, a rate might be imposed which, while not "confiscatory," would still involve the railroad in irreparable loss. "In common justice to the railroads," they should have the right of appeal to the courts to determine whether a rate was "justly compensatory." Without broad review, William Truesdale of the Lackawanna told Spooner, the bill would "work great injury to the transportation interests of the country."[59] Shippers, on the other hand, did not want crucial decisions transferred to the courts, from which past experience had taught them to expect little redress, and urged Senators, in the words of an Iowa livestock dealer, to "stand as firm as adamant" against attempts to diminish the authority given to the

---

[55] See the speech by Spooner in *C.R.*, 59.1:5887–99, 5945–53; *New York Times*, 27 April 1906; New York *Tribune*, 27 April 1906; Roosevelt to Edward P. Bacon, 9 March 1906, *Letters*, 5:173–4.

[56] Roosevelt to Edmund H. Hinshaw, 20 February 1906; to Knute Nelson, 11 April 1906; to William B. Allison, 12 April 1906, *Letters*, 5:158–9, 209–11; Roosevelt, *Works*, 15:226, 276.

[57] *C.R.*, 59.1:3959; Stephenson, *Aldrich*, 297, 469–70; *New York Times*, 7 March 1906.

[58] Phillips, *Treason of the Senate*, 141. Cf. Kolko, *Railroads and Regulation*, 133–4.

[59] Alexander J. Cassatt to Roosevelt, 19 and 26 February 1906, METRP, Reel 63; William H. Truesdale to John C. Spooner, 7 February 1906, Spooner MSS, LC. See also Frederick D. Underwood to Spooner, 9 February 1906; Victor Morawetz to Spooner, 9 April 1906, Spooner MSS, LC; A. J. Earling to Jonathan Dolliver, 5 January 1906; J. W. Blythe to William B. Allison, 6 April 1906, Allison MSS, ISDHA.

Commission. To allow the courts to decide the level of "just compensation," claimed a spokesman of Western livestock interests, would defeat the whole purpose of the law.[60] Thus the issue of court review involved the question of whether the process of regulation should be geared to protecting the interests of the carriers or the shippers.

More significantly still, the ICC was the first of a new species of government agency which, as the more timorous conservatives noted with foreboding, mingled legislative, executive and judicial powers in a manner which seemed contrary to the spirit of the American Constitution. It was to have the "quasi-legislative power" of setting railroad rates, the executive power of investigation and enforcement, and the judicial power of hearing complaints and adjudicating disputes. To Aldrich and other Old Guard Republicans this entailed a dangerous consolidation of power. They preferred to trust the wisdom of the courts and rely on traditional means of resolving economic conflicts. On the other hand, Roosevelt insisted that the function of supervising railroad rates was "unequivocally administrative." The procedural form to be established was as significant as its substantive results. What gave the question of court review such importance, then, in the eyes of Roosevelt and many of his supporters, was the implications that its resolution would have for shaping the institutions that would be entrusted with the regulation of the developing industrial society.[61]

The Search for Compromise

During most of February and March Roosevelt advised against the insertion of any review amendment, thereby leaving intact the sketchy formula in the House bill. By the end of March the deficiencies of this strategy had become evident. The speeches of Knox and Spooner had begun to convince wavering Republicans that it would be dangerous to omit an explicit statement on the role of the courts.[62] Therefore, the Administration and its Republican supporters decided that they must accept a review amendment and that that amendment must preclude the possibility of a broad review. The formula agreed upon at a White House conference at the end of March, presented to the Senate as the Long amendment, authorized the circuit court merely

[60] E. L. Beard to William B. Allison, 3 March 1906; Silas W. Gardiner to Allison, 1 February 1906, Allison MSS; ISDHA; A. K. James to Robert M. La Follette, 5 March 1906, La Follette Papers, SHSW. See also Edward P. Bacon to Allison, 8 May 1906, Allison MSS, ISDHA; H. P. Berwald to La Follette, 21 February 1906, La Follette Papers, SHSW; Edward P. Bacon to John C. Spooner, 5 March 1906, Spooner MSS, LC.

[61] Skowronek, *Building the New American State*, 254–5; Blum, *Republican Roosevelt*, 87–105; Stephenson, *Aldrich*, 290; *New York Times*, 21 January, 1 March 1906; Roosevelt, *Works*, 275.

[62] *New York Times*, 2, 25 March 1906; Stephenson, *Aldrich*, 301–3; Leon C. Richardson, *William E. Chandler: Republican* (New York: Dodds, Mead, 1940), 660–1.

to consider "whether the order complained of was beyond the authority of the Commission or in violation of the rights of the carrier secured by the Commission."[63]

When it became apparent that sufficient Republican votes could not be obtained to pass such an amendment, Roosevelt opened secret negotiations with Benjamin R. Tillman, the Democratic manager of the bill, in the hope of assembling a coalition of progressive Republicans and Democrats behind a narrow review formula which would combine elements of the Long and Bailey amendments.[64] This seemingly unnatural alliance was in the end abortive. Its collapse was a matter of sensational recrimination. Roosevelt in his efforts to cover his traces was guilty, it seems undeniable, of several quite generous distortions of the truth, disclaiming any role in initiating negotiations with Bailey and Tillman and accusing Bailey of negotiating with the "railroad Senators."[65] More fundamental was the failure of Tillman and Bailey to muster the promised number of Democratic votes. At a conference on 18 April only twenty-five Democratic votes endorsed the alliance program, one short of the bare minimum needed to carry it through.[66]

When it became clear to Roosevelt and his supporters, and equally to Aldrich, that a majority could be assembled on neither a broad nor a narrow review amendment, the Republican factions came together behind a formula which, though wordy, effectively left the position as it was in the House bill. Both factions were conscious of the desirability of restoring the unity of the Republican party and ensuring that the bill would go out into the world under its signature, rather than allowing the Democrats to claim credit. Allison, who had urged the importance of party solidarity so strongly to Aldrich before the session began, was one of those who, with Spooner, worked to restore the unity that had been fractured in the course of the review struggle.[67] The compromise amendment, which had a mixed authorship but went out under Allison's name, provided for appeal to a federal circuit court, which could

---

[63] *New York Times*, 3 April 1906; Ross, *Dolliver*, 211; Stephenson, *Aldrich*, 303.

[64] Roosevelt to Kermit Roosevelt, 1 April 1906; to William B. Allison, 12 April 1906, *Letters*, 5:204, 210–11; *New York Times*, 17 April 1906; Richardson, *Chandler*, 661–4; Acheson, *Bailey*, 192–9; Francis B. Simkins, *Pitchfork Ben Tillman: South Carolinian* (Baton Rouge: Louisiana State University Press, 1944), 425–6, 432.

[65] For the statements of Bailey, Tillman and the chief Republican participants, see C.R, 59.1: 6774–80, 6787, 6885–7, 6936–8, 7010–11; Roosevelt to William B. Allison, 14 May 1906, *Letters*, 5:270–2; to Henry Cabot Lodge, 19 May 1906, *Letters*, 5:273–6; *New York Times*, 13, 14, 15, 17 May 1906. See also Richardson, *Chandler*, 667–73; Acheson, *Bailey*, 200–8; Simkins, *Tillman*, 436–9; Sullivan, *Our Times*, 3:264–75.

[66] *New York Times*, 13, 19 March, 6, 7 April 1906; New York *Tribune*, 19 March 1906; *Railroad Gazette*, 23 March 1906; Biographer's Notes, Aldrich MSS, LC; Stephenson, *Aldrich*, 308.

[67] C.R., 59.1:6774–8, 6885–7; *New York Times*, 5 May 1906; New York *Tribune*, 1 May 1906; Roosevelt to William Boyd Allison, 12 April 1906, *Letters*, 5:210–11; to Philander C. Knox, 22 April 1906, *Letters*, 5:215; Ross, *Dolliver*, 211–12; Sage, *Allison*, 301–6.

"enjoin, set aside, annul, or suspend any order or requirement of the commission." Nothing was said about the scope of review, which was left to the courts themselves to determine. It empowered the ICC to set rates that were just and reasonable "in its judgment"; removed the requirement that they be "fairly remunerative"; prevented the issue of a restraining order without five days notice; and expedited judicial procedures arising from cases under the interstate commerce law by granting them the same priority accorded to antitrust cases.[68]

At the press conference at which Roosevelt announced his adherence to the compromise amendment a leading Washington correspondent asked quite bluntly why he had surrendered. So, not surprisingly, did the Democrats whom he had so abruptly left in the lurch.[69] Naturally the President defended himself against such charges, arguing consistently that the amendment gave him what he had always fought for, namely a statement which explicitly opened access to the courts but did not define their jurisdiction. While he would have preferred a narrow review amendment such as Long's, he could not complain unduly about a solution which so closely corresponded to his position of two months earlier.[70] Allison himself contended that "the amendment... confines absolutely the jurisdiction of the Court to two points, namely: whether the Constitutional rights of the carrier have been violated, or whether the Interstate Commerce Commission has exceeded its authority." Chester Long of Kansas argued that Supreme Court decisions in state cases had confirmed that it would not undertake the determination of precise rates but would investigate only whether the rate was extortionate or confiscatory and within the commission's delegated authority. In other words, no statement on review was effectively tantamount to narrow review.[71]

If Roosevelt was forced to compromise, then so were his adversaries. If the bill failed to limit the courts' jurisdiction, then neither did it offer the explicit invitation to a broad review that Knox and Aldrich had looked for. Indeed,

---

[68] *C.R.*, 59.3:6671, 6783–93; Chicago *Tribune*, 8, 9 May 1906, Robert M. La Follette MSS, LC; *New York Times*, 5, 8, 9 May 1906; *Railroad Gazette*, 11 May 1906, Biographer's Notes, Nelson W. Aldrich MSS, LC; Sage, *Allison*, 301–5; Richardson, *Chandler*, 665; Ripley, *Railroads*, 507–12; Blum, *Republican Roosevelt*, 102–3.

[69] *New York Times*, 5 May 1906; Isidor Rayner, "The Railroad Rate Debate in the Senate," *Independent* 60 (14 June 1906): 1408–11. For similar assessments, see Albert J. Beveridge to Albert J. Shaw, 20 May 1906, LC; Edward P. Bacon to John C. Spooner, Spooner MSS, LC; *C.R.*, 59.1:6686, 6695, 6769, 6780–1; *Nation*, 10, 17, 24 May 1906.

[70] Roosevelt to William B. Allison, 14 May 1906, *Letters*, 5:270–2. See also Roosevelt to Allison, 5 May 1906, *Letters*, 5:258–9; to Edward P. Bacon, 8 May 1906, *Letters*, 5:260; *New York Times*, 7 May 1906; Chicago *Tribune*, 9 May 1906, Robert M. La Follette MSS, LC.

[71] William B. Allison to J. M. Hume, 1 June 1906, Allison MSS, ISDHA; *C.R.*, 59.1:6686–92, 6763–6, 6773, 6778–80; Jonathan P. Dolliver, "The Battle over the Railway Rate Bill," *Independent* 61 (12 July 1906): 65–7; *New York Times*, 13, 18 May 1906.

the latter had been much more insistent on the need to clarify the position than had Roosevelt and his allies. The Democrats' disgruntlement followed partly from a difference in priorities. Whilst the narrow review Republicans had never laid particular emphasis on the restriction of the injunction power, to Democrats like Bailey this had always been the main concern. The Allison amendment gave way on this substantially. On the other hand, it offered greater comfort to those whose principal concern was to establish the administrative authority of the Interstate Commerce Commission, that is to Roosevelt and his Republican supporters.[72]

Senate Voting on the Hepburn Bill

In order to embarrass their opponents, the Democrats proceeded to offer the various amendments which the President and his Republican supporters had considered and then rejected in favor of the compromise formula, thereby forcing Republicans like Long to vote against propositions that they had previously espoused and for which they still, perhaps, entertained a sneaking regard. Bailey's amendment was rejected by 23 votes to 54, with twenty Democrats voting in favor along with three Republicans: La Follette, Burkett and Hansborough. Further anti-injunction amendments went down by votes of 29–50 and 24–52, with La Follette the only dissident Republican. Then Isidor Rayner put forward what was, almost word for word, Long's narrow review amendment, challenging Long to reject his own handiwork. This Long, after a lengthy and convoluted explanation, duly did, along with forty-nine other Republicans. Thus the vote on each of the narrow review amendments found an almost united Democratic minority arrayed against a solid Republican majority, weakened hardly at all by the regular defections of La Follette.[73]

The pattern reproduced itself when La Follette offered a series of amendments designed to put teeth into what he saw as a distinctly toothless bill: by revivifying the moribund long and short haul section of the 1887 Interstate Commerce Act; by restoring the imprisonment clause removed in 1903; by prohibiting parties appealing against an ICC order from bringing forward new evidence previously unseen by the Commission; by barring judges with railroad holdings from hearing cases under the act; and, most importantly, by requiring a physical valuation of railroad property as the basis for determining precisely what a "reasonable" rate should be. In each case a handful of Republicans voted with the Democrats in opposition to the solid rump of the Republican party.[74]

---

[72] Blum, *Republican Roosevelt*, 102–3; Skowronek, *Building the New American State*, 257–8.
[73] C.R., 59.1:6672–3, 6674, 6678, 6695–6, 6774.
[74] C.R., 59.1:6571, 6949–52, 6697, 6774, 6797, 6809.

It is clear from a cursory examination of the eighteen recorded Senate votes relating to the rate-making power and judicial review that voting mostly followed party lines (see Table 3.1). In all but two the majority of Democratic Senators supported more rigorous controls over railroad rates and practices and enlargement of the authority and effectiveness of the ICC, going a long way to substantiate their claim that railroad regulation was a "Democratic policy."

Since the Republicans united behind the Allison amendment and turned their face against any of the broad or narrow review proposals that they had argued about for the previous two months, it is difficult to identify intraparty divisions.[75] However, an amendment introduced by the Democratic Senator Henry M. Teller threatened to shatter the precarious compromise enshrined in the Allison formula. The operative sentence empowered the ICC to "determine and prescribe what, in its judgment, shall be a just and reasonable rate or rates." The Teller amendment proposed to strike out the words "in its judgment." Allison insisted that "those are essential words to be retained in the bill," indicating that Congress expected the Commission to exercise its "administrative judgment" in setting a rate. Dolliver put the case equally strongly: "With that discretion vested in the Commission, it makes very little difference what jurisdiction you give the courts, because the opinions of the courts are almost uniform that they will not review a discretion confided to an administrative board, except where there has been abuse or the finding is in conflict with constitutional rights." Removing the phrase seemed to invite the courts to review the decisions of the Commission.[76] This concern was echoed by some conservative Senators. Spooner argued that the phrase declared an intention to confer upon the Commission a power that went beyond the mere administration of a standard and a set of rules defined by Congress. To both sides the amendment clearly raised the question of the relative powers of Commission and court, and it captures better than any other recorded vote the division on the issue within the Republican party.[77]

The votes of Republican Senators on the Teller amendment are listed in Table 3.2. They reveal a predictable sectional distribution, with members from the Midwest predominating in the narrow review camp, those from

[75] Widely differing estimates are given in New York *Tribune*, 30 April 1906; *Railroad Gazette*, 3 April 1906, Biographer's Notes, Nelson W. Aldrich MSS, LC; *New York Times*, 4 April 1906; Roosevelt to Kermit Roosevelt, 1 April 1906, *Letters*, 5:204.

[76] *C.R.*, 59.1:7023, 7025, 7063–70. On the significance of the phrase, see Charles A. Prouty to Roosevelt, 22 May 1906, METRP, Reel 65; Samuel H. Cowan to Roosevelt, 17 May 1906, METRP, Reel 64; Chicago *Tribune*, 8 and 9 May 1906, Robert M. La Follette MSS, LC; *New York Times*, 8, 18, 19 May 1906; New York *Tribune*, 8 May 1906; *Railroad Gazette*, 11 May 1906, Biographer's Notes, Nelson W. Aldrich MSS, LC.

[77] *C.R.*, 59.1:7026, 7065. See also *C.R.*, 59.1:7028, 7068; Henry Cabot Lodge to Lucius Tuttle, 5 June 1906, Lodge MSS, MasHS.

TABLE 3.1. *Senate Roll Calls on the Hepburn Bill*

Page in Record	Subject	Division of Vote			Index of Diff.
		Whole	Rep.	Dem.	
6370	*Pipe–line amendment (1)*	53–22	25–22	28–0	49
6373	Pipe-line amendment	75–0	49–0	26–0	0
6455	*Pass: Culberson amendment (2)*	38–35	12–35	26–0	64
6512	Procedure	51–29	39–12	12–17	35
6512–13	Procedure	49–29	24–26	25–3	41
6552	*Commodity: delay to 1909 (3)*	29–44	6–42	23–2	79
6559	Procedure	48–25	20–25	28–0	56
6568	Commodity: substitute	62–11	46–2	17–9	31
6570	Commodity: final version	67–6	42–5	25–1	7
6571	*Long and short haul (4)*	25–46	2–44	23–2	88
6627–8	Imprisonment as penalty	27–49	2–46	25–3	85
6628	Imprisonment as penalty	73–2	46–1	27–1	1
6672–3	*Review: suspension (5)*	23–54	3–46	20–8	65
6674	*Review: suspension (5)*	29–50	1–50	29–0	98
6678	*Review: suspension (5)*	24–52	1–50	23–2	90
6685	*Review:* intrastate freight	27–48	2–48	25–0	96
6695–6	*Review: scope (6)*	24–55	1–50	23–5	80
6697	*Review:* new evidence	26–49	1–45	24–4	84
6774	*Review:* venue and scope	22–46	1–47	21–1	93
6774	*Review:* judges' interests	40–27	3–40	24–0	93
6783	*Review:* judges' interests	23–49	2–46	21–2	87
6787	*Review:* Allison amendment	73–3	49–0	24–3	11
6797	*Review:* court order	30–41	5–40	25–1	85
6809	*Physical valuation (7)*	27–40	6–39	21–2	78
6811	*Review: refer to courts (8)*	56–10	30–9	26–1	19
6811	*Review:* private suits	23–41	4–35	19–1	84
6821	*Employers' liability (9)*	28–45	5–42	23–3	78
6944	*Pass: Bacon amendment (10)*	42–33	24–23	18–10	13
6945	*Pass: Culberson amend. (11)*	49–23	21–23	26–0	53
6949	*Pass: Fulton amendment (12)*	49–29	30–16	19–6	13
6949	*Pass: Culberson amend. (13)*	60–16	33–15	27–1	27
6956	Waterways	25–43	4–40	3–21	4
7014	*Commodity: extend scope (14)*	23–42	5–37	18–4	70
7070	*ICC: "in its judgment" (15)*	24–50	18–28	6–23	19
7070	*ICC: "ascertain and declare" (16)*	47–21	41–3	6–18	68
7088	Passage	71–3	44–1	27–2	5

Notes: In each case the number voting for an extension of ICC powers is listed first, which may be yea or nay according to how the question was put.

The Index of Difference is the difference between the percentages of the two parties voting yea in any particular roll call.

TABLE 3.2. *Voting of Republican Senators on the Teller*
Amendment to the Hepburn Bill

Yeas	Nays	Not Voting
Alger (Mich.)	Allison (Iowa)	Aldrich (R.I.)
Allee (Del.)	Beveridge (Ind.)	Burrows (Mich.)
Ankeny (Wash.)	Burkett (Neb.)	Gamble (S.D.)
Brandegee (Conn.)	Clapp (Minn.)	Heyburn (Ida.)
Bulkeley (Conn.)	Crane (Mass.)	Smoot (Utah)
Burnham (N.H.)	Cullom (Ill.)	Sutherland (Utah)
Carter (Mont.)	Dolliver (Iowa)	Warren (Wyo.)
Clark (Wyo.)	Elkins (W.Va.)	
Dick (Ohio)	Frye (Me.)	
Dillingham (Vt.)	Fulton (Ore.)	
Dryden (N.J.)	Hemenway (Ind.)	
Flint (Cal.)	Hopkins (Ill.)	
Foraker (Ohio)	La Follette (Wis.)	
Gallinger (N.H.)	Long (Kan.)	
Hale (Me.)	Nelson (Minn.)	
Hansborough (N.D.)	Perkins (Cal.)	
Kean (N.J.)	Piles (Wash.)	
Knox (Pa.)	Warner (Mo.)	
Lodge (Mass.)		
McCumber (N.D.)		
Millard (Neb.)		
Nixon (Nev.)		
Penrose (Pa.)		
Platt (N.Y.)		
Scott (W.Va.)		
Spooner (Wis.)		
Wetmore (R.I.)		

Source: C.R., 59.1, 7070

the East and Mountain West among their opponents. Reportedly one or two conservative Senators refused to vote for the Teller amendment as a matter of honor, declining to depart from the intraparty agreement so recently arrived at. This might explain the votes of Frye, Crane, and possibly Elkins.[78]

Although the Democrats were consistently more favorable to effective regulation of rates, several of their number were evidently reluctant to limit the scope of court review.[79] Eight, including Culberson and Bacon, voted against the Bailey amendment, five against the Rayner (Long) amendment,

[78] *New York Times*, 19 May 1906.
[79] For estimates, again worryingly diverse, see ibid., 13, 19 March, 7, 11 April, 19 May 1906; New York *Tribune*, 19 March, 28 April 1906; Acheson, *Bailey*, 201; Simkins, *Tillman*, 433.

which represented the other prong of the narrow review attack, though only three against both. Small though it was, the number of conservative Democrats was sufficient to disrupt the plans of Tillman and Bailey.

In only two votes did a majority of Democrats support amendments which restricted the discretionary powers of the ICC. One was the Teller amendment described above; the other was Stephen R. Mallory's proposal to replace the words "determine and prescribe" with the less definite "ascertain and declare." Each garnered substantial Democratic support, by votes of 23–6 and 18–6, respectively, including that of steadfast proponents of narrow review, like Tillman and Rayner.[80] The bill, said Augustus Bacon of Georgia, was framed upon the theory that Congress regulated rates, setting a standard that rates should be "just and reasonable" and delegating to the Commission the administrative responsibility of deciding whether particular rates met that standard. To instruct it to establish "just and reasonable" rates "in its judgment" would indicate that the Commission, not Congress, laid down the standard for rate making.[81] For these reasons they also favored the Mallory amendment. The words "determine and prescribe" suggested, respectively, judicial and legislative powers which would be improperly vested in an essentially administrative body, the scope of whose duties were more fittingly described by the words "ascertain and declare."[82]

The Democrats' position betrayed considerable ambivalence. For the most part, they desired a strong commission which would act to check perceived abuses in the structure of railroad rates, and they wished to prevent the courts from frustrating its operation. However, they had profound misgivings about the sort of legal entity that was being engendered in the shape of a revitalized ICC: a new kind of regulatory agency with broad discretionary powers in a designated area of public policy. These powers, deciding specific cases and laying down a set of regulations, embraced both judicial and legislative, as well as more recognizably administrative, functions. It was precisely this admixture of what were conventionally viewed as separate powers that disturbed most Democrats. Not only did it offend their delicate sense of legal propriety; it also evoked fears of centralized executive power which lay at the heart of the Jeffersonian tradition in American political thought. Hence Roosevelt's suspicions regarding his one-time Democratic allies' commitment to the principle of narrow review, as he defined it, were substantially justified.

The importance of the rate-making component in what was commonly referred to as the "rate bill" should not distract attention from other provisions which stood as significant pieces of legislation in their own right. The Senate amended the bill to make express companies, sleeping car lines

---

[80] C.R., 59.1:7070. Only three Republicans voted for the Mallory amendment.

[81] C.R., 59.1:7024, 7027, 7063–4, 7067, 7069.

[82] C.R., 59.1:7063, 7069.

and switching facilities subject to the interstate commerce law.[83] Pipe lines, too, were brought under ICC supervision, control of transportation having long been recognized as one of the principal mechanisms by which Standard Oil had attained its hegemony over the oil industry.[84] Similar in intent was the so-called commodity amendment, which debarred railroads from carrying across state lines coal, coke or other commodities in whose production or sale they had an interest.[85] The Senate also took action to eradicate the longstanding practice of issuing free passes to political allies and favorites, although it took a long time to decide upon an acceptable formula.[86]

On looking at the full record of Senate voting on the Hepburn bill one is struck at once by the prime importance of party, but party allegiance explains only a fraction, albeit a major fraction, of the votes cast. After the elimination of duplicate votes, especially on judicial review, sixteen roll calls were extracted for further analysis (marked in italics in Table 3.1). Values of Yule's Q were calculated for each pair, and the resulting matrix was subjected to hierarchical cluster analysis using the group average method. This suggested the presence of one huge cluster of including all but three of the sixteen roll calls.[87]

We can proceed from the identification of clusters to analyze the distribution of opinion in greater detail by building a unidimensional scale. Eight out of the thirteen roll calls in the main cluster fit into such a scale. Table 3.3 presents the votes of Senators on these roll calls. A vote to augment the powers of the ICC is scored as 1. The roll calls are arranged from left to right according to the proportion voting positively; individuals are listed from top to bottom according to the proportion of positive responses. The coefficient of reproducibility is a satisfying .97. Thus we have a listing of Senators in order of their commitment to the principal component of railroad regulation. This embraces readiness to invest the ICC with effective rate-making power, to alleviate long and short haul discrimination, to strengthen the commodity amendment, to bring pipe lines under ICC control, to debar local railroad counsels from receiving free transportation, and to enhance the prospects of injured workers securing compensation in the courts.

The top positions in the table are occupied almost wholly by Democrats: twenty-three Democrats and one Republican, La Follette, achieve scores of seven or eight; only Clark, McEnery and Pettus among the Democrats score six or less. Burkett and Gamble were the only Republicans, apart from

---

[83] Ripley, *Railroads*, 499–506.

[84] *C.R*, 59.1:6358, 6365–7, 7000, 7001; Henry Cabot Lodge to Lucius Tuttle, 7 April 1906, Lodge MSS, MasHS; *New York Times*, 5 May 1906.

[85] *C.R.*, 59.1:6455–6; *Independent*, 60 (22 February 1906): 415–17; (19 April 1906): 937–8; (25 April 1906): 991–2; *New York Times*, 30 January, 9 February 1906.

[86] *C.R.*, 59.1:6440–5, 6455, 6446–7, 6932–5, 6938–45, 6946–9.

[87] The exceptions were roll calls on the Teller amendment (#13) and free pass section (#10 and #12). See the Appendix for an explanation of statistical procedures.

TABLE 3.3. *Senate Voting on the Hepburn Bill*

Name	Party	8	2	7	3	9	4	6	5	Score
					Roll Call No.					
15 Democrats	D	1	1	1	1	1	1	1	1	8
La Follette (Wis.)	R	1	1	1	1	1	1	1	1	8
Bacon (Ga.)	D		1	1	1	1	1	1	0	7
Culberson (Texas)	D	1	1	1	1	1	1	1	0	7
Daniel (Va.)	D	1	1			1	1	1	0	7
Newlands (Nev.)	D	1		1	1	1		1	0	7
Taliaferro (Fla.)	D	1	1	1	1	1	1	1	0	7
Clarke (Ark.)	D	1	1	1	0	1	1	1	1	7[a]
Gearin (Ore.)	D	1	1	1	1	1	0	1	1	7[a]
McLaurin (Miss.)	D	1	1	1	1	0	1	1	1	7[a]
Pettus (Ala.)	D	1	1		1	1	1	0	0	6
Burkett (Neb.)	R	1	1	1	1	1	0	0	1	6
Foster (La.)	D	1	1	1	1			0	1	5[a]
Gamble (S.D.)	R	1		1	1	1		0	0	5
Clapp (Minn.)	R	1	1		1	0	0	0	0	4
Dolliver (Iowa)	R	1	1	1	1	0	0	0	0	4
Warner (Mo.)	R	1	1	1	0	0	0	0	0	3
Kittredge (S.D.)	R	1	1	0	0	1	0	0	0	3[a]
McEnery (La.)	D		1	0		0		0	1	3[a]
Frye (Me.)	R	1	1	0	0	0		0	0	2
Knox (Pa.)	R	1	1	0	0	0	0	0	0	2
Long (Kan.)	R	1	1	0	0	0	0	0	0	2
Nelson (Minn.)	R	1	1	0	0	0	0	0	0	2
Nixon (Nev.)	R	1	1	0	0	0	0	0	0	2
Sutherland (Utah)	R	1	1	0	0	0	0	0	0	2
Elkins (W.Va.)	R		0	1	0	0	0	0	0	2[a]
Clark (Mont.)	D	1			0		0	1	0	2[a]
Fulton (Ore.)	R		0	0	0	1	0	0	0	2[a]
Hemenway (Ind.)	R		0	0	0	0	0	0	1	2[a]
Cullom (Ill.)	R	1	0	0	0	0	1	0	0	2[a]
Lodge (Mass.)	R	1	0	0	1	0	0	0	0	2[a]
Beveridge (Ind.)	R				0		0	0	0	2
Penrose (Pa.)	R			0	0	0		0	0	2
Spooner (Wis.)	R			0			0	0	0	2
12 Republicans	R	1	0	0	0	0	0	0	0	1
16 Republicans	R	0	0	0	0	0	0	0	0	0

Key: 8. Foraker amendment transferring rate cases to courts (6811)

2. Culberson amendment prohibiting free transportation, with exceptions (6949)

7. La Follette amendment for physical valuation of railroad property (6809)

3. Dryden amendment delaying application of commodity clause until 1909 (6552)

9. La Follette amendment inserting employers' liability clause (6821)

4. La Follette amendment to long and short haul section (6571)

6. Rayner (Long) amendment limiting scope of review (6695–6)

5. Bailey amendment prohibiting interlocutory orders without hearing (6672)

a Case containing error response

Note: Owing to lack of evidence, Allison (Iowa), Carmack (Tenn.), Heyburn (Ida.), Mallory (Fla.), Money (Miss.), Morgan (Ala.), Patterson (Col.), Proctor (Vt.), and Warren (Wyo.) were not classified.

La Follette, to score five or more. Only in two roll calls did ten or more Democrats vote against the majority of their party. Nor were the dissenters consistent from one subject to another. The most egregious exceptions were Morgan and Pettus of Alabama, both of whom voted against the bill on final passage. Yet even these relics of the old-time Democracy voted with their party more often than with the opposition. Others to stand out were the notorious copper baron William Clark and Samuel D. McEnery of Louisiana, known as an "Aldrich Democrat."[88]

Voting on the Hepburn bill followed a clear sectional pattern: Senators from the South and, less consistently, the Midwest supported a closer federal supervision of railroad rates and services; those from the Northeast and the transmontane West did not. The average scale score for representatives of the East and the Old Northwest was .69, the South 7.29, the North Central region and Wisconsin 3.35, and the Mountains and Pacific Coast 2.81. While personal convictions and political connections often took priority, there is no denying the influence of geography. Nor is there anything mysterious about this. The existing pattern of rates was more advantageous to the settled regions of New England, the Mid-Atlantic states and the Old Northwest. It was in the area west of the Missouri and south of the Ohio that complaints of extortionate rates and intolerable local discrimination were most numerous. The newer states further west retained the desire, typical of recently settled regions, to promote railroad development and encourage investment, which often overrode other considerations, and, in the absence of substantial urban development, primary producers' interests in low distance rates remained paramount. The railroads played a prominent role in state politics, a role which was only now coming to be challenged by a series of reform movements, the impact of which by 1906 was uneven, and this unevenness is one reason for anomalies in their Senators' behavior in Congress.[89]

The Limitations of the Hepburn Act

After the conclusion of the Senate debate, some awkward hurdles remained. Differences between the House and Senate on over fifty amendments had to be resolved before the bill could be presented for the President's signature. Generally speaking, the Senate had extended the bill's coverage and made it stronger. What supporters of regulation feared was that the Republican conferees from both houses would conspire to emasculate the bill. In the

---

[88] *New York Times*, 4 March 1907.
[89] See, for example, La Forte, *Leaders of Reform*; Carl S. Chrislock, *The Progressive Era in Minnesota, 1897–1918* (St. Paul, Minn.: Minnesota Historical Society, 1971); Herbert Margulies, *The Decline of the Progressive Movement in Wisconsin, 1890–1920* (Madison: University of Wisconsin Press, 1968); Martin Shefter, "Regional Receptivity to Reform: The Legacy of the Progressive Era," *Political Science Quarterly* 98 (1983): 359–83.

event Stephen B. Elkins and Shelby M. Cullom showed a degree of resolution in defense of the Senate position which surprised their detractors, and the House conferees gave ground on almost every point. The central sections of the bill as it had emerged from the Senate remained unchanged.[90] Apart from a modification of the commodity amendment, which would make it possible for the owners of pipelines to carry their own oil, the protracted process of conferring in the end left little changed. Yet none of the Republican conferees was noted for their partiality to reform. The desire of Hepburn to weaken the Senate bill was no secret, while few trusted Elkins and Cullom to stand firm in its defense. Yet stand firm they did, except on the pipeline clause, while the House conferees receded on point after point. Whatever their personal views, they were not unmindful of the sentiment in their respective chambers, and behind that of public opinion and the impending prospect of the autumn elections.

That the new law was only a partial solution to the railroad problem few denied.[91] The pending bill, La Follette told the Senate, "will not solve the transportation problem. Unless greatly strengthened, it will not meet the expectations of the country." The major omission, in his view, was the failure to provide any means of establishing the precise value of a railroad's physical assets. The Supreme Court had established the right of a public service corporation to receive a "reasonable" return on its investments. It was therefore essential to investigate exactly what its investments were worth. In view of the amount of watered stock generated in the course of corporate consolidations, this required a physical valuation of its assets, rather than merely accepting their inflated book value. Failure to do so would result in an overall level of rates which was too high by a considerable margin. Those who suffered would not be the shippers, who merely passed on the excess charges, but the eventual consumers of the goods. Whereas shippers were concerned with questions of discrimination, of relative rates, what mattered to the general public, as consumers, was the overall level of transportation costs. If Congress was to look beyond the interests of the merchants and manufacturers who dealt immediately with the carriers and "protect the consumer as well as the shipper – then the foundation must be laid for ascertaining the reasonable rate, in fact," not "the relatively reasonable rate." This could not be achieved without a physical valuation of railroad property. La Follette condemned the bill as deficient in any "broad consideration of public interest." It was a product of expediency, of the felt need for some legislation to meet popular demand and the complaints of various interest

[90] *C.R.*, 59.1:7852–3, 7920–40, 7978–98, 8340–5, 9077–85; *New York Times*, 2, 3, 8, 12 June 1906; Briggs, *Hepburn*, 268–75.

[91] For a summary of its provisions, see Ripley, *Railroads*, 499–521; Sharfman, *Interstate Commerce Commission*, 1:44–8; Hoogenboom, *Short History of the ICC*, 52–3.

groups and localities. As the record showed, only a handful of his fellow Republicans were willing to go along with him.[92]

A still more radical alternative was presented by the Democratic Senator Francis G. Newlands, who showed, for a Democrat, a remarkable predilection for the exercise of national power. In a series of speeches and articles he expounded "The Common Sense of the Railroad Question." This lay in national incorporation of all railroads, in recognition of the consolidation movement which had transformed the industry over the previous decade. With national incorporation would come national control. This would entail a full physical valuation of railroad property and the setting of rates which would ensure a regular 4 percent return; the abolition of all state and federal taxes on railroads except for a uniform tax on receipts levied by the federal government and distributed among the states; and ICC approval of stock and bond issues. A portion of gross receipts would be set aside to create a pension and insurance fund for railroad workers, and industrial disputes would be made subject to compulsory arbitration.

So comprehensive a solution to the railroad problem, claimed Newlands, would take the railroads "out of politics" once and for all, since they no longer would need to protect themselves against the uneven incidence of local taxes and regulation. The railroads would benefit from a regular return on their investments, shippers from lower rates and better service, workers from better conditions. The railroad industry was a "natural monopoly." "Let it be no longer outlawed, but frankly recognized, welcomed and made legal. The way to do this is by means of national incorporation." Such a policy offered "nearly all of the benefits of Government ownership, with none of its dangers." To Newlands the problem was essentially one of efficiency: the elimination of stock speculation, overcapitalization, dangerous working conditions and political corruption, and the rationalization of the complex and conflicting array of state regulations. Efficient management was not consistent with "a confusion of taxation and a confusion of regulation." Federal control over interstate commerce included "the power to create the intrumentalities for the exercise of that power" in the shape of federal corporations, and then to exempt those federal corporations from state regulation or state taxation. A federal system of incorporation and control was constitutionally as legitimate for railroads as it was for banks.[93]

---

[92] *C.R.*, 59.1:5684–5723, 6805–9; *New York Times*, 20 and 24 June 1906; *La Follette's Autobiography: A Personal Narrative of Political Experiences* (Madison: University of Wisconsin Press, 1960), 171–9; Belle C. to Fola La Follette, 24 June 1906, La Follette MSS, LC.

[93] *C.R.*, 59.1:6891–5; speech on the rate bill, 11 January 1905, in Francis G. Newlands, *Public Papers* (Arthur B. Darling, ed., 2 vols., Boston: Houghton, Mifflin, 1932), 1:312–27; testimony before Senate Committee on Interstate Commerce, 23 May 1905, in ibid., 1:327–32; Newlands to Theodore Roosevelt, 20 May 1907, Newlands MSS, SLYU.

Such high nationalism alarmed fellow Democrats like Bacon and conservative Republicans like Spooner in almost equal degree. Newlands found that a bill for national incorporation offended "the narrow states rights men, who believe that the States should do all the regulating," as much as those who wished to defend existing conditions.[94] Interstate Commerce Commissioner Charles A. Prouty rightly observed that, while "a comprehensive system of federal regulation" might attract some support as a way of preventing "hostile legislation by the States," it would alienate many who favored the Hepburn Act, particularly in the South and West, "because they will hesitate to support any measure which tends to curtail the power of the individual States over the railways."[95] A suggestion like Newlands's probed essential fault lines in the movement for regulation. It fell foul not only of vested interests and laissez faire conservatism but also the attachment of many of his own party to the principles of states' rights and constitutionalism, as well as their fears of monopoly and the close involvement of government in business. Of course, his scheme was, for its time, revolutionary in its nationalism and its acceptance of comprehensive government control. But most Democrats shied away also from some of the constitutional and political implications of an invigorated ICC with wide discretionary powers, as their voting on the review amendments shows.

The fate of the La Follette and Newlands amendments points up the limitations of the Hepburn Act. As La Follette rightly observed, it was an act drawn up to protect the interests of shippers against the railroads and, to some extent, of the railroads against each other, rather than to promote the interests of the consuming public. This, of course, reflected the pressures that lay behind the bill, which emanated above all from shippers and localities aggrieved at the existing rate structure. More immediately, from the viewpoint of the Administration and congressional leaders, it served as a solution to the conflicting political pressures that the shippers' campaign, together with the widespread public anxiety regarding the political power of railroads and other big corporations, had created. The "railroad question" meant many different things to different people, but to political leaders it was essentially a political problem, one of mediating urgent and potentially explosive political demands. The refusal to consider Newlands's more radical proposal indicates the extent to which the agreed objective was to resolve immediate problems on an ad hoc basis, rather than to undertake a more systematic examination of the "railroad problem." The bill itself emerged from a series of compromises – from the initial adjustments between rival bills in the House committee, through the "Allison compromise" on judicial

---

[94] Newlands, *Public Papers*, 1:321–4; Newlands to James S. Harlan, 24 December 1906; to Theodore Roosevelt, 3 January 1906; to Edward A. Moseley, 11 May 1907; to editor of *Outlook*, 10 May 1907, Newlands MSS, SLYU.

[95] Charles A. Prouty to Roosevelt, 16 March 1907, METRP, Reel, 72.

review, to the long drawn-out bargaining in successive conference committees. At each stage radical solutions were dropped in favor of more widely
acceptable alternatives.

Given the widespread acquiescence in the principle of ICC rate making,
the main subject of controversy from the start was the extent of judicial
review. Such concern came naturally to politicians steeped in constitutionalism. But it also reflected their main priorities in wrestling with the problem.
Like Roosevelt himself, they were preoccupied with procedural questions:
of who was to hold power rather than what it was to be used for; of institutional arrangements rather than economic policy. From a structural point
of view the Hepburn Act had radical implications, prefiguring the growth of
the regulatory machinery of twentieth-century American government. From
a legal point of view it constituted a radical advance in that a federal agency
was given clear authority to instruct private corporations what prices they
might charge for their services, although the peculiar status of railroads as
public service corporations "affected with the public interest" had long been
recognized, and the actual grant of power was in this case partial. All in
all, the law's actual impact on the development of the railroad system was
probably much less than its significance for the development of the American
state.

Mr. Taft's Railroad Bill

Although the Hepburn Act greatly enlarged the regulatory powers of the
Interstate Commerce Commission, it conspicuously failed to solve the "railroad problem." The Commission became much busier, achieving greater
success in settling a far larger number of complaints, many of them infor-
mally, than had been possible under the old law. The Supreme Court did
not avail itself of the opportunity left open to it by the Allison amendment
of insisting on a broad review of ICC decisions, accepting in 1910 that the
agency exercised essentially administrative functions and that the "expediency or wisdom" of its actions should not normally be a matter for judicial
scrutiny. But the Commission still had to tread gingerly within the parameters marked out by the earlier Supreme Court decision in *Smyth v. Ames*,
which held that a regulatory commission could only set railroad rates so
long as they were not so low as to amount to a "confiscation" of railroad
property. The Commission's interventions, which touched upon almost every
aspect of the business, went a long way to removing the more obvious abuses
and anomalies in contemporary railroad practice. However, it is difficult to
argue that, even in aggregate, they made much difference to the overall rate
structure. Devoting itself almost exclusively to the adjudication of specific
complaints, the Commission took as its starting point the existing pattern
of rates, accepting by and large the principles behind it. Lacking the power
to adjust rates on its own initiative, it confined itself to the examination

of abuses as they presented themselves to individual shippers or carriers, rather than considering the structure as a whole from the point of view of the "public interest." As Kolko notes, "the world of the I.C.C. was limited to shippers and railroads." Thus many of the deeper structural imbalances and injustices remained.[96]

Continuing pressure for modification of the interstate commerce law demonstrated that the Hepburn Act had failed to meet the hopes vested in it. Shippers found frustrating the inability of the Interstate Commerce Commission to intervene before the event to prevent the imposition of a higher rate, forcing them to undergo months of expense and inconvenience before they could secure relief by means of an ex post facto complaint. Shippers in the West and South also retained the hope that the long and short haul section of the original act might be revived.[97] Meanwhile, the railroads sought adjustments in their own interest. They wished not only to modify sections of the Hepburn Act, like the commodity clause and the provision for judicial review, but also to remedy omissions, from their point of view, like the failure to legalize traffic agreements.[98] Nevertheless, the railroads were less vocal in articulating their desires than they had been in 1905–6, and this is probably true of shippers' organizations as well. Nor was press coverage anything like so extensive. Although both major political parties came out in favor of amendment in their 1908 platforms, neither gave the issue priority during the campaign.[99]

To a considerable extent, the impetus for reform came from above, and particularly from Roosevelt's successor, President William Howard Taft. Taft's motives were not unlike those of Roosevelt in his campaign for railroad regulation, but he viewed the question from a different constitutional perspective. Like Roosevelt, Taft felt the need to balance competing interest groups; unlike Roosevelt, he was reluctant to entrust the resolution of conflicts of interest to an administrative agency. As a constitutional lawyer, he

---

[96] Kolko, *Railroads and Regulation*, 151–3, 155–76; *Outlook* 87 (7 September 1907): 1; 88 (18 January 1908): 105–6; Hoogenboom, *Short History of the ICC*, 53–9; Skowronek, *Building a New American State*, 259–61; Ripley, *Railroads*, 522–45; Berk, *Alternative Tracks*, 167–8. The number of formal complaints filed with the ICC rose from 82 in 1906 to 415 in 1907, while its staff and expenditure more than doubled. Sharfman, *Interstate Commerce Commission*, 1:40–4; Morton Keller, *Regulating a New Economy: Public Policy and Economic Change in America, 1900–1933* (Cambridge, Mass.: Harvard University Press, 1990), 48–9.

[97] See, for example, Commercial Club of Omaha to George Norris, 17 February 1908; W. S. Whitten to Norris, 15 April 1910, Norris MSS, LC; J. H. Kane to Robert M. La Follette, 12 April, 13 May 1910, La Follette MSS, LC; Philip A. Bates to Francis G. Newlands, 8 January 1908, Newlands MSS, SLYU; George M. Cornwall to J. J. Esch, 28 October 1907, Esch MSS, SHSW; Martin, *Enterprise Denied*, 146–7; Ripley, *Railroads*, 534–6.

[98] *Outlook* 92 (15 May 1909): 89–92; Kolko, *Railroads and Regulation*, 163–4; Ripley, *Railroads*, 552–9.

[99] Kirk H. Porter and Donald B. Johnson, eds., *National Party Platforms, 1840–1964* (Urbana: University of Illinois Press, 1966), 146–7, 159.

saw the American government as one founded on the principle of separation of powers, a principle which, in his eyes, was infringed by mixing in one agency what were essentially administrative and judicial powers. It was necessary to clarify the allocation of authority between the different agencies of government. The judiciary must maintain its role of scrutinizing the actions of executive agencies. However, at a time when the scale and complexity of government activity were expanding, this required the creation of specialized administrative courts competent to adjudicate the technical issues confronting government and to match the professional expertise of administrative specialists. Only then could traditional constitutional protections be maintained. Taft recognized the need to expand federal regulatory power but insisted on the necessity of controlling it. By creating such mechanisms he hoped more effectively to accommodate competing economic interests and, in doing so, to heal the growing divisions in his party.[100]

Hence Taft proposed to establish a Court of Commerce. All cases under the interstate commerce law previously heard by the federal circuit courts would go before the new tribunal. Not only would the proposed court provide more effective scrutiny of the actions of the Commission; it would also eliminate many of the inefficiencies and delays arising from the existing system. What was of "supreme importance," he declared, was that the judicial determination of such questions should be "as speedy as the nature of the circumstances will admit, and that a uniformity of decision be secured so as to bring about an effective, systematic, and scientific enforcement of the commerce law, rather than conflicting decisions and uncertainty of final result." In an oft-quoted comment, Taft declared that the function of his Administration would be "to complete and perfect the machinery" by which the Roosevelt reforms would be carried on. This meant the regularization of procedures, a clearer division of authority, and the establishment of the rule of law. The Commerce Court should be seen as part of a broader program of governmental reorganization. It was not designed, as it seemed to his enemies, as a mere sop to the railroads.[101]

There was never any doubt that the Commerce Court would stand as the centerpiece of any railroad bill emanating from the Administration. The question was what else would be included. Taft's strategy was to achieve a balance of elements attractive to railroads and shippers in order to construct a coalition potent enough to ensure its passage.[102] By September 1909 Taft and his advisers had drawn up a draft bill. This provided for a Commerce

---

[100] Skowronek, *Building a New American State*, 173-4; Donald F. Anderson, *William Howard Taft: A Conservative's View of the Presidency* (Ithaca, N.Y.: Cornell University Press, 1973), 59-67, 85-93, 229-35.

[101] James D. Richardson, *A Compilation of the Messages and Papers of the Presidents* (20 vols., New York: Bureau of National Literature, 1897-1914), 10:7822; Ripley, *Railroads*, 566-70; Skowronek, *Building a New American State*, 261-3.

[102] Kolko, *Railroads and Regulation*, 177, 179-80.

Court of five judges which would have original jurisdiction over all cases under the interstate commerce law, its decisions being subject to review only by
the Supreme Court. The Court would have all the powers of injunction previously vested in the circuit courts. Legal proceedings under the law would be
conducted by the Attorney General and his officers, not by the Commission.
This too was a reflection of Taft's desire to clarify lines of authority by divest-
ing the ICC of its judicial functions. Besides these procedural changes, several
major substantive amendments were proposed. Most importantly, the Commission would be empowered to suspend a new rate for thirty days pending
an inquiry into its reasonableness and to consider the justness of rates and
regulations on its own initiative. On the other hand, railroads would be permitted to make agreements covering rates, the outcome of which would be
subject to the same scrutiny as any other rates. No railroad company would
be permitted to hold stock in a competing railroad or to issue any new stock
or bonds without the assent of the Commission. This draft became the basis
for the Administration's legislative proposals during the ensuing session.[103]
Although further concessions were made to the railroads and although progressives in Congress condemned it, in La Follette's words, as "the rankest,
boldest betrayal of public interest ever proposed in any legislative body," the
President's bill, even before its amendment by Congress, constituted a very
considerable increase in federal regulatory power.[104]

Congress and the Mann-Elkins Bill

As in 1906, progressive Republicans and Democrats set out to defend and
enlarge the authority of the ICC. While some sections of the bill did, indeed,
strengthen the Commission, others undermined it, above all by creating the
overshadowing presence of the Commerce Court. Progressives feared that
the powers so carefully entrusted to the Commission four years earlier, as
well as in this bill, would be hijacked by the new judicial body, where the real
decisions over railroad rates and practices would now be made. Its creation
undermined the principle at the core of the new system of regulation. As
Bacon explained, "These are not in the proper sense law questions which are
going to be decided," but "questions of policy . . . questions of discretion."[105]
In the absence of provisions to the contrary, it was feared that the new court

---

[103] "Points of agreement reached at conference ... August 30, 31, and September 1, 1909,"
in La Follette MSS, LC; Kolko, *Railroads and Regulation*, 180–5; Ripley, *Railroads*, 557–79;
Messages and Papers, 10:7821–9.

[104] La Follette, *La Follette's Autobiography*, 180; Joseph L. Bristow to William A. White, 5
January 1910, White MSS, LC; George E. Mowry, *Theodore Roosevelt and the Progressive
Movement* (Madison: University of Wisconsin Press , 1946), 94–6.

[105] C.R., 61.2:6336, 6326–31, 6335–45, 7359–65; *Outlook* 94 (12 March 1910): 640–1, 816–19;
Kenneth Hechler, *Insurgency: Personalities and Politics of the Taft Era* (New York: Columbia
University Press, 1940), 166–8; Ross, *Dolliver*, 274–5; Ripley, *Railroads*, 567–9.

would assume more extensive powers of review than the circuit courts had claimed under the Hepburn Act. The bill was modified in the Senate to ensure that it should "not be construed as enlarging the jurisdiction possessed by the courts to review and set aside the orders of the commission" and to prohibit the Court from granting an interlocutory injunction or temporary restraining order without five days' notice and a hearing.[106]

Equally objectionable was an apparent imbalance in access. The bill, remarked La Follette, "created a new court, open to the railroads, to enjoin the orders of the Interstate Commerce Commission, and it denied the public admission to that court upon the same terms." After a lengthy debate, Cummins, now representing Iowa in the Senate, secured an amendment allowing "communities, associations, corporations, firms and individuals" to "intervene in any said suit or proceedings at any time."[107]

Not only were shippers denied access to Commerce Court hearings in the original bill; the Commission itself was "absolutely barred from appearing in court, even to defend its own orders." Instead the Attorney General would decide whether or not to prosecute, whether or not to contest a court order, and whether or not to appeal against it to a higher court. The ICC's absence would deprive the court of necessary expertise in resolving complicated issues. "Manifestly," noted La Follette, it was to the railroads' advantage "to get rid of [the] Attorneys for [the] Interstate Commerce Commission and substitute the untrained attorneys of a political department of the government instead."[108] By removing its right to defend itself, protested Newlands, "you strike at the very vitals of this commission." At stake was the vary nature of the ICC as a regulatory body. Whereas to conservative Senators, as to Taft, it appeared anomalous for a "quasi-judicial tribunal" to defend its own judgments on appeal, to progressives it was precisely because the Commission was not a judicial but an administrative body that it was wholly appropriate for it to appear in court to explain the grounds, often highly technical in nature, for its decisions. Here, too, the insurgents succeeded in amending the bill to provide authorization for the ICC to defend its decisions before the Commerce Court and to prevent the Attorney General from discontinuing suits or proceedings without its consent.[109]

---

[106] C.R., 61.2:4501–8, 7373; Joseph L. Bristow, "Speech at the Winfield Chautauqua, 9 July 1910," in Albert J. Beveridge MSS, LC; Herbert Margulies, *Senator Lenroot of Wisconsin* (Columbia: University of Missouri Press, 1977), 100–2. That progressive fears of the Commerce Court were warranted became clear when the newly established body proceeded, during its brief existence, to overrule nearly every ICC order that came before it. Ripley, *Railroads*, 580–94.

[107] C.R., 61.2:7360–4, 7373.

[108] C.R., 61.2:6444, 6346–7, 6389–6409, 6444–62, 7373; Bristow, "Speech at the Winfield Chautauqua"; George Norris to H. M. Bushnell, 13 May 1910, Norris MSS, LC; "Analysis of Relative Merits of Entrusting Cases to ICC or Attorney-General," n.d., Robert M. La Follette MSS, LC; Sayre, "Cummins," 360–3; Ripley, *Railroads*, 570–1.

[109] C.R., 61.2:6391–3, 6403, 6452; Newlands, *Public Papers*, 1:352–9.

As for the legalization of tariff agreements, this, exclaimed Cummins, was "the most startling, the most destructive proposal that has been in regard to this subject for years." It was tantamount to repealing the antitrust law, by which, according to Joseph L. Bristow of Kansas, "the government was able to protect the American people from the tyranny of a great and gigantic railroad combination . . . fixing every rate in the United States."[110] If such agreements were to be permitted, they, and the schedule of rates agreed under them, should be subject to ICC approval. Cummins offered an amendment to that effect, which was rejected in favor of a more modest demand by Coe Crawford of South Dakota for ICC approval of rate agreements but not of the resulting rates. Cummins then put forward a formula whereby ICC scrutiny would be required if rates were increased. When it appeared that this would command a majority Aldrich and Elkins elected to remove the section altogether, in accordance with a shadowy deal with the Democrats, which also included the elimination of the securities section.[111]

Besides modifying the original terms of the bill, the progressive coalition added important new sections. The ICC was authorized to suspend any advance in railroad rates for a period of up to ten months, instead of the sixty days provided in the initial bill.[112] The burden of proof was placed upon the carrier to show that the new rate was just and reasonable, rather than on the shipper to show that it was not — a major shift in the balance of power in the transportation marketplace.[113] Telephone and telegraph companies were brought under ICC control, just as pipelines and express companies had been in 1906.[114] Finally, a more effective long and short haul section was added. Nineteen or twenty Western Republicans combined with a majority of Democrats to compel acceptance of an amendment which forbade the levying of higher short haul rates unless the ICC found that special circumstances warranted them and so long as it was satisfied that the higher rates were not unreasonable or unjustly discriminatory in themselves.[115]

---

[110] Ralph M. Sayre, "Albert M. Cummins and the Progressive Movement in Iowa" (Ph.D. diss., Columbia University, 1958), 363; Bristow, "Speech at the Winfield Chautauqua"; C.R., 60.1:5559, 7373; Martin, *Enterprise Denied*, 185–6.

[111] C.R., 61.2:5564, 5559–67; Newlands, *Public Papers*, 1:359–60; Albert J. Beveridge to William D. Foulke, 4 May 1910, Beveridge MSS, LC; Claude E. Barfield, "The Democratic Party in Congress, 1909–1913" (Ph.D. diss., Northwestern University, 1965), 169–85; Sayre, "Cummins," 372–4; Sanders, *Roots of Reform*, 207; Mowry, *Theodore Roosevelt and the Progressive Movement*, 101; Hechler, *Insurgency*, 170–2.

[112] C.R., 61.2:6777–92, 6914–21; Bristow, "Speech at Winfield Chautauqua"; Martin, *Enterprise Denied*, 192.

[113] C.R., 61.2:7136–8.

[114] C.R., 61.2:6972–7, 7264–6. See also Jeffrey E. Cohen, "The Telephone Problem and the Road to Telephone Regulation, 1876–1917," *Journal of Policy History* 3 (1991): 57–63.

[115] C.R., 61.2:4497–8, 6331–4, 7374; Barfield, "Democratic Party," 174–9; Hechler, *Insurgency*, 169–73.

Despite its substantive complexity, the 1910 railroad bill produced a simpler voting pattern than that of 1906. The thirty-four roll calls taken in the Senate are listed in Table 3.4. The omission of duplicates leaves us with a sample of eighteen for further analysis. The Q-matrix reveals at once that fifteen, no pair of which gives a value of less than .90, are closely associated with one another. Votes on these are presented in Table 3.5. They do not generate a very useful scale, even though the coefficient of reproducibility is an impressive .96, because the proportion voting for stricter regulation does not vary greatly. In most cases a concerted Democratic minority combined with nine to twelve insurgents against the solid rump of the Republican party, a pattern which prevails with regard to almost every question put.

Most Democrats responded positively to every item in the scale. All but one, Charles Hughes of Colorado, accumulated scores of fourteen or fifteen – scores matched by only seven Republican insurgents. The three remaining roll calls were more divisive. Most Democrats voted against progressive Republican attempts to reinstate an amended version of the section relating to stock ownership, chiefly on the grounds that such matters were, as Bailey put it, "wholly beyond the jurisdiction of the General Government."[116] Although most Democrats preferred a strengthening of the long and short haul section, six voted against it, of whom all but Hughes represented the Gulf and Atlantic states.[117]

Republican voting, in contrast, displays a clear pattern of factionalism. The chief distinguishing mark of the hard-core insurgents was their adamant opposition to the Commerce Court, the core of the Administration program. Beveridge, Borah, Bristow, Clapp, Crawford, Cummins, Dixon, Dolliver, and La Follette voted to strike it out of the bill. They also voted together with Bourne to restrict the court's jurisdiction and with Bourne and Burkett against vesting control of litigation in the hands of the Attorney General. These eleven were joined by Gamble in voting to strengthen the suspension clause and to subject rate schedules arising from traffic agreements to ICC approval. Finally, Brown and Jones were among the fourteen who supported the physical valuation of railroad property. The remainder voted solidly against progressive amendments, except for that covering telegraph and telephone companies. The insurgents were a clearly defined group who had cooperated on other occasions, notably in the tariff debate of 1909. With the exception of Bourne, Dixon, and Borah, they were all Midwesterners. The Midwesterners who did not join them, like Curtis, Nelson, Stephenson, and Warner, now stood out as deviants from the sectional norm. In other words, the incipient sectional divisions of 1906 were now more starkly apparent, largely because of the trend in national politics, rather more because local

---

[116] C.R., 61.2:6921–3, 6962–72, 7132–3, 7135, 7191–5, 7197–9; "Democratic Party," 186–9; Sanders, *Roots of Reform*, 207.

[117] C.R., 61.2:6213, 6331–4; Barfield, "Democratic Party," 174–9.

TABLE 3.4. *Senate Roll Calls on the Mann–Elkins Bill*

Page in Record	Subject	Whole	Rep.	Dem.	Index of Diff.
		Division of Vote			
4501	Creation of land courts	27–34	18–25	9–9	8
4507	*Commerce Court: jurisdiction (1)*	25–40	9–36	16–4	60
4507	*Commerce Court: jurisdiction*	30–39	8–38	22–1	79
4508	*Commerce Court: jurisdiction*	28–36	8–36	20–0	82
4659	Through routes	51–9	38–5	13–4	12
5567	*Traffic agreements (2)*	29–35	10–35	19–0	78
6213	Long/short haul: Dixon amend.	57–10	44–5	13–5	21
6342	*Commerce Court: strike out (3)*	28–37	8–37	20–0	82
6346	*Commerce Court: three judges*	25–35	9–34	16–1	73
6462	*Representation before Court (4)*	40–23	39–10	1–13	73
6914	Suspension: 6–month limit	18–54	0–50	18–4	82
6915	Suspension: *no time limit (5)*	29–43	12–39	17–4	50
6920	Suspension	35–40	12–40	23–0	77
6921	Suspension: final version	72–0	51–0	21–0	0
6923	Stock issue: strike out section	68–1	47–1	21–0	2
6972	Stock issue: *Dolliver sub. (6)*	19–47	15–31	4–16	13
6975	*Telephone and telegraph (7)*	37–22	21–21	16–1	44
7135	*Stock ownership in competing lines (8)*	20–41	11–33	9–8	28
7196	Physical valuation	25–30	10–30	15–0	75
7199	Physical valuation	28–30	12–30	16–0	71
7203	Water competition	54–1	41–1	13–0	2
7218	*Commodity amend. (9)*	25–31	11–31	14–0	74
7257	Federal and state jurisdiction	31–28	14–28	17–0	67
7258	Federal and state jurisdiction	33–28	14–28	19–0	67
7258	*Federal and state jurisdiction (10)*	33–28	14–28	19–0	67
7264	*Shipper's representation (11)*	29–33	11–33	18–0	75
7266	Telephone and telegraph	34–28	14–27	20–1	61
7271	Physical valuation	29–31	11–31	18–0	74
7271	*Time when act effective (12)*	25–32	9–32	16–0	78
7341	*Long/short haul (13)*	32–26	22–22	10–4	21
7347	*Judges' interests (14)*	29–32	13–32	16–0	71
7351	Commerce Court: appointment	18–39	6–39	12–0	87
7355	*Hours of rail employees (15)*	14–31	12–30	12–1	63
7365	*Commerce Court: strike out (16)*	25–38	6–38	19–0	86
7369	Long/short haul: Heyburn amendment	8–47	7–36	1–11	8
7372	*Physical valuation (17)*	24–32	13–31	11–1	62
7375	*Passage (18)*	12–50	0–44	12–6	67

TABLE 3.5. *Senate Voting on the Mann-Elkins Bill*

Name	Party	7	10	17	2	11	14	5	1	9	12	15	3	16	4	18	Score
12 Democrats	D	I	I	I	I	I	I	I	I	I	I	I	I	I	I	I	15
Fletcher (Fla.)	D	I	I	I	I	I	I	I	I		I	I	I	I	o	I	14[a]
Bailey (Tex.)	D		I	I	I	I	I	o	I	I			I	I			14[a]
Borah (Ida.)	R	I	I	I	I	I	I	I	I	I	I	I	I	I	I	o	14
Bristow (Kan.)	R	I	I	I	I	I	I	I	I	I	I	I	I	I	I	o	14
Clapp (Minn.)	R	I	I	I	I	I	I	I	I	I	I	I	I	I	I	o	14
Cummins (Iowa)	R	I	I		I			I	I			I			I	o	14
Dolliver (Iowa)	R	I	I	I	I	I	I	I	I	I	I	I	I	I	I	o	14
La Follette (Wis.)	R	I	I	I	I	I	I	I		I	I	I	I	I	I	o	14
Paynter (Ky.)	D	I		I	I	I	I	I	I	I	I	I	I	I	I	o	14
Simmons (N.C.)	D	I	I	I	I	I	I	I	I	I	I	I	I	I	I	o	14
Clay (Ga.)	D		I	I	I	I	I	I	I	I	I	I	I	I	I	o	14
Beveridge (Ind.)	R	I	I	I	I	I	I	I	I	I		I	I	I	I	o	14
Chamberlain (Ore.)	D	I	I	I	I	I	I	I	I		I	I		I	I	o	14
Gore (Okla.)	D	I	I	I	I	I	I	I	I		I	I	I	I		o	14
Stone (Mo.)	D	I	I	I	I	I	I	I	I	I	I		I	I		o	14
Dixon (Mont.)	R	I	I	I	I	I	I	I		I		I	o	I	I	o	13[a]
Bourne (Ore.)	R	I	I	I	I	I	I	I	I	I	I	I	o	o	I	o	12[a]
Crawford (S.D.)	R	I	I	I	o	I	I	I	I	I	I	I	I	o		o	11[a]
Gamble (S.D.)	R	I	I	I	I	I	o	I	o	I	I	I	o	o	o	o	9[a]
Burkett (Neb.)	R	I		I	I		I	I	o			o	o	o	I	o	8[a]
Jones (Wash.)	R	I	I	I	o	o	I	o	o	o	o	o	o	o	o	o	4[a]
Nelson (Minn.)	R		o	I	I	o	o	o	I	o	o	o	o	o	o	o	4[a]
Burton (Ohio)	R	I	I	o	o	o	I	o	o	o	o	o	o	o	o	o	3[a]
Perkins (Cal.)	R	I	o	o	o	I	o	o	o	o	o	o	o	o	o	o	2[a]
Flint (Cal.)	R	o	o	o	I	o	o	o	o	o	o	o	o	o	o	o	1[a]
Piles (Wash.)	R	o	I	o	o	o	o	o	o	o	o	o	o	o	o	o	1[a]
Warner (Mo.)	R	o	I	o	o	o	o	o		o	o	o		o		o	1[a]
5 Republicans	R	I	o	o	o	o	o	o	o	o	o	o	o	o	o	o	1
24 Republicans	R	o	o	o	o	o	o	o	o	o	o	o	o	o	o	o	0

Key: 7. bring telephone and telegraph companies under the terms of the law (6975)

10. prevent interlocutory injunctions in cases arising under state laws (7258)

17. physical valuation of railroad assets (7372)

2. Cummins amendment to section legalising traffic agreements (5567)

11. permit shippers to be represented in cases before the Commerce Court (7264)

14. bar judges holding railroad securities from membership of Commerce Court (7347)

5. Cummins amendment preventing any increase in rates without ICC approval (6915)

1. restrict jurisdiction of Commerce Court to that held by circuit courts (4507)

9. Bailey amendment to the commodity section (7218)

12. delay application of law for sixty days (7271–2)

15. limit the hours of work of railroad employees (7355)

3. strike out Commerce Court (6342)

16. strike out Commerce Court (7365)

4. allowing for ICC intervention in cases before the Commerce Court (6462)

18. passage (7375)

[a] Cases containing error responses

Note: Owing to lack of evidence, Bankhead (Ala.), Bradley (Ky.), Clarke (Ark.), Culberson (Tex.), Daniel (Va.), Davis (Ark.), Foster (La.), Lorimer (Ill.), McCumber (N.D.), McEnery (La.), Money (Miss.), Oliver (Pa.), Penrose (Pa.), Richardson (Del.), Root (N.Y.), Smith (Md.), Smith (Mich.), Taliaferro (Fla.), Taylor (Tenn.), Tillman (S.C.), Warren (Wyo.), and Wetmore (R.I.) were not classified. Brown (Neb.) and Hughes (Col.) produced too many error responses to be assigned meaningful scores.

reform movements had made it more difficult for Midwestern politicians to be associated with the defense of railroad interests.

Only the long and short haul clause produced a different alignment, one that was still more sectional in nature. This, declared Joseph Dixon of Montana, was a matter which meant "more to the country west of the Missouri River than all the pending bill put together." Of nineteen Republicans voting for the Sutherland amendment eleven were Midwestern insurgents, while eight were Midwestern and Mountain Republicans with regular voting records, like Clark, Smoot and Stephenson. Bourne, on the other hand, deserted his fellow insurgents to vote with other West Coast Senators against the amendment. Heyburn was the only member from between the Sierras and the Missouri, the region worst affected by this kind of discrimination, to oppose the amendment, and then only because he favored a still more drastic formula. On no other issue were sectional lines so sharply drawn.[118]

The clarity of the sectional alignment on that issue shows that sectionalism offers only a partial explanation of the broader alignment of votes on the railroad question. Almost all Democrats voted for, approximately three-quarters of Republicans against, tighter regulation. Indeed, the Administration notoriously made the issue a test of party loyalty. This certainly did not deter the hard-core insurgents, but it might have influenced some of the so-called near-insurgents, who were under considerable pressure not to waver.[119]

While the bill was being reshaped in the Senate, a similar process was under way in the House. James Robert Mann, who had inherited Hepburn's position as chairman of the House Committee on Interstate and Foreign Commerce, proved a much more flexible manager than Elkins and one much more sympathetic to railroad regulation. A coalition of Democrats and progressive Republicans added a long and short haul section and more stringent controls on stock watering, mergers with competing railroads and rate agreements, struck out the section providing for antitrust exemptions, defined telephone and telegraph companies as common carriers, provided for physical valuation of railroad properties, and narrowly failed to strike out the Commerce Court. Norris acknowledged that what emerged was "a very great improvement over the bill as originally prepared by the Attorney General and the President."[120]

---

[118] Heyburn favored simply removing the "substantially similar" phrase altogether. *C.R.*, 61.2:7272–3, 7332–41, 7369.

[119] Hechler, *Insurgency*, 163–77; Mowry, *Theodore Roosevelt and the Progressive Movement*, 102; Braeman, *Beveridge*, 177–81.

[120] George Norris to William Owen Jones, 8 May 1910; to Isaac W. Carpenter, 26 April 1910; to Byrne and Hammer Dry Goods Company, 30 April 1910; to Perry L. Hale, 3 June 1910, Norris MSS, LC; Irvine Lenroot to W. R. Foley, 24 March 1910, Lenroot MSS, LC; Herbert F. Margulies, *Reconciliation and Revival: James R. Mann and the House Republicans*

As in the Senate, the minority was consistent in its support for stricter regulation, except for an embarrassing defection on a crucial vote to concur with the Senate amendments, which, in aggregate, enhanced the powers of the ICC. Twenty-five Republicans voted for the same resolution to concur, twenty-four of whom were Midwestern insurgents. It was not that they regarded the Senate bill as superior to their own, but, as Irvine Lenroot put it, it was "a better bill than we can expect will come out of a conference committee."[121] A smaller number of insurgents voted with the Democrats against the stock ownership section, preferring a more categorical condemnation of stock purchase in competing lines than was offered in the committee's bill, and to strike out the Commerce Court.[122]

The failure of the motion to concur took the bill to a conference committee. However, the insurgents made it clear that they would vote against any conference report which did not include the greater part of their amendments, keeping the elderly Republican leaders in Washington throughout the long hot summer. In the event, whether concerned for their health and their European holidays or, more likely, for the electoral consequences of stalemate, the conference committee, stiffened by Mann's desire to pass a meaningful law, retained almost all the progressive amendments except for physical valuation.[123]

The final Mann-Elkins Act was, like all legislation, a compromise, but it was one that the progressives could take more pleasure in than the President and his allies. La Follette proclaimed triumphantly that "the administration bill, framed in the interest of the railroads, has been torn to pieces and rewritten in the interest of the people." The Court of Commerce remained, but its powers of injunction were counterbalanced by the demand for notice and a hearing and the provision for immediate appeal to the Supreme Court. Indeed, after a record of confrontation with both the Commission and the Supreme Court, the ill-fated tribunal was legislated out of existence in 1913. The securities section fell, but so did that legalizing traffic agreements. The authority of the ICC was extended to interstate telephone and telegraph systems. A strict long and short haul clause was adopted, following the House bill in removing the "under substantially similar circumstances and conditions" clause and insisting that exceptions be granted only by the

in the Wilson Era (Westport, Ct.: Greenwood, 1996), 27–31; Margulies, *Lenroot*, 98–102; Richard Lowitt, *George W. Norris: The Making of a Progressive, 1861–1912* (Syracuse, N.Y.: Syracuse University Press, 1963), 186–7; Mowry, *Theodore Roosevelt and the Progressive Movement*, 97.

[121] C.R., 61.2:6032, 7568–77; Irvine Lenroot to T. L. Gilbert, 13 June 1910, Lenroot MSS, LC; Margulies, *Senator Lenroot*, 96–104; Hechler, *Insurgency*, 173–7; Lucas, *Lindbergh*, 62–4; Barfield, "Democratic Party," 141–55, 193–4.

[122] C.R., 61.2:5859–67, 5882–5901, 6030–2, 6033.

[123] Irvine Lenroot to T. L. Gilbert, 12 June 1910, Lenroot MSS, LC; Margulies, *Reconciliation and Revival*, 32; Hechler, *Insurgency*, 174–7.

Commission. The Commission had the authority to investigate rates on its own initiative, and, above all, it could suspend rate increases for up to ten months, leaving the railroads to demonstrate the reasonableness of a new rate.[124] The economist William Z. Ripley, writing at the time, saw the suspension clause as a "a radical extension of the authority of the Commission" and the measure as a whole as "really radical in character." Such also, from a more critical perspective, is the view of Albro Martin, who sees it as forging a critical link in the regulatory chains that bound and incapacitated the railroads.[125]

The Mann-Elkins Act marked a significant shift in the politics of railroad regulation. Confronted by a series of joint rate demands by the major trunk railroads, the Commission used its new-found power of suspension repeatedly to block the proposed increases. Seeing its duty as that of protecting the consuming public against overcharging by monopolistic corporations, it concerned itself more frequently with the overall level of rates, rather than with questions of discrimination. Commission and carriers commenced a ritual dance of confrontation which, in the end, did little service to either railroads or the public. As Gerald Berk explains, "The Gilded Age struggle over rate *structures* . . . was replaced by a Progressive Era struggle over rate *levels*."[126] This was a result more than a precondition of the legal changes of the Progressive Era.

Conclusion

The "railroad problem" in 1910 was addressed in much the same terms as the "railroad problem" in 1906. Congressional deliberations echoed the railroad debates of 1906, covering many of the same subjects, such as judicial review, physical valuation and long and short haul discrimination. Although a growing number of, particularly Democratic, Congressmen alluded to the interest of consumers in preventing unwarranted and inflationary rate increases, the problems of shippers still held center stage.[127] The Mann-Elkins Act was an extension of the Hepburn Act, building on the principles laid down in the earlier statute, above all by augmenting the Commission's control over rates. Once more both President and Congress showed a compelling interest in the legal mechanisms by which regulation was to be carried out. The Court of Commerce was both the centerpiece of the bill and its most controversial feature. Once more the principal problems which the bill was expected to solve, at both ends of Pennsylvania Avenue, were essentially political rather than economic.

---

[124] For a summary, see Ripley, *Railroads*, 560–79.

[125] Ripley, *Railroads*, 563–4, 578; Martin, *Enterprise Denied*, 183–93. Cf. Kolko, *Railroads and Regulation*, 193–4.

[126] Berk, "Constituting Railroads and Markets: Railroads in Gilded Age Politics," *Studies in American Political Development* 1 (1986): 165; Berk, *Alternative Tracks*, 162–77.

[127] See, for example, *C.R.*, 61.2:5741, 5841, 5858–9.

Once more the principal support for extension of the powers of the Interstate Commerce Commission came from Southern Democrats and Midwestern Republicans; once more opposition centered on the Republican heartland north of the Ohio and east of the Mississippi. The demand for rate regulation was in part a sectional movement speaking to the inequities in transportation facilities felt by shippers in the South and Midwest and the sense of "regional injury" felt by local populations – but only in part.[128] Sectional grievances were given added validity by a broader sense of unease with corporate power. They were, at the same time, channeled and utilized by political leaders like Theodore Roosevelt, who were able to exploit the factional balance in Congress to devise regulatory institutions more appropriate to the management of a modern industrial society.

Discussion of railroad regulation was permeated with the language of "public interest." Although it is notoriously difficult to define, those interpretations of the history of regulation which dismiss its importance neglect the simple truth that a concept like the "public interest" is relevant so long as a substantial number of people believe that it is and act accordingly. The origins and practice of regulation cannot easily be separated from ideas about regulation.[129] Its advocates believed themselves to be acting to protect the "people" against powerful railroad interests. According to Tillman, rate regulation was necessary to protect the people from "oppressive and exacting and tyrannical and outrageous robberies by the railroads."[130] The "people" were identified by most supporters of the bill with the shippers who were the immediate customers of the railroads. Big shippers were usually content with the existing rate structure. The demand for regulation therefore came mainly from smaller shippers, including small businessmen and farmers, who were poorly organized for much of the period and therefore relied on generalized appeals to political leaders. Advocates of legislation clearly envisaged small shippers as the victims of railroad power, and their conception of this category seems to have shaded off into more general notions of the "people." Both Democrats and progressive Republicans were prone to draw on the language of nineteenth-century republicanism in composing their narratives of popular interests menaced by corporate power.

Railroad spokesmen naturally resisted suggestions that their behavior was detrimental to the "public interest." Most of the abuses associated with the rating practices of the railroads, they maintained, were unavoidable

---

[128] Cf. Sanders, *Roots of Reform*, 179–216.

[129] Wilson, "Politics of Regulation," 384–7, 593–4; Samuel P. Hays, "Political Choice in Regulation," in Thomas K. McCraw, ed., *Regulation in Perspective* (Cambridge, Mass.: Harvard University Press, 1981), 131–2. On the difficulty of defining the "public interest," see McCraw, *Prophets of Regulation*, 300–1; McCraw, "Regulation in America," 180; Barry Mitnick, *The Political Economy of Regulation* (New York: Columbia University Press, 1980), 1–20; Wilson, "The Politics of Regulation," 367–72; Hoogenboom, *Short History of the ICC*, ix–x.

[130] *C.R.*, 59.1:2425.

consequences of the market conditions under which the industry operated. "The fact of transcendent importance stands that freight charges are absolutely controlled by commercial conditions," the railroad statistician Joseph Nimmo, Jr. told Spooner.[131] Such considerations have persuaded some historians. Albro Martin observes, for example, that such practices as "charging more . . . for a short haul confined to the lines of the railroad company than for a long haul which the shipper was free to send over a competing line" were "firmly rooted in the economic realities of railroad competition." He believes that "a repressive policy of rate regulation" starved the railroads of investment capital, leaving them unable to offer an efficient and competitive service or to meet the mounting challenges of the new century. Politicians blinded by the shibboleths of "archaic Progressivism" and conscious of "the unpopularity of higher railroad rates," failed to "apply the principles of economics" to the railroad industry. Their failure to comprehend the nature of the problem led reformers of the Progressive Era to interfere with the mechanism in ways that were ultimately damaging to the railroads' future health and usefulness. "The most damning line of criticism" of federal regulation, observes McCraw, "has rested on claims that the ICC has worked to impede economic efficiency" as a result of "its concern for fairness," whether to shipper or carrier or both.[132]

The problem, he concludes, was that the logic of railroad economics and the logic of American politics ran in opposite directions. The huge economies of scale involved in railroading, and the consequent gap between fixed and variable costs, left scope for wide differentials in the rates charged, while creating intensely competitive conditions. Railroads responded by charging very low rates on competitive routes and recouping their losses where competition did not operate. This gave rise to a set of intensely felt but highly localized grievances of precisely the kind to which the system of political representation was most sensitive. Any solution, however, had to acknowledge the industry's natural tendency towards monopoly; it must therefore involve some provision for rate agreements, in other words pooling. Many commentators observed that the principle behind effective railroad regulation ran contrary to that behind the antitrust law. As Interstate Commerce Commissioner Martin A. Knapp acknowledged,

It is not too much to say that every important railroad rate in this country is made in deliberate disregard, if not open violation, of the anti-trust law. . . . On the other hand

[131] Joseph Nimmo, Jr. to John C. Spooner, 9 March 1906; J. W. Midgley to Spooner, 22 March, 27 April 1906, Spooner MSS, LC; Spencer, "Railway Rates and Industrial Progress"; Wilcox, "Government Rate-Making Is Unnecessary."

[132] Martin, *Enterprise Denied*, 42–5, 355–60; McCraw, *Prophets of Regulation*, 63–4, 71–5. Cf. Hovenkamp, *Enterprise and American Law*, 131–7, 150–6; Eugene L. Huddleston, "'The Generals up in Wall Street': Ray Stannard Baker and the Railroads," *Railroad History* 145 (1981): 69–80.

it is obvious that competitive rates must be the same by all lines or must differ only by agreed amounts, otherwise the result would border on transportation chaos. As a practical matter the interstate commerce law cannot be complied with by competing roads without that concert of action which the anti-trust law prohibits. If they do agree they break one law, if they do not agree they break another.[133]

Many inside the railroad industry, and some outside it, including several members of the Interstate Commerce Commission, saw pooling, under ICC supervision, as a prerequisite for any orderly system of rates.[134] However, their voices were drowned by the tide of jeremiads against railroad consolidation and monopoly. Any notion of collusion between railroads aroused a storm of protest from shippers and the public at large, alarmed at any accentuation of monopolistic tendencies in the railroad industry. The proposal in the Mann-Elkins bill to legalize traffic agreements elicited a predictable response. "We have believed that a certain competition was necessary in the industrial life of the United States," pronounced Cummins. In the face of assertions by Elihu Root and Theodore Burton that the antitrust laws were unworkable in the railroad industry, progressives like Cummins and La Follette insisted that "the principle of competition" was inviolate. Pooling was the principal casualty in the legislative struggle over the Mann-Elkins bill.[135]

That the rating decisions of the railroads were influenced by competitive considerations that lay partially outside their control is undeniable, but it must be remembered that the structure of rates and the flow of economic activity were themselves a cumulative product of the actions of the railroads over a period of decades, actions which had a compelling influence on the development of communities all over the United States. As well as the railroads responding to the pattern of demand, they themselves shaped that demand by their own rating decisions, in particular by privileging long hauls over short-distance routes over a period of years. Over time the railroads shaped, as much as they responded to, the framework of economic possibilities.[136] For such arbitrary power to lie in private hands was unacceptable. After all, as Roosevelt himself pointed out, the railroad was the primary "highway of commerce... and we must do our best to see that it is kept open to all on equal terms."[137] This was a governmental responsibility that could not be wholly left in private hands. The contribution of preferential railroad rates to the rise of the Oil Trust, argued the *Independent*, completely confounded the

---

[133] Ibid., 49; Martin A. Knapp to Ray S. Baker, 11 September 1905, Baker MSS, LC.

[134] *Outlook*, 79 (14 January 1905), 110–11, 119–21; 81 (14 October 1905), 353–4; Theodore Roosevelt to Benjamin I. Wheeler, 18 January 1905, *Letters*, 4:1105; *New York Times*, 24 December 1905. Cf. Berk, *Alternative Tracks*, 153–5.

[135] *C.R.*, 61.2:5559–62, 5565. See also Dobbin, *Forging Industrial Policy*, 79–84.

[136] For a parallel argument, see Berk, *Alternative Tracks*; Berk, "Constituting Railroads and Markets."

[137] Roosevelt, *Works*, 15:281; *Outlook* 79 (18 February 1905): 407–8; 80 (1 July 1905): 563–5.

case against government rate making.[138] In the last analysis, regulation was a necessary response to the economic and political pressures on government leaders.

Nevertheless, it is hard to avoid the conclusion that, as an exercise in state building, railroad regulation in the Progressive Era was seriously flawed. Whether arbitrating disputes between individual railroads and shippers or judging the claims of the trunk railroads for an across-the-board increase in rates, the Interstate Commerce Commission was most of the time preoccupied with immediate problems and responded to immediate pressures from shippers, carriers and the general public. Its actions were almost invariably reactive rather than proactive. The Commission was given neither the legislative authority nor the administrative capacity to plan for the railroads as a system. Without the power to investigate the rate structure as a whole, without authority over the capitalization and consolidation of railroad companies, it was necessarily restricted to tinkering with the machine, rather than dealing systematically with its faults.

Yet this is no more than Congress asked of it. Congressmen, in their approach to the "railroad problem," sought ways of easing the political pressures placed upon them by constituents and interest groups rather than a comprehensive solution. As representatives, they were naturally responsive to the interests of local shippers and consumers, sometimes local railroads, rather than reflecting on the nation's transportation requirements as a whole. They were naturally conscious of the widespread public suspicion of corporate power. Many of the Democratic Congressmen who were the most loyal supporters of railroad regulation were both fearful of bureaucratic aggrandisement and reluctant to trespass on the rights of the states. Their antistatist proclivities, evident, for example, in the removal of the section of the Mann-Elkins Act covering consolidation and capitalization, were reflected in both of the major railroad measures of this period. Both emerged from a complex series of bargains and compromises, between Congress and the Executive and between various factions within Congress itself. The regulatory regime that emerged from such a process was inevitably piecemeal and incoherent – in a fashion which was all too characteristic of the emerging American state. It did nothing to alleviate, and maybe even exacerbated, the underlying inefficiencies in the system and the deteriorating financial and physical condition of much of the network. It would take the transportation crisis produced by the wartime mobilization of 1916–18 to propel Congress toward a more comprehensive solution. By then, however, it was probably too late.[139]

---

[138] "The Oil Trust and the Railroads," *Independent* 60 (10 May 1906): 1116–17.
[139] On railroad regulation after 1910, see Hoogenboom, *Short History of the ICC*, 62–99; Berk, *Alternative Tracks*, 166–78; K. Austin Kerr, *American Railroad Politics, 1914–1920* (Pittsburgh: Pittsburgh University Press, 1968).

4

Congress and the "Labor Question"

Prologue

On 21 March 1906 in the Speaker's Room of the House of Representatives an encounter took place that held profound significance for the place of organized labor in American politics. A delegation from the American Federation of Labor (AFL), led by its president Samuel Gompers, laid before Speaker Cannon an elaborate "Bill of Grievances" setting out the Federation's legislative demands and protesting at their neglect by Congress. Cannon received these proposals with unconcealed disdain, responding angrily to the allegation that he had discriminated against organized labor in his committee appointments. In his own eyes he had been perfectly faithful to the promise, given to Gompers on his accession to the Chair, that labor would receive a just hearing and that the laws enacted by Congress would favor no one class. But Gompers's organization seemed to demand special privileges: a Labor Committee packed in the interest of organized labor and the passage of "class legislation" for its benefit alone. It did not even represent all industrial workers: "Organized labor is not the whole shooting match. There are the workmen to be considered who refuse to wear the shackles of unionism." For such men Cannon and the Republican party, with its longstanding commitment to the protection of American labor and the promotion of American industry, claimed to speak with as much authority as the president of the AFL. Gompers, he pronounced, was no more than "a pestiferous fellow who hangs around here and presumes to control the whole American Congress, when in fact he does not control anybody but a few damned cowards who are afraid to tell him the truth." According to some accounts, Cannon was only restrained from more violent remonstration by Jim Watson tugging at his coat-tail. An outburst of what Gompers described as "rather lurid language" terminated the interview.[1] This dialogue of the deaf prefigured many of the frustrations that labor leaders were to endure in their dealings with a Republican Congress.

There was nothing unprecedented about the AFL delegation's appearance at the Capitol. One of the explicit aims of the Federation from its foundation had been to lobby for legislation in the interests of working men, and Gompers himself had regularly appeared before congressional committees for that purpose.[2] What was novel was the scale and scope of the political campaign which the presentation of the Bill of Grievances initiated. An alarming conjunction of circumstances induced a more urgent approach. Employers were more effectively organized through the National Association of Manufacturers (NAM), which maintained full-time lobbyists in Washington, cultivated close relations with influential Congressmen, orchestrated letter-writing campaigns, and claimed credit for defeating labor legislation. Federal and state courts had issued a series of judgments highly prejudicial to labor, culminating in the Danbury Hatters case, in which a federal circuit court found against the Hatters Union for conspiracy in violation of the Sherman Antitrust Act, and they had shown an increasing willingness to issue injunctions in labor disputes. Other grievances included widespread violation of the federal eight-hour law and its abrogation in the Panama Canal Zone. The overall drift of federal policy seemed highly inimical to the interests of organized labor.[3]

The AFL found Congress increasingly unresponsive to its demands. At the close of the first session of the Fifty-ninth Congress, in July 1906, Gompers reported in the *American Federationist* that all labor's bills were "hanging fire." A bill to strengthen the eight-hour law had fallen into the tender keeping of the House Committee on Labor, which persisted in holding exhaustive hearings, despite the fact that some five thousand words of testimony on

---

[1] *New York Times*, 22 March 1906; Samuel Gompers, *Seventy Years of Life and Labor* (2 vols., New York: Dutton, 1925), 2:243–4; James E. Watson, *As I Knew Them* (Indianapolis: Bobbs-Merrill, 1936), 98–9; Janice A. Petterchak, "Conflict of Ideals: Samuel Gompers and 'Uncle Joe' Cannon," *Journal of the Illinois Historical Society*, 71 (1981), 31–40; Bernard Mandel, *Samuel Gompers: A Biography* (Yellow Springs, Ohio: Antioch, 1963), 284–6; Marc Karson, *American Labor Unions and Politics, 1900–1918* (Carbondale, Ill.: Southern Illinois University Press, 1958), 42–3; Scott William Rager, "The Fall of the House of Cannon: Uncle Joe and His Enemies" (Ph.D. diss., University of Illinois, 1991), 108–10.

[2] Julie Greene, *Pure and Simple Politics: The American Federation of Labor and Political Activism, 1881–1917* (Cambridge: Cambridge University Press, 1998), 80–1, 93–4; Karson, *American Labor Unions and Politics*, 29–31; Mandel, *Gompers*, 174–95.

[3] Greene, *Pure and Simple Politics*, 88–93, 97–9; David Brian Robertson, *Capital, Labor, and State: The Battle for American Labor Markets from the Civil War to the New Deal* (Lanham, Md.: Rowan and Littlefield, 2000), 95–124; Philip S. Foner, *History of the Labor Movement in the United States* (5 vols., New York: International Publishers, 1947–80), 3:308–13; Karson, *American Labor Unions and Politics*, 31–41; Mandel, *Gompers*, 215–32; Robert H. Wiebe, *Businessmen and Reform: A Study of the Progressive Movement* (Cambridge, Mass.: Harvard University Press, 1962), 167–71.

the subject had already been accumulated. Its chairman showed no sense of urgency, allowing opposing witnesses "time without limit" and refusing to press the committee towards a decision. Privately he admitted "that he was sitting on the lid and preventing labor measures from being reported to Congress." The AFL's anti-injunction bill had been consigned to a Judiciary subcommittee, which was instructed to carry out an exhaustive review of the legal principles, effectively burying it for the foreseeable future. In the face of these dilatory tactics, H. R. Fuller, the legislative representative of the railroad brotherhoods, concluded "that it is not the intention of the present Republican organization of the House to permit any legislation on this important subject to come before the House for a vote."[4] Gompers had no hesitation in placing blame squarely on the shoulders of the congressional leadership. As he explained, "the way the House is made up, both in committee and rules, it is not possible to get through constructive legislation in the interest of labor unless it is with the consent of the speaker and a few of his colleagues who control practically all legislation." Cannon had publicly declared his opposition, making it clear that no anti-injunction bill would pass while he was Speaker. Thus, even when labor legislation emerged from committee and secured a place on the calendar it was denied recognition by those who controlled the business of the House. Nor was the upper chamber any more hospitable. According to Gompers, no labor measure had come up before the Senate during the last three sessions.[5]

When the AFL delegation presented its Bill of Grievances it was not with any expectation of an immediate change in policy, but as a preliminary step in its forthcoming election campaign. Ostensibly an intensification of the Federation's established "nonpartisan" strategy, this called for "the independent use of the ballot by the trade unionists and workingmen, united regardless of party," to "stand by our friends and administer a stinging rebuke to men or parties who are either indifferent, negligent or hostile." In practice, it came to mean an almost comprehensive endorsement of the Democratic party and its candidates.[6]

The stakes were high. Labor historians have become conscious of the extent to which the progress of trade unions was inhibited by the exercise of

---

[4] *American Federationist* 13 (July 1906): 464–6, (December 1906): 978–83; Gompers, *Seventy Years*, 2:236; H. R. Fuller to John Jacob Esch, 16 May 1906, Esch MSS, SHSW; *New York Times*, 7 June 1906; Samuel Gompers to D. A. Hayes, 5 October 1906, SGL, 116:43ff.

[5] Samuel Gompers to Thomas C. Bale, 15 August 1906, SGL, 114:806–7; to John H. Walker, 11 October 1906, SGL, 116:407–8; to Cal Wyatt, 25 September 1906, SGL, 115:670–1; to Charles C. Simpson, 3 October 1906, SGL, 115:944–6; *American Federationist* 13 (December 1906): 983; Gompers, *Seventy Years*, 2:239.

[6] *American Federationist* 13 (May 1906): 319, 293–4, (August 1906), 536–7; Julia Greene, "'The Strike at the Ballot Box': The American Federation of Labor's Entrance into Election Politics, 1906–1909," *Labor History* 32 (1991): 166–71; Mandel, *Gompers*, 284–9; Foner, *History of the Labor Movement*, 3:314–319.

state power, particularly that of the federal courts. A reliance on the judiciary to settle perplexing questions of social and economic policy was perfectly typical of the nineteenth-century "state of courts and parties." However, in areas like railroad regulation, legislatures stepped in during the Progressive Era, laying down principles of conduct, creating new institutional arrangements and new structures of decision making to deal with problematic issues of economic and social policy. In the field of labor relations this conspicuously did not happen. Here the courts continued to lay down policy and to do so in a fashion which was decidedly invidious to the interests of organized labor. Although neither the right of association nor the right to strike was, under most circumstances, held in question, many of the methods employed by unions in industrial disputes, such as mass picketing, sympathy strikes and secondary boycotts – methods which deployed the economic and cultural resources of working-class communities to the greatest effect – were ruled out of order. At the same time, the courts had devised a procedure, the labor injunction, which worked with devastating effect to cripple strike actions.[7]

The manner in which Congress and Congressmen responded to this new importunity on the part of organized labor forms the subject of this chapter. The claims of the union movement raised especially serious issues for policy-makers. The need to come to terms with the clash of interests was one of the most important challenges facing government in the Progressive Era, and the confrontation between capital and labor, which reached a special intensity in this period, constituted the most obvious, the most violent and the most urgent form of interest group conflict. The issue, despite its evident importance, was rarely in the foreground of political debate. Precisely because it raised complex legal and economic issues and had disturbing political implications, politicians preferred not to address it directly. The AFL's attempt to place them on record forced at least some to do so, providing invaluable evidence of the ways in which Congressmen of varying persuasions responded to the "labor question."

The "Bill of Grievances"

During the summer of 1906 the American Federation of Labor forwarded a copy of its Bill of Grievances to each Member of Congress, inviting them to

---

[7] On the impact of the state, see Melvyn Dubofsky, *The State and Labor in Modern America* (Chapel Hill: University of North Carolina Press, 1994), 1–60; Robert Harrison, *State and Society in Twentieth-Century America* (Harlow, Essex: Longman, 1997), ch. 3. The legal position and its implications are explained in Christopher L. Tomlins, *The State and the Unions: Labor Relations, Law, and the Organized Labor Movement in America, 1880–1960* (Cambridge: Cambridge University Press, 1985), 44–57; William E. Forbath, *Law and the Shaping of the American Labor Movement* (Cambridge, Mass.: Harvard University Press, 1991); Herbert Hovenkamp, *Enterprise and American Law, 1836–1937* (Cambridge, Mass.: Harvard University Press, 1991), 207–38; Robertson, *Capital, Labor and State*, 184–201.

place their responses on record. In the absence of other information, these answers formed the basis for the evaluation of members by the Federation's legislative representation committee. "Labor's campaign," explained Gompers, "is based on this fundamental query: 'Is the candidate pledged to carry out Labor's demands as set forth in the Bill of Grievances?'"[8] The answers serve a similar function for the historian seeking to analyze congressional opinion on the "labor question."

The Bill of Grievances itemized a number of sins of omission and commission. It complained of frequent infractions of the federal eight-hour law, particular exception being taken to an amendment to an appropriation bill passed early in the previous session which effectively nullified the law in the construction of the Panama Canal, "the greatest public work ever undertaken by our government." The Federation also asked for an extension of the eight-hour law to private contractors working for the federal government. It called for protection from the competition of convict labor, relief from the harmful effects of "induced and undesirable immigration," vigorous enforcement of the Chinese exclusion law and protection for American seamen. Condemning judicial interpretation of the antitrust laws in a manner prejudicial to labor organizations and condemning equally the judicial practice of issuing injunctions in labor disputes, the Federation called for corrective legislation.[9]

A substantial number of Congressmen accepted the invitation, and the September edition of the *American Federationist* reprinted 120 replies.[10] Some evinced a general sympathy for labor; others commented in detail on the items in the Bill of Grievances. Charles E. Fuller of Illinois may serve as an example of the first category: "My sympathies are all with the man who toils and creates the wealth of the country, and so far as my feeble efforts go they will be for whatever affects his interests." Such protestations failed to satisfy Gompers, who pointed out that Fuller's sympathy for labor did not prevent his voting to annul the eight-hour law on the Panama Canal.[11] On the other hand, when the Texas Democrat Morris Sheppard pronounced himself "heartily in favor of every measure looking to the advancement of the laboring man" Gompers saw no reason to question his sincerity.[12] Some Congressmen pointed to their record as testimony to their friendliness to labor. "You know my record on labor legislation," wrote William S. Bennet of New York, who claimed never to have voted against a measure endorsed by the AFL. He

[8] *American Federationist* 13 (November 1906): 879. The AFL's strategy is explained in ibid., 13 (September 1906): 691–3; and (November 1906): 879–83. See also Karson, *American Labor Unions and Politics*, 42–6.
[9] *American Federationist* 13 (September 1906): 689–90.
[10] Ibid., 646–89. Unless otherwise stated, the following references are to this source.
[11] Fuller (663).
[12] Sheppard (674). Cf. Gordon Russell (663) and J. Thomas Heflin (660).

too, it transpired, had forgotten his vote on the Panama rider.[13] Several members declined to offer unreserved support, promising instead, like Ebenezer J. Hill of Connecticut, to give each matter "thoughtful and careful consideration" as it came up and cast his vote "without prejudice and partiality, in such as a way as . . . may seem fair to all concerned and for the best interest, material, social, and moral, of our beloved country." Such promises of impartiality were common from conservative Republicans. "I am a representative of all the people in my district," Frederick Landis of Indiana reminded the AFL leaders. To Landis, as to Hill, organized labor was only one among a number of interests and could establish no special claim to government favor.[14]

Most of the remaining letters followed a common pattern and iterated common sentiments. They contained an unqualified declaration in support of the eight-hour law and its enforcement in all cases, with an exception made by most Republicans for the Panama Canal; a resolute desire to protect workingmen from the competition of convicts; an endorsement of Chinese exclusion; acceptance of the need to reduce the volume of "induced and undesirable immigration," though with little consensus as to what precisely those terms meant; and support for whatever measures might be necessary to improve the conditions of American seamen. They condemned abuses of court injunctions in connection with labor disputes and agreed on the need for some kind of corrective legislation, though not on its precise form. Reading through the replies, one is struck by the uniformity of sentiment and often by the uniformity of language, mainly produced by generous plagiarism from the text of the Bill of Grievances itself.

Voters, suggested Champ Clark, should accord more attention to men's records than their protestations. A Republican candidate "would promise anything under the shining sun to get elected. Yet, when he reached Washington, [he] would vote exactly as the Republican machine wished him to vote, promises or no promises." Labor organizations and their supporters should distinguish between "a man with a record" and "a man without a record," however they answered the questions. That was Gompers's view entirely: "Let us stand by our friends, our true friends, not those who simply mouth their pretended friendship now and whose past course has given their pretensions the lie."[15] The trouble was that labor measures came before the House too rarely to provide enough information to distinguish false friends from true.

---

[13] Bennet (649).
[14] Hill (667), Landis (764). See also William H. Draper (661), George W. Cromer (659), John W. Weeks (686), George L. Lilley (674), and Augustus P. Gardner (664). For Gompers's reactions see Gompers to John M. O'Hanlon, 15 September 1906, SGL, 115:465; *American Federationist* 13 (November 1906): 880.
[15] Clark, with editorial comment by Gompers (649–50).

Only one vote in the present Congress appeared to offer a useful test. "This, however," claimed Gompers, "was so clear-cut and important an issue that it furnished an ideal ground work for a campaign."[16] It was taken in January 1906 on an amendment to the Urgent Deficiency bill designed to expedite construction of the Panama Canal by exempting alien workers from the restraints of the eight-hour law. The rider was passed over the votes of the Democratic minority, who claimed that it constituted, as Clark put it, "an effort to break down the eight-hour law," since American workers on the isthmus would inevitably be affected, besides the dangerous precedent for other works of national importance.[17] Every Democrat who answered the roll voted against the amendment, along with twenty Republicans.[18]

Several Republicans claimed in justification that "Panama Canal labor stands on a different basis from labor in the United States." Panama was a "miasmatic and pestilential country," unsuited for white labor. The canal would be built by Chinese or West Indian laborers. "I did not think that your organization would be very interested in having the Eight-Hour Law apply to them," remarked Grant Mouser of Ohio. Some such exemption was necessary if the Panama Canal was to be completed within a reasonable time.[19] Others explained that they had not been in the chamber when the roll was called. To Gompers, however, absence was tantamount to "dodging the issue." "Had he the interest of labor at heart he could have been present and voted on this bill," he remarked of one Republican.[20] The use of this test vote was highly prejudicial to Republicans. Whatever their sympathy for the principle of the eight-hour day, they were inevitably subject to pressures from Administration and congressional leaders, together with a natural desire to expedite a major project with which their party was so closely identified.[21] Many of those who claimed to have been taken by surprise were no doubt telling the truth. It is hard to avoid the conclusion that Gompers had substantially prejudged the issue and found the Republican party guilty, laying upon its members the burden of proving themselves innocent of the charge of indifference or hostility to the cause of organized labor.[22]

---

[16] *American Federationist* 13 (November 1906): 880.

[17] *C.R.*, 59.1:1603–11; Greene, *Pure and Simple Politics*, 100–2.

[18] *C.R.*, 59.1:1629.

[19] Remarks of Grant Mouser (653), Edgar D. Crumpacker (657–8), J. J. Esch (661–2), Elias S. Holliday (668–9), W. L. Jones (672), W. Aubrey Thomas (685), and Lucius Littauer (*C.R.*, 59.1:1604–6).

[20] Campbell L. Weems and Charles S. Wharton, with Gompers's comments (686–7).

[21] Roosevelt, to whom urgent completion of the Canal was paramount, was surprised at labor's objections. Theodore Roosevelt to William Howard Taft, 27 July 1906, in Elting E. Morison et al, eds., *Letters of Theodore Roosevelt*, (8 vols., Cambridge, Mass.: Harvard University Press, 1951–4), 5:337–8.

[22] Cf. Dick, *Labor and Socialism in America*, 123. Gompers fervently denied the charge. Gompers to J. F. Sheridan, 26 October 1906, SGL, 116:993–5. See also Greene, *Pure and Simple Politics*, 133–4.

The Federation received from Democratic members forty-seven responses to the Bill of Grievances. Thirty-seven were reprinted without comment (which generally signified approval), three with favorable comments and four with a note of explanation. Only three received even the mildest criticism, one for omitting any reference to injunctions and two for supporting the wrong anti-injunction measure.[23] Of 73 Republican replies 23 passed without comment; 50 did not. Some were taken to task for their position on injunctions, a few for their position on labor issues in general. In most cases Gompers restricted himself to drawing a pointed contrast between the respondent's professions of sympathy and his actual vote on the Panama rider.[24]

Besides the comments attached to letters reprinted in the *American Federationist*, Gompers corresponded directly with union members about the congressional campaign. The Gompers Letterbooks from April to October 1906 contain comments on 123 Congressmen: 102 Republicans and 21 Democrats. None of the Democrats was subject to adverse comment, and fifteen received more or less enthusiastic endorsements. With regard to most Republican Congressmen he did no more than refer correspondents to their votes on the Panama rider and their responses to the Bill of Grievances, which was effectively to damn them with silence, while thirty-eight were singled out for special criticism. The only Republicans to be favorably appraised were the Chicago Congressmen William W. Wilson and William A. Rodenberg and George Pearre of Maryland, the sponsor of labor's anti-injunction bill.[25] John J. Gardner of New Jersey, the chairman of the Labor Committee, was commended for his consistent support of the eight-hour bill in earlier Congresses. If he now resorted to delaying tactics and cast doubt on the constitutionality of a bill that he himself had helped to frame, this, believed Gompers, was not because his inner faith was shaken but because he found it prudent to bend to the wishes of the party leadership. That might read like an exculpation of Gardner, but it entailed an implicit dismissal of the possibility of substantial reform from a Republican Congress and a presumptive argument for advising workingmen to vote Democratic.[26]

Only a minority of Republicans received the Federation's approval. The addition of those whose response to the Bill of Grievances met with no adverse comment to those voting against the Panama eight-hours rider and

[23] These were David Finley (652), Frank Clark (650) and John Gill Jr. (655).
[24] For example, Chaney (654), Henry A. Cooper (657), Crumpacker (658), Esch (662), Holliday (669), Jones (670), James C. Needham (680), Llewellyn Powers (682), Irving P. Wanger (686), Weems (686).
[25] Gompers to J. F. Grimes, 29 May 1906, SGL, 112:10; to William Rossell, 14 July 1906, SGL, 113:554–8; to Pearre, 15 June 1906, SGL, 112:612; to F. M. Zihlman, 11 May 1906, SGL, 111:537.
[26] Gompers to D.A. Hayes, 5 October 1906, SGL, 116:43ff; portion of letter, 29 May 1906, SGL, 112:36–7; to John J. Gardner, 19 June 1906, SGL, 112:708; to Joseph R. Buchanan, 21 June 1906, SGL, 112:843; Gompers, *Seventy Years*, 2:231–8.

TABLE 4.1. *Republican "Friends of Labor," 1906*

Voted against abrogation of eight-hour law in construction of Panama Canal[a]

Allen, N.J.	Greene, Mass.	Pearre, Md.
Bennett, Ky.	Hogg, Col.	Prince, Ill.
Brooks, Col.	Howell, N.J.	Rhodes, Mo.
Campbell, Kan.	Kennedy, Neb.	Rodenberg, Ill.
Capron, R.I.	McCall, Mass.	Samuel, Pa.
Cooper, Wis.	McGavin, Ill.	Smith, Pa.
Dale, Pa.	McLachlan, Cal.	Stafford, Wis.
Dickson, Ill.	Michalek, Ill.	Townsend, Mich.
Edwards, Ky.	Murdock, Kan.	
Goebel, Ohio	Murphy, Mo.	

Responded favorably to Bill of Grievances[b]

Bates, Pa	Dawson, Ill.	Michalek
Bradley, N.Y.	Dickson	Pearre
Buckman, Minn.	Hayes, Cal.	Rodenberg
Capron	McGavin	Smith
Cocks, N.Y.	McKinney, Ill.	

Endorsed in Gompers's Private Correspondence

Pearre	Rodenberg	Wilson, Ill.

Notes:
a. *C.R.*, 59.1, 1629.
b. Those listed had no critical remarks appended to their answers. *American Federationist*, 13 (September 1906), 646–88.

those who were commended by Gompers in his correspondence with labor activists leaves us with a list of thirty-seven names (see Table 4.1). The various sources of evidence are in some cases contradictory, but they enable us to compile a tentative list of Republican "friends of labor." It includes a number of Midwestern insurgents, such as Henry A. Cooper and Victor Murdock, and working-class Republicans, some like Hayes and Michalek with union connections themselves. Although several Republican "friends of labor" represented mining and industrial districts, there was little in their personal or constituency characteristics to distinguish them clearly from the main body of the party in Congress.

Most Democratic Congressmen received the Federation's approval. The congressional party, taken as a whole, had shown itself willing to support labor measures, both on the stump and on Capitol Hill, and it was clearly determined to reap the electoral benefits. "You can certainly find no fault with the attitude of the Democratic party," claimed William C. Adamson of Georgia, urging Gompers to eschew a strategy of "counseling independent non-partisan action by your folks. They ought unanimously to vote the Democratic ticket at every opportunity."[27] While still professing loyalty to

---

[27] Quoted in Gompers to William C. Adamson, 1 August 1906, SGL, 114:107–8.

its "nonpartisan" strategy, in practice the AFL leadership had come close to accepting that position.

The AFL and the Campaign of 1906

Although most incumbent Republican Congressmen incurred the AFL's displeasure, a few "known and persistent opponent[s] to the cause of labor" were marked out for special attention. Gompers profusely denied the existence of a "blacklist," but the limited resources available to the national federation virtually compelled a concentration of effort.[28] Cannon was an obvious target. There was, said Gompers, "no greater enemy to organized labor in the present Congress." "No measure in the interest of labor can pass Congress as long as 'Uncle Joe' interposes his objection."[29] As for Cannon's lieutenant John Dalzell, "whatever labor asked for met with his violent opposition." Also singled out for condemnation were James Kennedy of Ohio, "another of Labor's conspicuous opponents," Martin L. Smyser of Ohio, James W. Wadsworth of New York, Albert Dawson of Iowa and Zeno Rives of Illinois.[30] "Of all the members of Congress," declared the *American Federationist,* "no one stood more conspicuous as an antagonist to the interests of Labor and the people" than Charles E. Littlefield of Maine. As chairman of the Judiciary subcommittee responsible for injunction legislation he had "vindictively and persistently opposed all measures in Congress seeking better conditions for the workers." Hence he merited a "stinging rebuke" at the polls.[31]

Workingmen were heartily recommended to vote for Smyser's Democratic opponent William A. Ashbrook. Benjamin F. Caldwell, narrowly defeated by Rives in 1904, was also worthy of endorsement in view of his "untiring efforts" to pass eight-hour and convict labor bills during a previous term. Other friendly Democrats opposing conservative Republicans were William B. Wilson in the Pennsylvania anthracite region and former Congressman William C. Hughes of New Jersey.[32] Elsewhere the AFL Labor

---

[28] *American Federationist* 13 (June 1906): 386, (November 1906), 881. State and local federations drew up their own blacklists. On the organization of the campaign, see Greene, *Pure and Simple Politics,* 107–41.

[29] Gompers to W. E. Taylor, 6 September 1906, SGL, 115:280–1; to John P. Neff, 28 June 1906, SGL, 113:69.

[30] Gompers to Cal Wyatt, 25 September 1906, SGL, 115:670–1; to Samuel de Nedre, 13 October 1906, SGL, 116:522; to John Callaghan, 4 October 1906, SGL, 116:144–5; to H. J. Buckhardt, 30 July 1906, SGL, 114:41–3; to Joseph F. Valentine, 31 August, 1906, SGL, 115,230–3; to John P. Frye, 8 October 1906, SGL, 116:239–42.

[31] *American Federationist* 13 (September 1906): 675; (October 1906), 801–3; Gompers to M. F. Pettingill, 25 April 1906, SGL, 110:864–5; to John J. Kennedy, 28 May 1906, SGL, 111:1017; Karson, *American Labor Unions and Politics,* 46–7.

[32] Gompers to John Callaghan, 4 October 1906, SGL, 116:144–5; to Elmer Ellis, 14 August 1906, SGL, 114:734–5; to John P. Frye, 8 October 1906, SGL, 116:239–42; Thomas F. Tracy

Representation Committee itself initiated the process of finding sympathetic candidates to unseat labor's enemies, urging local organizations to find candidates to run against James S. Sherman in New York, Herschel M. Hogg in Colorado, and Washington Gardner in Michigan.[33]

Republican leaders responded to the campaign with a determination not to submit to "bulldozing" and "blackmail." Cannon was convinced that "the sensible element among the labor unions will not follow Gompers if the issue is made." Whatever labor votes might be lost by taking a firm stand against the importunate demands of the AFL leadership would be compensated for by an accession of votes from "the conservative element."[34] Republicans who were less committed to a stalwart position, like Taft and Roosevelt, were equally adamant that the challenge should be met outright. Taft feared that the defeat of Littlefield "would enable Gompers to wield an influence which would be dangerous and detrimental to the public weal." Therefore Littlefield must be reelected, and so, for all his deficiencies, must Cannon.[35] After the election Roosevelt exulted in his party's victory over "Gompers and the labor agitators."[36] However, unlike Cannon, he was loath to antagonize the union movement. "I do not think that Congress was quite wise in their treatment of the labor people," he observed. "I need hardly tell you that I believe in refusing any unjust demand of labor as quickly as I would refuse any unjust demand of capital; but great care must be taken when assuming a position antagonistic to labor on one point to make it clear as a bell that we are not as a whole antagonistic, but friendly to labor." He urged Republican speakers to stress what the party had done for workers, including passage of an employers' liability act and vigorous enforcement of the eight-hours law.[37] Evidently Roosevelt and Cannon differed significantly in the extent to which they were willing to recognize organized labor as a legitimate political interest.

The campaign was an unusual one by the standards of the past. Old Guard Republicans did their best to conduct it on traditional lines. Cannon offered John F. Lacey "the best general Republican speech that it is in my power to make" bringing out "the fact that the Republican party

to William B. Wilson, 28 August 1906, SGL, 115:138–9; Gompers to Paul Green, 17 October 1906, SGL, 116:686–8.

[33] Gompers to Calvin Wyatt, 7 August 1906, SGL, 114:368–70; to Max Morris, 7 August 1906, SGL, 114:383–4; to William H. McKinstry, 5 October 1906, SGL, 116:121.

[34] Joseph G. Cannon to John F. Lacey, 16 September 1906, Lacey MSS, ISDHA; Rager, "Fall of the House of Cannon," 109; Henry Cabot Lodge to Theodore Roosevelt, 10 September 1906, in Henry Cabot Lodge, *Selections from the Correspondence of Theodore Roosevelt and Henry Cabot Lodge* (2 vols., New York: Scribner's, 1925), 2:230.

[35] Taft quoted in Foner, *History of the Labor Movement*, 3:325.

[36] Roosevelt to Alice Roosevelt Longworth, 7 November 1906, *Letters*, 5:488–9. See also Roosevelt to Henry Cabot Lodge, 9 August 1906, *Letters*, 5:349–50.

[37] Roosevelt to James Wilson, 11 September 1906, *Letters*, 5:403–4; to Joseph G. Cannon, 17 September 1906, *Letters*, 5:413–14; to James E. Watson, 18 August 1906, *Letters*, 5:372–8.

is the true friend of labor and that its policies have resulted in the present condition of prosperity for laboring people throughout the country." But he realized that even "the best general Republican speech" might not work in a mining district like Lacey's, with a strong labor element.[38] The party's traditional claim to represent the interests of industrial workers through its policies of protection and promotion of enterprise became less convincing as the interjection of the conflict between capital and labor into electoral politics visibly splintered the "harmony of interests" on which that claim was based.

In November both sides claimed victory. Cannon and Littlefield retained their seats, but labor leaders could point to the election of five trade union members, including Wilson and Hughes, and a Republican majority cut by half. Many of their enemies suffered substantially reduced majorities. Littlefield's lead was cut from 5400 to 1362, although the losses were shared with other Maine Republicans that the AFL had not singled out. This, indeed, was the pattern throughout the nation. Incumbents targeted by labor did not fare consistently worse than other Republicans. Labor's campaign had little impact that could be clearly distinguished from the overall pro-Democratic trend.[39] Where local labor organizations made a special effort and put forward acceptable candidates, as in the anthracite region of Eastern Pennsylvania and some Chicago districts, they made substantial inroads into Republican strength. In many constituencies, however, the labor campaign was too half-hearted and Democratic candidates too unattractive to labor voters – like Littlefield's opponent in Maine, who agreed only at the last minute to endorse the AFL's demands – to shift them from their traditional allegiance or their increasing electoral apathy. It could not be said on the evidence of the election campaign of 1906 that the labor movement had clearly demonstrated its capacity to "defeat labor's enemies and to reward its friends."

"Government By Injunction"

The beneficent writ of injunction, intended to protect property rights has, as used in labor disputes, been perverted so as to attack and destroy personal freedom, and in a manner to hold that the employer has some property rights in the labor of the workmen.[40]

---

[38] Joseph G. Cannon to John F. Lacey, 16 September 1906, Lacey MSS, ISDHA. Cf. Henry Cabot Lodge to Theodore Roosevelt, 27 October 1906, in Lodge, *Selections from the Correspondence*, 2:257–8.

[39] *American Federationist* 13 (December 1906): 970–3; Karson, *American Labor Unions and Politics*, 46–9; James Weinstein, *The Corporate Ideal of the Liberal State, 1900–1918* (Boston: Beacon, 1968), 21–3; Foner, *History of the Labor Movement*, 3:327–31.

[40] *American Federationist* 13 (September 1906): 690.

Of all the subjects in Labor's Bill of Grievances the issue of court injunctions in labor disputes rankled most. Although labor injunctions had been in use since the 1880s, their number was increasing at an alarming rate. Writs of injunction are court orders enjoining individuals to desist from certain actions which the court is persuaded would bring about "imminent and irreparable damage" to a complainant's property. The courts were willing to accept a very wide definition of "property rights," including not only material assets but also the right to carry on a business, greatly extending the range of actions in connection with labor disputes that might be considered enjoinable. The injunction power is founded upon the courts' traditional right to exert jurisdiction in equity over "nuisances." Each and every method employed by trade unions to enforce their demands would inevitably cause some injury to employers and "nuisance" to the public. In considering complaints the courts assessed the objectives of an industrial action and the methods that were employed to carry it through. They tended to regard sympathetic strikes or strikes to secure the union shop as unlawful, having "no direct relation" to the legitimate purposes of a labor organization, and to condemn any element of coercion, through boycotting or "intimidatory" picketing, in the conduct of a strike. In effect, judges were assuming the responsibility to pass upon the most delicate areas of public policy and resolve highly complex and problematic socioeconomic issues, ostensibly as questions of abstract law.[41]

Judicial procedures were equally objectionable. A court would issue an ex parte restraining order without a hearing if it could be persuaded that irreparable damage, for which there was no adequate remedy in law, would result from the delay. A temporary and then a permanent injunction would follow after further hearings. All too often the preliminary injunction would in itself be fatal, engaging strike leaders in tedious legal proceedings and dissipating the organizational momentum. Refusal to obey would place individuals immediately in contempt of court and leave them subject to trial, without the benefit of a jury, by the judge whose authority they had challenged.

Offered such invidious alternatives, union leaders naturally sought changes in the law. To labor leaders the use of injunctions represented an infringement of the "inalienable rights of free citizens": to strike, to assemble freely in public places, to engage in peaceful persuasion of fellow workers, and even to publish their views without restraint. If a withdrawal of labor by workers infringed an employer's property rights, argued Gompers, then this implied that he had a proprietary right to their services. "This is a theory of slavery, and organized labor will not rest until it is abolished."[42] They sought

---

[41] Felix Frankfurter and Nathan Greene, *The Labor Injunction* (New York: Macmillan, 1930), 17–53; Witte, *Government in Labor Disputes*, 13–59.

[42] George Kibbe Turner, "What Organized Labor Wants: An Interview with Samuel Gompers," *McClure's* 32 (November 1908): 27–8; *American Federationist* 13 (December 1906): 979;

redress primarily from Congress because federal courts, which were accessible to any complainant able to show diversity of citizenship, had proved themselves more "hostile to organized labor" than state courts. The Sherman Antitrust Act and other laws relating to interstate commerce also provided scope for intervention by the federal judiciary. That is why injunctions found their place in Labor's Bill of Grievances.[43]

For reasons of political expediency as well as natural justice, politicians of both parties had come to support legislation to correct what they admitted to be abuses of the injunction power. Theodore Roosevelt in his Annual Message to Congress in December 1905, while he accepted that "depriving courts of the power to issue injunctions in labor disputes...would be most unwise," favored legislation "to regulate the procedure by requiring the judge to give notice to the adverse parties before granting the writ," although the delay should not be such as to permit "violation of the law or the jeopardizing of life or property."[44] Various bills barring injunctions without due notice and requiring a hearing for the opposing parties were introduced in the Fifty-ninth, as in earlier Congresses.[45]

Even such limited proposals as these aroused the indignant wrath of business groups. The Citizens' Alliance of Peoria, Illinois warned the chairman of the House Judiciary Committee that insistence on the provision of "due notice" would render injunction proceedings ineffective, permitting lawless strikers "to destroy property, intimidate persons and make unlawful threats or demands contrary to the law, and for the sole purpose of forcing, through fear of personal safety or property loss, acquiescence to their demands."[46] Conservative Republicans in Congress expressed similar fears. Spooner was deeply alarmed at attacks on the authority of the courts to issue injunctions, both in railroad cases and labor disputes, a challenge which he considered both "far-reaching and dangerous." His fellow Senator Joseph B. Foraker described the judiciary as "the conservative and preservative force in our Government." Occasional abuse should not lead the American people to "strip the courts of their wholesome and beneficent power to restrain

Tomlins, *State and the Unions*, 61–7; Forbath, *Law and the Shaping of the American Labor Movement*, 136–41.

[43] Frankfurter and Greene, *Labor Injunction*, 5–17, 53–133; Witte, *Government in Labor Disputes*, 84–104; William G. Ross, *A Muted Fury: Populists, Progressives, and Labor Unions Confront the Courts, 1890–1937* (Princeton, N.J.: Princeton University Press, 1994), 70–5.

[44] Fifth Annual Message, in *The Works of Theodore Roosevelt*, (National Edition, 20 vols., New York: Scribner's, 1926), 15:284–5. See also Irving Greenberg, "Theodore Roosevelt and Labor" (Ph.D. diss., Harvard University, 1959), 398–403.

[45] See Witte, *Government in Labor Disputes*, 266–8 and 280; Frankfurter and Greene, *Labor Injunction*, 140–1, 154–7, 182–3.

[46] Citizens' Alliance, Peoria, Ill. to John J. Jenkins, 7 March 1906, Docket 8E3 7/13/5277, RG 292, NARA. See also Chester M. Culver to George W. Norris, 22 May 1908, Norris MSS, LC; Simmons Manufacturing Co. to John C. Spooner, 12 March 1906, Spooner MSS, LC; Wiebe, *Businessmen and Reform*, 25–31, 161–73.

threatened violations of personal and property rights."[47] Proposals to regulate labor injunctions appeared to exempt one section of the population from the normal operation of the legal process. "The Pearre anti-injunction bill," declared Cannon, "is thoroughly vicious class legislation. It proposes to make in the matter of labor disputes the members of the American Federation of Labor subject to one law enacted for their benefit, and the other people subject to the law as it has been time out of mind in English-speaking countries."[48]

The Pearre bill to which Cannon referred was based on rather different principles from those described above. During the spring of 1906 the AFL leadership concluded that earlier measures were not only ineffective but dangerous. Labor disputes would still be liable to judicial intervention, while procedural legislation would constitute a statutory validation of injunctions. The Gilbert bill favored by the Administration, claimed Gompers, was an attempt "for the first time to legalize the granting of injunctions in labor disputes." Thus many "so-called Anti-Injunction Bills . . . were really in fact pro-injunction bills." Injunctions should be swift and effective where they were properly applicable, but they should not apply to actions that would be perfectly legal when performed outside the context of a labor dispute. Hence the AFL, rather abruptly, changed course and placed its weight behind a measure quite different to those that it had supported previously.[49] The new wisdom was embodied in a bill introduced by Pearre in April 1906. This prohibited the issue of a restraining order in any case between an employer and employee over terms of employment "unless necessary to prevent irreparable damage to property or to a property right" for which there was "no adequate remedy at law." For the purpose of the bill "no right to continue the relation of employer and employee . . . or to carry on business of any particular kind" was to be considered as "constituting a property right." Agreements or actions in connection with a labor dispute would not be regarded as constituting a criminal conspiracy unless they "would be unlawful if done by a single individual."[50]

Many Congressmen were ready to contemplate some form of anti-injunction legislation, but this was both a legal question of some complexity

---

[47] John C. Spooner to Albert S. Batchelor, 18 June 1906, Spooner Letterbooks, LC; Joseph B. Foraker, *Notes of a Busy Life* (2 vols., Cincinnati: Stewart and Kidd, 1916), 2:116–17.

[48] Joseph G. Cannon to John F. Lacey, 16 September 1906, Lacey MSS, ISDHA; Busbey, *Uncle Joe Cannon*, 278–9.

[49] Gompers to J. C. Dyer, 6 September 1906, SGL, 115:273–4; to Theodore Roosevelt, 12 May 1906, SGL, 111:549–55; *American Federationist* 13 (December 1906): 978–9; Forbath, *Law and the Shaping of the American Labor Movement*, 154; Frankfurter and Greene, *Labor Injunction*, 153–5.

[50] Copy of HR 18171 enclosed in Gompers to Executive Council of the American Federation of Labor, 13 April 1906, SGL, 110:419–21; Gompers to Executive Council, 14 April 1906, SGL, 110:486.

and a sensitive social and economic issue with serious political ramifications. The confusion and hesitancy with which they approached the subject is evident in their responses to the Bill of Grievances. Thirty-one Republicans commented on the subject. Most resorted to variations on a common formula: A defense of the "beneficent writ of injunction" as a necessary protection against violence or the destruction of property balanced by an admission that abuses did exist and should be legislated against, though often admitting that they did not know precisely what form corrective legislation should take. They varied according to which side of the equation received the greater stress. Wesley Jones of Washington stood alone in his curt dismissal of injunction reform, although we may assume that many who refrained from comment held similar views.[51] A second group was similarly fulsome in praise of the courts' beneficent authority but prepared to acknowledge the need for some form of corrective legislation. The views of Edgar D. Crumpacker of Indiana may be taken as typical:

I am not in favor of such a limitation of the power of the courts to issue injunctions as will materially impair the value of that proceeding in the protection of life and property. The courts are the most important factor in our government in the preservation of the rights and liberties of the people. It is likely that the power to issue injunctions has been abused on some occasions, and I would not object to having some reasonable safeguards thrown about so as to prevent its abuse and yet not prevent its beneficent exercise.

He did not indicate what those "reasonable safeguards" should be.[52] The remarks of Everis A. Hayes of California best encapsulate the views of the next group, wherein the two propositions are more evenly balanced. He maintained that injunctions should be available equally to all persons "under such rules as will prevent this writ from being used as an engine of oppression or injustice." This may be described as the median Republican position.[53]

Compare with the above statements that of Charles McGavin of Illinois: "While I recognize some merit in the writ of injunction, I am convinced that the writ has been frequently abused and the rights of our citizens have been abused thereunder. I shall support any anti-injunction measure which will limit or restrict the use of the writ to the cases which it was originally intended it should reach." McGavin was one of five Republicans in whose replies the rhetorical emphasis was placed on demands for correction rather than

[51] Jones (670).

[52] Crumpacker (658). Cf. John C. Chaney (653–4), Llewellyn Powers (682) and Irving Wanger (685).

[53] Hayes (666). Cf. J. J. Esch (662), Henry A. Cooper (656), Joseph M. Dixon (660), Thaddeus M. Mahon (675), James C. Needham (680) and Charles S. Wharton (686).

defense of the injunction power.[54] Finally, a few Congressmen acknowledged the need for reform of the injunction process without any counterbalancing reference to its virtues. Richard Bartholdt of Missouri declared himself "opposed to court injunctions for the purpose of preventing labor from enforcing its rights," while Victor Murdock favored any modification that would prevent abuses of the injunction power.[55]

Few of those who endorsed an anti-injunction bill felt able to say which. Indeed, some admitted to outright bewilderment. The handful who moved beyond generalities favored providing due notice and the opportunity for a hearing to the parties whose conduct was to be enjoined, but only as long as no irreparable damage would result from the delay. None, except for McGavin and Pearre himself, ventured comments which could be read as an endorsement of the Pearre bill favored by the AFL.

A higher proportion of Democrats made reference to the issue, and their comments showed a greater degree of conformity than did those of their Republican opponents. The overwhelming majority agreed with Dorsey Shackleford of Missouri "that the writ of injunction has been shamefully abused in labor disputes" and that "Some effectual legislation should be enacted to stop these abuses." Even their language showed a striking uniformity, in some cases drawing heavily on that of the Bill of Grievances itself. The words of Charles L. Bartlett of Georgia will stand for most of his fellow Democrats: "I am opposed to government by injunction, and will vote for any bill which will prevent the federal courts from perverting that writ so as to attack and destroy the personal freedom of the citizens."[56] A few made comments which constituted a clear endorsement of the Pearre bill.[57] The remainder, though less equivocal than most Republicans, were hardly more specific.

Events over the next two years brought no further encouragement to organized labor. Injunctions were granted by federal courts in ten further cases, culminating in the crippling injunction handed out in December 1907 against a boycott of the Buck's Stove and Range Company called by the International Molders Union. In the Sixtieth Congress the Federation continued to press for passage of the Pearre bill, according it pride of place in the Protest to Congress presented in March 1908.[58]

---

[54] McGavin (679). Cf. Elias S. Holliday (669), Charles B. Law (673), William A. Rodenberg (683) and George A. Pearre (688).

[55] Bartholdt (648), Murdock (678). Cf. Blackburn B. Dovener (661), John L. Kennedy (672), George W. Smith (684), and George W. Prince (687).

[56] Shackleford (674), Bartlett (647–8).

[57] George W. Burgess (649), John A. Moon (666), and Eaton J. Bowers (648)

[58] *New York Times*, 25 February and 20 March 1908; Greene, *Pure and Simple Politics*, 152–6; Karson, *American Labor Unions and Politics*, 50–1; Frankfurter and Greene, *Labor Injunction*, 155; Foner, *History of the Labor Movement*, 3:335–42, 346.

Most Republicans appeared willing, and in some cases eager, to contemplate some form of corrective legislation, but, as in the previous session, that which they envisaged was not the Pearre bill but something akin to the Gilbert bill of 1906. George Norris, for example, felt that "it would be a serious mistake to cripple our courts by taking away from them the power of issuing the writ of injunction," but he too was anxious to see some regulation. He would not prohibit the courts from issuing restraining orders without notice "where without the giving of such orders damage would result." But "the application for the writ should be heard as soon thereafter as possible and such hearing should not be delayed longer than the necessities of the case require." He would not support any proposal "to enact a different law for labor organizations than for other people."⁵⁹ Norris was one of a number of House Republicans who pressed strongly for the passage of some kind of anti-injunction legislation, along with a number of other reform measures, in preparation for the election campaign of 1908. "If we do this," he said, "I believe we will be in shape to go before the people on our record."⁶⁰ The Michigan Congressman Charles E. Townsend collected sixty-two signatures on a petition requesting a conference of Republican members to consider injunction legislation. The resulting conference, however, adjourned without a vote. The measure favored by Townsend and Norris, modest as it was, was denounced by Littlefield as an unreasonable incursion into the prerogatives of the judiciary. Once more the Judiciary Committee, under its chairman John J. Jenkins, whose "manly and courageous stand" received a warm commendation from Littlefield, refused to act, and Congress adjourned without giving serious consideration to the subject.⁶¹

A call for anti-injunction legislation was one of eight proposals laid by the Federation before the Republican National Convention at Chicago. Although many Old Guard Republicans would have been content to ignore its demands, Roosevelt and Taft were reluctant unnecessarily to antagonize labor. In consultation with Taft and Roosevelt, as well as Gompers, a draft plank was drawn up which went some way to meet anti-injunction sentiment. This called for an amendment of the injunction procedure which would "prevent the summary issue of such orders without proper consideration" but would "preserve undiminished" the power of the courts to enforce their orders – in other words, for the kind of legislation which Roosevelt and his supporters in Congress had been working for. Even so innocuous a

---

⁵⁹ George Norris to J. E. Costello, 20 May 1908; to O. T. Kountzee, 23 May 1908, Norris MSS, LC. Cf. Theodore Roosevelt, Sixth Annual Message, *Works*, 15:346–8; Seventh Annual Message, *Works*, 15:431–2; Albert J. Beveridge to Edward A. Perkins, 30 January 1908; to A. M. Glossbrenner, 19 February 1908, Beveridge MSS, LC.

⁶⁰ George Norris to F. P Carrick, 1 May 1908, Norris MSS, LC.

⁶¹ *New York Times*, 1, 2, 12, 20, 21 May 1908.

proposal as this provoked fierce resistance from conservative Republicans and, predictably, from the NAM, whose president, James W. Van Cleave, lobbied assiduously against any mention of the issue in the platform. He enjoyed the support of influential elements within the party, including the Convention's temporary chairman, Senator Julius C. Burrows of Michigan, who defended the integrity of the courts in his keynote address, and the chairman of the platform committee, Illinois Senator Albert J. Hopkins, who had promised to resist the inclusion of any anti-injunction plank. Only the persistence of Taft, the party's presumptive presidential candidate, compelled the platform committee to yield any ground at all. The result was a platform which promised to "uphold at all times the authority and integrity of the courts" but also called for a more exact definition of the procedures governing the issue of labor injunctions: "no injunction or temporary restraining order should be issued without notice, except where irreparable injury would result from delay, in which case a speedy hearing should thereafter be granted." Despite the provision for notice and a hearing, the "irreparable injury" clause effectively ratified existing practice. In view of the "conservative temper" of the delegates, Roosevelt probably took pleasure in the inclusion of any injunction plank at all.[62]

The AFL delegation received a warmer reception at the Democratic National Convention a few weeks later. All but two of their eight demands were incorporated into the platform, including an injunction plank which could be interpreted as an endorsement of the Pearre bill: "Injunctions should not be issued in any case in which injunctions would not be issued if no industrial dispute was involved." It also demanded jury trials in cases of contempt arising out of the infringement of labor injunctions.[63] Gompers had no hesitation in advising union members to vote for the Democratic presidential ticket and, in most cases, for Democratic candidates for Congress.[64]

Despite their disappointment, Roosevelt and Taft were confident that the issue would rebound to their advantage. As Roosevelt had told Hopkins on the eve of the convention, "We are not advocating an anti-injunction

---

[62] For the Republican injunction plank, see Kirk H. Porter and Donald B. Johnson, eds., *National Party Platforms, 1840–1964* (Urbana: University of Illinois, 1966), 160. On the maneuvers leading up to its adoption, see Theodore Roosevelt to Henry Cabot Lodge, 15, 16 June 1906, *Letters*, 6:1076–7, 1078–9; to Frank B. Kellogg, 16 June 1906, *Letters*, 6:1078; Gompers, *Seventy Years*, 2:259–62; Rager, "Fall of the House of Cannon," 72–6; Bolles, *Tyrant from Illinois*, 126–36; Henry F. Pringle, *The Life and Times of William Howard Taft* (2 vols., New York: Farrar and Rhinehart, 1939), 1:350–2.

[63] Porter and Johnson, *National Party Platforms*, 147–8. See also *Outlook* 89 (1 August 1908): 731; David A. Sarasohn, "The Democratic Surge, 1905–1912: Forging a Democratic Majority" (Ph.D. diss., University of California, Los Angeles, 1976), 86–94; Foner, *History of the Labor Movement*, 3:350–1; Karson, *American Labor Unions and Politics*, 58–60.

[64] Greene, *Pure and Simple Politics*, 159–62.

plank at all, but a singularly moderate and reasonable provision which in its essence merely asks that judges shall think before they act, but which does not in any way hamper their action when once they have thought." Such a plank he expected to please neither "the extreme labor agitators" nor "the equally extreme representatives of the Manufacturers' Association," as indeed it did not. The plank which emerged, though more restricted than he had desired, could nonetheless be treated as a plea for the kind of legislation that he had wanted all along, as against the Pearre bill, which he had not.[65] What "Labor" was contending for, he claimed, and what the Democratic platform had endorsed, was a removal of "the protection heretofore afforded by the courts of equity to the right to carry on a lawful business in a lawful way." The Pearre bill would free actions in connection with labor disputes from prosecution as criminal offenses or conspiracies unless they would be unlawful when performed by a single individual. This, said Roosevelt, by making legal "the black list and the sympathetic boycott," would permit the destruction with impunity of the business of innocent third parties. The AFL demanded "class legislation" predicated on the assumption "that organized labor has interests apart from, and hostile to, the interests of the great mass of the American people." Patriotic and intelligent American workingmen, he was convinced, would never endorse such claims.[66]

As in 1906, labor's electoral efforts, scantily financed as they were and bedeviled by local divisions between unionists supporting rival parties, bore little fruit. Taft was elected with a massive majority. In those congressional campaigns where labor was most active the Democrats made important gains; four further union men were elected to the House.[67] But they and their allies were still not numerous enough to shake the conservative Republicans' hold on the House nor powerful enough to force consideration of injunction legislation during the following Congress.

The injunction issue raised in an acute form the question of the status of trade unions in American society: how far they were to be allowed to act in a fashion damaging to the property rights of an employer and causing a "nuisance" to the public; how far their actions would be restrained by judicial orders or remain unchallenged, except in cases of criminal conduct. Whether or not they had fully thought through the implications of their position, congressional Democrats were prepared to countenance a restriction of judicial authority to enjoin actions in connection with an industrial

---

[65] Roosevelt to Albert J. Hopkins, 16 June 1908, *Letters*, 6:1078.

[66] Roosevelt to Philander C. Knox, 21 October 1908, *Letters*, 6:1305–13; to Thomas J. Dolan, 15 October 1908, *Letters*, 6:1286–7.

[67] On the campaign, see Greene, *Pure and Simple Politics*, 142–214; Foner, *History of the Labor Movement*, 3:351–9; Karson, *American Labor Unions and Politics*, 60–7; Sarasohn, "Democratic Surge," 101–5.

dispute and, thereby, to enhance the legal position and effective power of trade unions. Such a position was, in any case, consistent with their states' rights philosophy and their desire, in particular, to restrict the interventions of the federal courts. Apart from its author, few Republicans supported the Pearre bill. An injunction plank incorporating its terms submitted by La Follette's supporters at the Chicago Convention received only twenty-eight votes, twenty-five of them from his own Wisconsin delegation.[68] The majority of Republicans did believe some sort of corrective legislation to be necessary; a smaller number publicly denied the need for any reform, including some of the most influential Republican leaders in both chambers, like Cannon, Jenkins, and Spooner. However, all but a few Republicans defended the legitimacy of the injunction power, believing that its misuse did not remove the need to provide protection in equity for property rights.

"Conspiracies in Restraint of Trade"

A related issue was the liability of trade unions to prosecution under the Sherman Act as "conspiracies in restraint of trade." For some years labor organizations had sought immunity from the antitrust law. The Bill of Grievances included the complaint that a law designed to protect the people against monopoly had by judicial interpretation been "perverted, so far as the laborers are concerned, so as to invade and violate their personal liberty as guaranteed by the constitution."[69] This item went largely unnoticed; only four respondents offered any comment at all. The silence of the remaining members is striking. Either they shied away from the legal and ethical complexities of the issue, or the sanctified status of the antitrust laws deterred them from suggesting modification.

The anxiety of union leaders was further intensified in February 1908 when the Supreme Court confirmed the decision of the lower court in the Danbury Hatters case that the Sherman Act did cover labor organizations. "The Act makes no distinction between classes," declared the Court. Any industrial action with an interstate dimension was now liable to prosecution as a "conspiracy" under the act, leaving unions and their members subject to crippling damages.[70] From that point modification of the antitrust law became a paramount political concern of AFL leaders. It featured prominently

---

[68] Richard C. Bain, *Convention Decisions and Voting Records* (Washington: Brookings Institution, 1960), 173–4.

[69] *American Federationist* 13 (September 1906): 690. See also Witte, *Government in Labor Disputes*, 61–3.

[70] Martin J. Sklar, *The Corporate Reconstruction of American Capitalism, 1880–1916: The Market, Law and Politics* (Cambridge: Cambridge University Press, 1988), 223–8; Hovenkamp, *Enterprise and American Law*, 228–36; Witte, *Government in Labor Disputes*, 63–5; Karson, *American Labor Unions and Politics*, 50–2.

in Labor's Protest to Congress, drawn up the following month, which asked for an amendment to the Sherman Act explicitly excluding farmer and labor organizations.[71]

Their campaign converged with a movement, led by officials of the National Civic Federation and warmly supported by Roosevelt, to amend the antitrust laws so as to permit certain "reasonable" combinations under close federal supervision. In March 1908 a bill drafted by representatives of the National Civic Federation in consultation with Roosevelt's Commissioner of Corporations was introduced in the House by William P. Hepburn and in the Senate by William Warner.[72] The officials of the National Civic Federation were willing to incorporate a formula that also removed some of the uncertainty concerning the status of trade unions. The bill included a declaration to the effect that nothing in the new law or in the original Sherman Antitrust Act was intended to "interfere with or restrict the right of employees to strike for any cause or to combine or to contract with each other or with employers, for the purpose of peaceably obtaining from their employers satisfactory terms for their labor or satisfactory conditions of employment." Thus the right to strike was explicitly legalized, but nothing was said about the secondary boycott or any form of sympathetic action in support of fellow workers. This was by no means satisfactory to Gompers and his colleagues, but they resolved, though without much enthusiasm, to support the bill.[73]

The Hepburn bill aroused fierce opposition and collected few friends. Business groups of almost every kind, except the National Civic Federation itself, criticized it in congressional hearings and in the public press. Martin J. Sklar believes that hostility to its labor provisions may well have been decisive. Many businessmen, like NAM president Van Cleave, complained that the bill would "legalize the boycott, the black list, the malicious and sympathetic strike" and encourage an "orgy of crimes" by labor. The

---

[71] Turner, "What Organized Labor Wants," 29–30; *New York Times*, 20 March 1906.

[72] On the background to the Hepburn bill, see Theodore Roosevelt to Seth Low, 30 October 1907 and 28 March 1908, *Letters*, 5:824–5; 6:983–4; Eighth Annual Message, *Works*, 15:491–9; *New York Times*, 24 March 1908; Philip S. Post Jr., "Trusts and Trade Unions," *Outlook* 88 (21 March 1908): 231–5; Sklar, *Corporate Reconstruction*, 203–53; Arthur M. Johnson, "Antitrust Policy in Transition, 1908: Ideal and Reality," *Mississippi Valley Historical Review* 48 (1961): 415–34; Gerald Kurland, *Seth Low: The Reformer in an Urban and Industrial Age* (New York: Twayne, 1971), 258–68; Weinstein, *Corporate Ideal of the Liberal State*, 72–9; Marguerite Green, *The National Civic Federation and the American Labor Movement, 1900–1925* (Washington: Catholic University Press, 1956), 197–205; Wiebe, *Businessmen and Reform*, 79–83; William Letwin, *Law and Economic Policy in America: The Evolution of the Sherman Antitrust Law* (New York: Random House, 1965), 244–50.

[73] Gompers to Seth Low, 6 March 1908, enclosed in Low to Roosevelt, 7 March 1908; Low to Roosevelt, 7 March 1908, METRP, Reel 81; Sklar, *Corporate Reconstruction*, 233, 255–8; Kurland, *Low*, 264–6, 268–9; Green, *National Civic Federation*, 205–8; *New York Times*, 5, 7 April 1908.

New York Board of Trade condemned the exemption of labor organizations as "a dangerous and ill-advised piece of legislation."[74] By this time Roosevelt himself was cooling towards what he had earlier described as "in substance a very good bill," and for some of the same reasons. He shared the unease about the possible legalization of the blacklist and boycott, and he too was unhappy to see trade unions placed beyond the scope of the antitrust law.[75]

Introduced in the House towards the end of March, the Hepburn bill was referred to the Judiciary Committee, which placed it in the keeping of a subcommittee chaired by that old adversary of organized labor Charles E. Littlefield. Van Cleave's confidence that the bill "would never get out of committee" was not misplaced.[76] Few of the majority members were noted for their sensitivity to the demands of labor, but even relatively sympathetic Republicans were reluctant to liberate unions entirely from the constraints of the antitrust law. Richard Bartholdt, a member of the Labor Committee at times regarded as "friendly" to labor, found obnoxious "the idea of enacting a general law and exempting a particular class of the population from its operation by special legislation." This was a position held by many of his colleagues, who could not see why general laws should not apply to labor and, as might have been predicted from their replies to the Bill of Grievances two years previously, showed a marked inclination to ignore the issue altogether.[77]

Legislation promoted by organized labor had no more favorable a reception from the following Congress. However, the issue of union exemption from the antitrust law received an unusual airing in June 1910 when William Hughes, a New Jersey Democrat and former union official, offered an amendment to the Sundry Civil Appropriation Bill: "That no part of this money shall be spent in the prosecution of any organization or individual for entering into any combination or agreement having in view the increasing of wages, shortening of hours, or bettering the condition of labor, or for any act in furtherance thereof, not in itself unlawful." It had never been the purpose of the authors of the Sherman Act, Hughes argued, to apply it to trade unions. Associations of working men were fundamentally different to business combinations "formed for the purpose of monopolizing necessities

---

[74] James W. Van Cleave to Albert J. Beveridge, 1 April 1908, Beveridge MSS, LC; *New York Times*, 9, 20 April 1908; Sklar, *Corporate Reconstruction*, 253–85; Kurland, *Low*, 269–70. But cf. Wiebe, *Businessmen and Reform*, 81; Weinstein, *Corporate Ideal of the Liberal State*, 80–2; Johnson, "Antitrust Policy in Transition," 428–33.

[75] Roosevelt to Low, 28 March, 1 and 9 April 1908, *Letters*, 6:983–4, 986–7, 997; to Herbert Knox Smith, 14 April 1908, *Letters*, 6:1007–8; Green, *National Civic Federation*, 204–5.

[76] *New York Times*, 24 March and 5 April 1908; Green, *National Civic Federation*, 206–8; Kurland, *Low*, 270–2.

[77] Richard Bartholdt, *From Steerage to Congress* (Philadelphia: Dorrance, 1930), 212; *New York Times*, 5, 12 May 1908.

of life in order to wring additional profits from the pockets of the people."
In the wake of the Danbury Hatters' verdict, union members could not afford to be complacent. The Court's interpretation of the Sherman Act meant
that "any organization of laboring men entering upon a strike where the
commodity may be the subject of interstate commerce are offenders under
this law."[78]

James A. Tawney, the chairman of the Appropriations Committee, led the
opposition to what he described as "class legislation of the most pernicious
and the most vicious character. It proposes to exempt those who belong to organizations formed for the purpose of increasing wages from the effects of an
unlawful conspiracy formed for that purpose." Unlawful conspiracies should
be punished, and clearly Tawney believed that unions sometimes engaged in
unlawful conspiracies which merited prosecution under the antitrust law. To
him, as to many other Republicans, the central issue was that of equality
before the law, a principle as valuable to working men as to anybody else.[79]
The Kansas insurgent Edmond Madison agreed that the law should offer
equal protection to "the capitalist in the mansion" and the "wage-earner
in the cottage." Hughes's amendment, in effect, would "absolutely repeal
the law of conspiracy." Actions which were quite harmless and quite legal
when performed by individuals could, when performed collectively, destroy
a man's business. Such, for example, was the effect of the secondary boycott.
Strikes for improved pay and conditions, conducted peacefully, would not
fall foul of the Sherman Act; it would not interfere with the rightful activities
of trade unions. Madison, like Tawney, evidently had a more limited view
of what constituted their rightful activities than that held by Hughes or, for
that matter, Gompers.[80]

The rider passed the House on a voice vote but was rejected in the Senate, where only five Republicans voted in its favor. When the conference
report appeared Hughes moved that the House persist in its disagreement
and demanded a separate roll call on this section, which carried by 154–
105. Thirty-eight Republicans supported him, of whom twenty-four were
insurgents and nine, including five of the above, had been "friends of labor" in 1906 (see Table 4.2). But several Republican "friends of labor" and
several insurgents voted against the exemption of labor organizations from
the antitrust law. When, after continuing disagreement, Tawney moved that
the House recede and consent to the removal of the clause he succeeded in
winning a second vote by 138–130. This time only twenty-two Republicans
held firm.[81]

---

[78] C.R., 61.2:7325–7, 8654–6, 8848–9; Sarasohn, "Democratic Surge," 160–2; Gompers, *Seventy Years*, 2:290–3.
[79] C.R., 61.2:7326, 8847–8.
[80] C.R., 61.2:8849–50. See also the remarks of Martin B. Madden in C.R., 61.2:8851–2.
[81] C.R., 61.2:8656–7, 8852–3.

TABLE 4.2. *Republicans Voting to Exempt Labour Organisations from Prosecution under the Antitrust Law, 1910*

Austin, Tenn.	Hinshaw, Neb.[b]	Murdock, Kan.[ab]
Campbell, Kan.[a]	Hollingsworth, Ohio[b]	Murphy, Mo.[a]
Cary, Wis.[b]	Hubbard, Iowa[b]	Nelson, Wis.[b]
Cooper, Wis.[ab]	Kendall, Iowa[b]	Norris, Neb.[b]
Davis, Minn.[b]	Kennedy, Iowa	Pearre, Md.[a]
Dawson, Iowa[ab]	Kinkaid, Neb.[b]	Poindexter, Wash.[b]
Driscoll, N.Y.	Kopp, Wis.[b]	Reynolds, Pa.
Fish, N.Y.[b]	Kronmiller, Md.	Rodenberg, Ill.[a]
Focht, Pa.	Langley, Ky.	Southwick, N.Y.
Good, Iowa[b]	Lenroot, Wis.[b]	Stafford, Wis.[a]
Greene, Mass.[a]	Lindbergh, Minn.[b]	Steenerson, Minn.[b]
Haugen, Iowa[b]	Lundin, Ill.	Wilson, Ill.[a]
Hayes, Cal.[ab]	Mondell, Wyo.	Woods, Iowa[b]

Key: a. Designated as "friends of labor" in Table 4.1.
    b. Voted for the Norris rules resolution (*C.R.*, 61.2, 3436).
Source: C.R., 61.2, 8656, 8856.

Conclusion

Speaker Cannon's irascible reaction to the AFL delegation in March 1906 prefigured much that was to follow. It was all too evident that he and Gompers differed fundamentally in their approach to the labor problem, indeed were barely speaking the same language. When Gompers referred to "labor" he meant organized labor, which, while it might have enrolled a small minority of industrial workers, could, in his eyes, rightly claim to speak for the unorganized multitude who would naturally be members of trade unions could they only overcome the obstacles of inertia, ignorance, the oppressive power of employers, and the discriminatory actions of government. The union movement was the one agency which would secure better conditions for the "toiling masses." It was not only necessary to alleviate the wages and working conditions of industrial workers but also to protect them in the enjoyment of their full and equal rights as citizens of the Republic, and thereby ultimately the integrity of republican institutions themselves. In the absence of such protection, workers would be "forced into the maelstrom of wage-slavery." To Gompers organization was the "the very essence of our industrial and our commercial life." Labor organizations were therefore as legitimate as business or professional associations.[82]

To Cannon, on the other hand, "labor" had meaning in terms of the "free labor" ideology which lay at the heart of the founding creed of the

---

[82] Turner, "What Organized Labor Wants"; Tomlins, *State and the Unions*, 61–7; Stuart B. Kaufman, *Samuel Gompers and the Organization of the American Federation of Labor* (Westport, Conn.: Greenwood, 1973).

Republican party. Early Republicans, of whom Cannon was one of the few surviving examples, laid great stress on the dignity of labor but also on the opportunities that a dynamic capitalist society offered for individual enterprise and industry. As Eric Foner has shown, the free labor ideology was centered on the possibilities for individual advancement in what was perceived as an essentially fluid society with broadly equal economic opportunity. Although they were well aware that they lived in a very different society from that which had given birth to the party, elements of the free labor ideology retained their appeal to Republican politicians of this generation. Equally, they found it difficult to accept the reality of class conflict. Even Roosevelt, though prepared to recognize organized labor as a legitimate interest in American industrial society, was unwilling to acknowledge that it might have interests which were directly antagonistic to those of capital.[83]

This made it difficult for Republican Congressmen to accede to organized labor's demands for relief from court injunctions and exemption from prosecution under the Sherman Act. They accepted that situations might arise when legal action against trade unions might be necessary and desirable to protect the rights of employers and the general public. Certain kinds of industrial action, especially secondary actions and strikes in support of the closed shop, were regarded as illegitimate; certain modes of industrial warfare, such as mass picketing or boycotts, were regarded as unacceptable. In response to the suggestion that the labor injunction be outlawed, most Republicans cited the secondary boycott or the blacklist as evils that would be unleashed and raised the fear of an upsurge of labor violence. Even those who accepted that the injunction power had been abused in labor disputes were reluctant to see its teeth removed. Republican reformers of the injunction process would require notice and a hearing in advance of a restraining order, but not in cases where "irreparable damage" would result from delay, which, since the danger of "irreparable damage" was always presented as the grounds for an injunction, would have little practical effect. They would not accept legislation eliminating labor disputes as a subject for injunction, as proposed in the Pearre bill. Similarly, they declined to exempt unions from the antitrust laws on the grounds that certain kinds of action – again the blacklist and the boycott were cited – were properly describable as conspiracies in restraint of trade.

[83] Eric Foner, *Free Soil, Free Labor, Free Men: The Ideology of the Republican Party before the Civil War* (New York: Oxford University Press, 1970), 11–39; Charles W. Calhoun, "Political Economy in the Gilded Age: The Republican Party's Industrial Policy," *Journal of Policy History* 8 (1996): 298–301; Alan Trachtenberg, *The Incorporation of America: Culture and Society in the Gilded Age* (New York: Hill and Wang, 1982), 70–8; Gerald Friedman, *State-Making and Labor Movements: France and the United States, 1876–1914* (Ithaca, N.Y.: Cornell University Press, 1998), 6–11, 64–77; John Gerring, *Party Ideologies in America, 1828–1996* (Cambridge: Cambridge University Press, 1998), 57–64; Greenberg, "Theodore Roosevelt and Labor."

Apart from La Follette, the leading insurgents were "ambivalent" on labor issues, and some, like Norris, even found themselves on an AFL "blacklist."[84] On these matters, with very few exceptions, Republicans had more in common with one another that with members of the opposition.

Democratic Congressmen from all sections and types of constituency offered their support to the AFL's reform program. They were prepared, by endorsing the Pearre bill, to restrict the issue of labor injunctions and, in principle, to exempt labor organizations from prosecution under the Sherman Act. Yet one cannot but question the depth of their commitment. On the one hand, it was clear that electoral interest was a motivating force. On the other hand, one suspects that their conception of "labor" also differed from that of union leaders. When a rural Southerner like Tom Heflin of Alabama observed that "my whole life... is evidence that I am the friend of labor" he probably had in mind something akin to the Jacksonian vision of the "industrial classes," encompassing a wider constituency than industrial workers, few of whom inhabited Heflin's district in any case. They were prone to conceive of society in terms of a conflict between the "people" and the "interests," between "producers" and "non-producers." The traditions of the party left them readier than their Republican opponents to contemplate the existence of class divisions.[85] The Democratic party of William Jennings Bryan, and even that of Woodrow Wilson, with its Jeffersonian tradition, its heterogeneous composition, and its highly instrumental reasons for soliciting the support of organized labor, was, as events would prove, an uncertain ally. When it finally took power, the unhelpful results of its attempt to reform the injunction and antitrust laws, in the shape of the Clayton Act of 1914, would indicate how shallow was the party's support for the political demands of organized labor.[86]

According to Melvyn Dubofsky, "as unions grew in size and their conflicts spread into a larger national arena, the policies and actions of the federal government proved decisive to the cause of labor."[87] During the period in which Republicans controlled the federal government its policies and actions remained mostly inimical to the interests of organized labor. For all the efforts of urban liberals inside and outside the Wilson Administration, this would also largely be the case during the period when Democrats held power in Washington, with the brief exception of the war years. Equally significantly, the mechanisms by which policy was formulated and executed

[84] Braeman, *Beveridge*, 137; Lowitt, *Norris*, 110; Robert S. La Forte, *Leaders of Reform: Progressive Republicans in Kansas, 1900–1916* (Lawrence: University Press of Kansas, 1974), 5–6.

[85] *American Federationist* 13 (September 1906): 660. See also Gerring, *Party Ideologies*, 200–3.

[86] Dubofsky, *State and Labor*, 51–60; Harrison, *State and Society*. For a more positive evaluation of the labor legislation of the Wilson years, see Elizabeth Sanders, *Roots of Reform: Farmers, Workers and the American State, 1877–1917* (Chicago: Chicago University Press, 1999), 340–86.

[87] Dubofsky, *State and Labor*, 39.

were unchanged. Labor law remained substantially judge-made law. Indeed, the scale of judicial intervention expanded; the employment of injunctions in labor disputes increased at an almost geometric rate between the 1880s and the 1920s. Congress repeatedly failed to legislate on trade union rights. There was no American equivalent of the British Labour Disputes Act until the Clayton Act of 1914, whose labor provisions were, in any case, so hedged around with qualifying clauses as to leave the law effectively unchanged. Nor was there any serious attempt to replace judicial resolution of industrial disputes with administrative processes, except in the special case of railroad workers. Even efforts by Administration officials and Republican moderates like Townsend to introduce a system of compulsory federal investigation, though not arbitration, of especially disruptive industrial disputes fell foul of the indifference of Republican conservatives, the states rights sensitivities of Democrats, and the unanimous opposition of organized labor.[88] During this period, the dominant elements in the trade union movement wished to curtail, not increase, the influence of the state in labor relations. Rather than seeking federal intervention, they sought only to be left alone. Hence, rather than seeing the creation of new political institutions to resolve these problems, the Progressive Era witnessed a campaign by organized labor and its Democratic allies to free themselves of the interference of old ones.[89]

In this they largely failed. The actions of the state remained predominately inimical to organized labor, at least until the 1930s. This had profound implications for the continuing expansion of the union movement, which ground to a halt after 1904, before resuming briefly during the war years and then sputtering out after the Armistice. In that respect, then, the decisions, or rather the "non-decisions," taken by Congress in the Progressive Era had significant repercussions for the future development of the labor movement in the United States. As Gerald Friedman concludes, "Political processes, not economic structures shaped early unionization." It was from the first decade of the twentieth century that the rate of growth of American trade unions began to diverge markedly from that of its Western European counterparts.[90] Therefore, in declining significantly to amend the legal status of trade unions, Congress contributed to the process by which the dramatic turn-of-the-century expansion of union numbers was stemmed and the labor movement marginalized as an agent protecting the standard of living of American workers.

[88] C.R., 60.2:114–34.

[89] William E. Walling, "Why American Labor Unions Keep Out of Politics," *Outlook* 80 (20 May 1905): 183–6; Robertson, *Capital, Labor and State*, 66–73; Greene, *Pure and Simple Politics*, 80–5; Sanders, *Roots of Reform*, 71–8; Forbath, *Law and the Shaping of the American Labor Movement*, 37–57.

[90] Friedman, *State-Making and Labor Movements*, 62.

5

The Ideal of a "Model City": Congress and the District of Columbia

Toward a Federal Social Policy

The Progressive Era was a formative period in the history of American social policy during which state governments exercised their "police power" on a mounting scale to protect the health and welfare of their citizens. However, campaigns for regulatory legislation were all too often frustrated by interstate variations, the consequences of which were prejudicial, both to the welfare of disadvantaged citizens in those states which lagged behind in their social provision and to employers in the more progressive commonwealths who labored under the competitive disadvantage of higher taxes and stricter regulation. Such inequalities were regularly cited as arguments against state action. It seemed as if the federal system was out of tune with the requirements of a national economy.[1]

The alternative of prescribing national standards by federal statute appeared to be ruled out by the Constitution. Social policy was almost universally regarded as a preserve of the states. In several cases the Supreme Court had affirmed that the protection of public health, morality and order was "a power originally and always belonging to the States, not surrendered by them to the general government." Admittedly it had muddied the waters somewhat in the *Champion v. Ames* case of 1903 by upholding a federal law banning the interstate shipment of lottery tickets as "a reasonable and

---

[1] David B. Robertson, "The Bias of American Federalism: The Limits of Welfare State Development in the Progressive Era," *Journal of Policy History* 1 (1989): 261–91; David Brian Robertson, *Capital, Labor, and State: The Battle for American Labor Markets from the Civil War to the New Deal* (Lanham, Md.: Rowan & Littlefield, 2000); Norman Graebner, "Federalism in the Progressive Era: A Structural Interpretation of Reform," *Journal of American History* 64 (September 1977): 333–43; Elisabeth S. Clemens, *The People's Lobby: Organizational Innovation and the Rise of Interest Group Politics in the United States, 1890–1925* (Chicago: University of Chicago Press, 1998), 67–73; Martha Derthick and John J. Dinan, "Progressivism and Federalism," in Sidney Milkis and Jerome M. Mileur, eds., *Progressivism and the New Democracy* (Amherst, Mass.: University of Massachusetts Press, 1999), 81–102.

proper prohibition of immoral and unsafe trade through the channels of interstate commerce." This judgment opened the possibility that the interstate commerce clause of the Constitution might provide the basis for a "federal police power" which would permit quite extensive incursions by the national government in the field of social policy. The federal pure food and meat inspection laws of 1906 could be regarded as merely the first installment of this nationalizing trend.[2] Albert Beveridge was the most enthusiastic advocate of federal legislation which, by laying down a "National standard," would establish an "equality of economic competition." In the second session of the Fifty-ninth Congress he introduced a federal child labor bill based on the interstate commerce clause, arguing that "the decision of the Supreme Court in the Lottery Cases absolutely settled its constitutionality."[3] This was a view shared by hardly anyone else. Even Theodore Roosevelt, a self-avowed nationalist, would not identify himself publicly with this position. The refusal to consider Beveridge's child labor bill demonstrated the lack of congressional support for the idea of a federal "police power." Indeed, far from supporting national legislation, Congressmen of both parties felt it necessary to warn against the dangers of "federal aggression" against states' rights and proclaim the virtues of local self-government.[4]

Such was the purpose of Secretary of State Elihu Root in a speech delivered in December 1906. He, too, lamented "the tendency of the people of the country to seek relief through the National Government" but insisted that the only remedy was for the states to adjust their legislation to the growing interdependence of American economic and social life. He urged them to cooperate to establish uniform standards. Root's speech gave impetus to a wide-ranging movement to secure a greater uniformity in state legislation in areas ranging from divorce and marriage to workingmen's compensation and factory inspection. "The basic response of the Progressive Era," argues

[2] Loren P. Beth, *The Development of the American Constitution, 1877–1917* (New York: Harper, 1971), 40–6, 138–65; James E. Anderson, *The Development of the Modern Regulatory State* (Washington, D.C.: Public Affairs Press, 1962), 41–70; Morton Keller, "Powers and Rights: Two Centuries of American Constitutionalism," *Journal of American History* 74 (1987): 675–96; John Braeman, "The Square Deal in Action: A Case Study in the Growth of the 'National Police Power,'" in John Braeman, Robert Bremner and David Brody, eds., *Change and Continuity in Modern America* (Columbus: Ohio State University Press, 1964), 36–43; Stephen B. Wood, *Constitutional Politics in the Progressive Era: Child Labor and the Law* (Chicago: University of Chicago Press, 1968).

[3] Albert J. Beveridge to Harriet Lake, 22 November 1907, Beveridge MSS, LC; Braeman, "The Square Deal in Action," 57, 77–9. See also Beveridge to William Loeb, Jr., 12 November 1906; to Theodore Roosevelt, 24 November 1906, 22 October 1907, Beveridge MSS, LC.

[4] See, for example, Samuel W. McCall, "The Fifty-ninth Congress," *Atlantic Monthly* 98 (November 1906): 579–81; Lawrence B. Evans, *Samuel W. McCall: Governor of Massachusetts* (Boston: Houghton Mifflin, 1916), 80–96; summary of a speech by Philander C. Knox, in *Outlook*, 86 (6 July 1907), 483–4; Eugene Hale to James Tawney, 15 July 1907, Tawney MSS, MinHS.

William Graebner, "to the specific problem of interstate competition and, indeed, to its general economic and political environment, was uniform state action." By such means national social problems could be handled within the framework of a federal system.[5]

To this program of state-centered reform the national government made a limited but significant contribution. It could influence the social policy of the states by investigation and the dissemination of information. Such a role was performed by the Industrial Commission of 1901 and the federal investigation of child and woman labor conducted in 1907. Reformers called for, but did not secure until 1912, the creation of a federal Children's Bureau. As Theodore Roosevelt said, in endorsing the enabling bill, "public sentiment, with its great corrective power, can only be aroused by full knowledge of the facts."[6] But the federal government had another important role. In one particular territory – the District of Columbia – it too wielded the authority of a state government. If the states were "laboratories" for social experimentation, then the District was a laboratory in which the federal government itself could perform legislative experiments for the enlightenment of the nation as a whole.

A "Model City"

If prevailing conceptions of the limits of federal power barred the Government of the United States from exercising authority over wide areas of policymaking, there were no such restrictions on its sovereignty in the District of Columbia. Here it held plenary power, serving as national, state and municipal authority all in one. Here, unencumbered by the rival claims of other governmental authorities, it was free to formulate its own social and municipal policy as a model for emulation by the cities and the states. By such means it could endeavor to influence and harmonize the policies of independent sovereignties – to achieve indirectly by example what it could not achieve directly by legislation.

In December 1904 Roosevelt devoted several paragraphs of his Annual Message to this theme, urging that "the District of Columbia government should be a model for the other municipal governments of the nation." He went on to list a number of measures required to achieve this, including the

---

[5] Elihu Root, "How to Preserve the Local Self-Government of the States," in Root, *Addresses on Government and Citizenship* (Cambridge, Mass.: Harvard University Press, 1916); *Outlook* 84 (22 December 1906): 948–50; Derthick and Dinan, "Progressivism and Federalism," 87; Graebner, "Federalism in the Progressive Era," 343, 345–6; Clemens, *People's Lobby*, 65–73.

[6] Walter I. Trattner, *Crusade for the Children: A History of the National Child Labor Committee and Child Labor Reform in America* (Chicago: University of Chicago Press, 1970), 95–8; Edward D. Berkowitz, "Social Welfare and the American State," in Donald T. Critchlow and Berkowitz, eds., *Federal Social Policy: The Historical Dimension* (University Park: Pennsylvania State University Press, 1988).

establishment of a juvenile court, laws permitting the condemnation of un-sanitary buildings, a modern building code, a compulsory school attendance law, and the provision of parks and playgrounds.[7] He returned to the theme twelve months later:

> The National Government has control of the District of Columbia . . . and it should see to it that the city of Washington is made a model city in all respects, both as regards parks, public playgrounds, proper regulation of the system of housing, so as to do away with the evil of alley tenements, a proper system of education, a proper system of dealing with truancy and juvenile offenders, a proper handling of the charitable work of the district. Moreover, there should be proper factory laws to prevent all abuses in the employment of women and children in the district. These will be useful chiefly as object-lessons, but even this limited amount of usefulness would be of real national value.[8]

The image of a model city was one that he regularly returned to when dis-cussing the affairs of the District.

Nearly everybody else commenting on District affairs made obeisance to the ideal of a model city. Charles F. Weller, the secretary of the Asso-ciated Charities, hoped that, in the absence of "party politics, gag rule or 'graft' of any sort" and with "the cordial interest and, to some extent, the resources of the entire nation," the capital could be made "a worthy model in the matter of wholesome social conditions and municipal legislation."[9] The District, urged John Sharp Williams, should have "a model child-labor law." Its schools, declared Congressman David J. Foster, should be "an ob-ject lesson for the rest of the country."[10] The Superintendent of Insurance offered to draft a model insurance code: "If such a code were adopted here, it would doubtless be followed, soon by some, and perhaps later by all of the States; thus making a substantially uniform system of insurance laws, which would be advantageous to insurance companies, insurance departments, and policy holders." Thus the exemplary potential of legislation for the District was explicitly linked to the movement for uniform state legislation.[11] It was the duty of Congress, claimed Jonathan Dolliver, to give the District "the most modern and efficient code of laws applicable to its local affairs" in order that the federal capital might "present to the world a model system of government." Williams was equally enthusiastic that the District should be

[7] Fourth Annual Message, *The Works of Theodore Roosevelt* (National Edition, 20 vols., New York: Scribner's, 1926), 15:228, 227–31.

[8] Fifth Annual Message, *Works*, 15:284.

[9] Charles F. Weller, "Neglected Neighbors: In the Alleys, Shacks and Tenements of the National Capital," *Charities and the Commons* 15 (3 March 1906): 792.

[10] *C.R.*, 60.1:603 (Williams); 59.1:5755 (Foster). Cf. Henry Cabot Lodge to Curtis Guild, Jr., 8 December 1905, Lodge MSS, MasHS; Henry S. Curtis, "The Playgrounds of Washington," *Charities and the Commons* 15 (3 March 1906): 831; *Annual Report of the Commissioners of the District of Columbia for the Year Ended June 30, 1905*, 1:445–6.

[11] *Annual Report of the Commissioner, 1905*, 5:x; Washington *Evening Star*, 25 January 1907.

made into a "model territory"; it should be "like a city on a hill."[12] Such a metaphor fell oddly from the lips of a Mississippi planter's son; it was also singularly inappropriate to Washington's topography. More seriously, it bore scant likeness to the actual condition of affairs in Washington, which was far from being a model city and showed little immediate likelihood of becoming one.

Implicit in many of the proposals for model legislation was the premise that the District of Columbia was actually, in important respects, quite backward. What was desired was not so much that it should set a shining example, but that it should cease to be such a shameful disgrace. Henry B. McFarland, chairman of the Board of Commissioners, told members of the National Child Labor Committee in December 1905 that "we seek a law...which shall take us out of the black list of states and territories that have no child labor laws."[13] Washington was the only large city in the country which made no provision for the care of juvenile offenders, and it was one of the few jurisdictions not to require compulsory school attendance. "We ought not to be behind other communities as we are today in the matter of providing for the children of the District," declared Senator Jacob Gallinger.[14] In all too many areas of social policy the story was one of neglect, not exemplary achievement. While Washington was probably not, as Champ Clark maintained, "the worst-ruled city on the continent," the conduct of its affairs, by the highest standards of the day, left much to be desired.[15]

Nor was it wholly exempt from the problems that afflicted other large cities. Though as yet spared the congestion of population in large and noisome tenement blocks, Washington had its own form of bad housing in the shape of the alley dwellings that clustered out of sight of the main thoroughfares. Although few of its children were employed in factories and sweatshops, according to the 1900 census over two thousand worked in hotels, offices and stores or in the various street trades. At 22.8 per thousand its death rate was higher than that of comparable cities like Philadelphia, Cincinnati, and Indianapolis. The city attracted few immigrants, but black migrants from the rural South swelled the population of the alley slums and exacerbated the problems of both social and racial adjustment that the community

---

[12] C.R., 60.1:6032; *Evening Star*, 7 March 1906. See also *Evening Star*, 25 February 1908; *Washington Post*, 4 December 1905.

[13] Samuel McCune Lindsay, "The National Child Labor Meetings," *Charities and the Commons* 15 (16 December 1905): 368; *Annual Report of the Commissioners, 1906*, 1:7; U.S. Congress, House Committee on the District of Columbia, *Report of Hearing of March 13 and 16, 1906 on S.1243, Providing for Compulsory Education in the District of Columbia* (Washington, 1906), 47.

[14] C.R., 59.1:3703, 3325.

[15] C.R., 59.1:5761. Cf. *Charities and the Commons* 15 (3 March 1906): 739–40; *Outlook* 79 (21 January 1905): 147–8; *Evening Star*, 13 February 1907.

faced at the turn of the century.[16] The dedicated and influential citizens who addressed themselves to the social problems of the city, through such organizations as the Associated Charities, the Civic Center, the Monday Evening Club, the Committee on the Improvement of Housing Conditions, and the Citizens' Child Labor Committee, assembled a formidable list of legislative demands, most of which were endorsed by the District Commissioners and supported by what passed for public opinion in the District.[17] The way in which Congress responded to the needs of the District offers a critical test of its competence in the field of social policy.

The Alleys of Washington

Washington's distinctive solution to the problem of housing its poor was its alley dwellings. In 1905, 286 alleys housed 19,076 inhabitants. A maze of minor streets, in the center of the spacious city blocks and largely hidden from the main thoroughfares, contained a motley collection of shacks and shanties which varied greatly in their mode of construction and fitness for habitation. Many alley dwellings were in a horribly dilapidated condition, exhibiting, according to Charles Weller, "every housing evil known to man," and so unsanitary that the death rate in the alleys was nearly double that in the streets. Yet the physical state of the houses, though often deplorable, was not in the eyes of reformers the principal problem; much more harmful was their segregation from the rest of the community. As Weller explained,

The [G]ordian knot is the alley itself rather than detailed physical defects, such as dilapidation or lack of paving, sewers, water supply and ventilation. The basic evil is the alley system, the segregation, the hiding away of little communities which are thus encouraged to develop their low standards of life without much interference from the general community.

The human stories gathered of scores of families who live in [the] average alley indicate that segregation has an unfortunate effect upon moral relations, industrial conditions, the spread of tuberculosis, school attendance and the training of children for future citizenship.

---

[16] Weller, "Neglected Neighbors"; *Reports of the President's Home Commission* (Washington, 1908); Charles P. Neill, "Child Labor at the National Capital," *Charities and the Commons* 15 (3 March 1906): 795–800; George M. Kober, "The Health of the City of Washington," *Charities and the Commons* 15 (3 March 1906): 802–13; Constance M. Green, *The Secret City: A History of Race Relations in the Nation's Capital* (Princeton: Princeton University Press, 1967), 119–67.

[17] Constance M. Green, *Washington: Capital City, 1879–1950* (Princeton: Princeton University Press, 1962), 61–76, 149–52; *Outlook* 79 (11 March 1905): 625–6; Howard Gillette, Jr., *Between Justice and Beauty: Race, Planning, and the Failure of Urban Policy in Washington, D.C.* (Baltimore: Johns Hopkins University Press, 1995), 109–29. See particularly the special edition of *Charities and the Commons* published on 3 March 1906 devoted to social reform in the District.

These were private worlds which even the police hardly dared enter, resorts of immorality and crime whose residents escaped contact with "the wholesome standards of life which characterize the general community."[18] The fact that the majority of their population was African-American seemed merely to exacerbate the problem, which, as Weller's comments suggest, was perceived essentially as one of social control. Only by opening them to public scrutiny and supervision could the social and moral condition of their inhabitants be improved.

The first requirement was a law providing for the condemnation of unsanitary dwellings. Bills for this purpose had been before Congress since 1897 but had not passed "owing to the opposition of a few householders and the inertia of a few Congressmen."[19] In 1906, as a result of the promotional activities of men like Weller and Jacob Riis, who testified before a joint session of the House and Senate Committees on the District of Columbia that the worst of Washington's alley dwellings were as noisome as even the grimiest slums of New York, and, with the support of the President, a bill creating a board with authority to condemn unsanitary buildings was reported and passed after perfunctory debate.[20]

During the next two years the Board for the Condemnation of Unsanitary Buildings ordered 224 houses to be repaired and 545 to be demolished. As Thomas Jesse Jones, the secretary of the Monday Evening Club's housing committee, noted, at this rate it would take over forty years to eliminate the alley problem. Slow progress was partly due to a lack of building and sanitary inspectors. But there were also serious deficiencies in this mode of procedure. For one thing, no provision was made for, indeed little thought was given to, the 1056 alley residents, 1042 of them black, who had formerly inhabited the condemned buildings. As William H. Baldwin of the

---

[18] Weller, "Neglected Neighbors," 765, 769 and passim. See also Charles F. Weller, *Neglected Neighbors* (Philadelphia: J. C. Winston, 1909); James B. Reynolds, "Report on the Housing of the Poor in the District of Columbia," *Reports of the President's Home Commission*; George M. Kober, *The History and Development of the Housing Movement in the District of Columbia* (Washington, D.C. 1927); Grace V. Bicknell, *The Inhabited Alleys of Washington, D.C.* (Washington, D.C.: Ideal Printery, 1912); Thomas Jesse Jones, "The Alley Homes of Washington," *Survey* 28 (19 October 1912): 67–9; U.S. Congress, Committee on the District of Columbia, *Report on Hearings of March 30, 1906 on H.R.4467: To Create a Board for the Condemnation of Unsanitary Buildings and for Other Purposes* (Washington, D.C. 1906); Jacob A. Riis, "Backing up the President," *Charities and the Commons* 15 (3 March 1906): 754–5; Gillette, *Between Justice and Beauty*, 111–23. James Borchert's examination of alley life goes some way to refuting the picture of social disorganization painted by Progressive Era reformers. *Alley Life in Washington* (Urbana: University of Illinois Press, 1980).

[19] Kober, *Housing Movement*, 52–3; Associated Charities and Citizens' Relief Association, *Joint Annual Report for the Year July 1, 1904 to July 1, 1905*, 43–6; House Committee on the District of Columbia, *Hearings on H.R.4467*; Gillette, *Between Justice and Beauty*, 113–18; Green, *Washington*, 152–3.

[20] C.R, 59.1:4936, 5201, 7745–6; *Evening Star*, 3, 6 April 1906.

Civic Center also pointed out, the criterion of public health was an inadequate one for bringing about fundamental changes in housing conditions.
After all, unsanitary dwellings were only part of the problem.[21] Reformers
believed that there would be no lasting improvement as long as people continued to inhabit closed alleys. To Weller, "no treatment of the alley problem
will be at all adequate which does not provide for the complete elimination, root and branch, of all the hidden alley slums." What was needed
was to open up the alleys and convert them into wider streets clearly visible from the main avenues. Existing laws already gave the Commissioners
authority to "condemn, open, extend, widen or straighten alleys" if they
considered it "necessary for the preservation of peace, good order and public morals" or "for the public health." All that further progress required was
action by the Commissioners and an appropriation to meet the initial costs of
improvement.[22]

The laws of 1892 and 1894 providing for the conversion of alleys into
minor streets had not been acted upon, indeed had been largely forgotten,
until the matter was taken up in 1905 by the Associated Charities' Committee on the Improvement of Housing Conditions. In response, the Commissioners appointed a board to recommend which alleys should be opened
up and, on its advice, proceeded with twelve. It was hoped that the cost
of demolishing alley buildings could be met by an assessment on neighboring property, the value of which would supposedly be enhanced, although
an appropriation would be required for work to proceed in advance of the
assessment. Congress granted $50,000 for that purpose in 1906. Unfortu-
nately, a Supreme Court decision in 1907 left property holders exempt from
assessment for benefits which could not be shown to result directly from the
conversion. The remaining costs would have to be met out of public funds.
This entailed applying to Congress for an appropriation in connection with
the opening of each alley, a daunting prospect. Congress was notoriously
indisposed to spend money on the District, especially when it appeared to
redound to the benefit of private individuals. Moreover, each improvement
would require separate legislation to be passed in the face of the immense
inertia of Congress.[23]

A committee of the President's Home Commission drafted a bill allowing
a public grant of 25 percent toward the expense, if the rest could be raised
from an assessment on the surrounding property. The plan was endorsed

---

[21] Jones, "Alley Homes of Washington," 68–9; William H. Baldwin, "Report of the Committee
on Improvement of Existing Houses and Elimination of Insanitary and Alley Houses," 3–8,
9, *Reports of the President's Home Commission*; Associated Charities, *Joint Annual Report,
1906–1907*, 40–1; Gillette, *Between Justice and Beauty*, 119–20.

[22] Weller, *Neglected Neighbors*, 93–114; Kober, *Housing Movement*, 20–3, 50–3.

[23] Baldwin, "Report," 10–11; Weller, *Neglected Neighbors*, 113–17; *Annual Report of the Commissioners, 1907*, 1:7; Associated Charities, *Annual Report, 1907*, 40–1; *Charities and the
Commons* 18 (6 April 1907): 3–4.

by the Commissioners and approved by the chairman of the House District Committee. However, owing to a combination of inertia and parsimony, no action was taken by Congress. The campaign against alley dwellings remained stalled. "To refuse to remove them because it costs something is like refusing to escape blindness by the removal of a cataract because of the fees of the oculist," argued Baldwin. However, Congress, in District affairs, worried more about bills than blindness.[24]

The Right to Play

Public playgrounds offered one way of utilizing land from which foul and offensive dwellings had been removed; they were also regarded as an important part of the equipment of the model city of the Progressive Era. Social workers and educationalists had become convinced of the significance of play in child development. In the absence of suitable and wholesome outlets for their natural instincts, children, especially in crowded urban neighborhoods, would find unsuitable and anti-social forms of amusement through the medium of street gangs and indulgence in petty crime. Hence the community must provide the facilities for healthy and constructive play. By 1905 this had become a veritable orthodoxy among social and municipal reformers. A further refinement was the insistence that children, especially the children of poor, immigrant or black families, required supervision if their play was to be constructive and healthy, rather than destructive, anarchic and possibly violent. A trained supervisor was as necessary to the social usefulness of the playground as a trained teacher to that of the schoolroom.[25]

Washington duly followed the example set by other cities. The first public playground was organized by Charles Weller in 1901 in association with Neighborhood House, a local social settlement. Two years later, a Public Playgrounds Committee was formed. By 1905 it had raised enough money, including an appropriation of $3500 from Congress, to open, equip and furnish supervision for nineteen playgrounds. However, dependence on private donations, voluntary and part-time assistance and, most worrying of all, borrowed land made their status precarious. Therefore, the committee requested public funds to maintain the playgrounds and acquire land for permanent sites. The District Commissioners heartily endorsed this proposal. In their

---

[24] Baldwin, "Report," 9–20; Weller, *Neglected Neighbors*, 117–20; *Annual Report of the Commissioners, 1907*, 1:18–19.

[25] On the playground movement and the "philosophy of play," see Paul Boyer, *Urban Masses and Moral Order in America, 1820–1920* (Cambridge, Mass.: Harvard University Press, 1978), 242–51; Judith Sealander, *Private Wealth and Public Life: Foundation Philanthropy and the Reshaping of American Social Policy from the Progressive Era to the New Deal* (Baltimore: Johns Hopkins University Press, 1997), 190–9; Dominick Cavallo, *Muscles and Morals: Organized Playgrounds and Urban Reform, 1880–1920* (Philadelphia: University of Pennsylvania Press, 1980).

annual report for 1905 they recommended an appropriation to buy sites and to enable the city government to take over from private charities the provision of this valuable service. "Large expenditures for this form of popular education have been made in a number of the large cities of the country with such satisfactory results that the practice of making such appropriations has been well established and with general approval." Washington, they urged "should not be behindhand in this important matter."[26]

In 1906 the Commissioners persuaded Congress to allocate $15,000 for the "maintenance, supervision and equipment" of public playgrounds.[27] The following winter the sum of $75,000 for the purchase of land for three playgrounds was included in the District Appropriation Bill. Champ Clark, however, raised the point of order that this was "new legislation"; money was being appropriated for a purpose not approved by general legislation, contrary to the rules of the House. In practice, a great deal of "new legislation" was commonly smuggled into appropriation bills without any objection. Clark feared "that this was merely a beginning, an entering wedge of a scheme that would ultimately cost in all probability a million dollars." He might also have suspected that the proposed transactions were part of an insalubrious real estate deal of a kind not unknown in the history of the District. As it was more or less compelled to do once it had been made, the Chair sustained the point of order. Clark was clearly acting under a misapprehension, as he later acknowledged, yet his one objection was enough to defeat the measure, supported though it was by the Washington Playground Association, the Commissioners and a majority of local residents, and to jeopardize the future of the whole playground project.[28] Fortunately, the Senate restored the appropriation, which was duly accepted by the House conferees, and the Commissioners went home with $75,000 for the purchase of new sites and $10,000 for their improvement. But the incident demonstrated very forcefully the perils of legislating for the District.[29]

The intensive use of existing playgrounds emboldened the Commissioners to ask in 1908 for $75,000 for the purchase of additional sites, arguing that their success had demonstrated the case "for making these outdoor schools a part of the municipal system of public education." Their reward was an item of $1500 for maintenance and equipment of existing playgrounds in the District Appropriation Bill. The New York Congressman Jacob Olcott

---

[26] Associated Charities, *Joint Annual Report, 1904–1905*, 26–9; Curtis, "Playgrounds of Washington"; *Annual Report of the Commissioners, 1905*, 1:15; *Annual Report of the Commissioners, 1906*, 1:11–12, 182–5; Washington *Post*, 11 March 1906.

[27] *Annual Report of the Commissioners, 1906*, 1:11–12.

[28] C.R., 59.2:1226–7, 1297–9; *Evening Star*, 18 January 1907; *Charities and the Commons*, 17 (26 January 1907), 726–7 and (2 March 1907), 967–8. To make amends, Clark introduced a separate bill appropriating $100,000 for playgrounds. This, of course, had no chance of passing. *Evening Star*, 22 January 1907.

[29] C.R., 59.2:3994–6, 4134–8.

moved to increase that sum to $10,000 to cover the cost of supervision also. After a brief but vigorous debate, the amendment was rejected on a voice vote.[30] In the District Appropriation Bill reported to the House in January 1909 the same amount was set aside for playground maintenance. Another New York Congressman, Herbert Parsons, moved to increase the sum to $15,000. Surprisingly, in view of the tiny amount involved, his amendment provoked a passionate debate lasting over two hours, affording Congressmen a rare opportunity to air their views on a significant aspect of social policy.[31]

Big-city Congressmen like William S. Bennet, representing the Lower East Side of New York, and Andrew J. Peters of Boston rehearsed the well-tried arguments for the provision of civic playgrounds, noting the lack of open space for children to disport themselves and the harmful effects of their playing on the streets. The experience of other cities, they maintained, had demonstrated the value of playgrounds in checking crime and juvenile delinquency and in promoting healthy physical and moral development, as well as the necessity for careful supervision if the facilities were to be put to constructive use. The costs of this necessary and valuable public service should be assumed by the municipality. "We can afford to be liberal," insisted Frederick H. Gillett of Massachusetts; "we cannot afford to be niggardly in anything which promotes the healthy development of children on whom depends the whole future of the nation."[32]

Opponents of the increased appropriation, mostly Southern Democrats augmented by a number of conservative Republicans, argued against it with surprising vehemence. Some, like Edward Vreeland of New York and Albert S. Burleson of Texas, wondered why citizens should apply for a subvention from the Treasury instead of displaying their "civic pride" by the voluntary support of playgrounds. Fears that the Treasury would be drained by such appropriations, remarkable in view of the paltry sums in contention, featured prominently in their arguments. "Is there never to be any retrenchment or reform in paying out public money?" asked John Wesley Gaines of Tennessee in the tones of a nineteenth-century Jacksonian Democrat. He and others of like mind condemned the alarming propensity of pressure groups of all sorts to make importunate demands on the Treasury, without regard to the plight of the poor benighted taxpayers who had to foot the bill.[33] Nor did critics see the need for children to be tutored in the arts of constructive play. "Do you mean to say you are going to employ teachers to teach the children how to play?" asked Gaines in astonishment, warning that such meddlesome supervision would "sissify" the American boy and "chloroform his genius and

---

[30] *Annual Report of the Commissioners, 1908*; C.R., 60.1:4383–6.
[31] C.R., 60.2:859–75.
[32] C.R., 60.2:868. See also C.R., 60.1:4583 (Norris), 4584 (Gillett, Mass.); 60.2:859–62 (Parsons), 862–3 (Peters), 864–5 (Foster, Vt.), 869–70 (Mann).
[33] C.R., 60.2:863 (Gaines), 865–8 (Vreeland), 872 (Burleson).

TABLE 5.1. *Voting on the District of Columbia Playground Appropriation, 60th Congress*

Percentage Urban in Constituency	Republican	Democratic	Both Parties
0–19.9	10–18	7–44	17–62
20–29.9	8–10	6–13	14–23
30–49.9	16–16	6–9	22–25
All members	34–44	19–66	53–110

Source: C.R., 60.2, 918–19.

his character." Burleson, who regarded the project as inherently "paternalistic and socialistic" in its tendencies, asked, "if you take this step now, and coddle and supervise him and direct him and manage him when he is on the playground, where is he to learn the lesson of self-reliance that makes for sturdy Americanism and self-reliant American citizenship?"[34] Equally fundamental objections were raised by James Tawney, who insisted that such "solicitude" would do the children of the District a positive disservice. Their physical and mental growth would benefit from application and hard work; they should not be encouraged "to devote too much time to play." Such remarks indicate that opposition to public playgrounds flowed not only from a desire to safeguard the public treasury, powerful though that was, but also from a fundamental lack of sympathy with the concepts of child nurture that animated the playground movement of the Progressive Era.[35]

Not content with debating the amendment at length, the House insisted on taking a roll call. This confirmed the impression that the main opposition to the clause came from Southern Democrats, support from big-city Representatives of both parties (see Table 5.1).[36] The Senate later added an appropriation of $10,000 for playgrounds. However, despite the efforts of dedicated supporters like Senator Francis G. Newlands, who pleaded in vain with Burleson to withdraw his opposition, the House conferees, who were all confirmed adversaries of the playground appropriation, stood firm, and the final amount was little more than the measly sum originally allocated by the House committee. A continuation of such parsimony over the years left Washington with a playground system which, as Hastings Hart reported in 1924, was still greatly inferior to those of other cities of comparable size and resources.[37]

[34] C.R., 60.2:860, 863–4 (Gaines), 872 (Burleson).
[35] C.R., 60.1:4385. See the comments in Jacob A. Riis, "Playgrounds in Washington and Elsewhere," *Charities and the Commons* 20 (18 March 1908): 101–4.
[36] C.R., 60.2:918–19. Cf. C.R., 61.2:2930, 5970.
[37] Henry S. Curtis to Francis G. Newlands, 23 February 1909; Newlands to Albert S. Burleson, 6, 23 February 1909, Newlands MSS, SLYU; Hastings H. Hart, *Child Welfare in the District of Columbia* (New York: Russell Sage Foundation, 1924), 138–9.

Child Labor in the District

As the movement to regulate child labor gathered momentum during the early years of the century, those responsible for administering the affairs of the District became aware that theirs was one of the few jurisdictions in the nation with no legislation whatsoever on the subject. By 1905 it shared that distinction with Georgia, Idaho, Nevada, and three of the territories. In successive messages Roosevelt urged Congress to pass a strict child labor law for the District, noting that its failure to do so was "discreditable to the National Government." His call was echoed by Samuel McCune Lindsay, the secretary of the National Child Labor Committee, who hoped that, "if Congress says that a certain standard is desirable for the District of Columbia, it will have a beneficial effect upon similar legislation in the Union." The capital of the nation should "stand for the best that we have produced in the legislative remedies applicable to the growing evils of child labor," not the worst.[38] The absence of large-scale industry did not mean that child labor in the District was not a serious problem. Some two thousand children worked there, many in the various street trades which, in the reformers' eyes, subjected them to particular moral dangers. Regulation would be more than a symbolic gesture.[39]

In 1905 the Citizens' Child Labor Committee of the District of Columbia agreed on a draft bill, which was presented to both houses of Congress. Its provisions closely followed the model law recommended by the National Child Labor Committee: It prohibited the employment of children under fourteen during school terms and at any time in certain undesirable occupations; it permitted the employment of children between the ages of fourteen and sixteen for no more than eight hours a day, with a ban on night work, and only after the submission of documentary evidence of age and educational attainment. The President, the District Commissioners and several civic groups gave their approval. The National Child Labor Committee urged its members throughout the country to write asking their Senators and Representatives to give it favorable consideration: "It will mean much to the cause in every State to have at the National Capital a reasonably strong and fair law on the subject of child labor."[40] Whether moved by such pressures

---

[38] Theodore Roosevelt, Sixth Annual Message, *Works*, 15:360; Samuel McCune Lindsay, "When Congress Acts as a State Legislature," *Charities and the Commons* 15 (3 March 1906): 756–7. See also Lindsay, "National Child Labor Meetings"; S. W. Woodward, "A Businessman's View of Child Labor," *Charities and the Commons* 15 (3 March 1906): 800–1. On the wider movement, see Trattner, *Crusade for the Children*; Wood, *Constitutional Politics in the Progressive Era*; Hugh C. Bailey, *Edgar Gardner Murphy: Gentle Progressive* (Coral Gables, Fla.: University of Miami Press, 1968), 65–108.

[39] Neill, "Child Labor at the National Capital"; House Committee on the District of Columbia, *Report of Hearings on S.1243*.

[40] Report of the Secretary, 16 November 1905, Minute Book No. 1, National Child Labor Committee MSS, LC; *Charities and the Commons* 15 (2 December 1905): 270–1.

or merely by its intrinsic merits, the House acted promptly. The Committee on the District of Columbia reported in March 1906 an amended version that was, if anything, stronger than the original, and this was passed after only a brief discussion.[41] It experienced a much stormier passage in the Senate, where it encountered opposition sufficient to delay its passage for two years.

Generally speaking, child labor legislation was advanced on humanitarian grounds and on the basis of a progressive conception of the protective role of the state. Children, said Henry Cabot Lodge, must be protected and provided "that education on which, according to our American belief the safety of the country and of the States rests," in order to produce good citizens for the future. Dolliver agreed: "the question is not only one of their occupation, but one of their moral character and their preparation for the business and for the duties of American citizenship."[42] Beveridge, too, looked at the matter, not only from the point of view of sympathy for the children, but for "the future of the Republic." Children would only grow up to be good citizens "if their bodies are not broken and their souls are not crushed and their minds are not stunted in the meantime." Otherwise, they would turn into a class "dangerous to free institutions."[43]

Criticism of the bill, mostly enunciated by conservative Republicans, exhibited a similar inhospitability to contemporary thinking on the subject of child welfare to that evinced by the playground scheme. Several Senators propounded the virtues of hard work. Nathan B. Scott after treating the Senate to a glowing description of the "active, energetic set" of children in his West Virginia glass factory, warned that it was unwise to "compel boys to desist from labor" and that enforced idleness would lead to bad habits and moral ruination. Knute Nelson, likewise, thought it unwise "to educate children away from work," citing the benefits derived from his own early career as a newsboy. Samuel Piles of Washington evoked the same American tradition of self-help and self-reliance, insisting that "if a boy desires to fight his own way in the world he should have that opportunity." He must be permitted to develop those manly qualities of independence and self-reliance" which characterized "the great men of this country." In other words, to prohibit poor boys from seeking gainful employment would be to deny them access to the bottom rungs of the ladder of opportunity.[44] Others objected to government intrusion in the affairs of the family. The proposed law, said Weldon Heyburn of Idaho, would go "a long way toward taking the ordinary and proper custody of a child from the parent who is responsible for feeding and

[41] C.R., 59.1:4967–71; *Evening Star*, 23 March 1906.
[42] C.R., 59.2:199–204 (Lodge); 60.1:5786, 5791 (Dolliver), 5795–6 (Lodge).
[43] C.R., 59.2:1795.
[44] C.R., 59.1:8339 (Nelson); 59.2:198–9 (Scott), 208 (Piles); 60.1:5786–8 (Nelson), 5790, 5797 (Piles).

clothing and providing a home for the child," and it would wrongfully "take away from the parent the right to those services at the hands of the child that are natural and proper because the child is a part of the household." Eugene Hale condemned such legislation as "a step in the direction . . . of the Government assuming control and management here of the domestic relations." Objections to the regulation of child labor were very various, but they shared a common attachment to a set of traditional values and institutions and a traditional model of American society.[45]

Many Senators gave their support to the Piles amendment, which would allow a judge to issue a permit for the employment of a child between the ages of twelve and fourteen in any occupation not injurious to his or her health or morals if such employment was necessary to support a disabled or dependent relative.[46] "There could," protested Dolliver, "be no more serious weakening of the proposed law than to amend it in such a way as to allow people to permit their children to work when they are under the pressure of poverty and necessity." But he was unable to muster sufficient votes to defeat the amendment.[47] Nor could he prevent adoption of the Nelson amendment permitting the employment of children in "mercantile establishments, stores, and business offices," while the schools were not in session. As Lodge pointed out, in a city like Washington, the exemption of offices and stores would drastically reduce the law's scope.[48]

This was one of the few District bills on which votes were recorded. Senate voting on the Nelson and Piles amendments followed no particular sectional pattern, except for a tendency for Southern members to support the weakening amendments in greater numbers than those from other parts of the Union. This was, as much as anything, an expression of the region's general backwardness in social policy. Southern Senators were either more conservative in their personal opinions or, as Lindsay suggested, reluctant to register their votes in favor of a model child labor law which would inevitably "cast a reflection upon the lower standard in their home communities." There was a modest correlation between Senators' votes and the strictness of the child labor codes that operated in their own states.[49] Generally speaking,

[45] C.R., 59.1:7914–15 (Hale); 60.1:5790–1 (Heyburn).

[46] C.R., 60.1:5795.

[47] C.R., 60.1:5797–8 (Dolliver), 5795–6 (Lodge); 59.2:201–4 (Lodge).

[48] C.R., 60.1:5786–90 (Nelson), 5795–6 (Lodge); 59.2:205–8 (Dolliver).

[49] Lindsay, "When Congress Acts as a State Legislature," 756. The votes are recorded in C.R., 60.1, 5792, 5802. Republicans voted 19–26 in favor of the Nelson amendment, Democrats 13–4; for the Piles amendment, 26–14 and 9–5, respectively. If state child labor laws are coded 1 to 6 according to how many of the NCLC's principal requirements they met (minimum age 14, documentary proof of age, certificate of schooling, ban on night work, no exemption for support of dependent relatives, and an eight-hour day), the correlation between those scores and their Senators' voting on the Nelson amendment is $r = -.42$; on the Piles amendment $r = -.33$. Information about state laws is derived from Elizabeth Brandeis, "Labor Legislation," in John R. Commons et al., *History of Labor in the United States* (4 vols.,

it is probably true to say that Senators, in their speeches and votes on this measure were doing no more than venting their personal prejudices and presuppositions. This, of course, was the problem. The District was all too vulnerable to the miscellaneous prejudices of members of Congress drawn from remote and very diverse communities.

The bill's sponsors were even more embarrassed by the behavior of one of the more ardent advocates of child labor legislation, Albert J. Beveridge. Convinced of the potentiality of the interstate commerce clause as a constitutional mandate for wide-ranging social legislation, Beveridge offered a national child labor law based on that clause as an amendment to the District bill.[50] He spoke to his amendment for the best part of three legislative days. Thereafter, for the remainder of the session, whenever the bill came up one of his colleagues successfully moved that it lie over. Supporters of the bill attributed its demise to Beveridge's insistence on interposing his wider and more controversial measure. This he emphatically denied, arguing that his amendment could easily have been voted down: "in no way should it at any time have prejudiced the District Bill unless it was that Senators were unwilling to go on record as to my measure." It was predictable, however, that his colleagues should be unwilling to vote for a measure which they believed to be unconstitutional and, at the same time, fearful that a vote against a national child labor law might be interpreted as hard-hearted indifference to the plight of toiling infants by a public less sensitive than themselves to the niceties of constitutional exegesis. It was equally predictable that those responsible for the management of legislative business would soon become impatient with the seemingly interminable constitutional wrangles and wish to move to other matters. Presumably, Beveridge was well aware of this, but he valued passage of the District bill much less than the opportunity to give a public airing to his own more comprehensive measure. His insistence delayed for two years the control of child labor in the District.[51]

Only insistent pleading by Roosevelt, together with a change of heart on the part of the National Child Labor Committee, which had initially supported him, persuaded Beveridge to desist from offering his amendment when the bill came up before the next Congress.[52] This he did reluctantly.

New York: Macmillan, 1918–35), 3:409–37; Edward N. Clopper to Albert J. Beveridge, 8 October 1910, Beveridge MSS, LC.

[50] John Braeman, *Albert J. Beveridge: American Nationalist* (Chicago: University of Chicago Press, 1971), 112–16; Claude G. Bowers, *Beveridge and the Progressive Era* (New York: Literary Guild, 1932), 250–5.

[51] C.R., 59.2:1552–7, 1792–1826, 1867–83, 2965, 3300, 4100; Albert J. Beveridge to Mary G. Hay, 7 March 1907, Beveridge MSS, LC.

[52] Roosevelt to Beveridge, 12 November 1907, 30 March 1908, *Letters*, 5:844, 6:985–6; Reports of Meetings of Board of Trustees, 23 November, 6 December 1906, 25 October, 26 November 1907, National Child Labor Committee MSS, LC; Trattner, *Crusade for the Children*, 87–93; Murphy, *Gentle Progressive*, 94–101, 107–8; Braeman, *Beveridge*, 116–21. Roosevelt urged

While he accepted the need to legislate against child labor in the District, he insisted that, "in comparison with the general evil," it was trivial. Privately he dismissed the District bill as "for all practical purposes a mere fake." Passage would set back, not advance, the movement for reform. "People will then say, 'Now Congress has given the states an example of what ought to be done; let us wait for some years for the states to follow that example.' Meanwhile the murder of the innocents will go on." Beveridge, in other words, was highly skeptical of the practical value of model legislation for the District, which he regarded as a bogus alternative to effective national action.[53]

It was doubtful, in any case, whether the child labor law that finally emerged could be described as model legislation. Along with the compulsory education law of 1906, the new law, apparently, had an immediate and substantial effect on child labor in the District itself.[54] However, in its broader aims it was less successful. Though broadly in line with the most progressive legislation of the day, it had serious defects. The allowance made for the care of dependent relatives was much regretted by reformers like Florence Kelley, as were the clauses permitting employment of children in certain supposedly noninjurious occupations and, most anomalously of all, as pages on the floor of the Senate. Moreover, Congress had neglected to make an appropriation for inspectors to enforce the law, an omission which the experience of other states had shown was likely to render it nugatory. The sad truth was that the child labor law passed by Congress for the District was not a model law. While registering its disapproval of the practice, it failed to provide the nation with a model which could unequivocally be followed by the citizens of other states. As in many other areas of social policy, Congress, rather than setting a lead, did no more than follow trends set elsewhere.[55]

Education and Welfare

More rapid progress was made by the related compulsory education law. Here, too, the District had fallen seriously behind. "It is mortifying to

the expediency of passing the local measure unencumbered by Beveridge's national bill but showed no constitutional scruples regarding "the use of the interstate commerce clause" as "an ultimate resort for control of child labor." Seventh Annual Message, *Works*, 15:438; Roosevelt to G. H. Davis, 2 March 1908, *Letters*, 6:957–8.

[53] *C.R.*, 59.2:1552; Beveridge to Owen R. Lovejoy, 14 March 1908; to Harry Van Hook, 13 March 1908, to Roosevelt, 28 October 1907, Beveridge MSS, LC. See also Beveridge's explanatory remarks in *C.R.*, 60.1:5801.

[54] *Annual Report of the Commissioners, 1910*, 1:36; *Evening Star*, 18 October 1908.

[55] Florence Kelley, "The Senate's Monopoly of Child Labor," *Charities and the Commons* 20 (4 July 1908): 429–30; *Evening Star*, 25 May 1908. On proceedings in the House and in conference, see *C.R.*, 60.1:6030–5, 6665, 6918. There was at one stage a possibility that the House might reduce the age limit to twelve. This Roosevelt was quick to scotch. Roosevelt to Joseph G. Cannon, 29 April 1908, *Letters*, 5:1019–20.

remember that Washington has no compulsory-school-attendance-law," Roosevelt told Congress in December 1904. By 1906 this was true of only eleven states, all but one of them in the South. Out of twenty large cities Washington ranked thirteenth in the proportion of its children attending school and eighteenth in the level of literacy, ahead only of Louisville and New Orleans. The various civic leaders who testified at the hearings held by the House Committee on the District of Columbia were almost unanimous in their insistence on the importance of education in "the proper preparation of American citizens for the duties of life," as William Baldwin put it. This was especially true of the very children who were most likely to be absent from the rolls, those from alley homes or with dependent or indigent parents. Compulsory school attendance was therefore one way of tackling a broader social problem.[56]

A compulsory education bill, requiring the attendance at school of all children between the ages of eight and fourteen, was reported to the Senate early in the first session of the Fifty-ninth Congress. There was no vocal dissent to its passage.[57] The bill faced more serious criticism in the House, particularly over a committee amendment lowering the age of entry to six. A few members, like John Sharp Williams, worried that at that "tender age" many children were physically unready to enter the schools and preferred, like Franklin Brooks of Colorado, to leave that decision to "the good judgment and sound common sense of the parents." However, only the egregious John Wesley Gaines objected to the principle of compulsory education.[58]

Congressmen and Commissioners alike took pride in the new law. But, like much legislation for the District, it was defective, principally in its failure to provide for a force of attendance officers to deal with truants. Over the years Congressmen showed themselves highly distrustful of educational innovation, of what John Fitzgerald called "the introduction of a lot of useless and unnecessary fads to the schools." Such sentiments stood in the way of the development of a progressive school system in the District.[59] More serious than a suspicion of pedagogical "fads and frills" were budgetary constraints which hobbled the school-building program required to accommodate the additional pupils. In 1910 Washington ranked fifty-third in per capita expenditure on education among cities over 30,000. The result was chronic overcrowding and inadequate facilities which left Washington with far from a model school system.[60]

---

[56] Fourth Annual Message, *Works*, 15:230; Emily Young O'Brien, "Legalized Ignorance in the National Capital," *Charities and the Commons* 15 (3 March 1906): 822–4; *Report of Hearings on S.1243*; *Washington Post*, 2 February 1906; *Evening Star*, 2 March 1906.

[57] C.R., 59.1:3325–6.

[58] C.R., 59.1:7570–80.

[59] C.R., 59.1:6853–4.

[60] C.R., 61.2: 229–33. See also Hart, *Child Welfare in the District*, 1–5.

The District government, like other municipalities, supported a bewildering range of eleemoynsary institutions, most the product of private initiative but relying in varying degrees on public funds. These commitments had been assumed in a decidedly piecemeal fashion. In tune with the contemporary desire to rationalize the administration of relief, Congress had in 1900 established a Board of Charities to manage public institutions and supervise its grants to private agencies. The Board set out to reorganize the charities of the District in order to establish, as it declared in its report for 1905, "such a model of public charity and reformatory work as everyone believes should mark the capital of the nation." To this end it proposed to replace the lump sums previously handed out to the several agencies to spend as they saw fit with a system of contracts by which funds would be allocated in return for specific services rendered. The contract system would enable the public authorities, rather than the officials of private institutions, to determine who should be the recipients of public aid. What the Board thought it imprudent to mention was that the category of recipients most neglected by private charities was the city's large black population. Provision was also less generous for men than for women and children. Less favored groups had to seek help from the overcrowded and underprovided public facilities.[61]

Although the contract system allowed for a greater degree of coordination in the work of the District's charities and a more efficient use of public funds, there remained a great deal of uncertainty regarding their application. Increasingly, the Board came to advocate direct control of the institutions in receipt of public money. In 1908 it called for the creation of a complete set of charitable institutions wholly under the direction of the District government, "broad enough in their aims and complete enough in their equipment, to take care of all who should be the object of public charity." This would include the improvement of existing public institutions, like the workhouse and the Washington Asylum, and the construction of a school for feeble-minded children and new hospital facilities to accommodate indigent consumptives, alcoholics and the insane. Such a policy, claimed the Board, would make for a more efficient and equitable use of public resources. But it represented a radical shift of control of the administration of care from private to public hands.[62]

Attracted largely by the prospect of greater economy, Congress approved the substitution of payments on a contract basis for block grants to private

---

[61] *Annual Report of the Commissioners, 1905,* 1:445–6, 449–50; *Annual Report of the Commissioners, 1906,* 1:13–15. For an excellent description of the District's charities, see Green, *Washington,* 61–73. On the charity organization movement and related developments in public philanthropy, see Boyer, *Urban Masses and Moral Order,* 143–61; Trattner, *From Poor Law to Welfare State,* 77–107, 201–18; Michael B. Katz, *In the Shadow of the Poorhouse: A Social History of Welfare in America* (New York: Basic Books, 1986), 66–84.

[62] *Annual Report of the Commissioners, 1906,* 1:268–73; *Annual Report of the Commissioners, 1908,* 1:21–3, 454–6.

agencies, though not without some qualms. A provision in the 1906 appropriation bill for medical charities met angry opposition in the Senate. Hale complained of the intrusive behavior of "this ambitious and engrossing Board of Charities" and demanded that its supervisory authority over hospitals and asylums be removed. The private charities were, he claimed, well-managed, "prudent and conservative" institutions. Henry M. Teller argued that Congress was as fit to distribute the money as the Board of Charities and should maintain the practice of appropriating for separate institutions. This the Senate agreed to do. However, its amendment was retracted in conference, and the final measure allowed the Board the discretion that it had asked for.[63] Congress was less willing to replace private with public institutions. Many of the District's charities possessed influential friends, including Congressmen, who fought tooth and nail to protect the cherished institutions to which they had committed so much time and money. Considerable hostility was displayed in Congress, for example, to proposals to cease aid to the Columbia Hospital for Women and the Home for Incurables. Such resistance largely prevented the diversion of resources to public institutions, which remained unloved and underequipped – sad testimony to the reluctance of Congress to promote innovations in social policy.[64]

Government and Finance

For all the demerits of being totally subject to external rule, the citizens of Washington enjoyed, by common consent, a fairly efficient and honest government. The capital, admitted Burleson, was spared the "extravagance and graft, high taxes and ever increasing bonded indebtedness" commonly associated with municipal government. Indeed, government by the Board of Commissioners anticipated and shared many of the advantages of the commission plan adopted in Galveston and Houston in his own state of Texas. Despite the absence of a local civil service law, for which the Commissioners had repeatedly pleaded, most branches of the city government were reasonably efficient in the conduct of their affairs.[65]

Of course, it was not a democratic regime; the inhabitants of the District had no direct voice in the management of their affairs. As a writer in the *Atlantic Monthly* noted, "Washington, the capital city of our nation, instead of affording, as it should, the most striking model of self-government in

[63] C.R., 59.1:5504–5, 8253–5, 8948–51; *Evening Star*, 17 April 1906.

[64] C.R., 59.1:8153–5; Green, *Washington*, 159–60.

[65] C.R., 59.1:5525–8; C.H.A. Forbes-Lindsay, *Washington: The City and the Seat of Government* (Philadelphia: J. C. Winston, 1908), 142–6, 151–3. For a more critical view, see Lawrence Schmeckebeier, *The District of Columbia: Its Government and Administration* (Baltimore: Johns Hopkins University Press, 1928).

the whole country, is as a matter of fact a most horrible example of just the reverse." Even though it enjoyed "good government," it did not enjoy "democratic good government." And "this, happening at the seat of a nation which boasts of its democratic government, constitutes a solecism of the first magnitude."[66] Champ Clark regarded the state of affairs that existed "right under the Dome of the Capitol" as a severe condemnation of the principle of representative government. He would prefer the citizens to work out their own salvation and "cease to be wards of the nation." Burleson, too, favored a popularly elected government for the District, although, as a Southern Democrat, he would have liked to see educational and poll tax qualifications in place to eliminate the influence of the potentially large black vote.[67]

Such enthusiasm for local democracy was not often voiced by citizens of the District. One possible reason was a fear of the political influence of that third of the population that was black. In Washington, as nowhere else, wealthy taxpayers were free from the demands of propertyless voters and the schemes of machine politicians. Such considerations dampened the ardor of influential Washingtonians for home rule. As Clark noted, "the people who rule public sentiment in this city" consistently opposed such a step. Of course, such persons were never without a voice. In the absence of formal channels of representation, well-organized groups of citizens, like the Board of Trade and the Associated Charities, claimed to speak for the whole community and could expect to be listened to by the Commissioners and the District Committees of the House and Senate. In particular, the Board of Trade, a "commercial-civic organization" which acted, in effect, as an informal city council, cultivated close relations with influential Senators. In contrast, the voice of the District's poorer inhabitants, and above all its African-American population, was rarely heard.[68]

Municipal reformers praised the "concentration of authority" in the hands of the Commissioners, who had full authority over all aspects of municipal government, subject only to the superior power of Congress. However, the trend in the early part of the century was toward a greater dispersion of authority. For example, in 1906 Congress responded to criticism of the management of the public schools by transferring the power of appointing members of the Board of Education to the judges of the District Supreme Court. To Foster "this little body of 'peanut politicians' known as District Commissioners" had proved its unfitness to choose men and women

---

[66] Clinton R. Woodruff, "Charter-Making in America," *Atlantic Monthly* 103 (May 1909): 631–3.

[67] *C.R.*, 59.1:5761 (Clark); 59.2:1228–9 (Burleson).

[68] *C.R.*, 59.1:5761; Alan Lessoff, *The Nation and Its City: Politics, "Corruption," and Progress in Washington, D.C., 1861–1902* (Baltimore: Johns Hopkins University Press, 1994), 208–25; Green, *Washington*, 4–5, 171–86.

competent for the job.[69] Two years later a school reorganization bill took the severance still further, authorizing the Board of Education to submit separate estimates and in other respects to manage its own affairs.[70] By the 1920s, through the superimposition of other agencies, the government of the District had attained an almost baroque complexity. According to Laurence Schmeckebier, its principal defects included a "failure to centralize in a single office the responsibility for the conduct of administrative affairs . . . Inadequate and unsystematic grouping of the local administrative services into coordinate departments; the absence of the merit system; and the failure to distinguish clearly between the responsibilities of the District courts and the federal judiciary." Thus the District was moving in directions opposite to those prescribed by contemporary conceptions of a model municipal government.[71]

The determining feature of the structure of government for the District was the jealous refusal of Congress to yield any but the most routine discretionary powers to any local agency. Although the Commissioners had the authority to issue municipal ordinances and police regulations, there was no decision that they could take that might not be countermanded by Congress. Nor was Congress averse to legislating on the most trivial and particular areas of conduct. A law of 1892, for example, prohibited the flying of kites over the streets of Georgetown. Thus the District was subject to congressional supervision not only in principle but in quite minute detail.[72] This scrutiny was most rigorous in matters of finance. The Commissioners were forbidden to enter into any contracts or incur any liabilities without congressional assent. They were required to submit detailed estimates of expenditure to Congress, which, after careful deliberation, would appropriate sums that deviated substantially from those recommended. Even on the floor of the House members, determined to allow no possible scope for extravagance in the use of the taxpayers' money, would question the need for a given number of tax officials or court messengers and monitor the provision of water meters or library books.[73]

Since 1878 District finances had operated on a "half-and-half" principle, with local taxpayers and the United States Treasury contributing equally to the costs of government. The rationale for this sharing of the burden lay in

[69] C.R., 59.1:5755–63. For the Commissioners' opposition, see Henry B. McFarland to Joseph Babcock, 9 February 1906, Office of the Commissioners of the District of Columbia, Letters Sent, Vol. 69, RG 351, Series 19, NARA.

[70] *Evening Star*, 8 February 1908. For evidence of local opposition, see John L. Weaver to Francis G. Newlands, 10 February 1908; Washington Chamber of Commerce to Newlands, 25 February 1908; W. C. Dodge to William S. Greene, 16 December 1907, Newlands MSS, SLYU.

[71] Schmeckebeier, *District of Columbia*, 27 and passim.

[72] Ibid., 3–6, 26; Lessoff, The *Nation and Its City*, ch. 5; Forbes-Lindsay, *Washington*, 142–6.

[73] See, for example, C.R, 59.1:5610–14, 6531–4, 5665–9; 59.2:1287–92.

the fact that approximately half of the real estate in the District was in federal hands and therefore exempt from local taxation. Furthermore, Washington incurred expenses not faced by other cities because of its status as seat of the national government. As Martin B. Madden put it, "it would not be just to... force the local citizens to create a city, such as the nation's capital should be, unaided."[74] This arrangement became increasingly precarious as the city's financial needs increased. The new century brought mounting demands: for the extension of sewers and water mains to the suburbs; for the reclamation of Anacostia Flats and the improvement of Rock Creek; for the installation of a high-pressure water system for the control of fires; for new school buildings following the compulsory attendance law of 1906; for a new almshouse and reformatory and expanded hospital facilities. By 1909 the Commissioners were recommending a series of projects the aggregate cost of which would amount to $20,282,000. Meanwhile, the cost of present services increased, especially in the areas of education, law enforcement and fire protection. During the brief period between 1906 and 1909 the estimates submitted by the Commissioners rose from $11 million to $16 million, but congressional appropriations remained consistently around $10 million.[75]

By 1909 affairs had reached crisis point. The Commissioners asked in their estimates for $16 million; tax revenues would bring in no more than $6 million, which would be matched by the federal contribution, leaving a deficit of $4 million. Citizens of the District contended that they paid taxes at a rate comparable to other cities, but the tax base was restricted by the large population of servants and day laborers and the absence of substantial commercial and industrial enterprises, the largest enterprise in the city, the United States Government, being, of course, untaxed. Hence it would be fair "for the citizens to pay a reasonable tax on what they own, and the Government to pay the balance."[76] An alternative strategy favored by the Commissioners was for current expenditures on the day-to-day provision of services to be distinguished from extraordinary expenditures on permanent improvements, such as schools, sewers and parks. For the latter purpose the Commissioners hoped to be able to borrow from the Treasury, just as other cities issued bonds to finance improvements without prejudicing the provision of existing services. However, the practice of Congress was to charge such advances to the District's general account and demand their liquidation within a short time span. No other municipal or business corporation,

---

[74] C.R., 59.1:5530 and 5528–33 passim; Green, *Washington*, 4–5. It was also pointed out that the District did not have a school fund such as Congress had provided for most states. W. C. Dodge to William S. Greene, 16 December 1907, Francis G. Newlands MSS, SLYU.

[75] Green, *Washington*, 40–1, 178–80.

[76] W. C. Dodge to William S. Greene, 16 December 1907, Newlands MSS, SLYU.

commented the Washington *Evening Star*, paid for improvements in such a fashion.[77]

Members of Congress tended to regard the government and people of the District as chronically prone to extravagance. "It has seemed," remarked Frederick H. Gillett, the chairman of the House Appropriations subcommittee responsible for the District, "that nobody in the District of Columbia is interested in economical expenditure of money, and everybody is interested that more expenditure shall be made in one line or another." Burleson, his Democratic counterpart, accused the District Commissioners of "irresponsibility" and the citizenry of a wanton disregard for economy. Congressmen of both parties were alert to any possible danger of extravagance in any part of the District budget, from policing to playgrounds. The victims of swollen payrolls and lavish improvements, as they saw it, were the taxpayers, whom they felt obliged to protect – not only the disfranchised and "helpless" taxpayers of the District but their own constituents in every state of the Union.[78] Many Congressmen had come to question whether the "half-and-half" system was equitable. Gillett believed that the commercial growth of the city had made it obsolete: "if the rate of taxation was made as high here as in the average city throughout the country we would have money enough in the next few years to make this really a model city." His successor as manager of the District appropriation, Washington Gardner, also believed that the tax rate was unusually low. At 1.5 percent on two-thirds of an out-of-date valuation, real property was leniently treated, while personal property was hardly taxed at all. The District, it was claimed, had acquired something of the status of a tax haven.[79]

Organs of local opinion, like the *Evening Star*, accused Congressmen of a woeful ignorance of local finances. Many, indeed, coming as they did from rural areas, showed little appreciation of the problems of municipal finance.[80] This could not be said of the members of the committees responsible for the District appropriations, who were both conscientious and informed. But theirs was a double responsibility, both to their charges in the District and their constituents back home. The latter obligation predisposed them to financial caution. This was especially true at a time when Congress was concerned about the advancing trend in federal expenditures as a whole; the District budget was not alone in feeling the effects of the paring knife. Be that as it may, the consequence was that, year after year, the District estimates were severely cut. The *Evening Star* summarized the pattern: "The

---

[77] *Annual Report of the Commissioners, 1905*, 1:8–9; *Annual Report of the Commissioners, 1908*, 1:7–8; *Evening Star*, 22 May 1908.

[78] C.R., 59.1:5502 (Gillett), 6849 (Burleson); 59.2:1229–30 (Burleson); *Evening Star*, 12 February 1906.

[79] C.R., 59.1:5502–3 (Gillett); 60.2:818–19 (Gardner). See also C.R., 59.1:5528–30; 59.2:1229–30; 60.2:820–1; Green, *Washington*, 180–5.

[80] *Evening Star*, 17, 19, 25 February, 11 April 1906.

House slices the estimates beyond recognition, the Senate restores them to a semblance of their original form, and the conference strikes the balance in compromise." Far from allowing generous loans for further improvements, Congress insisted that the District devote a large share of its revenue to paying off existing debts, even at the expense of current expenditure. In 1908, for example, the House cut the estimates for repairs and improvements by $250,000, for road repairs by $100,000, for the police force by $100,000, for playgrounds by $186,000 and for schools by $1,700,000. Schools and sewers took the heaviest cuts the following year, along with provisions for libraries and policing. Such a process left the District of Columbia without a complete modern system of sewers, seriously short of school accommodation, and in other ways bereft of the physical equipment and services to be expected of a model city in the Progressive Era.[81]

Congress and the District

In their report for the year 1907–1908 the Commissioners pointed with some satisfaction at the achievements of the eight years since the District centennial in 1900. These included new parks and sewers, substantial reorganization of the system of public relief, and improved educational and public health facilities. Congress had played its part by passing compulsory education and child labor laws, authorizing the condemnation of unsanitary buildings, regulating employment agencies, creating a system of juvenile courts, and appropriating money for public playgrounds, alley clearance and numerous other improvements.[82] Yet, in the next breath, the Commissioners presented a list equally long of things yet to be done. These included a civil service law for the District, regulation of life insurance companies, cheaper gas, control of the liquor traffic, and the reorganization and enlargement of the public health department. They also stated the need for the establishment of an effective public utilities commission, resolution of the legal impasse in the campaign to eliminate alley dwellings, and the creation of more complete facilities for the chronically sick, alcoholics, and the "mildly insane." Moreover, all of the social programers of the District were seriously underfunded and understaffed.[83] That the federal government had failed to create a model city in the District of Columbia was widely admitted. At best Congress placed its imprimatur on lines of policy tried and developed elsewhere, rather than setting an example. Even here the record was patchy. If, as Clark suggested,

[81] *Evening Star*, 22 May 1908. See also ibid., 30 March, 8, 16, 17 April 1908, 6, 15 January 1909; C.R., 60.1:4352–4, 6776–7; 60.2:1831–2; Green, *Washington*, 149, 179–84; Lessoff, *The Nation and Its City*, 138–45, 250–2.

[82] *Annual Report of the Commissioners*, 1908, 1:10–11. Cf. *Joint Annual Report of the Associated Charities*, 1909, 12–13; *Evening Star*, 5 March 1907; Green, *Washington*, 156–7.

[83] *Annual Report of the Commissioners*, 1908, 1:12. Cf. *Evening Star*, 19 April 1908; Green, *Washington*, 160–1.

"this District [was] used as a legislative experiment station for the rest of the country," the experiments conducted were neither innovative nor systematic.[84] Instead, Congress responded in a piecemeal and reactive fashion to the challenges of the new century. If its record was no worse than that of many other municipalities, it was certainly no better.

It was easy to find fault with Congress's management of the District's affairs. The problem lay largely with its insistence upon an obsessively detailed scrutiny and its jealous refusal to delegate substantial authority to the agencies of local government. Any but the most trivial municipal regulation, any institutional development, any item of spending required legislation which had to compete for congressional time and attention with a host of other business, ranging from individual claims and pension bills to questions of national importance. Much worthy and widely supported District legislation languished helplessly on the House calendar. It is true that, under the rules, every second Monday was "District day" when only District business was in order for two hours after the reading of the Journal. But even this supposedly sacred hour, when the House was supposed solemnly to assume the status of a local assembly and devote itself conscientiously to the requirements of its wards in the District, was often diverted to other matters. By a mere majority vote the House could resolve to move to other business, in the event that the leadership discovered more urgent priorities. Thus on 23 January 1906 it voted to set aside District day in order to proceed with consideration of the statehood bill. When the regular order of business was followed it was with no great enthusiasm. A quorum was rarely in attendance, which meant that business had to proceed by unanimous consent; a call of "no quorum" could bring it to a standstill or, at the very least, lead to the waste of precious time while members were brought in to make up the numbers. Often time was wantonly expended on irrelevant speeches, for campaign purposes, with the complacent acquiescence of the House. The informal procedures of the Senate sometimes allowed more business to be transacted. Here, too, much of the business was done by unanimous consent, and the ruling principle of "senatorial courtesy" prevented the discussion of any measure in the absence of an avowed opponent who had expressed a wish to be heard. "When this narrow channel of legislation is thus measured," observed the *Evening Star*, "what wonder remains that the District needs today many laws to give it a full equipment to bring it up to date with other municipalities, to correct the faults of the past, and to set high standards for the future."[85]

---

[84] C.R., 59.2:2728.

[85] *Evening Star*, 13 February 1907. See also ibid., 8 February 1908, 13 January 1909; *Washington Post*, 23 January 1906; C.R., 59.1, 5761; Schmeckebeier, *District of Columbia*, 3–6; Lessoff, *The Nation and Its City*, 149; DeAlva S. Alexander, *History and Procedures of the House of Representatives* (Boston: Houghton Mifflin, 1916), 213–25.

Normal channels being so restricted and strewn with obstacles, members often sought to secure legislation for the District by more indirect means. Much of it took the form of riders to appropriation bills, which, being privileged, found an easier path through the congressional thicket. Thus the policy of creating a system of public playgrounds developed piecemeal through a series of provisions in District appropriation bills, while the reorganization of charities was related to the way in which funds were allocated by Congress. This too was a precarious route: any innovative use of money, which had the slightest flavor of "new legislation" was liable to a point of order. Therefore, unanimous consent was necessary. Nor could legislation concocted in so haphazard a fashion follow any coherent plan. "As a result," noted Hastings Hart with reference to one important area of social policy, "the legislation of the District of Columbia on behalf of children is in a hopeless state of confusion."[86]

Most members showed a lack of interest in District affairs which was either lamentable or inevitable, depending upon one's point of view. Not only did they owe a prior loyalty to their distant constituents, but those same constituents imposed upon them an almost unmanageable burden of personal and local business that left no time to cultivate an interest in the personal and local business of somebody else. In many important respects they were quite ignorant of conditions in the District. What passion they did show in District debates was liable to be an expression of their own, or their constituents', prejudices – against railroad companies, against real estate speculators, against African-Americans, against social workers or against bureaucrats.[87]

In such a sea of indifference and ignorance, the District relied heavily on those few individuals whose duty, and in some cases inclination, involved them particularly in its affairs. Most prominent, of course, were the members of the House and Senate Committees on the District of Columbia, which were, in effect, Washington's city councils. The House District Committee was characteristically composed of representatives of big-city districts who might therefore be expected to show some knowledge and understanding of urban problems. They were by no means equally attentive to the onerous duties of a committee service on which brought neither public recognition nor political advantage and counted for little with their constituents in Missouri or Maine. Turnover was therefore high. The chairman, Joseph W. Babcock, showed some diligence in seeing to District business, although there were some grounds for suspicion that his interest lay partly in the prospect of profiting from investments in real estate and utility stocks about which his privileged position afforded special information. Judge Ben Lindsey found

---

[86] Hart, *Child Welfare in the District of Columbia*, 3; Lessoff, *The Nation and Its City*, 153–4.
[87] *Outlook* 79 (11 March 1905): 625–6; 93 (2 October 1909), 239–40; *Charities and the Commons* 15 (3 March 1906): 739–40; 20 (18 April 1908): 101–4; *Evening Star*, 2 June 1908.

him to have "little or no interest" in legislation relating to child welfare, but, in fact, in 1906 he introduced and guided through the House the child labor, compulsory education and unsanitary buildings bills.[88] Nobody impugned the attention to duty of the chairmen of the Appropriations subcommittee. Gillett showed some sympathy for social spending, Gardner rather less, but both, following the lead of the chairman of the full committee, James Tawney, saw their chief duty as that of curbing public spending. Their conscientious strivings did not necessarily serve the best interests of the District.[89]

Few of the Senate committee were residents of large cities. Indeed, the membership appeared to be almost willfully drawn from the most bucolic localities. That, however, did not stop men like Francis G. Newlands of Nevada from displaying both interest in and sensitivity to the needs of the capital. A number of Senators like Newlands and Allison became long-term residents of Washington, acquired houses, and sometimes other real estate, and became intimately involved in local affairs.[90] Chairman Jacob Gallinger had acquired a rather ambivalent reputation for shady real estate speculation and a tenderness for the interests of the local traction companies. However, he, too, managed many progressive measures in their progress through the Senate and gamely defended, whatever his sympathies, both the child labor and compulsory education laws.[91]

A further difficulty confronting any campaign to persuade Congress to convert the capital into a model city lay in the patent lack of consensus about what a model city would, in fact, look like. To many urban members, as to civic leaders in the District, it should boast an armory of advanced social legislation and a battery of social facilities to better the living and working conditions of the city's "neglected neighbors." However, to many Western Republicans and Southern Democrats a model city would be one which firmly checked utility "monopolies" and real estate speculation. There was no necessary incompatibility between these priorities, but in practice they tended to run counter to one another. Social reform and constraints on utility companies appealed to different elements in the membership. Thus, when the distribution of votes on the playground appropriation of 1909 is compared with a 1908 roll call on a provision requiring the street railroad

---

[88] House committees are listed in *C.R.*, 59.1:288; 60.1:428. For comments on their members' service to the District, see *Washington Post*, 22 December 1905; *Evening Star*, 8 November 1906, 17, 19, 20 December 1907. See also Lessoff, *The Nation and Its City*, 149–53. On Babcock, see *Washington Post*, 24 January 1906; Ben B. Lindsey, "Saving the Citizenship of Tomorrow," *Charities and the Commons* 15 (3 March 1906), 758; Green, *Washington*, 180.

[89] *C.R.*, 59.1:5501–6 and 5525; 60.1:4352–4, 6776–7; 60.2:818–21.

[90] For Senate committees, see *C.R.*, 59.1:537; 60.1:383. On Newlands's and other Senators' involvement in the District, see Lessoff, *The Nation and Its City*, 150–2, 158–63.

[91] Connolly, "Gallinger of New Hampshire."

companies to issue universal free transfers a distinctly negative association appears (Q = −.42). Most Southern Democrats voted in favor of universal transfers on the streetcars but against the playground appropriation. All but a score or so Republicans voted against free transfers, but they were equally divided on the playground issue, while the twenty-two Republicans, most of them Midwestern insurgents, who voted for free transfers and answered the roll on the playground vote divided almost evenly on the latter.[92]

In the eyes of Southern Democrats, a model city would be one whose racial arrangements conformed more closely to the prevailing Southern pattern. Though still very much a Southern city with a typically Southern population mix and typically Southern racial attitudes, Washington, under Republican rule, had failed to install the full paraphernalia of racial controls that were becoming normal in that section. Hence Southern Congressmen pressed hard for laws which would bring the District into line with the South's developing racial mores. These included Jim Crow laws, bans on interracial marriage and stricter vagrancy laws. It is fortunate that, although the District's Republican rulers seemed disinclined to take positive steps to tackle the worsening pattern of racial discrimination or to ensure that public agencies were even-handed in their treatment of African-Americans, they were still willing to pay lip service at least to the ideals of racial equality that had animated the party in the past, and thus to obstruct the passage of overtly discriminatory legislation.[93]

Many government leaders were preoccupied with the beautification of the city so that it might serve as a fit embodiment of a proud and potent American nationhood. Their interest was in parks and public buildings rather than schools and sewers. The McMillan Plan of 1902, which set the template for the further development of official Washington, promised few benefits to the majority of the city's inhabitants. No consideration was given to the housing of the poor, as if their very existence threatened the authors' "vision of a monumental capital." Alley dwellings were regarded as an eyesore rather than a social problem. It was a plan, says Alan Lessoff, to create a federal "city-within-a-city" rather than to "put the impress of the nation's capital" on the whole city. Even apart from the federal government's own expenditure on the construction of office buildings and monuments and the laying out of the Mall, the District spent a higher proportion of its budget on public works than almost any comparable municipality and a smaller proportion

---

[92] The roll call on universal transfers is at *C.R.*, 60.1:6686–7. For explanation of its context and significance, see *C.R.*, 60.1:2297–2355, 4980–7, 6680–6.

[93] Green, *Secret City*, 155–67; William E. Chancellor, "Washington's Race Question," *Collier's* 42 (3 October 1908): 24–5. The Republican party's ambivalence towards blacks is demonstrated by Richard B. Sherman, *The Republican Party and Black America from McKinley to Hoover* (Charlottesville: University Press of Virginia, 1973).

on health, education and welfare. The resulting contrast between public grandeur and private squalor has worsened rather than lessened during the intervening decades.[94]

The inability of Congress to develop a systematic and progressive social policy for the District, then, was more than an expression of a collective indifference to the welfare of its citizens. It stemmed from fundamental disagreements as to what a systematic and progressive social policy should be. It also reflected the essential conservatism of most Congressmen – their parsimonious attitude to the expenditure of public money on social projects, their skepticism towards progressive ideas of education and child welfare, and their fondness for old and sometimes idiosyncratic charitable foundations. Nor must we forget the influence of racism in shaping congressional attitudes to social policy – sometimes crude and blatant, as in Democratic demands for segregation laws, more often implicit, as in the discourse about alley dwellers, working children, and the recipients of public charity. Finally, the construction of a coherent social policy for the District fell foul of the formidable inertia of Congress as an institution and the low status accorded to District affairs in its listing of priorities.

The decentralization of governing authority is often cited as a principal cause of the arrested development of the American welfare state.[95] Yet the experience of the District of Columbia, where federal authority ruled supreme and unchallenged, suggests that a social policy formed in its entirety by Congress would not necessarily have been any more progressive than one constructed piecemeal by the states. The strength of traditional social attitudes and fiscal conservatism among its members, along with their widely divergent prejudices and purposes, leads one to doubt whether, in the absence of constitutional constraints, a national social policy could ever have been as far-reaching and enlightened as the more nationalist-minded reformers imagined. The common liberal assumption of the greater wisdom and benignity of federal action would not apply to federal social policy in the Progressive Era. The condition of Washington, D.C. at the end of the Roosevelt Administration stands as testimony to its deficiencies. In any case, the reform initiatives of the Roosevelt era tended to wither away in the years that followed, and with them withered, as an immediately practicable ideal,

[94] William A. Tobin, "In the Shadow of the Capitol: The Transformation of Washington, D.C. and the Elaboration of the Modern Nation-State" (Ph.D. diss., Stanford University, 1993), 66–7; Lessoff, *The Nation and Its City*, 267 and passim; Gillette, *Between Justice and Beauty*, 88–108.

[95] See, for example, Charles Noble, *Welfare as We Knew It: A Political History of the American Welfare State* (New York: Oxford University Press, 1997), 14–16, 28–30; Robertson, "Bias of American Federalism"; Robertson, *Capital, Labor, and the State*; Theda Skocpol, *Social Policy in the United States* (Princeton: Princeton University Press, 1995), 72–135.

the dream of a "model city" on the banks of the Potomac.[96] And with that, in turn, faded the possibility of using the national capital as a proving ground for a national social policy, of setting national standards by example where they could not be laid down by federal decree, and laying the preliminary foundations of a modern welfare state.

[96] Green, *Washington*, 157–70.

6

The Senate and Progressive Reform

The twentieth-century American state was not a product of autogenesis, emerging spontaneously from a peculiar conjunction of economic and social forces. Certain individuals were responsible for constructing the new governing institutions and crafting the legal framework within which they were to operate; certain other individuals worked to obstruct that process and preserve older modes of decision making inherited from the "state of court and parties" that preceded it. Many of the formative acts of creation were carried out in Congress. It is important to identify who was responsible for the reform legislation that constituted the blueprint for the new American state and to investigate, so far as we can, the constituencies that they represented, the social pressures that they were subjected to, and the reasons that they gave for supporting reform. In short, who were the progressives, and who and what did they stand for? Such an exercise will help us to locate the process of state building within the field of partisan conflict and to relate movements for progressive reform to the distribution of opinion within the Republican and Democratic parties.

The political parties in Congress retained a pronounced tendency to stick together even when confronted by the new, and supposedly divisive, issues of progressive reform, which makes the analysis of congressional voting particularly difficult. Examination of both parties together does little more than register their tendency to oppose one another. Therefore they are best considered separately. The purpose of this chapter is to examine the response of Senate Republicans to a variety of reform issues from the Fifty-ninth to the Sixty-first Congress, focusing especially on the growing division between progressives and conservatives. It employs roll call evidence to identify Republican factions and to investigate the relationship between the various reform proposals set before the chamber. The following chapter carries out a similar analysis for the House of Representatives. The central theme in each is the evolution of an increasingly discrete and coherent body of progressive Republicans, known at the time as "insurgents," who, though relatively small in number, had a disproportionate impact on the tenor of congressional debate, on the formulation of policy, and on the decision-making process in both houses of Congress. They were able to do this primarily because their objectives partially coincided with those of the Democratic minority, which was consistently more sympathetic to progressive reform than all but a handful of congressional Republicans. However, progressivism Democratic-style had its own peculiar stamp. The fact that reform legislation, and therefore the creation of the new American state, depended heavily on Democratic support had important consequences for its ultimate complexion. Chapter 8 therefore reflects on the distinctive character of Democratic progressivism.

Republican Voting in the Senate

At the close of the highly productive first session of the Fifty-ninth Congress the *New York Times* observed that it had "been difficult to draw party lines... in sizing up the attitude of the legislators to these reformatory measures."[1] The issues of progressive reform appeared to divide the two main parties, threatening to produce a major party realignment. Even so shrewd a political commentator as Lincoln Steffens confidently expected this to happen. "A political realignment is going on here," he informed his readers. "There is a great slanting crack across the face of both the old parties."[2]

When we turn to examine congressional voting, however, we discover a striking degree of party cohesion. In the Senate during the course of the Fifty-ninth Congress 115 roll calls were taken, in 90 of which three-quarters and in 63 of which nine-tenths of the Republicans voted together. Three-quarters or more of the Senate Democrats voted together in 92 divisions, nine-tenths in 66. The median value of the Rice Index of Cohesion stood at 83 for the Republicans and 88 for the Democrats.[3] It is true that by 1909 serious cracks were opening up in the Republican ranks, the average Rice Index sliding from 72 in the Fifty-ninth and the first session of the Sixtieth Congress to 64 in the second session of the Sixtieth and the Sixty-first Congress, but this was accounted for by the errant behavior of a relatively small number of Republican insurgents. Even these levels were high by historical standards.[4]

---

[1] *New York Times*, 25 June 1906.

[2] Lincoln Steffens, "Forming New Political Parties," proof of article dated 28 January 1906, La Follette MSS, LC. Cf. Woodrow Wilson, "Politics 1857–1907," *Atlantic Monthly* 100 (November 1907): 643–4.

[3] The Rice Index of Cohesion is calculated by subtracting the minority of a group from the majority and converting to a percentage. A value of 100 represents unanimity and 0 a fifty-fifty split.

[4] For comparative data, see Patricia Hurley and Richard Wilson, "Partisan Voting Patterns in the U.S. Senate, 1877–1986," *Legislative Studies Quarterly*: 14 (1989): 225–50; Howard W. Allen and Jerome M. Clubb, "Progressive Reform and the Political System," *Pacific Northwest*

TABLE 6.1. *Classification of Senate Roll Calls, 59th and 60th Congresses*

Cluster	No.	Subject	Cluster	No.	Subject
1A	3	Railroad (pipe-line)	2	4	Railroad (pass)
	7	Railroad (pass)		22	TCIC merger
	8	Railroad (review)		23	Country Life Commn.
	9	Railroad hours		24	Forest reserves
	10	Railroad hours			
	11	Railroad hours	3	5	Railroad (pass)
	12	Railroad hours		13	Railroad hours
	15	Employers' liability			
	18	Forest reserves	4	6	Railroad (pass)
	20	Railroad (commodity)		19	Long/short amendment
	21	Direct election			
			5	16	Child labor
1B	1	Pure food		17	Child labor
	2	Pure food			
	14	Emergency currency	6	25	Forest reserves

Note: The above classification was derived from the CLUSTER program of SPSS-X using the group average method.

Most Republicans voted together most of the time, but that still leaves a sizeable number of roll calls from which useful information about intraparty divisions can be gleaned. A sample was drawn by taking all those votes on identifiable issues of progressive reform during the Fifty-ninth and Sixtieth Congresses in which eleven or more Republicans opposed the majority of their party. Three roll calls on the Hepburn bill were removed in order to prevent duplication. The sample includes all the measures which have featured prominently in the historical literature and which produced significant divisions in the Republican ranks when the roll was called.

Values of Yule's Q were calculated for each pair of roll calls. Cluster analysis was employed to sort out this miscellaneous set of items into more manageable groups. Table 6.1 presents a classification array produced by the group average method, which identifies six clusters, most consisting of two to four items, the largest of fourteen. These fourteen roll calls do not form a satisfactory scale; there are far too many error responses. Many deviations from the perfect scale pattern are evidently due to random factors, such as individual eccentricities, ignorance, tactical voting or the passage of time. It is, after all, unrealistic to expect Senators, who have to negotiate an ever-changing field of constituency pressures, factional disputes, legislative compromises and executive demands, to show a high level of ideological consistency over a four-year period during which their political universe was

Quarterly. 65 (1974): 132–3; Jerome M. Clubb et al., *Partisan Realignment* (Beverly Hills, Cal.: Sage, 1980), 235–8, 239–49.

undergoing dramatic change. At a lower level of aggregation it is possible to identify a number of subclusters which better satisfy the criteria of scalarity. The largest forms a scale of six items (#8, #12, #15, #18, #20, and #21), mostly concerning railroad issues.

Table 6.2 displays the votes of Republican Senators in the six roll calls, arranged according to the proportion of members voting in favor of an extension of federal regulatory powers (which might mean a vote of yea or nay according to how the question was put). One signifies a vote for, zero a vote against progressive reform. Following the demanding Goodenough-Edwards criterion the coefficient of reproducibility is .92. In other words, 92 percent of the votes conform to a scale pattern, which is a striking display of orderly conduct on the part of so self-willed a body of individuals as United States Senators. It is possible to conclude, therefore, that, apart from individual vagaries, which are not surprising in view of the range and complexity of the issues, most members regarded these questions as closely connected. The information in Table 6.2 also enables us to rank Senators according to how far in support of reform they were prepared to go. Moses Clapp of Minnesota responds positively to all six propositions; Foraker, Gallinger and Hale cannot bring themselves to assent to any; the others assume positions in between. Also listed are the proportions of positive votes recorded on twelve of the fourteen items in the cluster. These are closely correlated with scale scores ($r = .92$), which provides confirmation of the extent to which the items test a broadly similar range of issues.[5]

What can we say, then, about the progressives and conservatives – progressives and conservatives, that is, as far as these issues are concerned? Progressives tended to be slightly younger – the average age of those scoring four and over on the scale was 52.6, of those scoring three or less 55.5 – and to have spent less time in the Senate. Those with substantial business interests were mostly to be found at the conservative end of the scale, as were most of the Senate's rather numerous contingent of millionaires.[6] What most clearly distinguished progressives from conservatives was the section of the country which they represented. A cursory examination of Table 6.2 reveals that most of the conservative Republicans represented New England, the Mid-Atlantic states or the Rocky Mountain West. The average scale score for New England and the Mid-Atlantic states is 1.18 (.18 for the full cluster); for the older states of the Midwest 2.57 (.55); for the West North Central region 4.93 (.83); for the Mountain West 1.74 (.21); and for the Pacific coast 4.64 (.68). "There is a new spirit here," proclaimed Robert M. La Follette, "and it comes from the middle west." The evidence presented here demonstrates

---

[5] The two votes on the pure food bill (#1 and #2) were excluded for the purpose of calculating cluster scores. The remaining twelve roll calls maintain an average intercorrelation of $Q = .73$.

[6] For a listing of Senate millionaires, see *New York Times*, 27 May 1906.

TABLE 6.2. *Votes of Republican Senators on Scale Items, 59th and 60th Congresses*

| | Roll Call | | | | | | Score | |
Name	#18	#12	#20	#8	#15	#21	Scale	Cluster
Clapp (Minn.)	1	1	1	1	1	1	6	.82
Beveridge (Ind.)	1	1	1	1	1	1	6	1.00
Piles (Wash.)	1	1		1	1	1	6	.73
Fulton (Ore.)	1	1		1		1	6	.88
La Follette (Wis.)		1	1	1		1	6	1.00
Burkett (Neb.)	1	1	1	1	1		5	1.00
Dolliver (Iowa)	1	1	1	1	1		5	.91
Hopkins (Ill.)	1	1	1	1	1	0	5	.75
Flint (Cal.)	1	1	1	0	1		4[a]	.73
Elkins (W.Va.)		1	1	1			4	.88
Frye (Me.)	1	1		1	0		4	.50
Nelson (Minn.)	1	1	1	1	0	0	4	.83
Warner (Mo.)		1	1	1		0	4	.89
Carter (Mont.)	1	1	1	0	0	0	3	.55
Penrose (Pa.)	1		1	0		0	3	
Ankeny (Wash.)		1	0	0	0	1	2[a]	.45
Smoot (Uta.)	1	0	0		1		2[a]	.30
Brandegee (Conn.)	1	1	0	0	0	0	2	.42
Knox (Pa.)	1		0	0	0	0	2	.30
Nixon (Nev.)	1		0	0			2	
Sutherland (Uta.)	1	1	0		0		2	.20
Wetmore (R.I.)	1		0	0	0	0	2	.13
Dick (Ohio)	0	1	0	0	0	0	1[a]	.17
Kean (N.J.)	1	0	0	0	0	0	1	.17
Lodge (Mass.)	1	0	0	0		0	1	.18
11 Republicans	0	0	0	0	0	0	0	
Long (Kan.)	0	0	1	1	0	0		.33
Perkins (Cal.)	1	1	0	1	0	1		.64

Key: 18. Agricultural Appropriation: for roads within forest reserves (60.1, 6076)
   12. Railroad hours: exclude lines lying entirely within one state (59.2, 893)
   20. Bill suspending enforcement of commodity clause of Hepburn Act (60.1, 6754)
   8. Railroad bill: remove "in its judgment" from clause on ICC powers (59.1, 7070)
   15. Employers' liability: substitute bill reported from Senate committee (60.1, 4538)
   21. Direct election of Senators: refer resolution to committee (60.1, 6806)
   a Cases containing error responses
Note: Cullom (Ill.), Dillingham (Vt.), Gamble (S.D.), Hansborough (N.D.), Hemenway (Ind.), Kittredge (S.D.), and McCumber (N.D.) recorded insufficient votes to be included.

the extent to which this dimension of progressivism was a sectional, and especially a Midwestern, phenomenon.[7]

Principally Concerning Railroads

It is necessary to inquire why the division of opinion on this particular set of issues should have so strongly sectional a character. The question is perhaps most easily answered with reference to railroad regulation. The pattern of rate differentials, or discrimination, as it might be interpreted, largely shaped the pattern of responses to the proposal, which formed the core of the Hepburn bill, that a government agency, the Interstate Commerce Commission, should be empowered, under certain circumstances, to set rates. The most striking instances of local discrimination were to be found in the South and West. According to C. L. Davidson, the president of the Wichita Chamber of Commerce, "the railroads have forced the people of this state to take an advanced position on this question" and to insist that their representatives in Congress adopt an "advanced position" in turn. Even reliably conservative Midwestern Senators like William B. Allison and Chester Long, men with longstanding political and professional connections with the railroads, felt obliged to bend to local pressure.[8] It was quite natural also for those benefiting from the prevailing system to be suspicious of change. New England Senators like Henry Cabot Lodge feared that a federal rate-making agency would respond to Midwestern demands by prohibiting the low through rates which they considered essential to the industrial prosperity of their section.[9]

Only Joseph B. Foraker among the Republicans voted against the Hepburn bill. Many more followed Aldrich and Knox in support of amendments which would enable the courts to review ICC orders in full. As we have seen, the clearest test vote on judicial review was taken on an amendment (#8) to strike out the words "in its judgment" from the section authorizing the Commission to "determine and prescribe . . . a just and reasonable rate or rates." To both sides the amendment clearly raised the question of the relative powers of the Commission and the courts, and it captures better

---

[7] Robert M. La Follette to O. J. Schuster, 19 March 1906, La Follette MSS, SHSW, Microfilm Edition. Cf. Elizabeth Sanders, *Roots of Reform: Farmers, Workers, and the American State, 1877–1917* (Chicago: University of Chicago Press, 1999); Jerome M. Clubb, "Congressional Opponents of Reform, 1901–1913," (Ph.D. diss., University of Washington, 1963), especially 195–211, 295–6.

[8] Unidentified clipping dated 25 January 1906, in Chester I. Long to Theodore Roosevelt, METRP, Reel 62. See also William Allen White, *The Autobiography of William Allen White* (New York: Macmillan, 1946), 351–3; Robert S. La Forte, *Leaders of Reform: Progressive Republicans in Kansas, 1900–1916* (Lawrence: University Press of Kansas, 1974), 24–8, 70, 97–9.

[9] *C.R.*, 59.1:2414–23; Henry Cabot Lodge to Lucius Tuttle, 10 January 1906, Lodge MSS, MHS; Lodge to Roosevelt, 1 December 1905, METRP, Reel 61; John A. Garraty, *Henry Cabot Lodge* (New York: Knopf, 1953), 227.

than any other record vote the division within the Republican party over the
question of judicial review.[10] Two other votes on the Hepburn bill find their
way into this cluster: on an amendment to the pipeline section restricting its
application to the movement of petroleum (#3); and on the free pass amendment (#7). Also included is a later roll call (#20) on an attempt to secure a
stay of execution for railroads which had still not disposed of their holdings
in manufacturing and mining companies as required by the "commodity
clause" of the Hepburn Act.[11]

It is rather less easy to relate the railroad hours bill to this sectional pattern. Its purpose was to restrict the periods of continuous duty that railroad
employees were expected to perform, with harmful consequences not only
for their own physical and social welfare but also for the safety of the general public. To some extent it expressed the same resentment against the
railroads that had fuelled support for the rate bill. Certainly the conservative Senator Jacob Gallinger of New Hampshire believed so, attributing
the movement for such legislation to "a disposition and determination" in
certain quarters "to make an indiscriminate raid upon corporations."[12] A
similar animus might explain why Midwestern Republicans also supported
the tougher Senate version of the 1908 employers' liability bill (#15).[13]

Nobody, in view of the public concern about the accident rate and the
pressure placed on Congressmen by the railroad brotherhoods, opposed the
railroad hours bill outright. As La Follette explained to his wife, "they don't
like to go on record against a bill which all the railway employees petition
for and which the public itself is so much interested in."[14] Debate focused on
amendments offered by Jacob Gallinger and Frank Brandegee which sought
to make allowance for the exigencies of the railroad business. Gallinger's
amendment (#11) made exceptions for extra hours caused by an "unavoidable accident . . . or resulting from a cause not known to the carrier" when the
journey began. Brandegee's (#9) made allowance for any "emergency which
by reasonable care on the part of such carrier" could not be avoided.[15] As
Francis E. Warren of Wyoming explained, "there are a great many contin-
gencies and incidents and intricate details that come up in railroad business,
impracticable to regulate by legislation." Thomas Carter of Montana feared
that the legislation would "at once disorganize and paralyze the entire railway operating system of the United States." He shared with Gallinger and
Brandegee a desire that the bill should be drafted so as to minimize inconvenience to the railroads.[16] La Follette himself offered an amendment (#10)

[10] *C.R.*, 59.1:7023–9, 7063–70.
[11] *C.R.*, 60.1:6754.
[12] *C.R.*, 59.1:9361, 9365.
[13] *C.R.*, 60.1:4526–45; *New York Times*, 10 April 1908; *Outlook* 88 (18 April 1908): 844.
[14] Robert M. La Follette to Belle C. La Follette, 28 June 1906, La Follette MSS, LC.
[15] *C.R.*, 59.2:757–83, 889–95, 882; *New York Times*, 11 January 1907.
[16] *C.R.*, 59.1:9264–5 (Warren), 9667 (Carter).

in the form of a substitute for the bill reported from committee, which he found to be loosely worded and "faulty in construction." Different in substance was the Bacon amendment (#12), which, in response to concerns about the bill's constitutionality, excluded railroad lines lying wholly within one state.[17] This also attracted a mainly conservative Republican vote. Indeed, voting on all these amendments followed a fairly consistent pattern, which closely mirrored that on the central issues of rate regulation.

The railroad hours bill was advanced, above all, as a measure to promote public safety at a time when a mounting accident rate provoked concern. Supporters of the bill, like La Follette and Dolliver, contended that most such accidents were caused by fatigue due to overwork and marshaled impressive arrays of statistics to substantiate their claim.[18] As we have seen, La Follette also urged Congress to consider the welfare of "the great body of the American people who constitute the consumers of the country" in framing its railroad regulation. The pure food bill was, of course, specifically designed "to secure the health and welfare of the consuming public."[19] The progressive publicist Walter Weyl was one of many to identify "a new insistence ... upon the rights of the consumer" as a common element in many of the political movements of the day.[20]

It remains to identify the other items in the cluster. One (#14) is a roll call taken on the 1908 emergency currency bill, designed to alleviate the shortages of circulating currency which had contributed to the financial panic of the previous autumn by permitting groups of national banks, under carefully controlled conditions, to issue emergency currency backed by state, municipal and railroad bonds. Barely anybody found this scheme attractive, but opposition was strongest in the West and South. To some extent this opposition reflected agrarian suspicion of the "Money Trust" and a belief that the emergency currency would serve the interests of speculators rather than ordinary commercial bankers. More specific was the objection that the bonds required to guarantee the emergency issue were of a type more commonly to be found in the portfolios of Eastern, and especially New York City, banks than of those in other parts of the country.[21] Several Western Republicans

[17] C.R., 59.2:765–7, 819–20, 883–6, 891, 893; Robert M. La Follette to Belle C. La Follette, 17 January 1907, La Follette MSS, LC.

[18] C.R., 59.1:9267–70, 9365; 59.2: 811–19 Carl Snyder, "The Growing Railway Death Toll: Who Is Responsible?" *Everybody's* 16 (April 1907): 504–14.

[19] Theodore Roosevelt, Fifth Annual Message, *The Works of Theodore Roosevelt* (National Edition, 20 vols., New York: Scribner's, 1926), 15:326.

[20] Walter Weyl, *The New Democracy* (New York: Macmillan, 1913), 251; Walter Lippman, *Drift and Mastery* (New York: M. Kennerley, 1914), 54–5. Cf. David P. Thelen, "Social Tensions and the Origins of Progressivism," *Journal of American History* 56 (1969): 323–41; Thelen, *Robert M. La Follette and the Insurgent Spirit* (Boston: Little, Brown, 1976), 21–6, 52–78.

[21] For examples of Western opposition, see Carl K. Bennett to Knute Nelson, 9 January 1908; W. L. Hixon to Nelson, 13 January 1908; Thomas Tonneson to Nelson, 16 January 1908; E. W. Davies to Nelson, 27 January 1908; E. T. Buxton to Nelson, 18 February 1908, MinHS.

spoke out against the bill, and fourteen recorded their votes in favor of an amendment offered by Knute Nelson of Minnesota which would add real estate to the list of assets which might be offered as security, while a smaller number voted against the bill altogether.[22]

During the same session a Democratic resolution initiating the process of amending the Constitution so that Senators would be elected by popular vote, rather than by state legislatures, came before the Senate. Demands for direct election of Senators were grounded in a belief in the intrinsic corruptibility of state legislatures, which were all too easily subverted, it was charged, by the influence of powerful political bosses and wealthy corporations, and the intrinsic incorruptibility of the people as a whole. The Senate, it was widely believed, represented moneyed "interests" rather than the people. Direct election was consistent with other political reforms designed to secure a more immediate expression of democratic impulses, such as direct primary legislation and the initiative and referendum. The process of electing Senators produced so many deadlocks, disputes and charges of malpractice that by 1908 two-thirds of the legislatures, including all but one of those west of the Missouri, had asked to be relieved of the responsibility. This was the first time that such a resolution had reached the floor of the Senate. From there it was summarily consigned to its final resting place in the Committee on Privileges and Elections (#21). Half of the twelve Republicans who voted against committal represented states in the Midwest and on the Pacific littoral where direct primary legislation had already effectively submitted the choice of candidates to public choice.[23]

Pure Food and Drugs

The federal Pure Food and Drug Act, which demanded truthful labeling of food products and medicines, while prohibiting certain deleterious ingredients, emerged from the same congressional session as the Hepburn Act.

See also *New York Times*, 8, 9, 14 January 1908. On the background to the bill, see Robert C. West, *Banking Reform and the Federal Reserve, 1863–1913* (Ithaca, N.Y.: Cornell University Press, 1977), 49–51; Robert H. Wiebe, *Businessmen and Reform: A Study of the Progressive Movement* (Cambridge, Mass.: Harvard University Press, 1962), 72–5; Stephenson, *Aldrich*, 325–31.

[22] *C.R.*, 60.1:3874–6, 4003–13, 4018–20; *New York Times*, 27, 28 February 1908.

[23] *C.R.*, 60.1:6803–6; *New York Times*, 24 May 1908; Philip L. Allen, "The Trend Toward a Pure Democracy," *Outlook* 84 (15 September 1906): 120–5. On the background, see George E. Mowry and Judson Grenier, introduction to David Graham Phillips, *The Treason of the Senate* (Chicago: University of Chicago Press, 1964), 41–4; Mowry, *Era of Theodore Roosevelt*, 51–3, 70–82; C. H. Hoebeke, *The Road to Mass Democracy: Original Intent and the Seventeenth Amendment* (New York: Transactions, 1995); Daniel Wirls, "Regionalism, Rotten Boroughs, Race, and Realignment: The Seventeenth Amendment and the Politics of Representation," *Studies in American Political Development* 13 (1999): 18–20.

Its passage offers a useful illustration of the development of the modern regulatory state.

The food products consumed by the American public were increasingly processed outside the home, distributed over great distances, and preserved with the aid of a bewildering variety of chemicals. At the same time, numerous proprietary medicines competed for custom, promising miraculous cures for a variety of afflictions but deriving much of their impact from impressive quantities of alcohol and even morphine. Muckraking journalists like Samuel Hopkins Adams and Mark Sullivan, as well as committees of medical practitioners, revealed how misleading and dangerous patent medicine advertising sometimes was. Such exposures did a great deal to arouse public anxiety regarding patent medicines and processed foods. Reform groups like the General Federation of Women's Clubs, the Women's Christian Temperance Union, and the National Consumers' League lobbied extensively for food and drug regulation. So did important elements within the food industry. They exploited the "strategic uses of public policy" as a means of gaining competitive advantage. Manufacturers of "legitimate" products like baking powder made with cream of tartar, rather than alum, and "straight," rather than "rectified" or "blended," whiskeys sought to regulate the marketplace so as to prohibit or disadvantage "illegitimate" competitors. More generally, food manufacturers looked to regulation to allay public anxiety about their products and to relieve themselves of the inconvenience of diverse state laws. Various professional groups also developed an interest in regulation. For example, agricultural chemists played a major role in the pure food movement, for reasons which had as much to do with enhancing their own status and prestige as protecting the public health. In particular, Harvey W. Wiley, head of the Department of Agriculture's Bureau of Chemistry, seizing on pure food as the area of expertise best fitted to enhance the power and prestige of his agency, formed alliances with companies that might gain from legislation, like H. J. Heinz and the "straight" whiskey manufacturers, cultivated consumer groups, placed favorable copy in friendly journals, and organized testimony before congressional committees. Regulation therefore grew out of the activities of a complex coalition whose members harbored very different motives.[24]

---

[24] James Harvey Young, *Pure Food: Securing the Federal Food and Drug Act of 1906* (Princeton: Princeton University Press, 1989); Young, *The Toadstool Millionaires: A Social History of Patent Medicines in America before Federal Regulation* (Princeton: Princeton University Press, 1961), 205–44; Clayton A. Coppin and Jack High, *The Politics of Purity: Harvey Washington Wiley and the Origins of Federal Food Policy* (Ann Arbor: University of Michigan Press, 1999); Lorine S. Goodwin, *The Pure Food, Drink, and Drug Crusaders, 1879–1914* (Jefferson, N.C.: MacFarland, 1999); Peter Temin, *Taking Your Medicine: Drug Regulation in the United States* (Cambridge, Mass.: Harvard University Press, 1980), 18–34; Donna J. Wood, *The Strategic Use of Public Policy: Business Support for the 1906 Food and Drug Act* (Marshfield, Mass.: Pitnam, 1986); Mark Sullivan, *Our Times* (6 vols., New York: Scribner's, 1926–35),

In 1906, following a campaign lasting over ten years, Congress passed the Pure Food and Drug Act. Earlier legislation had been shelved owing to the influence of the patent medicine and other lobbies and the hostility of influential Senators like Nelson Aldrich, himself a wholesale grocer. By 1906, however, pressure from the American Medical Association and other groups, along with personal appeals from the President, forced the Senate leadership to relent.[25] The object, said Weldon Heyburn, the law's sponsor, was "to prevent the manufacture of articles that were deleterious to health and to prevent the combination of articles that would deceive and defraud the public." Porter McCumber desired to ensure "that when we go out into the market to buy an article of food or a drug to be used in the family, we shall get what we call for" and not "some poisonous substance in lieu thereof." Today, he pointed out, the citizen's health and welfare were "threatened at every step by the greed and the avarice of the manufacturers of drugs and many kinds of food products." He and others described the ingenious variety of food adulteration to which the defenseless public was subjected: the hams containing as preservative up to ten times the normal dose of boracic acid, the jars of "potted chicken" and "potted turkey" which were quite innocent of the presence of any such fowl, the fruit jellies containing "nearly everything but fruit juice," and all the other triumphs of "creative chemistry" uncovered by state food commissioners and Wiley's USDA "Poison Squad."[26] Judging by the press reaction, this measure enjoyed widespread public support; even so conservative a paper as the New York Times spoke in its favor.[27]

Opposition reflected the interests of specific sections of the food and drug industries. For example, Lodge spoke for the sacred codfish of New England, whose preservation apparently required the liberal application of boracic acid. Aldrich represented the interests of wholesale grocers, Frye and Hale the canners of "imported French sardines" caught off the coast of Maine. James Hemenway of Indiana, who had links with patent medicine manufacturers, demanded that the bill should not penalize "statements made in good faith" about the "therapeutic qualities" of their products. Gallinger,

2:483–534; Harvey Wiley, *An Autobiography* (Indianapolis: Bobbs-Merrill, 1930), 199–230; Louis Filler, *The Muckrakers: Crusaders for American Liberalism* (2nd. edn., State College: Pennsylvania State University Press, 1976), 150–68; Oscar E. Anderson, *The Health of a Nation: Harvey Wiley and the Fight for Pure Food* (Chicago: University of Chicago Press, 1958), especially 148–71; John A. Braeman, "The Square Deal in Action: A Case Study in the Growth of the 'National Police Power,'" in Braeman et al., eds., *Change and Continuity in Twentieth-Century America* (Columbus: Ohio State University Press, 1964), 36–47; Robert M. Crunden, *Ministers of Reform: The Progressives' Achievement in American Civilization, 1889–1920* (New York: Basic Books, 1982), 163–200.

[25] Sullivan, *Our Times*, 2:533–6; Young, *Pure Food*, 160–5, 205–6; Anderson, *Health of a Nation*, 176–94.

[26] *C.R.*, 59.1:894 (Heyburn), 1218, 1415–16 (McCumber).

[27] *Literary Digest* 32 (3 March 1906): 311–12; *New York Times*, 2 July 1906.

whom Samuel Hopkins Adams described as a "patent medicine doctor," worried that the bill might "by indirection... utterly destroy the so-called 'patent-medicine business.'"[28] Foraker and Boies Penrose spoke for the producers of rectified and blended whiskeys. To demand that they publish their ingredients, as the bill required, argued Foraker, would impose an "unfair, unreasonable, and uncommercial requirement" upon the rectifiers which the distillers of "straight whiskey" would not have to meet. Foraker therefore offered an amendment permitting rectifiers to market their product as "rectified," "blended," or "vatted" whiskey without having to own up to its true composition. This was the one section to call forth significant record votes (#1 and #2), which divided the Senate in a similar fashion to the railroad votes.[29] Since most of the producers opposing regulation were located in the Eastern and older Midwestern states, it was Senators from those regions who were most concerned to protect manufacturing interests by amending the legislation before Congress. On the other hand, several Western states, like McCumber's state of North Dakota, had themselves passed strict regulatory laws, which the federal statute was designed to complement.[30]

Although federal meat inspection never came to a vote, it was a closely parallel issue. The public had a right, declared Heyburn, to demand that meat products were prepared "under cleanly and healthful conditions."[31] "The railroad rate bill, meat inspection bill and pure food bill, taken together, mark a noteworthy advance in the policy of securing Federal supervision and control of corporations," claimed Roosevelt in July 1906. Writing to the chairman of the Republican Congressional Committee the following month, he repeated that all three measures were "really along the same general lines." Beveridge agreed, arguing that each of them recognized the principle that "when any business becomes so great that it affects the welfare of all the

---

[28] *C.R.*, 59.1:2720–1 (Lodge), 2722 (Gallinger), 2724–8 (Hemenway); Samuel Hopkins Adams to Robert M. La Follette, 26 June 1906, La Follette Papers, SHSW, Microfilm Edition, Reel 93; Henry B. Needham, "The Senate of Special Interests," *World's Work* 11 (February 1906): 7206–11; Edward Lowry, "The Senate Plot against Pure Food," *World's Work* 10 (1905): 6215–17. See also Young, *Pure Food*, 207–9; Ralph L. McBride, "Conservatism in the Mountain West: Western Senators and Conservative Influences in the Consideration of Progressive Legislation, 1906–1914" (Ph.D. diss., Brigham Young University, 1976), 41–5.

[29] *C.R.*, 59.1:2647–52; Young, *Pure Food*, 165–8, 172–3; Anderson, *Health of a Nation*, 174–6; Wood, *Strategic Uses of Public Policy*, 174–6; Jack High and Clayton A. Coppin, "Wiley and the Whiskey Industry: Strategic Behavior in the Passage of the Pure Food Act," *Business History Review* 62 (1988): 286–309. The votes are at *C.R.*, 59.1: 2770.

[30] See McCumber's explanation of the bill's objectives in *C.R.*, 59.1:2661–5. On state regulation, see Young *Pure Food*, 168–73, 281–2.

[31] *C.R.*, 59.1:9026, 8763–9. On the history of the measure, see Braeman, "Square Deal," 47–80; John A. Braeman, *Albert J. Beveridge: American Nationalist* (Chicago: University of Chicago Press, 1961), 101–9; Sullivan, *Our Times*, 2:471–83, 535–52; Gabriel Kolko, *The Triumph of Conservatism: An Interpretation of the Progressive Movement* (New York: Free Press, 1963), 98–108; Crunden, *Ministers of Reform*, 189–95; Young, *Pure Food*, 221–52.

people, it must be regulated by the Government of all the people."[32] Each of them also involved a sizeable augmentation of the regulatory authority and administrative capacity of the new American state.

The Conservation of Children and Trees

A scattering of tiny islands lie off the continental land mass of the main cluster. Two votes on the District of Columbia child labor bill form one of these. The most revealing roll calls were taken on the Nelson and Piles amendments, which respectively exempted employment in shops and offices from its terms, on the grounds that such work was not "prejudicial" to health or morals, and relieved children with "dependent relatives" from the restrictions imposed by the bill. Both substantially weakened its effectiveness as protective legislation.[33] The votes on these two amendments (#16 and #17) are closely correlated to one another ($Q = 1$), but not with those included in Table 6.2. Warner, Clapp, and Nelson among the progressives listed there voted for the amendments; Burnham, Gallinger, and Kean among the conservatives voted against them. The overall correlation between voting on items in the two clusters is $r = .07$. This was not really a sectional issue as far as the Republicans were concerned; opponents of regulation were not concentrated in any particular region.

Another issue which does not fit the dominant pattern is conservation. Two votes in the second session of the Sixtieth Congress (#24 and #25) touched upon aspects of the Administration's forestry policy.[34] These were taken on amendments offered by Heyburn to the 1909 Agricultural Appropriation Bill ordering the removal of untimbered land from the national forest reserves and reducing the appropriation for the Forest Service. In each case Republican opponents mostly represented the Western states where the forest reserves lay, together with a few Eastern conservatives like Foraker, Gallinger, Hale, and Kean. However, other conservatives, such as Aldrich, Knox, Lodge, and Penrose, voted with the Administration.[35]

Much of the animosity felt by Western Senators toward the Forest Service centered upon what they regarded as abuses in the exercise of its legal authority. The forest reserves incorporated large tracts of agricultural land, users of which had to submit to an elaborate array of rules and regulations, as well as valuable streams and water-power sites, whose exploitation was

---

[32] Roosevelt to Lyman Abbott, 1 July 1906, in Elting E. Morison et al., eds., *The Letters of Theodore Roosevelt* (8 vols., Cambridge, Mass.: Harvard University Press, 1951–4), 5:328; to James E. Watson, 18 August 1906, *Letters*, 5:375; Beveridge quoted in Braeman, *Beveridge*, 110.

[33] C.R., 60.1:5790–1, 5797–8, 5795–6. The votes are at 5792 and 5802.

[34] C.R., 60.2:3252, 3253.

[35] The correlations between Republican voting on the conservation votes and scores on the railroad scale are $r = .355$ (#24) and $-.317$ (#25).

carefully guarded. Those who leased grazing, mineral or water-power rights were charged fees which many settlers found exorbitant. Many found fault with the "unwise and unjust regulations" imposed upon settlers by the agents of a bureaucracy governed from Washington and remote from the needs and concerns of ordinary settlers.[36] There was, as can be seen, a noticeable anti-statist undertone in Western anticonservationist rhetoric. Although local business groups took the lead in condemning the Administration's forestry policy, they were largely supported by a local population imbued with values of rugged individualism and hostile to central control.[37] Instead of enjoying the same opportunity to develop their natural resources that the settlers of older commonwealths had gleefully exploited, the people of the Western states, protested Heyburn, were "hampered and driven back by onerous conditions, by prohibitions, and closed areas" and treated as if they were "freebooters and marauders intent only upon the destruction of the country and its resources." Heyburn and other Western Senators demanded the return of these resources to the states, insisting that local people could best manage and dispose of them, in accordance with American principles of self-government.[38]

Defenders of the Administration's forestry policy denied that it either hindered the sound and lasting development of the West or barred the way to settlement by "genuine homesteaders." The aim of federal policy, declared Reed Smoot of Utah, was to ensure that "the national forests will be handed down to the next generation with their resources intact and the rights of the people to enjoy them inviolate." Without some such scheme to preserve the resources of nature, their prosperity would be short-lived. In view of the "reckless improvidence" that they had shown in the past, Lodge was extremely reluctant to entrust resource management to "the tender mercies of the States or the settlers." Ultimately, the resources in question belonged to, and should be managed in the interests of, "the entire people of the United States."[39]

This was a policy of what Beveridge called "scientific forest preservation." It was designed to benefit the whole American people and not just part;

---

[36] *C.R.*, 59.2:3188 (Fulton), 3200 (Carter). See also *C.R.*, 59.2:1959–62, 2015–23, 2198–2207 (Heyburn), 3183–8 (Fulton) and 3514–22 (Clark, Wyo.); 60.2:3086–3105 (Carter). On the background to the attack on the Administration's forestry policy, see Samuel P. Hays, *Conservation and the Gospel of Efficiency: The Progressive Conservation Movement, 1890–1920* (Cambridge, Mass.: Harvard University Press, 1959), 133–8; Geoffrey R. Graves, "Anti-Conservation and Federal Forestry in the Progressive Era" (Ph.D. diss., University of California, Santa Barbara, 1987); Harold T. Pinkett, *Gifford Pinchot: Private and Public Forester* (Urbana: University of Illinois Press, 1967), 75–80; Lewis L. Gould, *The Presidency of Theodore Roosevelt* (Lawrence: University Press of Kansas, 1990), 199–203.

[37] Graves, Anti-Conservation," 67–8.

[38] Weldon B. Heyburn, "Forest Reserves," *Independent* 60 (22 March 1906): 667–71; *C.R*, 59.2:3188; 60.2:3233; Graves, "Anti-Conservation," 233–41.

[39] *C.R.*, 59.2:3299, 3515–16 (Lodge); 60.2:3240 (Smoot).

it was designed to benefit future generations of Americans "in a scientific way," by empirical investigation and systematic planning.[40] Roosevelt, in his brief to the National Conservation Commission, declared that "every effort should be made to prevent destruction, to reduce waste, and to distribute the enjoyment of our national wealth in such a way as to promote the greatest good of the greatest number for the longest time." In this sense, he told the Governors' Conference on Conservation in 1908, conservation was part of a "another and greater problem . . . the problem of national efficiency, the patriotic duty of insuring the safety and continuance of the Nation."[41] This echoes some of the arguments for child labor legislation. Indeed, social welfare measures of that kind were sometimes described as measures for the "conservation of human resources."[42] The link is a tenuous one, but not entirely figurative. Both reforms were founded on a broad conception of the public interest, as largely defined by organized groups of interested specialists, like foresters, hydrologists, or social workers; both envisaged planning for the long term, rather than immediate benefits to any group in society; both demanded some sacrifice of individual or sectional interests for the sake of the nation as a whole.

Conservatives and Progressives

"Historians must constantly remind themselves," observes David Levine, "that men's actions are not a very precise guide to their ideas."[43] We cannot with confidence infer a particular ideological position from a set of legislative votes. That a Senator should vote for a progressive measure might not testify to a sincere personal commitment to reform so much as a yielding to his constituents' desires, to interest-group pressures, or to presidential persuasion. We must be wary when the results of roll call analysis contradict evidence of another kind. Lodge, for example, on the basis of Table 6.2 appears solidly conservative, but he pronounced himself ready to support "moderate reforms" and staunchly defended the "Roosevelt policies" against the criticism of his friend the banker Henry Lee Higginson, arguing that "Government control and regulation" were necessary to check the "unquestionable abuses" and "indifference to law" which had characterized the behavior of some business magnates. Roosevelt felt quite happy to compliment

---

[40] *C.R.*, 59.2:3532.

[41] Roosevelt to Theodore E. Burton, 8 June 1908, *Letters*, 6:1068; Seventh Annual Message, *Works*, 15:443–4.

[42] As in the 1912 Progressive Party platform. Kirk H. Porter and Donald B. Johnson, eds., *National Party Platforms, 1840–1964* (Urbana: University of Illinois Press, 1966), 177.

[43] Daniel Levine, *Varieties of Reform Thought* (Madison: University of Wisconsin Press, 1964), viii.

his friend as "on the whole the best and most useful servant of the public to be found in either house of Congress."[44]

Several of those who stand out as devotees of reform had contemporary reputations of quite a different character. Some, like Allison, Long, and the California Senators Perkins and Flint, sustained intimate relations with local railroad interests. Allison had long acted as the attorney and political representative of a number of Iowa railroads. Long, who, according to William Allen White, was associated with the "conservative faction" in the state Republican party, was known in Kansas as a "railroad Senator." "It is not surprising that the railroads elected Long or that Long supported the railroads," commented J. M. Oskison in *Collier's*. "To him they have always represented a greater and more enduring power than resides with the people.... The point of view of the railroads is his own point of view." Flint and Perkins, too, supposedly owed their election to "the organization." The North Dakota Senators Hansborough and McCumber enjoyed a similar reputation. "They are machine men with a big 'M,'" alleged one of their constituents.[45]

It is largely a matter of perspective. La Follette saw none of his Republican colleagues as truly progressive – by his own standards. Although Elmer J. Burkett figures here as one of the more progressive Republicans, La Follette was highly critical: "His record shows him voting quite as often with the special interests as in the public interest."[46] Knute Nelson also fell foul of La Follette, who "read the roll" against him, as he did against the more obviously conservative Ankeny and Hemenway. To La Follette the tests of fidelity were support of his amendments to the Hepburn bill covering physical valuation, imprisonment and judicial qualifications and resolute opposition to the railroad bonds clause of the Aldrich currency bill. Few passed these tests.[47] The view of the Administration was rather different, being colored more by votes on battleships than banks and by defense of the President's

---

[44] John A. Garraty, *Henry Cabot Lodge* (New York: Knopf, 1953), 225–9; *C.R.*, 59.1:8767–9; Henry Cabot Lodge to Henry Lee Higginson, 7 January 1908, Lodge MSS, MasHS; Theodore Roosevelt to Lyman Abbott, 23 February 1906, *Letters*, 5:163; Richard M. Abrams, *Conservatism in a Progressive Era: Massachusetts Politics, 1900–1912* (Cambridge, Mass.: Harvard University Press, 1964), 31–7.

[45] On Allison see Sage, *Allison*. On Long see White, *Autobiography*, 352–3, 394–5; Joseph R. Burton to Victor Murdock, 19 December 1906, Murdock MSS, LC; J. M. Oskison, "Senate Undesirables: Long of Kansas," *Collier's* 41 (18 July 1908): 8–9; La Forte, *Leaders of Reform*, 26–8, 70, 97–9. On Perkins and Flint see Frank F. Oster to J. J. Esch, n.d. November 1905, Esch MSS, SHSW. On Kittredge, Hansborough and McCumber see E. A. Trow to Robert M. La Follette, 30 April 1906; E. H. Kent to La Follette, 29 June 1906, La Follette MSS, SHSW, Microfilm Edition.

[46] Robert M. La Follette to William Husenetter, 2 November 1910, La Follette MSS, LC; La Follette to Irvine Lenroot, 8 January 1908, Lenroot MSS, LC.

[47] See Belle C. and Fola La Follette, *Robert M. La Follette* (2 vols., New York: Macmillan, 1953), 1:211–13, 218–20, 230–4, 304–5.

executive actions rather than his railroad policy. The special nature of these criteria is evident from Roosevelt's encomium on Lodge. Albert J. Hopkins may have been regarded by *Collier's* as a spoilsman and a party hack worthy of inclusion in its series on "Senate Undesirables," but he received a presidential endorsement as "one of the most constant and loyal supporters" of the Administration's policies.[48]

In many respects La Follette was right. In 1906, indeed in 1908, few Republicans wished to be identified as progressives. On the other hand, most did not wish to be identified as conservatives either. They carefully avoided too close an association with either wing of the party and were greatly embarrassed by the emerging factional split. Frank P. Flint, for example, explained to Beveridge in September 1908 just how difficult he found the present political situation: "I am unable to subscribe to a great many of the doctrines of the radicals like La Follette and his followers, and on the other hand, I am not so conservative as a great many of our party who carry their conservatism so far that they are really reactionaries." Flint's predicament was that of a railroad attorney connected to the Southern Pacific machine confronting a growing progressive sentiment in his own state, and it was a predicament shared by many of his colleagues. They had been raised in a certain school of politics; they had become accustomed to certain established political procedures and relationships, for example with the railroads. Many shared Flint's unease in the face of intraparty divisions and did their best to steer a middle course through the stormy sea of Progressive Era politics. Their pleas were neither for "radical" reform nor for "standpat" conservatism. "A steady progress along the lines that we have followed during the past seven years, and at the same time not to the extent of disturbing business affairs, seems the ideal course to pursue," continued Flint in his letter to Beveridge.[49] It was no surprise that the position assumed by such men seemed a little wobbly. Burkett's opportunistic attempts to work both sides of the street in Nebraska politics had gained him the soubriquet "slippery and slimy Elmer." To Roosevelt, Flint's senior colleague George C. Perkins had "no more backbone than a sea anemone." But these were troublesome times when the penalty of excessive rigidity promised to be especially punitive. Many, like the veteran Shelby Cullom, found it prudent to occupy the position of "the man on the fence," declining to commit themselves irrevocably to either side.[50]

---

[48] A. S. Henning, "Senate Undesirables: Albert J. Hopkins," *Collier's* 40 (7 March 1908): 11–12 and (14 March 1908): 13–14; Theodore Roosevelt to Cornelius J. Tron, 15 February 1909, *Letters*, 6:1521.

[49] Frank P. Flint to Albert J. Beveridge, 7 September 1908, Beveridge MSS, LC.

[50] Richard Lowitt, *George W. Norris: The Making of a Progressive, 1861–1912* (Syracuse, N.Y.: Syracuse University Press, 1963), 190; Theodore Roosevelt to William Kent, 4 February 1909, *Letters*, 6:1504; James W. Neilson, *Shelby M. Cullom: Prairie State Republican* (Urbana: University of Illinois Press, 1962), 238. On another Midwestern Senator's attempts to find a middle way, see Millard L. Giecke and Steven J. Keillor, *Norwegian Yankee: Knute Nelson*

Perhaps the lesson of all this is the great danger involved in seeking to divide legislators into progressive and conservative factions when their dearest wish and the object of their most carefully devised strategies was to avoid identification with either.

The Payne-Aldrich Tariff

After 1909 such strategies became less tenable. The insurgent group in the Senate was more clearly demarcated, factional lines sharper and more consistent. The split between insurgents and regulars, which later became assimilated to the conflict between friends and foes of the embattled Taft Administration, accounts for the greater part of intraparty divisions.[51]

It all started with the tariff. Ever since the promulgation of the highly protectionist Dingley Tariff of 1897 the case for revision had been steadily mounting. At the most fundamental level it arose out of the growing discrepancy between the rates of duty imposed in 1897 and the changes in products, markets and relative costs over the intervening years. All but the deepest-died "standpat" protectionists admitted that some compensatory adjustments were necessary. In many industries, it was claimed, domestic costs of production had fallen to a point at which the existing level of duties allowed extortionate profits and provided a barrier behind which monopolistic combinations might be formed. Excessive tariffs were therefore blamed both for the seemingly inexorable rise in prices and the growth of trusts. Hence tariff revision was a popular cause which spoke to a wide range of public concerns.[52] More specifically, revisionism was a political movement which marshaled the sometimes conflicting campaigns of a variety of manufacturers, traders and agricultural exporters to influence American trade policy in ways which would improve their competitive position in overseas markets. This involved, on the one hand, making concessions to European importers so as to prevent retaliatory measures against American goods and,

and the Failure of American Politics, 1860–1923 (Northfield, Minn.: Norwegian-American Historical Association, 1995), 251–86.

[51] See especially George E. Mowry, *Theodore Roosevelt and the Progressive Movement* (Madison: University of Wisconsin Press, 1946); Donald F. Anderson, *William Howard Taft: A Conservative's View of the Presidency* (Ithaca, N.Y.: Cornell University Press, 1973); Henry F. Pringle, *The Life and Times of William Howard Taft* (2 vols., New York: Farrar and Rhinehart, 1939); Kenneth Hechler, *Insurgency: Personalities and Politics of the Taft Era* (New York: Columbia University Press, 1940); Gould, *Reform and Regulation*, 87–120; Sullivan, *Our Times*, 4:349–540.

[52] David W. Detzer, "The Politics of the Payne-Aldrich Tariff of 1909" (Ph.D. diss., University of Connecticut, 1970), 1–45; John D. Buenker, *The Income Tax and the Progressive Era* (New York: Garland, 1985), 35–9; Judith Goldstein, *Ideas, Interests, and American Trade Policy* (Ithaca, N.Y., 1993), 115–18; Morton Keller, "Trade Policy in Historical Perspective," in Keller and Melnick, eds., *Taking Stock*, 15–25; Frank W. Taussig, *The Tariff History of the United States* (8th edn., New York: Putnam's, 1931), 361–408.

on the other hand, allowing access to cheaper imported raw materials for American industry.[53]

The Payne tariff bill, passed by the House in fulfillment of promises made by Taft and the Republican party during the 1908 election campaign, was subjected at the hands of Aldrich's Finance Committee to a process of amendment which blunted its, admittedly modest, revisionist thrust almost completely. The Payne bill was hardly satisfactory to any committed revisionist, but at least it offered measurable reductions on a wide range of commodities and allowed for the free admission of hides, coal and iron ore. The bill reported by the Finance Committee and eventually passed by the Senate raised 847 duties and left the overall level of protection comparable to that of the prevailing Dingley Act. How the insurgent Senators, outraged at what they regarded as a gross betrayal of party promises, struggled in vain through the long hot summer to shame the standpat leadership into concessions is a familiar story. So is the outcome. Although Taft secured significant reductions in conference, particularly in raw material duties, the resulting Payne-Aldrich bill was much more Aldrich than Payne.[54] Whether one concludes that in aggregate the Dingley duties were raised slightly, lowered slightly, or left pretty much as they were depends on the mode of calculation employed. What was beyond argument was that, if the Republican party had pledged itself to significant downward revision in 1908, it failed to fulfill that pledge in 1909.[55]

This failure troubled Aldrich and his lieutenants hardly at all. Many, indeed, denied that downward revision was what the party had pledged itself to. "I think that we shall bring out the Dingley bill with some improvements in detail and classification," predicted Lodge, now a member of the Finance Committee, at the beginning of the session. Adjustment of certain individual rates, rather than an overall downward movement, was what standpatters

---

[53] Paul Alan Wolman, *Most Favored Nation: The Republican Revisionists and United States Tariff Policy, 1897–1912* (Chapel Hill: University of North Carolina Press, 1992). See also David W. Detzer, "Businessmen, Reform and Tariff Revision: The Payne-Aldrich Tariff of 1909," *Historian* 35 (1973): 196–204.

[54] Stanley D. Solvick, "William Howard Taft and the Payne-Aldrich Tariff," *Mississippi Valley Historical Review* 50 (1963): 424–42; Anderson, *Taft*, 104–25; Pringle, *Taft*, 1:421–67; Hechler, *Insurgency*, 99–145; Bowers, *Beveridge and the Progressive Era*, 333–73; Stephenson, *Aldrich*, 346–61.

[55] For varying computations, see the table presented to the House by Champ Clark in *C.R.*, 61.1:4700–5 (who found no difference); Samuel W. McCall, "The Payne Tariff Law," *Atlantic Monthly* 104 (October 1909): 562–6 (decreases in duty outnumbered increases); "The New Tariff," *Outlook* 92 (14 August 1909): 872–6 ("substantial and far-reaching reductions"); Robert B. Porter, "The Payne Tariff Law: At Home and Abroad," *Outlook* 92 (21 August 1909): 926–31; Albert J. Beveridge to Walter Bradfute, 18 February 1910; "Imports and Revenues by Principal Articles and Classes, 1909 and 1910," 26 September 1910; to Robert A. Brown, 15 March 1910; to H. D. Tichenor, 10 August 1910, Beveridge MSS, LC; Taussig, *Tariff History*, 407–8 (no substantial difference).

maintained, somewhat disingenuously, was meant by revision. Naturally, they interpreted revision of the tariff, or at least "revision by the party of its friends," in relation to what they saw as the true philosophy of Republican protection, which, said Aldrich, "was to extend a proper protection to every American industry." Who was to determine what constituted a "proper protection"? Heyburn, for one, contended that "the producer should fix it." Rather than seek some kind of objective standard, high protectionists preferred to use as the starting point for tariff making the demands of the protected industries themselves. Any enterprise deserved protection against foreign competition. Even the prospect of nurturing American tea plantations and pineapple groves was not too fanciful for sizeable numbers of Republican Senators. Protection, they maintained, was "a broad national policy," a system which should cast its benefits equally among the various sections of the community. Therefore, those requesting protection for themselves should look kindly on the requests of others.[56]

Such assumptions determined the fashion in which tariff bills were put together. The task, as Aldrich saw it, was not one of applying abstract criteria to the level of duties, but the very different one of compiling a majority in favor of legislation by offering a satisfying level of protection to a sufficient number of industries. Rather than a readjustment based on principle, complained *The Outlook*, "the Senate is acting as if revision meant a mere accommodation between conflicting interests." Essentially it was an exercise in "log rolling." It involved, as David Detzer explains, welding together "through a series of interrelated deals, not only the members of the party itself, but also many of their Democratic colleagues." These negotiations were conducted behind closed doors in meetings of the Finance Committee and later in conference rather than in open Senate. According to Dolliver, Aldrich himself arranged the textile schedules, "every paragraph drawn by the parties in interest," and made up the rest of the bill by exchanging for votes "the privilege of naming the other rates." The outcome was that Aldrich, as Taft came to realize at the conference stage, was "loaded down by his relations to Senators who have particular predilections" and that "in dealing with the party and with local interests one must yield and be disappointed in certain things."[57]

---

[56] Lodge quoted in Mowry, *Theodore Roosevelt and the Progressive Movement*, 51; C.R., 61.1:1438, 1450 (Aldrich), 3092 (Heyburn), 2080 (Sutherland). See also Henry Cabot Lodge to William W. Wood, 14 May 1909, Lodge MSS, MHS; "The Senate and the People," *Outlook* 92 (26 June 1909): 432–3; Detzer, "Payne-Aldrich Tariff," 42–5, 132–7; Stephenson, *Aldrich*, 347–8. A shrewd analysis of Republican tariff orthodoxy is Charles W. Calhoun, "Political Economy in the Gilded Age: The Republican Party's Industrial Policy," *Journal of Policy History* 8 (1996): 291–309.

[57] "How Not to Revise the Tariff," *Outlook* 92 (3 July 1909): 541–2; "The Senate and the People"; Detzer, "Payne-Aldrich Tariff," 55–68, 108–9, 150–3; Jonathan P. Dolliver to Robert M. La Follette, 13 October 1909, La Follette MSS, LC; W. H. Taft to Albert J.

Such considerations obviously influenced the voting of Republican, and some Democratic, Senators. Even those who disapproved of certain schedules voted for them in order to retain provisions that mattered to their own constituents. Barely ten Senators, believed Beveridge, supported the increase in the cotton schedule; barely fifteen wished the woolen duties to remain at their current level. "Yet those men who were opposed to these things were coerced into voting for what they condemned by being threatened with refusals of perfectly proper duties on products in their own states." Even so senior a figure as Elkins admitted, "I voted for nearly everything prepared by the Senator from Rhode Island to get what I did for my state.... I could not get off the reservation during the consideration of the tariff. I was afraid to try."[58] This was why the Republican lines held so firm during the prolonged consideration of the bill. The great majority of Republican Senators supported the Finance Committee on nearly every vote. Thirty-three broke ranks no more than twice in 122 roll calls. On the other hand, ten Republicans voted against the leadership on at least fifty occasions. These ten individuals, all of whom went on to vote against the bill on final passage, were together responsible for 83 percent of all Republican defections.

Although the reimposition of the duty on hides, which had been removed by the House, divided Republicans along rather different lines, and although proposed duties on exotic products like tea and pineapples did not command majority support, divisions on other items followed an almost uniform pattern.[59] A small group of six to twelve insurgents, joined by at most one or two other Republicans, were to be found consistently voting against Aldrich and his carefully assembled majority. Table 6.3 shows the votes of insurgent Senators in selected roll calls. Their votes, suitably arranged, form a kind of truncated unidimensional scale. It is possible to discern a hard core of insurgents and a rather wispy penumbra of "near insurgents" who occasionally voted with them, but the table displays a clear pattern of bipolarity.

There was never any doubt in the insurgents' minds, though often in the minds of their standpat opponents, that they were true protectionists. While voting consistently against committee amendments to the House bill, they

Beveridge, 13 July 1909, Beveridge MSS, LC; Buenker, *Income Tax*, 83–5. Particularly recalcitrant in their opposition to Taft's demand for free raw materials were the Senators representing Western mining and livestock interests. Lewis L. Gould, "Western Range Senators and the Payne-Aldrich Tariff," *Pacific Northwest Quarterly* 64 (1973): 49–56.

[58] Albert J. Beveridge to Louis Howland, 16 April 1910, Beveridge MSS, LC; Elkins quoted in Ross, *Dolliver*, 279. Eugene Hale told Robert M. La Follette, "we have always felt that the Committee had the bill well in hand." Hale to La Follette, 12 June 1909, La Follette MSS, LC.

[59] A committee amendment increasing the duty on hides to 15 percent carried by 46–30, with thirteen Republicans in opposition, including Beveridge, Clapp, La Follette, Nelson, and nine Eastern conservatives. *C.R.*, 61.1:3667. For voting on pineapple and tea duties, see *C.R.*, 61.1:3706, 3934.

TABLE 6.3. *Voting of Selected Republican Senators on the Payne-Aldrich Tariff Bill*

	A	B	C	D	E	F	G	H	I	J	K	L	M	%	Score
La Follette (Wis.)	I	I	I	I	I	I	I	I	I	I	I	I	I	.87	8
Clapp (Minn.)	I	I	I	I	I	I	I		I	I	I	I	I	.83	8
Bristow (Kan.)	I	I	I	I	I	I	I	I	I	I	I	I	I	.81	8
Cummins (Iowa)	I	I	I	I	I	I	I	I	I	I	I	I	I	.77	8
Beveridge (Ind.)		I		I	I	I	I		I	I	I	I	I	.65	8
Dolliver (Iowa)	I	I	I	I	I	I	I	I	I	I	I	I	I	.61	8
Nelson (Minn.)	I	I	I	I	I	I	o	I	I	I	I	I	I	.58	7
Brown (Neb.)	I	I	I	I	I	I	I	I	I	I	I	I	o	.59	7
Burkett (Neb.)	I	I	I	I	I	I	I	o	I	I	I	I	o	.49	7
Crawford (S.D.)	I	I	I	I	I	I	I	I	I	I	o	o	o	.47	7
Gamble (S.D.)	I	I	I	I	I	I	I	I	o	o	o	o	o	.32	6
Curtis (Kan.)	o	I	I	I	I	o	o	o	o	o	o	o	o	.20	4
Johnson (N.D.)	I	I	I	I	o	o	o	o	o	o	o	o	o	.12	4
McCumber (N.D.)	I	I	I	I	o	o	o	o	o	o	o	o	o	.07	4
Root (N.Y.)	I	I	I	o	o	o	o	o	o	o	o	o	o	.04	3

Key: A 3717 Cut coal duty from 60 to 40 cents a ton (#5)
  B 3881 Decrease duties on metal goods
  C 3866 Cut duty on cash registers by half (#7)
  D 3680 Decrease duty on sawed lumber (#3)
  E 1995 Raise iron ore duty by 25 cents a ton (#2)
  F 2442 Strike out Dutch standard for grading sugar
  G 4225 Establish customs court (#8)
  H 3827 Raise petroleum duty to $\frac{1}{2}$ cent per gallon (#6)
  I 2865 Increase duty on varieties of cotton cloth
  J 4316 Passage
  K 3036 Decrease duties on woolen and worsted cloths
  L 3124 Decrease duties on wool
  M 4949 Conference report
  % Percentage of all tariff roll calls on which Senators voted for revision
  Score Score on a cumulative scale derived from the roll calls marked in italics.
Note: Six of the above roll calls are included in the sample listed in Table 6.5. Their numbers are given in brackets.

were nearly as firm in dismissing Democratic amendments. Nor were they timid in defending the products of their own states: the tinplate of Indiana, the sugar beet of Iowa, the zinc and barley of Wisconsin. "I have always favored adequate protection to the American farmer," explained La Follette, "and in the case of this schedule [barley] I believe that the thirty cent rate measures the protection which should be given."[60]

The Aldrich bill, they believed, went beyond a reasonable level of protection. The rates on many articles of common use were much too high, to the detriment of the consumer, the "American housewife," for whom they presumed to speak. Several insurgents subscribed to the belief that excessive tariff protection created an artificial hothouse atmosphere which encouraged the growth of monopolies and that reduction was, as La Follette put it, "one way of reaching trusts." Beveridge, however, had no faith in the trustbusting capacities of tariff reform, while Dolliver feared that the lowering of duties might actually strengthen the competitive position of the trusts by driving smaller firms out of business.[61]

Complaints against extortionate duties frequently took on the tone of a moral jeremiad. In the shape of the Aldrich bill, proclaimed Joseph L. Bristow, the protective system was "being contorted into a synonym for graft and plunder."[62] They exposed to public censure the numerous "jokers" in the bill, the instances where changes in classification or shifts from ad valorem to specific duties had the effect of raising duties, even where the average rates were unchanged or even lowered. Thus cotton cloth was judged to be "colored" even if it only had one colored thread, and therefore liable to a higher rate of duty; an obsolete color test to grade sugar placed unnecessary obstacles in the path of imported refined sugar; the duty on low-grade electric light carbons was reduced to 35 cents a hundred feet, a substantial "downward revision," but, since these were never imported, the effective duty was the 65 cents on high-grade carbons, which was 45 percent higher than the Dingley level – "a typical Aldrich tariff joker," explained La Follette. Such trickery, said Dolliver, constituted "a petty swindle on the American people."[63]

The level of duties that Republican revisionists approved of, although in this they did no more than follow the Republican platform, was one which, while still offering protection, did not raise tariff barriers beyond what was necessary to equalize the costs of foreign and domestic producers. Though an ancient idea, cost equalization was given added credibility by the development of more sophisticated methods of cost accounting. "All tariff duties," said La Follette, "should be measured by the difference in the cost of production here and abroad. I am in favor of maintaining a sufficient duty to keep American labor employed at American wages." Albert J. Cummins

[61] Hechler, *Insurgency*, 119; Detzer, "Payne-Aldrich Tariff," 142–5. See also Buenker, *Income Tax*, 85–7.

[62] Albert J. Beveridge to Louis Howland, 16 April 1910; to W. F. Adams, 3 May 1910; to Gifford Pinchot, 24 March 1910; to Walter Bradfute, 18 February 1910, Beveridge MSS, LC; Hechler, *Insurgency*, 100.

[63] A. B. Sageser, *Joseph L. Bristow: Kansas Progressive* (Lawrence: University Press of Kansas, 1968), 93; Albert J. Beveridge to Walter Bradfute, 18 February 1910, Beveridge MSS, LC; Robert M. La Follette to Hugh T. Halbert, 28 December 1909, La Follette MSS, LC; Ross, *Dolliver*, 251–2; Detzer, "Payne-Aldrich Tariff," 156–9; Hechler, *Insurgency*, 117–18, 143–4.

agreed that the object of protection was to maintain "a reasonable American level of prices." The duty on each product, therefore, should "measure the difference between the cost of production at home and abroad together with a fair manufacturer's profit."[64] But this was still a problematic formula. Costs varied from firm to firm and from year to year. Taking the costs of production of the most efficient firm might doom smaller and weaker units to extinction, reducing rather than extending the area of competition. Taking the cost differential in any one year would inevitably lead to rates that were either excessive or inadequate under altered trading conditions. It was for such reasons that high protectionists preferred to build in a substantial margin of error.[65]

The revisionists' adherence to the cost equalization formula led them logically to support the principle of a tariff commission. According to Cummins, "in order intelligently to apply the standard of the Republican platform we needed more information than individual members of congress could get through their own study ... we never will have a satisfactory revision of the tariff" without "a tariff commission ... that will carefully collect the information necessary to enable congress to know the difference between the cost of production here and elsewhere." A body of experts given wide investigative powers would determine exactly the difference between domestic and foreign costs, enabling Congress intelligently to set rates which provided adequate protection without relying on the interested parties themselves for information. Such a system would contribute to a more rational and "scientific" process of decision making based on accurate knowledge of the facts and drawing upon technical expertise in what most found a bewilderingly complex subject. It offered a way of finessing potential conflicts between different sections, industries, and types of firm within the revisionist movement itself. Finally it would compensate for the revisionists' weakness in the congressional arena by entrusting at least some tariff-making powers to a separate executive agency. The progressives, for all these reasons, were driven to support radical changes in the institutional arrangements for tariff making.[66]

Beveridge had for some years been involved in a movement to establish a tariff commission which incorporated the National Association of Manufacturers and several chambers of commerce and producers' associations.[67]

[64] Robert M. La Follette to Charles Westphal, 30 March 1909, La Follette MSS, LC; Albert J. Beveridge to Joseph L. Bristow, 3 September 1910; Albert B. Cummins, interview with Henry B. Needham, enclosed in Cummins to Beveridge, 6 October 1909, Beveridge MSS, LC.

[65] Detzer, "Payne-Aldrich Tariff," 145–9; Taussig, *Tariff History*, 363–8.

[66] Albert B. Cummins, interview with Henry B. Needham, enclosed in Cummins to Beveridge, 6 October 1909, Beveridge MSS, LC; *Outlook* 92 (1 May 1909) 4–5 and (3 July 1909): 541–2; Wolman, *Most Favored Nation*, 77–111; Detzer, "Payne-Aldrich Tariff," 159–66.

[67] Braeman, *Beveridge*, 122–33.

What emerged was a proposal for a fact-finding commission which Beveridge sought to attach to the tariff bill. At a conference in Aldrich's office, Beveridge and NAM president James W. Van Cleave reluctantly agreed to a compromise amendment which dropped the *sub poena* clause in his original proposal. This was then accepted by the Finance Committee and in due course by the Senate. Unsatisfactory as such concessions were to Beveridge, the work of the conference committee was even more so. Cannon and Payne's bitter opposition to a tariff commission led to its being stripped of the responsibility to secure "information useful to Congress in tariff legislation" and of the authority "to make thorough investigations and examinations into the production, commerce and trade of the United States and foreign countries," leaving only the duty of advising the President on the administration of the maximum-minimum section of the bill. The result was "little more than a scrawny mutation" of the original idea.[68]

High protectionists naturally abominated the idea of a tariff commission. An effective commission would greatly hamper their ability to deliver protection to local interests. At another level the system of log rolling, the interchange of tariff duties and other localized advantages, served as a form of congressional currency, the accumulation of which constituted power on the Hill, power which its holders were unwilling to relinquish. Tariff protection was a way of attaching powerful economic interests to the Republican party. It was, noted E. E. Schattschneider, "a dubious economic policy turned into a great political success."[69] It was opposition to this system, above all else, that bound the insurgents together. The tariff bill, said Dolliver, was not a piece of legislation so much as "a rank interchange of political larcenies." In that sense, the tariff was more potently a political than it was an economic issue. Revisionist already in response to constituency pressure, the insurgents were reinforced in their opposition to the leadership by their dissatisfaction with its methods.[70] According to Beveridge, they faced "ostracism, contempt, sneers, insults and every form of abuse." This was because their difference with the Old Guard was a difference of principle rather than a dispute over details of tariff schedules. Their criticism was leveled not so much at specific levels of duty as at some of the basic understandings that constituted the spider's web of congressional decision making.[71]

---

[68] Albert J. Beveridge to W. H. Taft, 22 July 1909; to George H. Lorimer, 13 September 1909; to Curtis Guild, 18 November 1909; to Frank A. Munsey, 24 April 1909, Beveridge MSS, LC; Detzer, "Payne-Aldrich Tariff," 166–9; Braeman, *Beveridge,* 158–60, 163–4; Bowers, *Beveridge and the Progressive Era,* 352–4, 362–3.

[69] Quoted in Buenker, *Income Tax,* 83.

[70] Jonathan P. Dolliver to Robert M. La Follette, 13 October 1909, La Follette MSS, LC; Albert J. Beveridge to Louis Howland, 16 April 1910, Beveridge MSS, LC.

[71] Albert J. Beveridge to Frank Schaffer, 21 May 1909, Beveridge MSS, LC; Detzer, "Payne-Aldrich Tariff," 100–7; La Follette, *La Follette,* 1:274–5; Ross, *Dolliver,* 249.

Patterns of Insurgency

In examining the relationship between voting on the tariff and other issues the same procedure was followed as before. A sample of twenty-five roll calls was selected by first isolating those in which eleven or more Republicans voted against the majority of their party, then removing procedural votes, votes of little apparent substantive interest, and several duplicates, especially on the tariff and railroad bills. This time cluster analysis of the Q-matrix turns up one enormous group of twenty items and five outriders whose closeness to each other is no greater than to the central cluster.

Two scales can be derived from the large cluster. One consists of eight roll calls: five on amendments to the Mann-Elkins railroad bill (#13, #14, #15, #17, and #18); one on a proposed investigation by the Tariff Board of the iron and steel, wool and cotton schedules (#24); and two relating to political reform (#23 and #25). The other scale, which was incorporated in Table 6.3, includes votes on six amendments to the tariff bill (#2, #3, #5, #6, #7, and #8) which stand proxy for a very large number, indeed a clear majority, of tariff votes in the Senate. The six remaining roll calls were taken on a proposal to reduce salaries in the 1909 Urgent Deficiency bill (#9), the postal savings bill (#10), an investigation into the capitalization of the Washington Gas-Light Company (#11), a long and short haul amendment to the railroad bill (#16), the ship subsidy bill (#21), and a procedural motion connected with the direct election resolution (#22). So tightly knit is the cluster that, even more than in the earlier analysis, it can be regarded as composing a single issue dimension and individuals awarded scores on the basis of their aggregate performance. These are closely correlated with the railroad scale scores ($r = .97$). The votes of Republican Senators on the items in the larger scale are presented in Table 6.4. The scale meets the established criteria of unidimensionality (the coefficient of reproducibility is .97), but the paucity of intermediate values, an expression of the deep factionalism that afflicted the party, results in a far from satisfactory scale. Also presented are the proportions of all cluster items on which individuals responded positively.

The issues raised by the Mann-Elkins bill closely resemble those raised by the Hepburn bill four years earlier, and so do Republican voting patterns. A group of from eight to fourteen insurgents opposed the rump of the Republican party in twenty-six out of thirty-five roll calls on amendments to the bill. Five of these are included in the scale: on a Democratic amendment regulating the issue of federal court injunctions against the operation of state laws (#15); a proposal by La Follette to limit further the hours of work of railroad employees (#17); the same Senator's valuation amendment (#18); Dolliver's substitute for the section relating to the capitalization and consolidation of railroad companies (#13); and the amendment bringing telephone and telegraph companies under ICC control (#14). These five roll calls reflect the dominant pattern of Republican voting on the Mann-Elkins bill (see Table 3.5).

TABLE 6.4. *Voting of Republican Senators on Scale Items, 61st Congress*

	Roll Call No.								Scores	
	23	14	15	13	17	18	25	24	Scale	Cluster
Beveridge (Ind.)	1	1	1	1	1	1	1	1	8	1.00
Borah (Ida.)	1	1	1	1	1	1	1	1	8	.80
Bristow (Kan.)	1	1	1	1	1	1	1	1	8	1.00
Clapp (Minn.)	1	1	1	1	1	1	1	1	8	1.00
Dolliver (Iowa)		1	1	1		1	1		8	1.00
La Follette (Wis.)	1	1	1	1	1	1	1		8	1.00
Cummins (Iowa)	1	1	1	1			1	1	8	1.00
Bourne (Ore.)	1	1	1	1	1	1		1	8	.69
Brown (Neb.)	1	1	1	1	1	1	1	1	9	1.00
Burkett (Neb.)	1	1	1	1	1	1	1		7	1.00
Dixon (Mont.)	1	1	1	1	1	1	1		7	.67
Jones (Wash.)	1	1	1	1	0	1	1	1	7[a]	.70
Crawford (S.D.)	1	1	1	1	1	1		0	6	.95
Gamble (S.D.)	1	1	1	1	1	1	0	0	6	.80
Burton (Ohio)	1	1	1	1	0	0	0	0	4	.50
Smith (Mich.)	1		1	0			0	0	3	.50
Curtis (Kan.)	1	1	0	0		0		1	3[a]	.41
Carter (Mont.)	1	1	0	0	0	0	0	0	2	.28
Clark (Wyo.)	1	1	0	0	0	0	0	0	2	.26
Cullom (Ill.)	1	1	0	0	0	0	0	0	2	.15
Perkins (Cal.)	1	1	0	0	0	0	0	0	2	.11
Nixon (Nev.)	1	0		0		0	1	0	2[a]	.19
Piles (Wash.)	1	0	0	1	0	0	0	0	2[a]	.26
Warner (Mo.)	1	0	0	1	0	0	0	0	2[a]	.21
Burrows (Mich.)	0	1	0	0		0	0	0	1[a]	.11
Bradley (Ky.)	1	0	0	0			0	0	1	.13
Briggs (N.J.)	1	0	0	0		0	0	0	1	.06
Frye (Me.)	1	0	0	0	0	0	0	0	1	.06
Guggenheim (Col.)	1	0	0	0	0	0	0	0	1	.11
Nelson (Minn.)	1	0	0		0	0	0	0	1	.47
Stephenson (Wis.)	1	0	0	0	0	0	0	0	1	.18
Sutherland (Utah)	1	0	0	0	0	0	0		1	.26
Dupont (Del.)	1		0	0		0	0		1	.19
18 Republicans	0	0	0	0	0	0	0	0	0	

Key: 23. Direct election of Senators: joint resolution submitting amendment to states (3639)
14. Railroad bill: include telephone and telegraph companies (6975)
15. Do.: prohibit issue of interlocutory injunctions by Commerce Court (7275)
13. Do.: regulate issue and ownership of stock in railroad companies (6972)
17. Do.: regulate hours of work of railroad employees (7355)
18. Do.: physical valuation of railroad property (7372)
25. Admission of Arizona and New Mexico (4319)
24. Direct Tariff Board to report on iron, steel, wool and cotton schedules (4029)
a Cases containing error responses.

Notes: Aldrich (R.I.), Lorimer (Ill.), McCumber (N.D.), Penrose (Pa.), Richardson (Del.), and Root (N.Y.) recorded an insufficient number of votes to be classified.

The other major reform measure considered by the second session of the Sixty-first Congress was the creation of a system of postal savings banks. Such a system, it was hoped, would make it easier for the less well off to save small amounts of money by depositing them at the local post office. Though opposed by banking interests and a few conservative Senators, this scheme had widespread popular and congressional support. The question at issue was not whether such depositories should be established but what should be done with the deposits. Many Senators, especially from the South and West, expected and demanded that they be placed in local banks for safekeeping, "at the service of the neighborhood where they belong," rather than being siphoned off to the major financial centers. The bill should not, insisted William E. Borah, "be used as a means by which the money collected at the different localities should be transported to foreign parts or foreign places." Taft, however, along with conservative Senators like Elihu Root, feared that small local banks might not provide secure repositories for the funds. Therefore Root demanded that the money be invested in government bonds, and when this fell on stony ground he gave his support to an amendment offered by Smoot permitting such action "when, in the judgment of the President, a war or other exigency involving the credit of the Government" required it. The vote included here (#10) was taken on an amendment which confined the emergencies warranting the withdrawal of deposits from the locality of origin under the Smoot amendment to outbreaks of war. Intense Administration pressure caused the bill to be modified in the House to give the president a free hand to purchase bonds and won over enough of what Bristow called "the wavering fellows" to force the House version through the Senate.[72]

Thirteen Republicans voted against the ocean mail subsidy bill, for many years a key component of the Republican party's program of subsidies and tariff protection.[73] The bill before the Sixty-first Congress sought to extend the subsidized mail service to South America, as a stimulus to commerce and as "a very important step . . . toward the rehabilitation of the American merchant marine." Shipping interests had, said Lodge, been treated unfairly by

[72] C.R., 61.2:2666–71, 2673–4, 2676–80, 2708–10, 2712–18, 2725–8, 8268–73; Albert J. Beveridge to Gifford Pinchot, 24 March 1910, Beveridge MSS, LC; Joseph L. Bristow to William Allen White, 23 June 1910, White MSS, LC; *Outlook* 94 (19 March 1910): 594; Sanders, *Roots of Reform*, 232–6; Ralph M. Sayre, "Albert Baird Cummins and the Progressive Movement in Iowa" (Ph.D. diss., Columbia University, 1958), 358–9, 378; Hechler, *Insurgency*, 158–62; Pringle, *Taft*, 1:516–20; Philip C. Jessup, *Elihu Root* (2 vols., New York: Dodd, Mead, 1937), 2:233–5; Braeman, *Beveridge*, 175–7.

[73] For the background, see William P. Frye, "The Meaning and Necessity of Ship Subsidy," *Independent* 60 (14 June 1906): 1459–63; William E. Humphrey, "The Pending Shipping Legislation," *North American Review* 182 (March 1906): 446–55; Marvin L. Bishop, "American Ships and the Way to Get Them," *Atlantic Monthly* 104 (October 1909): 433–41; "Ship Subsidies," *Outlook* 88 (11 April 1908): 815–16; Alfred Spring, "The Revival of Our Shipping," *Outlook* 94 (15 January 1910): 124–30.

the protective system. They were forced to compete on unequal terms with foreign vessels manned by cheap labor and fuelled by government subsidies. Cummins contended that it was against any "sound principle of government" to take the people's money and "devote it to private purposes... unless it is sure that all the people of the United States will share alike... in the advantages that might accrue from the subsidized business." This subsidy, however, would not put a single American flag on the high seas; it would merely constitute a donation to favored individuals.[74]

As in the previous Congresses, support for railroad regulation and tariff revision went hand in hand with a desire for political reform. The movement for direct election of Senators came closer to fruition when the Senate, for the first time, seriously debated a resolution proposing an amendment to the Constitution. With state primary laws already influencing the process of senatorial election – nearly half of the Senators elected in 1910 had been, in effect, chosen by popular vote – and with the Democratic party firmly committed to reform, its adoption by the Senate was now a matter of time. Progressive Republicans argued in favor of the principle of direct democracy and spoke of the need to remove the process of senatorial election from state legislatures which were often under the control of party bosses. "What judgment is so swift, so sure and so remorseless as the judgment of the American people?" asked Borah. There was no reason to question the "intelligence and patriotism" of the American people or to deny them a "more direct responsibility" for the conduct of government.[75]

On the other hand, conservatives like Root and Lodge pronounced themselves satisfied with existing practice. Root warned of the dangers of discarding the system of representative government devised by the Founding Fathers in favor of direct democracy. The Senate was designed to be a "deliberative body." It was constituted as it was specifically to provide a check on the passions of the moment and compel a more careful consideration of the consequences of proposed legislation – "opportunity for reflection," said Lodge, "a space for second thought." The upper chamber accommodated statesmen who were not compelled to cater to passing public whims but could offer their views candidly and without fear of the political consequences.[76] Thirty-two Republicans eventually voted for the joint resolution, including some like McCumber and Sutherland who made it fairly obvious that they were moved more by constituency pressure than personal conviction. Those who did feel so cross-pressured gladly supported

---

[74] C.R., 61.3:1824–5.
[75] C.R., 61.3:2178–80, 2251–9, 2494–5, 3307, 3639. See also Hoebeke, *Road to Mass Democracy*, 150 and 161–81; Claudius O. Johnson, *Borah of Idaho* (New York: Longmans, Green, 1936), 124–9; Marian C. McKenna, *Borah* (Ann Arbor: University of Michigan Press, 1961), 109–11.
[76] C.R., 61.3:1976–9 (Lodge), 2243–4 (Root).

a proviso introduced by Sutherland which, by imposing federal control of the time, place and manner of holding elections, drove away enough Democratic votes to prevent the resolution from obtaining the requisite two-thirds majority.[77]

The Insurgent Profile

The Senate insurgents, then, were a clearly defined group who worked together in a deliberate and organized fashion. By the end of the period under review moves were afoot to crystallize their inchoate organizational identity into what eventually, in January 1911, became the National Progressive Republican League. Along with national figures like Hiram Johnson, Gifford Pinchot, Louis Brandeis, Ray Stannard Baker, William Allen White, and a number of Representatives, Senators Beveridge, Borah, Bourne, Bristow, Brown, Clapp, Cummins, and La Follette were members of the League.[78] They, with Dolliver, who died in October 1910, constituted the hard core of the insurgent group. Borah and Bourne had lined up with the regulars on the tariff, but, in the case of Borah at least, this was compelled by the need to ensure protection for hides and wool, a matter of priority to his Idaho constituents. The insurgents were joined on several occasions by Burkett, Crawford, Dixon, Gamble, Jones, and McCumber, and more irregularly by Nelson, Burton, Smith, and Curtis.[79]

The insurgents differed markedly from other Republicans. The sectional bias evident in previous Congresses was still more pronounced. Senators from the Midwest were insurgent on average in 77 percent of the twenty roll calls, those from the Pacific Coast in 35 percent, those from the Old Northwest in 28 percent, those from the Mountain West in 27 percent, but those from the Mid-Atlantic states and New England ("Darkest America," as Lincoln Steffens called it) in 9 percent and 4 percent, respectively.[80] All but a handful of Midwestern Senators scored highly; even the region's conservatives, men like Nelson and Curtis, outscored any Republican from east of the Appalachians.

Insurgents were generally younger: the fifteen top scorers had an average age in 1909 of just over fifty, eleven years less than that of the remaining Senate Republicans. They were relative newcomers to the Senate,

---

[77] *C.R.*, 61.3:3307.

[78] On the National Progressive Republican League, see Robert J. Collier to Robert M. La Follette, 1 July 1910; Rudolph Spreckels to La Follette, 27 December 1910, La Follette to Alfred T. Rogers, 14 December 1910, La Follette MSS, LC; to Irvine R. Lenroot, 29 December 1910, Lenroot MSS, LC; to William Allen White, 28 December 1910, White MSS, LC; Mowry, *Theodore Roosevelt and the Progressive Movement*, 172–4.

[79] On Borah and the tariff, see Johnson, *Borah of Idaho*, 113–20; Gould "Western Range Senators and the Payne-Aldrich Tariff."

[80] Lincoln Steffens to Robert M. La Follette, 8 September 1909, La Follette MSS, LC.

averaging 3.60 years of service, as against the 8.95 years accumulated by the noninsurgents. Insurgency was to some degree a generational phenomenon. In a chamber where great wealth was commonplace, few of the insurgents possessed notable fortunes. A list of "Senate millionaires" compiled by one of La Follette's aides found room for only one of their number, Jonathan Bourne, while Crawford, McCumber, and Dixon, none of them consistent insurgents, were described as "fairly wealthy." On the other hand, twenty-seven of the forty-two noninsurgents were listed as "millionaires" and four as "fairly wealthy."[81] Of course, this was largely a function of the predominantly agricultural nature of the region that the insurgents had the honor to represent. Most were small-town lawyers, editors and businessmen, many of them raised on the farm and educated at local state universities. But many products of the same environment had managed to exploit their business acumen or political connections to make substantial fortunes in such fields as railroading, mining, lumbering and real estate. The Gilded Age style of distributive politics and the close connections between political influence and local "boosterism" had afforded many lucrative opportunities for politicians in the developing states west of the Missouri. The insurgents, however, chose to develop their careers in quite different directions and set themselves quite different standards of achievement.[82]

Last but not least, the states which sent insurgents to the Senate were almost invariably states where reform movements had overthrown the Old Guard machines that had controlled the Republican party for decades. In Wisconsin, Iowa, Kansas, Nebraska, Minnesota, South Dakota, and Oregon progressive elements had taken command of the party, and this was naturally reflected in their senatorial representation. Most of these states had already adopted direct primary laws, including preferential primaries which gave the electorate the opportunity to indicate which senatorial candidate they favored, an indication which the state legislature was, in varying degrees, obliged to act upon. By 1908 the primary was already in force in Wisconsin, Oregon, Iowa, Nebraska, Missouri, South Dakota, Washington, and Kansas, states represented by ten out of the fourteen leading insurgents in the Sixty-first Congress. By 1910 they were joined by California, Illinois, Michigan, North Dakota, several of the Rocky Mountain states, and New Hampshire.[83] The Payne-Aldrich tariff, by all accounts, met with almost unanimous hostility throughout the region. Clapp, according to Cummins, was "cocky as ever in the knowledge that nine out of ten of his constituents

---

[81] In A. O. Barton to Paul L. Benedict, 4 March 1910, Robert M. La Follette MSS, LC.

[82] Cf. Hechler, *Insurgency*, 83–91; Holt, *Congressional Insurgents*, 3–5; John A. Braeman, "Seven Progressives," *Business History Review* 35 (1961): 588–92.

[83] These primary laws varied a great deal in form. See *C.R.*, 61.2:7113–20; S. N. D. North, ed., *The American Year Book* (New York: T. Nelson & Sons, 1911), 140–1; Charles E. Merriam and Louise Overacker, *Primary Elections* (Chicago: University of Chicago Press, 1928).

are with him" in his tariff vote.[84] Beveridge was less fortunate. "It requires no particular courage for such men as Dolliver and myself to vote against the bill, but we all realize that in your case nothing but the superb quality of your mind and heart led to the result that you announced in your vote," Cummins told him. The complex social and demographic structure and political history of Indiana provided less fertile ground for insurgency. It was, Beveridge explained, "both progressive and conservative...the typical American commonwealth."[85]

The trouble was that progressive impulses in states like Indiana tended to gravitate toward the Democratic party. Indiana was a genuine two-party state, whereas many Midwestern states were virtual Republican satrapies. But then so were Eastern states like Maine and New Hampshire. It is sometimes suggested that insurgency thrived in localities where the Grand Old Party was so dominant that intraparty factionalism provided the principal focus for political dissent. That, however, is to underestimate the strength of the Bryan Democracy throughout the region. The insurgents did not, in fact, represent states in which the Republican party was unusually strong. On the basis of the Republican presidential vote in 1908, the party was, if anything, marginally weaker in insurgent states, and, equally significantly, its share of the vote had declined more markedly since 1904 than in the states represented by conservatives. Insurgents were responding to a sense of impending danger rather than exploiting the advantages of political hegemony. In the Western states Republican leaders were willing and able to provide a viable progressive alternative; in the East they were not. "The Democratic victories in the East," observed Louis Brandeis in November 1910, "are the result mainly of the absence of Republican Insurgency."[86]

Insurgency may be viewed, at least in part, as a sectional movement whose purpose was to redress the balance of economic advantage between East and West. It expressed, said Carl Chrislock, a strong sense of "regional injury" which overrode ethnic and class divisions.[87] Far from traditional Republican policies spreading their benefits indiscriminately across the nation, they

[84] Albert B. Cummins to Albert J. Beveridge, 13 September 1909, LC; La Forte, *Leaders of Reform*, 153; Holt, *Congressional Insurgents*, 5–8, 40–3; Detzer, "Payne Aldrich Tariff," 223–6.

[85] Albert B. Cummins to Albert J. Beveridge, 17 August 1909; Beveridge to J. C. O'Laughlin, 28 October 1909, Beveridge MSS, LC.

[86] Louis Brandeis to Robert M. La Follette, 9 November 1910; George L. Record to La Follette, 19 September 1910, La Follette MSS, LC. The fifteen insurgents represented states in which the average Republican presidential vote in 1908 was 54.7 percent; the figure for states represented by non-insurgents was 56.4 percent. The decline in the Republican share of the vote between 1904 and 1908 was 11.2 percent in the insurgent states, but only 4.9 percent in non-insurgent territory.

[87] Carl H. Chrislock, *The Progressive Era in Minnesota, 1897–1919* (St. Paul: University of Minnesota Press, 1971), 35–6. Cf. Sally F. Griffith, *Home Town News: William Allen White and the Emporia Gazette* (New York: Oxford University Press, 1989), 110–11, 132–5.

appeared to operate disproportionately to the advantage of the urban and industrial regions east of the Mississippi and north of the Ohio. Tariff revision, opposition to ship subsidies, railroad regulation, a desire for a graduated tax on incomes which would fall more evenly upon the nation's wealth, the demand for local retention of postal savings deposits – all of these addressed particularly the problems and interests of the Midwest and West. Ray Baker suggested that many in the East might tender their support also were it not for the feeling "that the insurgent movement thus far is largely an agricultural movement . . . in short many thoughtful eastern people look upon the movement as sectional in character."[88]

The political scientist Elizabeth Sanders sees a "conflict between core and periphery" as fundamental to the regulatory politics of the Progressive Era. It represented an "agrarian" effort to restrain the predatory actions of the powerful corporations of the industrial Northeast and correct "the regional maldistribution of wealth they entailed." The evidence here supports that hypothesis, at least in part. The insurgents mostly represented the lightly industrialized regions of the trans-Mississippi West; none at all had their base in the "Northeast-Great Lakes manufacturing belt." However, the periphery harbored far too many conservative Republicans for the core-periphery distinction to provide more than a crude approximation of the roots of Republican factionalism in the Progressive Era. Applying Sanders's classification of "trading areas" to the ranking of Senators in Table 6.4, we find that, while all of the twenty-three Republican Senators from the core region had cluster scores of .50 or less, so did thirteen of the twenty-three Senators from the periphery and seven out of twelve from the intermediate, or "diverse," region. In particular, the economic interests of many of the states of the Mountain West, with their extractive economies inextricably connected to the industrial core and dominated by large corporations, though assigned to the periphery by Sanders's criteria, diverged fundamentally from those of the Plains, and so did the political behavior of their congressional representatives. At the same time, many Republicans throughout the trans-Mississippi West, especially of the older generation, retained their allegiance to the party's traditional distributive policies, and in particular to tariff protection.[89]

In fact, Republican insurgency flourished best in states that had moved beyond frontier conditions and were beginning to exhibit more variegated patterns of economic development, that is in the West North Central region and on the Pacific littoral. It grew out of a popular reaction to the Republican regimes established in the late nineteenth century, especially after the 1890s realignment, which for a while had weakened the effectiveness of the

---

[88] Ray S. Baker to Robert M. La Follette, 29 November 1910, La Follette MSS, LC.

[89] Elizabeth Sanders, "Industrial Concentration, Sectional Competition, and Antitrust Policies in America, 1880–1914," *Studies in American Political Development* 1 (1986): 143, 150 and passim. For the delineation of core and periphery, see Sanders, *Roots of Reform*, 13–29.

Democratic opposition. Republican party organizations, with their seemingly incestuous relations with major corporate, and particularly railroad, interests, forged at an earlier stage of development, appeared unresponsive to the claims of a growing range of aggrieved interest groups which clamored for changes in policy, both at a local and a national level: a more equitable distribution of the burden of taxation, adjustments in tariff rates, regulation of railroads, controls on out-of-state insurance companies, labor legislation, and much else besides. Many of the groups which felt excluded from access to effective power, ranging from dairymen in Wisconsin to citrus-fruit growers in Southern California, provided the core constituencies for progressive governors like Cummins in Iowa, La Follette in Wisconsin, and Hiram Johnson in California, and likewise for insurgent Republicans in Congress. Insurgency therefore grew out of a complex interplay between economic interest and political organization whose outcome varied markedly from one state to another.[90]

Insurgency was not just a policy agenda but also a political discourse. The policies favored by the insurgents were not just conducive to their constituents' economic welfare; they were a challenge to the "special interests" which exploited government power to their own advantage. An editorial in the *Outlook* suggested that the insurgents were more than just a squabbling party faction. They represented a new political idea: "It is that the public interest is something else besides the sum total of all private interests." This was the principle that lay behind the controversies over the tariff, railroad regulation, conservation and many other issues of the day.[91]

Cummins accused the regular Republican leadership "of giving aid and comfort to every transportation company, every monopoly, every combination that Congress ever attempted to regulate or correct" and of being "enemies of every measure that has been projected to relieve the people from the tyranny, oppression, and injustice of the modern money-lover and money-getter."[92] Such rhetoric ran through progressive speeches on a variety of topics. Bristow, as preface to a detailed analysis of tariff and railroad legislation, stated the "fundamental question" to be: "shall this government be administered in the interest of the average man, or for the benefit of the special privileges"? For half a century before the Civil War special interests in the shape of the "slave power" had controlled national politics in order to fight off any threat to their institution.

[90] Martin Shefter, "Regional Receptivity to Reform: The Legacy of the Progressive Era." *Political Science Quarterly* 98 (1983): 359–83; Elisabeth S. Clemens, *The People's Lobby: Organizational Innovation and the Rise of Interest-Group Politics in the United States, 1890–1925* (Chicago: University of Chicago Press, 1998), 73–81; Griffith, *Home Town News*, 132–5.

[91] Edward H. Abbott, "The New Era in Congress," *Outlook* 94 (5 February 1910): 290.

[92] Albert B. Cummins, transcript of interview with Henry B. Needham, 6 October 1909, Beveridge MSS, Library of Congress. Cf. Holt, *Congressional Insurgents*, 11–12.

The conflict in American politics today is based upon the same fundamental principles as was that which preceded the civil war. The corporate interests of the country have dominated the affairs of the nation as completely as did the slave interest in the days of its greatest strength.... Just as every effort made for the restriction of slavery was resisted by the slave power, so every effort made to protect the people from the injustice of corporate greed is resisted by the great corporations of this time. The representatives of the slave power had seats in the halls of congress and contended for the perpetuity of slavery because of their financial interest in the institution. And now the gigantic monopolies of this day have representatives in the halls of congress whose sole purpose is to promote their interests and keep open the opportunity which they now have to plunder the American public.[93]

The central struggle was categorized not so much as one between warring sectional interests but as an ancient, almost Manichean, struggle between the "people" and the "interests," the insurgents thereby locating themselves in a longstanding tradition of republican virtue. To La Follette the issues of progressive reform involved one "great fundamental principle":

Our great fight is for democracy, always for a democratic form of government, always to restore control to the people.... Since republics were established, concentrated wealth and power have encroached upon the rights of the majority. The struggle in which the American people are engaged in their efforts to redeem government is as old as the history of democracy. With changing economic and social conditions, the form of the contest will vary, but in the final analysis it is always plutocracy against democracy. Today in this country it is corporate power and special interests dominating and suppressing the principle of popular government.

Hence the most urgent political task was to "break the hold of special privilege on legislation, and bring government back to the people."[94]

The insurgents invested their principles with a strong sense of moral purpose. "I feel that my life has been enriched and strengthened by the new light in which I have had a glimpse of your motives and purposes in American public life," Dolliver told La Follette in the wake of the tariff fight. His attachment to the insurgent faction he described as a conversion experience; as a good Methodist, he felt compelled to testify to the errors of his past. Although he had supported regulatory reforms ever since his election to the Senate in 1900, he now perceived himself as enlisted in a crusade against privilege and corruption, advancing similar policies but in a different spirit.[95]

---

[93] Bristow, "Speech at Winfield Chautauqua." See also Sageser, *Bristow*, 108–10.

[94] Notes on speech, February 1906, Robert M. La Follette Papers, SHSW, Microfilm Edition, Reel 90; La Follette to Thomas E. Watson, 7 May 1910, La Follette MSS, LC.

[95] Jonathan P. Dolliver to Robert M. La Follette, 13 October 1909, La Follette MSS, Library of Congress; Dolliver to Albert J. Beveridge, 14 September 1909, Beveridge MSS, LC. For differing interpretations of what produced Dolliver's "conversion" see Ross, *Dolliver*, 241–5, 265–6; Sayre, "Cummins," 326–30; La Follette, *Autobiography*, 184–6; Bowers, *Beveridge and the Progressive Era*, 329–30; Stephenson, *Aldrich*, 344–6; Sullivan, *Our Times*, 4:357–61.

This moralistic stance was dismissed by the regulars as mere posturing. Boies Penrose accused La Follette of neglecting his committee duties in order to make grand speeches in a manner more appropriate to a "vendor of patent medicine" than a United States Senator. La Follette, said Lodge, was "a plain crook, a mere adventurer," Dolliver a wrecker, Beveridge a flatterer and thoroughly untrustworthy.[96] While doggedly defending the economic interests of their own constituents, the insurgents inveighed from a stance of adamantine moral rectitude against the predatory behavior of the "special interests." Yet such apparent inconsistency did not reflect mere hypocrisy so much as changing perceptions of the legitimacy of public and private interests and the changing structure of interest-group competition. As Daniel T. Rodgers has demonstrated, the logical coherence and rhetorical consistency of progressive reform hinged on a sharp distinction between "the public weal" and selfish private interests. "The Interests were, by definition, alien and predatory: sores on the body politic." The "Interests" were predatory corporations which exploited political influence for private gain. They were quite distinct from the legitimate "interests" of farmers, industrial workers, smaller businessmen and consumers, who collectively constituted the "people." Even though segments of the "people," including farmers, industrial workers and women, were beginning to organize quite effectively as interest groups, many of which threw their weight behind progressive candidates and formed an important part of their constituency, progressives were still prone to regard the people's will as unitary, in juxtaposition to the particular claims of the "Interests."[97] Progressivism therefore emerged at a moment when the rhetorical and the organizational landscape of American politics was undergoing fundamental change.

---

[96] *C.R.*, 60.2:2622–3; Henry Cabot Lodge to Theodore Roosevelt, 25 April 1910, Lodge MSS, MHS; "Address of William Alden Smith, Oct. 6 1910," Beveridge MSS, LC.

[97] Rodgers, *Contested Truths*, 179–87; Thomas Goebel. "The Political Economy of American Populism from Jackson to the New Deal," *Studies in American Political Development* 11 (1997): 134–41; Clemens, *People's Lobby*, 1–8, 26–38 and passim.

7

Patterns of Republican Insurgency in the House of Representatives

Republican insurgents in the House of Representatives were celebrated in their day as leading protagonists in the struggle for progressive reform. "The Insurgent movement," proclaimed Mark Sullivan in the wake of the campaign to revise the House rules, "has come to mean much more than a change in parliamentary procedure . . . it is the crystallization of the people's demand for progress and for relief from control of the United States Government by and for organized wealth." William Allen White was still more fulsome: "The insurgent movement was nothing in God's world but implementation of the deepening moral intelligence of the American people."[1] Historians, too, were for a long time content to view the phenomenon within a frame of reference set by the participants themselves. James Holt, for example, described the insurgents as "outstanding reformers in an age of reform" and their revolt against the conservative leadership in Congress as "one of the most celebrated movements of the whole 'progressive era.'"[2]

Whereas earlier historians did not seriously question the insurgents' reform credentials, recent writing has adopted a more critical tone. David Sarasohn offers a salutary reminder that reform measures in Congress received more consistent support from Democrats than from their irregular Republican allies. In a study of the "Congressional Revolution of 1910," John D. Baker describes the movement to revise the House rules, not as "part of the progressive movement," but as "an isolated maneuver motivated largely out of political self-interest." Finding that the rules insurgents'

---

[1] Mark Sullivan, *The Education of an American* (New York: Doubleday, Doran, 1938), 361; White quoted in Kenneth W. Hechler, *Insurgency: Personalities and Politics of the Taft Era* (New York: Columbia University Press, 1940), 220.

[2] James Holt, *Congressional Insurgents and the Party System, 1900–1916* (Cambridge, Mass.: Harvard University Press, 1967), 1. See also George E. Mowry, *Theodore Roosevelt and the Progressive Movement* (Madison: University of Wisconsin Press, 1946); Hechler, *Insurgency*; Russel B. Nye, *Midwestern Progressive Politics, 1870–1950* (East Lansing, Mich.: Michigan State University Press, 1951).

votes on other issues displayed no unanimous commitment to reform, he concludes that their demands were inspired by political expediency mingled with personal resentment.[3] While most historians locate the rules revolt within a discussion of progressive reform, political scientists accord it a very different significance as a stage in what Nelson Polsby terms the "institutionalization of the House." Curtailment of the enormous discretionary power of the Speaker was an important element of a long-term transition "from particularistic and discretionary to universalistic and automated decision-making." Its timing was related to another important trend. As the turnover in membership fell off sharply around the turn of the century, the growing number of senior members seeking to establish permanent careers on Capitol Hill looked for less arbitrary ways of allocating power and prestige. From this perspective, the movement to liberalize the House rules appears as a function of the changing shape of "the congressional career" rather than as an expression of progressive impulses.[4]

The purpose of the present chapter is not to refurbish the historical reputation of the insurgents. Such a project would be otiose. It is rather to examine how House Republicans responded to the issues of progressive reform. The votes of Republican Congressmen, along with their public and private statements, will be used to analyze divisions within the party during the period leading up to the "congressional revolution" of 1910. We shall seek to identify the principal issues dividing the Republicans and determine how far they corresponded to familiar categories of reform. Did the insurgents form a cohesive faction, "a party within a party," as George Mowry describes it, or shifting and transitory groupings which changed according to the object in view?[5] By a systematic examination of patterns of Republican insurgency it is hoped not only to illuminate its history but also to sort out some of the ideological and programmatic components of progressivism, in so far as they found expression in the House of Representatives. This exercise reinforces and supplements the discussion of the Senate Republicans in

---

[3] David A. Sarasohn, "The Insurgent Republicans: Insurgent Image and Republican Reality," *Social Science History* 3 (1979): 245–61; John D. Baker, "The Character of the Congressional Revolution of 1910," *Journal of American History* 60 (1973): 679–91.

[4] Nelson W. Polsby, "The Institutionalization of the United States House of Representatives," *American Political Science Review* 62 (1968): 144–68; Polsby, Miriam Gallagher, and Barry S. Rundquist, "The Growth of the Seniority System in the United States House of Representatives," ibid. 63 (1969): 787–807; H. Douglas Price, "The Congressional Career Then and Now," in Nelson W. Polsby, ed., *Congressional Behavior* (New York: Random House, 1971), 14–27; Price, "Congress and the Evolution of Legislative 'Professionalism,'" in Norman W. Ornstein, ed., *Congress in Change* (New York: Praeger, 1975), 2–23; Joel Budgor et al., "The 1896 Election and Congressional Modernization: An Appraisal of the Evidence," *Social Science History* 5 (1981): 53–90; Allan E. Bogue et al., "Members of the House of Representatives and the Process of Modernization, 1789–1969," *Journal of American History* 63 (1976): 275–302.

[5] Mowry, *Theodore Roosevelt and the Progressive Movement*, 32.

the previous chapter by permitting closer analysis of the social and political roots of insurgency and a fuller examination of the impact of progressivism on the structure of congressional decision making.

Cannon, Roosevelt, and Reform

What gave particular meaning to congressional insurgency during this period, what, indeed, caused contemporaries to use the word "insurgency" to describe it, was the fact that departures from regular party voting were, by historical standards, rare. "When I first reached Washington," recalled George Norris, "it was the general practice of members to follow implicitly the decision of the caucus."[6] The average value of the Rice Index of Cohesion for House Republicans during the Fifty-ninth Congress was 82. More significantly, the median value was 98; that is, in nearly half the roll calls the party was quite unanimous. In only 19 percent of recorded votes, when the index fell below 60, were as many as 20 percent willing to vote against the main body of their party. Such habits of loyalty, though characteristic of the period 1897–1911, lie outside normal expectations of congressional behavior.[7] Even when, as with regard to the joint statehood proposal, Republican members were unhappy with elements of party policy, they were reluctant to break ranks. Norris believed that no more than one in ten of his Republican colleagues approved of the bill set before them, yet only forty-three would vote against it.[8] As we have seen, the reasons for their acquiescence were complex. Nevertheless, this background of habitual party regularity makes all the more significant those instances of independent voting that did occur.

Perhaps the most significant outbreak of insurgency before the rules "revolt" of 1909–1910 came during the winter of 1905–6 in reaction to proposals to reduce tariff duties on imports from the Philippines and to admit Arizona and New Mexico as one state. Republican opponents of the Philippine tariff bill represented beet sugar and tobacco-raising districts, fearful of the consequences of opening American markets to tobacco and sugar produced by what Joseph W. Fordney of Michigan called "the cheapest labor on earth."[9] Republican opponents of joint statehood objected to

---

[6] George Norris, *Fighting Liberal: The Autobiography of George W. Norris* (New York: Macmillan, 1945), 97.

[7] For a historical comparison, see David W. Brady and Philip W. Althoff, "Party Voting in the U.S. House of Representatives, 1890–1910," *Journal of Politics* 36 (1974): 753–75; Jerome M. Clubb and Santa Traugott, "Partisan Cleavage and Cohesion in The House of Representatives, 1861–1974," *Journal of Interdisciplinary History* 7 (1977): 375–401.

[8] George Norris to N. M. Ayers, 16 March 1906, Norris MSS, LC. See also Henry C. Adams to Robert M. La Follette, 6 December 1905; to William D. Hoard, 17 January 1906, Adams MSS, SHSW; *New York Times*, 15 March 1906.

[9] C.R., 59.1:740, 745.

a proposal which would force the people of Arizona into an "unwilling wedlock" with New Mexico, "in direct defiance of the principles of republican government."[10] Some of the insurgents protested vehemently against the pressures that they were subjected to and the tactics, including special rules limiting debate and precluding amendment, which were employed to "coerce the minority." Many Republicans, claimed Henry C. Adams, had grown "very restless under the arbitrary rules of the House machine" and had "made up their minds sooner or later to change the existing order."[11] John J. Esch and Henry A. Cooper were other insurgents who expressed themselves in favor of rules reform at this time. Both Esch and Cooper proposed changes – election of the Rules Committee by the House and restraints on the Chair's arbitrary power of recognition – almost identical to those promulgated a few years later.[12] There is little evidence that such views were widespread among their fellow Republicans. Nor did the "pretty strong revolt" that Adams discerned survive the passage of the bills in question or give rise to any more persistent pattern of insurgency.

At this stage Republicans sympathetic to progressive reform had few grounds for complaint. During the Fifty-ninth Congress the House leadership cooperated with the Administration in securing the passage of important regulatory legislation. The Hepburn railroad bill went through the House smoothly, and, although some Midwestern Republicans would have preferred a stricter measure, they did not openly attack it. Some apprehension was expressed at Cannon's delay in bringing up the pure food bill and the meat inspection amendment after they had been passed by the Senate, but both measures eventually went through in a form which the President and his supporters could accept. Although Cannon had antagonized the American Federation of Labor and the supporters of immigration restriction, he was not yet widely perceived as a stubborn barrier standing in the path of progressive reform or the "Roosevelt policies."[13]

---

[10] *C.R.*, 59.1:1545–7 (Kahn), 1547–52 (Mondell); Henry C. Adams to Ben Adams, 18 December 1905, Adams MSS, SHSW; Joseph W. Babcock, "Statehood Rights of Arizona and New Mexico," *Independent* 60 (1 March 1906): 505–8.

[11] *C.R.*, 59.1:1503 (Jones), 4124 (Humphrey); Henry C. Adams to Ben Adams, 18 December 1905; to Leslie "R," 29 December 1905; to William D. Hoard, 16 December 1905, 17 January 1906, Adams MSS, SHSW.

[12] J. J. Esch to A. D. Howard, 16 April 1906, Esch Letterbooks, SHSW; Henry A. Cooper to Samuel Gompers, n.d. 1906, Cooper MSS, SHSW.

[13] *New York Times*, 28 May, 5, 8 June 1906; *Literary Digest* 32 (16 June 1906): 894–5. See also J. Harvey Young, *Pure Food: Securing the Federal Food and Drug Act of 1906* (Princeton: Princeton University Press, 1989), 210–20, 246–62; John A. Braeman, "The Square Deal in Action: A Case Study in the Growth of the National 'Police Power,'" in Braeman et al., eds., *Change and Continuity in Twentieth-Century America* (Columbus: Ohio State University Press, 1964), 61–73; William R. Gwinn, *Uncle Joe Cannon: Archfoe of Insurgency* (New York, 1957), 109–13; Martin L. Fausold, "James W. Wadsworth Sr., and the Meat Inspection Act of 1906," *New York History* (1970): 43–61.

The next few years, however, saw mounting friction between Roosevelt and the Republican leaders in Congress. During the Sixtieth Congress the President intensified his demands for reform legislation, bombarding the legislature with a series of messages calling, among other things, for a revised employers' liability law, restrictions on labor injunctions, further enlargement of the powers of the Interstate Commerce Commission, amendments to the antitrust law, federal licensing of interstate corporations, and abolition of "stock gambling." Most of these proposals congressional leaders received with undisguised contempt, from time to time releasing statements that no major legislation, other than an emergency currency bill, would pass that session. Even though the House Democrats gleefully endorsed the President's program and nearly fifty Republicans were thought to be substantially in favor, the antagonism of Cannon and his associates was sufficient to block consideration of all but a few token measures.[14] It was during 1908 that "Cannonism" first entered public discourse. Powerful pressure groups, including labor organizations, supporters of temperance and women's suffrage, conservationists, and newspaper publishers anxious for the removal of duties on wood pulp and print paper, protested loudly at the Speaker's obstructive methods.[15] Newspaper and magazine articles critical of Cannon and the House rules began to proliferate. The same dissatisfaction infiltrated the correspondence of Republican Congressmen. "That the leaders in both houses are unfriendly with the Pres[ident] and are doing everything possible to discredit him seems an open secret," a Wisconsin postmaster wrote to Esch. "The fact that a small coterie of members in the House and a smaller one in the Senate constitute an oligarchy that rules the entire legislative body with a mailed hand is intensely offensive to the people and rapidly growing more so."[16] A series of much publicized confrontations between President and Congress during the lame-duck session of the following year served only to exacerbate the situation.

While Cannon felt few qualms about blocking measures that he did not approve of, many Republican Congressmen were distinctly embarrassed by his stance and wondered how they might explain to the voters their collective failure to respond to the President's initiatives. "There is a great deal of quiet

---

[14] *New York Times*, 1 February, 13, 22 March, 16, 28, 29 April, 31 May 1908; Gould, *Reform and Regulation*, 68–73; George E. Mowry, *The Era of Theodore Roosevelt, 1900–1912* (New York: Harper, 1958), 220–3; Blair Bolles, *Tyrant from Illinois: Uncle Joe Cannon's Experiment with Personal Power* (New York: Norton, 1951), 88–105.

[15] Ibid., 110–22; Gwinn, *Uncle Joe Cannon*, 132–41; Scott William Rager, "The Fall of the House of Cannon: Uncle Joe and His Enemies" (Ph.D. diss., University of Illinois, 1991), 43–9, 86–9; Watson, *As I Knew Them*, 116–18.

[16] D. C. Beebe to J. J. Esch, dated 23 April 1907 [but from the content clearly written in April 1908], Esch MSS, SHSW. See also "Government by Oligarchy," *Outlook* 89 (2 May 1908): 12–14. For an analysis of press comment on Cannon and the House rules, see C. R. Atkinson, *The Committee on Rules and the Overthrow of Speaker Cannon* (New York: Columbia University Press, 1911), 75–92; Rager, "Fall of the House of Cannon," 86–96.

agitation on the subject among the members," Norris informed an editor of the *Outlook* in May 1908. He and a few others spoke out openly against the rules and began to press for their reform.[17] During the ensuing election campaign several Republican candidates in the Midwest found it expedient to dissociate themselves from Cannon. Norris, for example, was compelled to repudiate Democratic charges that he was a "Cannon man."[18] After the election, a group of Republicans organized openly under the leadership of the veteran William P. Hepburn to work for parliamentary reform. The same individuals formed the core of the insurgent faction which succeeded a year later, with Democratic assistance, in achieving substantial modification of the House rules.[19]

Considerable dangers attend the analysis of roll call data for the House of Representatives during this period. Since the Speaker and the Rules Committee held such a tight grip on business, they could normally prevent votes being taken on controversial issues which might provoke opposition to their leadership or expose intraparty divisions. As Augustus P. Gardner complained, the Speaker's control over the order of business was so complete that "he can leave any contentious measure pending on the Calendar until adjournment." When a measure did reach the floor members were often denied an opportunity to vote on key provisions. Special rules frequently disallowed amendments, thereby presenting legislation "in such a form," according to Gardner, "that Members must choose between two evils."[20] This reluctance to go on record on controversial questions, which was shared, of course, by many ordinary members, greatly detracts from the usefulness of roll calls as evidence of the distribution of opinion. Thus we have no informative votes on important questions like railroad rates, pure food, meat inspection, child labor, employers' liability, and antitrust policy.

Nor must we forget, in evaluating members' votes, the role of such factors as ignorance or error, especially in the confused and chaotic atmosphere of the House Chamber. Unless the question before the House was one of special significance, members were to be seen reading, writing letters, or conversing with one another, while only a handful attended to debate. Such was the

[17] George Norris to E. F. Baldwin, 28 May 1908, Norris MSS, LC; *New York Times*, 4 and 30 April, 1 May 1908. Norris, Cooper, John Nelson, and Victor Murdock spoke out against the rules during the first session of the Sixtieth Congress. C.R., 60.1:6–7, 1649–52, 2835–7, 6440.

[18] "Speech Made by Hon. I. D. Lenroot at Superior, Wisconsin, July 29th, 1908," Lenroot MSS, LC; Herbert Margulies, *Senator Lenroot of Wisconsin* (Columbia: University of Missouri Press, 1977), 72–6; Lowitt, *Norris*, 131–2; Howard W. Allen, *Poindexter of Washington* (Carbondale: Southern Illinois University Press, 1981), 29–30, 33–4; Hechler, *Insurgency*, 43–4; Bolles, *Tyrant from Illinois*, 140–51, 164–70.

[19] *New York Times*, 8 December 1908, 6 January 1909; Hechler, *Insurgency*, 44–9; Lowitt, *Norris*, 139–46; John E. Briggs, *William Peters Hepburn* (Iowa City: State Historical Society of Iowa, 1919), 319–27.

[20] C.R., 60.2:600–1.

noise and confusion that few could hear precisely what was going on. It was natural in such circumstances for members, diverted from their correspondence or drawn in from the cloakrooms, to rely heavily on trusted friends, and especially party leaders, for cues as to how to cast their votes. Nevertheless, roll call analysis offers the only means by which we can approximate a reconstruction of the distribution of opinion and the nature of factional groupings within the Republican party.

The following analysis is applied to a sample of thirty-six roll calls drawn from the Fifty-ninth and Sixtieth Congresses. The sample includes every roll call in which over ten per cent of the Republican votes were cast against the majority of the party, with the exception of some duplicate votes and some whose substance was deemed trivial or expressly local in application. The prevalence of low values in the resulting Q-matrix points to the absence of any dominant factional division. In order to explore the data further, the matrix was subjected to cluster analysis using the group average method. This reveals the presence of one large cluster and several much smaller ones. The resulting classification is presented in Table 7.1.

"Subsidy Is Odious"

The first and largest cluster is dominated by a group of roll calls relating to subsidies. Three (#17, #25, and #36) were generated by a series of ocean mail subsidy bills which Republican leaders tried to force through over the combined opposition of the Democrats and a large body of Midwestern Republicans. Though ostensibly designed to improve postal services to South America and the Orient, they were universally recognized as attempts to subsidize the expansion of the American merchant marine. The object, explained Jesse Overstreet, chairman of the Committee on Post Offices and Post Roads, was "to stimulate the mail facilities, to encourage the shipping interests, to improve the trade relations with South America and the Orient, and to afford a valuable auxiliary to the navy in time of war." While advocates made full use of strategic and commercial arguments, they constantly reiterated the theme that American shipping deserved the same protection as was afforded domestic industries by the tariff. "Our foreign shipping is our only unprotected industry," observed William E. Humphrey of Washington, "and it is the only one from which American labor and American capital have been driven out by foreign labor and foreign capital." Now was the time "to bring it under the aegis of protection," so that it too might flourish.[21]

---

[21] C.R., 59.2:4156. See also C.R.:59.2:4049–55, 4141–4, 4146–57; 60.2:3688–94; William E. Humphrey, "The Pending Shipping Legislation," *North American Review* 182 (March 1906): 446–55.

TABLE 7.1. *Classification of House Roll Calls, 59th and 60th Congresses*

Cluster	No.	Roll Call Subject Matter	Cluster	No.	Roll Call Subject Matter
1 A	4.	Railroad monopolies	3 A	3.	Eight hours on Canal
	6.	Railroad mail subsidy		11.	Rate bill, conference
	8.	Anti-graft law			
	9.	Rate bill, conference	3 B	5.	Special rule
	10.	Panama Canal purchases		22.	Emergency currency
	13.	Congressional salaries		23.	Lilley charges
	16.	D.C. street railroads		31.	Secretary of State
	17.	Ship subsidy			
	20.	Army Appropriation	4	1.	Philippine tariff
	24.	D.C. street railroads		2.	Statehood bill
	25.	Ship subsidy			
	26.	Railroad mail pay	5	19.	Appalachian Forest
	32.	State Department		34.	Appalachian Forest
	33.	President's salary			
	36.	Ship subsidy		8.	Geological Survey
				21.	Naval Appropriation
1 B	28.	Rules of House		27.	Sundry Civil bill
	29.	Secret Service		30.	Bankruptcy Act
	35.	Rules of House			
2 A	7.	Naval purchases			
	12.	Compulsory pilotage			
2 B	14.	Naval purchases			
	15.	Railroad hours			

Note: The above classification was derived from the CLUSTER program of SPSS-X using the group average method.

Republican opponents of ship subsidies echoed the Jacksonian rhetoric condemning "special privileges" and "class legislation" favored by Democratic spokesmen. What this bill entailed, contended Halvor Steenerson of Minnesota, was "simply taking three and three-quarter million out of the public Treasury for the benefit of private firms." According to William H. Stafford of Wisconsin,

It is nothing more or less than voting the people's money to the extent of millions and millions of dollars in the interest of the favored few. For one I am opposed to that policy of conferring benefits upon the few at the expense of the many. Subsidy is odious to the American people because of its favoritism, because of the unmeasured and unmerited gratuity to the beneficiaries regardless of the services rendered.[22]

---

[22] *C.R.*, 60.2:3669 (Steenerson); 59.2:4370 (Stafford). See also *C.R.*, 59.2:4037–9 (Steenerson), 4267–71 (Birdsall).

However, the positions of Democratic and Republican opponents differed markedly. Republican insurgents devoted more attention to practical details of mail routes, relative costs of American and foreign shipping, and the value of naval auxiliaries, and they appeared readier to concede that subsidies might be acceptable if they promised to be more effective and cast their benefits more widely.[23]

Many of the same insurgents voted to reduce the compensation paid to the railroads for carrying the mails, by removing extra subsidies for the provision of "special facilities" and adjusting the formula by which the rate of compensation was calculated (#6 and #26). Whereas defenders insisted that generous subsidies were necessary to ensure a fast and efficient service, especially in less developed regions like the South, many Democrats and Republicans believed that the government was overcharged for the "special facilities" provided. The subsidies therefore constituted a form of "graft." Carrying the mails, said Steenerson, was "the most profitable business that the Southern railway has or will have."[24] The 1908 Post Office Appropriation bill, while removing a longstanding, and expensive, anomaly in the procedure for calculating the payments to the railroads for carrying the mails, included a clause providing for annual weighing of the mails, instead of every four years. This, argued Victor Murdock, would effectively increase the compensation by about three million dollars, since the current scale allowed for an increase in volume over a four-year period. Annual weighing was conclusively defeated on a record vote by a coalition of Democrats and insurgent Republicans.[25]

The five subsidy votes can be arranged in a cumulative scale. When the items are listed in order of "difficulty" and Republican members in order of party regularity the votes approximate fairly closely to a perfect scale, with 92 percent of all responses conforming to the expected pattern. These results are consistent with the assumption that the issues belong to a common "universe of content" and that each can be located on an underlying continuum of attitudes. Table 7.2 displays the responses of Republican members to the scale items, as well as the proportion of cluster items on which Republican members responded positively, which is highly correlated with the

[23] *C.R.*, 59.2:4200–5 (Gronna), 4365 (Prince); 60.1:6857–8; 60.2:3672–4 (Burton). Compare the remarks of Democratic members like John Sharp Williams and John H. Small. *C.R.*, 59.2:3945; 60.2:3088–90.

[24] *C.R.*, 59.1:4810–17, 5240–5, 55251.

[25] *C.R.*, 60.1:6755–9, 6855. On Murdock's campaign to modify the divisor used in calculating railroad mail pay, see *C.R.*, 59.2:264–7, 3140–4, 3232–5, 3469–72; 60.1:2835–40; Murdock to E. E. Higgins, 22 July 1909, Murdock MSS, LC; William Allen White to Roosevelt, 16 February 1907, METRP, Reel 72; Roosevelt to White, 6 March 1907, *Letters*, 5:607–8; *New York Times*, 19, 20 February 1907; Robert S. La Forte, *Leaders of Reform: Progressive Republicans in Kansas, 1900–1916* (Lawrence: University Press of Kansas, 1974), 137–43.

TABLE 7.2. *Votes of House Republicans on Scale Items, 59th and 60th Congresses*

Name	Roll Calls					Scores	
	6	26	17	25	36	Scale	Cluster
Burton (Ohio)	1	1	1	1	1	5	.70
Cooper (Wis.)	1	1	1	1	1	5	.83
Davidson (Wis.)	1	1	1	1	1	5	.56
Esch (Wis.)	1	1	1	1	1	5	.75
Gronna (S.D.)	1		1		1	5	.67
Hinshaw (Neb.)		1	1	1	1	5	.90
McKinney (Ill.)	1	1	1	1	1	5	.64
Mann (Ill.)		1	1	1	1	5	.73
Murdock (Kan.)	1	1	1	1	1	5	.91
Nelson (Wis.)		1	1	1	1	5	1.00
Perkins (N.Y.)		1	1	1	1	5	.70
Prince (Ill.)		1	1		1	5	.71
Stafford (Wis.)	1	1	1	1	1	5	1.00
Steenerson (Minn.)	1	1	1	1	1	5	.91
Wilson (Ill.)	1	1	1	1	1	5	.82
Woodyard (W.Va.)		1	1	1	1	5	.60
Campbell (Kan.)	0	1	1	1	1	4[a]	.70
Chapman (Ill.)	1	1	1	0	1	4[a]	.82
Haugen (Iowa)	1	1	0	1	1	4[a]	.89
Norris (Neb.)	1	1	0	1	1	4[a]	.83
Jenkins (Wis.)		1	0		1	4[a]	.33
Knopf (Ill.)		1	0		1	4[a]	.71
Davis (Minn.)		1	1	1	0	4	.80
Edwards (Ky.)		1	1	1	0	4	.78
French (Ida.)	1	1	1	1	0	4	.45
Graff (Ill.)	1		1	1	0	4	.55
Kinkaid (Neb.)		1	1	1	0	4	.70
Miller (Kan.)	1	1	1	1	0	4	.67
Reeder (Kan.)		1	1	1	0	4	.64
Townsend (Mich.)	1		1	1	0	4	.56
Volstead (Minn.)		1	1	1	0	4	.73
Calderhead (Kan.)		1	0	1	0	3[a]	.33
Dawson (Iowa)	1	1	0	1	0	3[a]	.60
Gilhams (Ind.)		0	1	1	0	3[a]	.75
Higgins (Conn.)	1	1	0	1	0	3[a]	.36
Darragh (Mich.)		1	1	0	0	3	.70
Hamilton (Mich.)	1	1	1	0	0	3	.58
McGavin (Ill.)		1	1	0	0	3	.57
McKinlay (Cal.)		1	1	0	0	3	.25
Marshall (N.D.)	1		1		0	3	.29
Mouser (Ohio)	1	1	1	0		3	.60
Foster (Vermont)	0	1	1	0	0	2[a]	.33

(continued)

TABLE 7.2 *(continued)*

Name	Roll Calls					Scores	
	6	26	17	25	36	Scale	Cluster
Lawrence (Mass.)	I	O	I	O	O	2[a]	.42
Driscoll (N.Y.)	I	I	O	O	O	2	.45
Acheson (Pa.)		I	O	O	O	2	.38
Bede (Mich.)		I	O	O	O	2	.20
Cushman (Wash.)		I	O	O	O	2	.27
Foss (Ill.)		I		O	O	2	.14
Gaines (W.Va.)		I	O	O	O	2	.10
Hill (Conn.)		I	O	O	O	2	.18
Humphrey (Wash.)		I	O	O	O	2	.27
Jones (Wash.)		I	O	O	O	2	.27
Parsons (N.Y.)		I	O	O	O	2	.13
Pollard (Neb.)		I	O	O	O	2	.44
Scott (Kan.)		I	O	O	O	2	.29
Wanger (Pa.)		I	O	O	O	2	.11
Fowler (N.J.)		I		O	O	2	
Crumpacker (Ind.)	I	O	O	O	I	2[a]	.55
Conner (Iowa)	I		O	I	O	2[a]	.63
Ellis (Oregon)	O	I	O	O	O	1[a]	.33
Knapp (N.Y.)	O	I	O	O	O	1[a]	.33
Allen (Maine)	O		I		O	1[a]	.22
Chaney (Ind.)		O	O	I		1[a]	.30
Holliday (Ind.)		O	I	O	O	1[a]	.50
Landis (Ind.)		O	I	O	O	1[a]	.44
Pearre (Md.)	O	O	I	O		1[a]	.25
Snapp (Ill.)	O	O	I	O	O	1[a]	.30
Stevens (Minn.)	O	O	I	O	O	1[a]	.30
12 members	I	O	O	O	O	1	
63 members	O	O	O	O	O	O	
Smith (Ill.)	O	I	O	I	I		.55

Key: 6 Post Office Appropriation, railroad mail subsidy (59.1, 5252)
 26 Do., calculation of railroad mail pay (60.1, 6854)
 17 Ocean mail subsidy bill, passage (59.2, 4377)
 25 Post Office Appropriation, ocean mail subsidy (60.1, 6761)
 36 Ocean mail subsidy, passage (60.2, 3694)
 a Cases containing error responses

scale scores (r = .92).[26] A pronounced sectional bias is apparent, with those accumulating the highest scores drawn almost exclusively from the region

[26] Twelve of the cluster items are included in computing these scores. The remaining three (#8, #20 and #31) are too marginal to the cluster and too weakly correlated with the remainder to warrant inclusion.

between Lake Michigan and the Continental Divide. All but three of those with a perfect record of insurgency represented that region. The average scale scores were: for New England .66; for the Mid-Atlantic states .55; for the Old Northwest 1.80; for the South and Border states 1.25; for the Midwest 3.18; for the Rocky Mountain states 1.56; and for the Pacific Coast.63. It is almost as if proneness to this particular brand of insurgency was a function of distance from the ocean.

A good number of those who questioned the efficacy of subsidies were also to be found in the revisionist camp. They commented regularly on the urgent need to revise the Dingley tariff rates, in order to reduce the prices charged to consumers and to curb the growth of tariff-protected trusts. "I am a tariff revisionist and not a stand-patter of the old school," declared Esch. Similar declarations were made by Adams, Cooper, Norris, and many other Midwestern Congressmen, who found it increasingly difficult to defend existing duties on the stump. James T. McCleary of Minnesota discovered to his chagrin during the 1906 election campaign that he was the only "stand-patter" in his delegation. He was also the only Republican to lose his seat.[27] Only one roll call during the Fifty-ninth and Sixtieth Congresses touched indirectly upon the tariff, and that was on a resolution giving preference to domestic producers in the purchase of materials used in the construction of the Panama Canal (#10).[28]

In the eyes of their supporters, tariff protection, ship subsidies, and railroad mail subsidies, like similar expenditures on river and harbor improvements, reclamation projects, and agricultural research, drew upon a common principle. Each, argued New York Congressman J. Sloan Fassett, initiated "its general blessing in universal benefits by blessing some one particular locality somewhere, somehow first." In such terms Fassett evoked the traditional Republican commitment to distributive policies designed to advance the "uniform general welfare and benefit of all the country" by aid to particular localities and economic groups.[29] The insurgents were more skeptical about the benefits of such policies and more suspicious of their discriminatory character. Benjamin P. Birdsall of Iowa regretted that

We have come to look too much for Government aid, to expect the Government to make us richer or poorer, and the consequence of it is to fill our halls with the representatives of special interests, capital and labor alike demanding some legislation

[27] J. J. Esch to John K. True, 12 February 1906, Esch Letterbooks, SHSW; Henry C. Adams to F. L. Phillips, 8 December 1905; to John Anderson, 3 February 1906, Adams MSS, SHSW; Edward P. Bacon to Henry A. Cooper, 24 November 1906, Cooper MSS, SHSW; George Norris to J. H. Mooney, 14 April 1908, Norris MSS, LC; James T. McCleary to John A. Lacey, [date illegible] 1906, Lacey MSS, ISDHA; *New York Times*, 30 April 1906, 16 February 1908; *Outlook*, 79 (21 January 1905), 147; David W. Detzer, "The Politics of the Payne-Aldrich Tariff of 1909" (Ph.D. diss., University of Connecticut, 1970), 33–42.

[28] C.R., 59.1:8655–60.

[29] C.R., 60.2:3690–1. Cf. C.R., 59.2:4052–3 (Pollard), 4155–6 (Humphrey).

which will enhance a particular interest. This is all wrong, and I hope the day is not far distant when our lobbies will be cleared of them and the money changers scourged from the temple.[30]

They condemned subsidies which, in their eyes, operated to the benefit of a privileged and powerful few without affording compensating advantages to the rest of the community. In a society becoming increasingly conscious of the conflicts of interest arising out of industrialization and the growth of giant corporations, the assumption of a "harmony of interests" which had served to validate such favors in the past no longer convinced a sizeable segment of the Republican party. Just as excessive tariff duties appeared merely to enable powerful industrial "trusts" to charge higher prices, so the ship subsidy seemed to be no more than "a donation to private enterprise."[31]

Also included in the first cluster are four roll calls relating to the regulation of railroad corporations. One (#4) was taken on a resolution, offered by a Texas Democrat while Republican floor leaders were sleeping on the job, which required the Interstate Commerce Commission to conduct an investigation of alleged combinations between the railroads engaged in the transportation of coal. This, claimed John Sharp Williams, offered an opportunity "to shed the light of publicity upon these corrupt details of corporate life."[32] The second (#9) was on a resolution forcing the House to vote on the Senate amendments to the Hepburn bill as a package, without permitting the separate consideration of those which some members wished to retain, especially that bringing express companies within the compass of the interstate commerce law.[33] Finally, many Republicans voted on separate occasions to require the Washington street railroad companies to restrict themselves to a standard three-cent fare and to furnish free transfers to connecting lines (#16 and #24).[34] The Midwest was the scene of several vigorous antirailroad campaigns; demands for more effective controls on the economic and political power of railroads and other public service corporations formed a central part of the platforms of progressive Republicans in states like Iowa, Kansas and Wisconsin. Hence it is not surprising that many Midwestern Congressmen were sympathetic to measures proposing to investigate railroad monopolies, cut railroad mail pay and tighten federal regulation. A background of local reform agitation aimed at readjusting the relationship between the states and their public service corporations made Midwestern insurgents particularly sensitive to similar issues at a national level.

[30] C.R., 60.2:4269.
[31] C.R., 59.2:4370 (Volstead).
[32] C.R., 59.1:1701–3, 2885–9; *New York Times*, 30 January 1906.
[33] C.R., 59.1:7428–33; *New York Times*, 26 May 1906.
[34] C.R., 59.2:4503–10; 60.1:6680–7.

Many have remarked on the shift in emphasis from policies designed to promote to policies designed to regulate private enterprise.[35] This, of course, had two aspects. One was an insistence, familiar to students of the Progressive Era, that private corporations should be subject to closer regulation in order to protect the public interest. The other was an equally insistent demand that government aid to private enterprise be more carefully circumscribed in order to prevent undue favoritism and "graft." That the former should feature more prominently in this set of roll calls is principally because the conservative House leadership was in a position to ensure that regulatory proposals did not come to a vote. The insurgents were most often cast in a negative role, seeking to stem the flow of favors rather than voting for regulatory controls. Nevertheless, it is justifiable to identify insurgency on this set of issues as corresponding to one major component of progressivism and to label those professing it "progressives."

The remaining groupings are small and their common features far from clear. The four items in the second cluster in various ways involve the interests of labor. The House Committee on Interstate and Foreign Commerce offered to substitute for the railroad hours bill passed by the Senate a version of their own which the legislative representative of the railroad brotherhoods described as full of "loose constructions, loop holes, and vagaries" and La Follette as "a very bad bill." It allowed the possibility of men working up to thirty-four hours over a two-day period; the allowance made for "unavoidable circumstances" and "unforeseen delays" would hamper any prosecution under the law; and it penalized only offenses that were committed "knowingly," thereby placing the burden of proof on the government. Nineteen Republicans joined the Democrats to deny the two-thirds majority required to pass the substitute under suspension of the rules (#15).[36] A much larger number of Republicans opposed a bill to abolish compulsory pilotage introduced by Charles E. Littlefield (#12). Littlefield's bill was vigorously opposed by his old antagonists in the AFL, to which the pilots' union was affiliated.[37] The other two roll calls (#7 and #14) concerned the relative merits of private and public sources for naval supplies.[38] Two votes in the third cluster also touched upon the rights of labor. One was taken on the rider

[35] Gould, *Reform and Regulation*, 14–22; Richard L. McCormick, *From Realignment to Reform: Political Change in New York State, 1890–1910* (Ithaca, N.Y.: Cornell University Press, 1981), 251–72.

[36] C.R., 59.2:3235–52; H. R. Fuller to Brotherhood lodges in Wisconsin, 6 April 1907, Esch Papers, SHSW; Robert M. La Follette to Belle C. La Follette, 4 March 1907, La Follette MSS, LC; *New York Times*, 17, 19 February 1907.

[37] C.R., 59.2:108–53; *New York Times*, 7 and 8 December 1906; *American Federationist*, 14 (1907), 38–9, 101; Samuel Gompers to John C. Spooner, 19 March 1906, Spooner MSS, LC; Charles E. Littlefield to John F. Lacey, 19 March 1906, Lacey MSS, ISDHA.

[38] C.R., 59.1:6327–30, 6543–4, 6574–96, 7030; 59.2:2911–13, 2990–8, 3068–9.

to the Urgent Deficiency bill, so roundly condemned by Gompers, which exempted work on the Panama Canal from the constraints of the federal eight-hour law (#3).[39] Debate on the final conference report on the Hepburn bill largely focused on the impact of the free pass ban on railroad employees and their families (#11).[40] It must be emphasized that these issues are only tenuously linked to one another. The demands of labor emanated from a variety of sources, involved a variety of considerations, and, in each case, were intermingled with a variety of other considerations. None of these roll calls offers a clear test of members' partiality towards organized labor.[41]

The other branch of the third cluster includes an ill-matched set of measures of which the most important was the Vreeland currency bill of 1908 (#22). This provided for an emergency currency issued by clearing house associations against the commercial assets held by their members (as against the bond-based currency in the Aldrich bill passed by the Senate). Eighteen Republicans voted against the bill. Those who spoke against it were mostly members of the Committee on Banking and Currency who complained both of technical defects of the bill and the irregular manner in which their committee had been bypassed in order to bring it before the House. They were joined by a number of Midwestern Republicans with a more persistent record of insurgency, like Cooper, Murdock, and Charles A. Lindbergh.[42]

The two votes on conservation that form the fifth cluster (#19 and #34) produced a very different sectional alignment to that evident in the subsidy votes.[43] It is not surprising to find unanimous support from New England delegations for a proposal to establish forest reserves in the White Mountains of New Hampshire, as well as in the Southern Appalachians. The reserves were planned not only to protect the rapidly diminishing stands of timber on their slopes but also the watersheds of the many rivers that drained them, furnishing power for the factories of New England.[44] Its opponents worried

---

[39] *C.R.*, 59.1:1603–11, 1629; *American Federationist* 13 (1906): 643–5, 980–1.

[40] *C.R.*, 59.1:9077–85; *New York Times*, 24 June 1906.

[41] The correlation between scores on the first cluster and voting on the Panama eight-hours bill is r = .17; on the railroad hours bill .09. The association between these two votes is Q = .59.

[42] For Republican opposition to the bill see the speeches by Ebenezer J. Hill, Charles G. Fowler, J. Warren Keifer, and Charles A. Lindbergh, *C.R.*, 60.1:6265–6, 6269–70, 6278–81, Appendix 58. See also Bruce C. Larson, *Lindbergh of Minnesota: A Political Biography* (New York: Harcourt, Brace, Jovanovich, 1971), 59–64; Richard B. Lucas, *Charles A. Lindbergh, Sr.: A Case Study of Congressional Insurgency, 1906–1912* (Uppsala: University of Uppsala Press, 1974), 40–3. On the bypassing of the Banking and Currency Committee, see *New York Times*, 3–12 May 1908; Edward B. Vreeland to Nelson Aldrich, 1 April 1908, Aldrich MSS, LC; Bolles, *Tyrant from Illinois*, 101–5.

[43] The correlation between individual scores on the items in this and the first cluster is r = −.12.

[44] The case for the bill is explained by John W. Weeks in *C.R.*, 60.2:3515–28. See also *C.R.*, 59.2:4483–9; *Outlook*, 85 (2 March 1907), 485–6; Harold T. Pinkett, *Gifford Pinchot: Private*

that the modest initial grant would act as an "opening wedge" which would inevitably "lead to unending expenses of enormous magnitude." Several Western and Midwestern Republicans protested against the partiality shown to this one section of the country. Frank Mondell saw it as "a monumental raid on the Treasury" by "a powerful, persistent and effective lobby" in the aid of a few private interests.[45] Many enemies of ship and railroad subsidies seemed to see in the Appalachian and White Mountain Forest project the same objectionable taint of government favoritism. Lindbergh, Murdock, and Norris were among those voting against it. Representatives from outside the Northeast who supported the scheme were by no means restricted to the ranks of the progressives: Henry A. Cooper, Asle Gronna, and Charles R. Davis voted in favor, but so did conservatives like Adam Bede, John F. Lacey, and Charles F. Scott. As in the Senate, the distribution of support for conservation was not at all closely related to other dimensions of progressivism.

The Despotism of the Rules

A small subgroup of the first cluster comprises one vote arising from the dispute between the President and Congress over the employment of the Secret Service (#29) and two relating to rules reform (#28 and #35).[46] These were taken on a resolution proposing a revision of the rules introduced surreptitiously by Gardner at the beginning of the second session of the Sixtieth Congress and a modest reform proposal emanating from the Rules Committee right at the end of the session. The Republicans who voted for Gardner's resolution and against the committee's were almost identical with the twenty-nine signatories of a resolution presented in February 1909 calling for the removal of the Speaker's power to appoint committees, their appointment instead by an enlarged Committee on Rules to be elected by the whole House, and the institution of a "Calendar Tuesday" when the consideration of bills on the House calendar would be in order without prior reference to the Chair (see Table 7.3).[47] It was this last suggestion which the leadership seized upon as a concession to appease discontent but which the insurgents dismissed as a "mere pretense" at reform. It was, said Norris, "a comic parliamentary

and Public Forester (Urbana: University of Illinois Press, 1970), 96–101; Charles G. Washburn, *The Life of John W. Weeks* (Boston: Houghton, Mifflin, 1928), 74–81; Bolles, *Tyrant from Illinois*, 118–22.

[45] C.R., 59.2:4486 (Burton), 4488 (Mondell); 60.2:3528–30 (Smith), 3530–1 (Madden), 3540–1 (Mondell); Geoffrey R. Graves, "Anti-Conservation and Federal Forestry in the Progressive Era" (Ph.D. diss., University of California, Santa Barbara, 1987), 241–7.

[46] On the Secret Service controversy, see C.R., 60.2:140–1, 373–5, 458–65, 645–84; William B. Gatewood, Jr., *Theodore Roosevelt and the Art of Controversy* (Baton Rouge: Louisiana State University Press, 1970), 236–87.

[47] C.R., 60.2:274–8, 2116, 3567–73. See also Hechler, *Insurgency*, 46–9; Lowitt, *Norris*, 142–4.

TABLE 7.3. *Republican Advocates of Rules Reform, 60th Congress*

Signed resolution demanding elective Rules Committee and "Calendar Tuesday" (C.R., 60.2, 2116)			Signed resolution for "Calendar Tuesday" (C.R., 60.2, 2116)
Boyd (Wis.)[a]	Hayes (Cal.)	Morse (Wis.)	Anthony (Kan.)
Cary (Wis.)	Hepburn (Iowa)[a]	Murdock (Kan.)	Campbell (Kan.)
Cooper (Wis.)	Hinshaw (Neb.)	Nelson (Wis.)	Foster (Vt.)
Davis (Minn.)	Hubbard (Iowa)	Norris (Neb.)	Howland (Ohio)
Ellis (Mo.)	Kinkaid (Neb.)	Pearre (Md.)	McLaughlin (Mich.)
Esch (Wis.)	Lindbergh (Minn.)	Pollard (Neb.)[a]	Parsons (N.Y.)
Fowler (N.J.)	Lovering (Mass.)	Steenerson (Minn.)	Scott (Kan.)
Gardner (Mass.)	McKinlay (Cal.)	Volstead (Minn.)	Townsend (Mich.)
Gronna (N.D.)	Madison (Kan.)	Waldo (N.Y.)[a]	
Haugen (Iowa)	Marshall (N.D.)[a]		

Key: [a] Members not reelected to the 61st Congress

joke . . . a homoeopathic dose of nothingness" because, taken in isolation, it left the powers of the Speaker largely intact. "You can not restore power to the individual here without taking it from the Chair," insisted Murdock.[48]

The Speaker possessed an "unreasonable and arbitrary power" over the business of the House, more power, said Cooper, "than ought to be given to any man in any government that pretends to be republican in form and democratic in spirit." This power had been assumed at the expense of the ordinary member, who, though representing some two hundred thousand constituents, was given little opportunity to influence legislation. He could vote but had little or no voice in deciding which questions should be voted on. To secure a hearing for his constituents' legislative business he had to become "a mendicant at the feet of the Speaker begging for the privilege" to be heard.[49] There must, insisted Gardner, be "some definite time when nothing is in order except matters which are not at present privileged under the rules." Then committees and individual members could bring up bills by right without having to beg for recognition. The Committee on Rules, which must admittedly be empowered to arrange the order of business, should be elective, not appointive, and its membership should reflect the partisan and sectional composition of the House.[50] Norris laid special emphasis on the appointment of committees by the Speaker, which enabled him to shape legislation and to reward and punish members. It was not surprising that a member "should strive to please the man who has the power to advance

---

[48] C.R., 60.2:3568, 3570.

[49] C.R., 60.1:6–7 (Cooper), 2837 (Murdock); 60.2:2653–5 (Hepburn). See also remarks of Augustus P. Gardner, George Norris, and Elbert H. Hubbard, C.R., 60.2:599–609, 1056–8, 2651–2; Norris, *Fighting Liberal*, 107–19.

[50] C.R., 60.2:603 (Gardner), 1057 (Norris).

or ruin his future political prospects." This power, too, should be removed from the Speaker and placed in the hands of an elected committee.[51]

What the insurgents complained of was not so much that the rules were too rigorous but that, in many respects, they were not rigorous enough to cope with an immense and increasingly problematic array of business. Existing methods of disposing of it were arbitrary, as well as unjust. Hepburn took exception to the growing reliance on unanimous consent to get legislation through, often by the bushel. Since each member knew that he in turn would have occasion to request this privilege he was reluctant to incur resentment by objecting, and so a great deal of business went through by means of a kind of "log rolling system," than which, he claimed, "no more faulty system of legislation" was possible. Some more orderly procedure for sifting measures was needed. John Nelson agreed that the business of the House was dispatched in an inefficient manner: "the rules have become so complicated, cumbersome, and unwieldy, that fully three-fourths of the business has to be done outside of the rules – under suspension of the rules, by unanimous consent, or by riders on appropriation bills." All these procedures were arbitrary and gave undue influence to the presiding officer. Hence many of the insurgents were conscious of the need to rationalize the manner in which the House did its business in response to the growing legislative demands placed upon it.[52]

Both Baker and, by implication, some of the political scientists who have examined the historical development of the House of Representatives attribute the movement for rules reform to the manner in which Cannon allocated committee places. So, in retrospect, did Cannon himself: "Many of the insurgents were honest and really believed they were the victims of the Speaker and a self-appointed cabal...more were dishonest and disgruntled and loaded their failures on the Speaker." According to his friend and protégé Jim Watson, they were "led into the fray by three men who were hostile to Speaker Cannon wholly because of blighted personal hopes and ambitions, and not because they were actuated by any principles." Victor Murdock was "thwarted in his overweening desire to be placed upon the Appropriations Committee," Norris wanted a place on Judiciary, and Gardner was "disappointed at not being made Chairman of the Committee on Immigration." Cannon ascribed Cooper's chronic insurgency to Speaker Reed's refusal to make him chairman of the Committee on Rivers and Harbors.[53] No doubt many Republican members harbored unsatisfied dreams of

---

[51] George Norris to Norman Hapgood, 17 November 1908, Norris MSS, LC; C.R., 60.2:1056.

[52] C.R., 60.1:1649 (Nelson); 60.2:2657 (Hepburn).

[53] Baker, "Congressional Revolution," 687–8; L. White Busbey, ed., *Uncle Joe Cannon: The Story of a Pioneer American* (New York: Holt, 1927), 256–7; James E. Watson, *As I Knew Them* (Indianapolis: Bobbs-Merrill, 1936), 256–7. Cf. Mark Sullivan, *Our Times* (6 vols., New York: Scribner's, 1928–35), 4:378–80; Rager, "Fall of the House of Cannon," 130–4.

grandeur. No doubt the accumulation of frustrated ambitions bred resentment. Some political scientists have suggested that the growing number of senior members seeking advancement had raised discontent to a dangerous level. Such considerations explain neither the timing nor the composition of the movement for rules reform. The "ageing of the House" had been proceeding for some years, while senior members were by no means disproportionately represented in the reformers' ranks.[54] Cannon was not, as we have seen, especially arbitrary in his committee assignments. Only towards the end of his regime did he depart more than occasionally from seniority, and that was in delivering retribution upon the insurgents themselves. In the Sixty-first Congress he removed Cooper, Charles G. Fowler, and Gilbert Haugen from their chairmanships and relegated Norris, Murdock, and Lindbergh to inferior positions because they had "failed to enter and abide by a Republican caucus." Loss of committee standing was a punishment for insurgency; it was not, in most cases, an independent factor causing it.[55]

The rules insurgents were not just personal victims of Cannon's power; they were also opponents of his policies. Cannon was a conservative who, in Cooper's opinion, was "never at all in sympathy with the remedial legislation of the Roosevelt Administration" and who used the power of his office to prevent the consideration of legislation called for by the people and a majority of the members of the House of Representatives. Roosevelt's reform program was doomed, insisted Nelson, as long as Cannon and his coterie controlled the House. "President Roosevelt has been trying to cultivate oranges in the frigid climate of the Committee on Rules, but what has he gotten but the proverbial lemons?" This bitter experience revealed the "great necessity of parliamentary reform in the House. . . . It is fundamental; it is a condition precedent to the passage in this House of all popular reforms."[56]

Sixteen of the twenty-nine signatories of the Gardner resolution also scored highly on the subsidy votes, as did five newcomers to the Sixtieth Congress. Most, in other words, had been continuously at odds with the party leadership over a set of issues which bore a significant relationship to some of the central elements of progressivism. Many of the remainder were

---

[54] Budgor, "1896 Election and Congressional Modernization," 81–6; Price, "Congressional Career."

[55] Victor Murdock to George Norris, 10 August 1909, Norris MSS, LC; Charles G. Fowler to Murdock, 28 May 1910, Murdock MSS, LC; Peter T. Harstad and Bonnie Lindermann, *Gilbert N. Haugen: Norwegian-American Farmer Politician* (Iowa City: State Historical Society of Wisconsin, 1992), 101–2, 109; Bolles, *Tyrant from Illinois*, 152; Ch'ang-Wei Ch'iu, *The Speaker of the House of Representatives since 1896* (New York: Columbia University Press, 1928), 66–71; Polsby, "Growth of the Seniority System," 798–802.

[56] Henry A. Cooper to Herbert Parsons, 20 July 1908, Cooper MSS, SHSW; George Norris to Norman Hapgood, 17 November 1908, Norris MSS, LC; *C.R.*, 60.1:1642, 1649.

closely identified with reform legislation of another kind – Gardner with immigration restriction, Pearre with injunction legislation, Fowler and Waldo with currency reform – and had come to regard the Speaker as an immovable obstacle in their path. There remain only four whose position cannot be related to some compelling reform interest. Of these, Hepburn, in other respects a confirmed "stand-patter," was moved by conscientious objections to "the undue and overgrown powers of the Speaker," tinged no doubt with a measure of personal jealousy, while William C. Lovering of Massachusetts was also said to be "more concerned about the autocracy of Cannon than about his conservatism."[57] Most of the rules insurgents, though, had come to differ from the majority on critical areas of policy. No longer confident that the leadership could be trusted to represent their views, they now demanded that the membership of key committees and the selection of bills for consideration should better reflect the increasingly heterogeneous character of the congressional Republican party.[58]

Rules Reform

Less than two weeks after the Sixtieth Congress expired, most of its members were back in Washington for the special session of the Sixty-first. An ad hoc coalition of Democrats and insurgent Republicans defeated the customary resolution to adopt the rules of the previous Congress but narrowly failed to force through a resolution creating an elective Rules Committee. A small group of Democrats, led by John Fitzgerald, were persuaded, partly, it seems, by the promise of favors in the tariff bill, to support a more limited revision which established a special unanimous consent calendar, so that members would not be obliged to plead with the Speaker for recognition, and reinforced Calendar Wednesday by requiring a two-thirds majority to override it. These changes, which hardly reduced the powers of the Speaker, the insurgents dismissed as "a mere drop in the bucket."[59] Though punished for their stance by deprival of patronage and committee places, the insurgents stuck to their last and during the following session, by virtue of Norris's parliamentary opportunism, secured consideration of a resolution embodying their longstanding demands for an elective Rules Committee on which the

---

[57] On Hepburn, see Briggs, *Hepburn*, 309–27; on Lovering, Norris, *Fighting Liberal*, 149; on Lovering and Gardner, Irvine Lenroot to Kenneth W. Hechler, 1 December 1938, Lenroot MSS, LC.

[58] Cf. David W. Brady and David Epstein, "Intraparty Preferences, Heterogeneity, and the Origins of the Modern Congress: Progressive Reformers in the House and Senate, 1890–1920," *Journal of Law, Economics, & Organization* 13 (1997): 26–49.

[59] C.R., 61.1:19–34. See also Hechler, *Insurgency*, 42–59; Bolles, *Tyrant from Illinois*, 179–82; Lowitt, *Norris*, 146–8; Herbert F. Margulies, *Reconciliation and Revival: James R. Mann and the House Republicans in the Wilson Era* (Westport, Ct.: Greenwood, 1996), 12–17.

TABLE 7.4. *Republican Advocates of Rules Reform, 61st Congress*

Voted for rules reform, March 1909 (C.R., 61.1, 20)		Voted for rules reform, March 1910 (C.R., 61.2, 3436)	
Cary (Wis.)	Kopp (Wis.)	Ames (Mass.)	Kopp
Cooper (Wis.)[a]	Küstermann (Wis.)	Barnard (Ind.)	Küstermann
Davidson (Wis.)	Lenroot (Wis.)	Cary	Lenroot
Davis (Minn.)[a]	Lovering (Mass.)[a]	Cooper	Lindbergh
Fowler (N.J.)[a]	Madison (Kan.)[a]	Davidson	McLaughlin (Mich.)
Gardner (Mass.)[a]	Morse (Wis.)[a]	Davis	Madison
Good (Iowa)	Murdock (Kan.)[a]	Dawson (Iowa)	Martin (S.D.)
Gronna (N.D.)[a]	Nelson (Wis.)[a]	Fish (N.Y.)	Miller (Minn.)
Haugen (Iowa)[a]	Norris (Neb.)[a]	Foelker (N.Y.)	Morse
Hayes (Cal.)[a]	Pickett (Iowa)	Fowler	Murdock
Hinshaw (Neb.)[a]	Poindexter (Wash.)	Gardner	Nelson
Hollingsworth (O.)	Steenerson (Minn.)[a]	Good	Norris
Hubbard (Iowa)[a]	Volstead (Minn.)[a]	Gronna	Parsons (N.Y.)
Johnson (Ohio)	Woods (Iowa)	Haugen	Pickett
Kendall (Iowa)		Hayes	Plumley (Vt.)
Kinkaid (Neb.)[a]		Hinshaw	Poindexter
		Hollingsworth	Steenerson
		Howland (Ohio)[a]	Taylor (Ohio)
		Hubbard	Townsend (Mich.)
		Johnson	Volstead
		Kendall	Woods
		Kinkaid	

Key: [a] Individuals who voted for rules reform in the Sixtieth Congress (C.R., 60.2, 275 and/or 3572)

Speaker would not sit. After a tense, and sometimes dramatic, struggle, the resolution passed.[60]

Forty-three insurgents voted for the Norris resolution in March 1910 (see Table 7.4). However, even at their moment of triumph, they constituted no more than a small minority of the congressional Republican party. Over three-quarters, 154 in all, voted to maintain the existing rules. This is surprising in view of the massive press support for reform and the apparently overwhelming public hostility to "Cannonism." The incoming correspondence, not only of an insurgent Congressman like Norris, but also of a stalwart leader like James A. Tawney, shows a preponderance of letters in favor of

[60] For an account of the events leading up to the adoption of Norris's resolution, see Atkinson, *Committee on Rules*, 99–121; Bolles, *Tyrant from Illinois*, 195–208, 217–24; Rager, "Fall of the House of Cannon," 134–45; Hechler, *Insurgency*, 65–78; Lowitt, *Norris*, 169–82; Holt, *Congressional Insurgents*, 16–19; Margulies, *Reconciliation and Revival*, 24–7; Margulies, *Senator Lenroot*, 91–6; Sullivan, *Our Times*, 4:373–82. See also "The Liberation of the House," *Outlook* 94 (2 April 1910): 750–4.

rules reform. Not only did muckraking magazines like *Collier's* and *Success*, as well as reform-minded journals like *Arena* and *The Outlook*, maintain a steady stream of criticism, but, as a Chicago *Tribune* poll taken early in 1910 revealed, the great majority of Republican editors west of the Alleghenies wished for Cannon's removal. In a poll of its subscribers taken by *Success* in March 1909, 95.3 percent declared themselves opposed to the reelection of Cannon as Speaker and 96.9 percent in favor of taking the power of appointing committees out of the Speaker's hands. Admittedly, the life subscribers of *Success* constituted a very selective sample of the electorate, and their verdict did not represent the "instant, spontaneous outpouring of public sentiment" that its editor, Edward E. Higgins, claimed. At the same time, as one of Tawney's constituents pointed out, Cannon's supporters in the country at large were "conspicuous for their silence."[61]

Higgins estimated that eighty percent of Republican members secretly raged against the Speaker's power but dared not rebel. "There are quite a number of Republicans," agreed Norris, "who would like to see us win, who will not dare to vote with us."[62] But even when success was certain insurgent numbers swelled only slightly. This suggests that fear of antagonizing the House machine, as Norris and Higgins claimed, accounted for only part of their reluctance. Many believed in the virtues of the existing rules, feeling like Tawney that to hand over the task of appointing committees to a panel appointed by the members themselves "would result in nothing but chaos and dissatisfaction." As Mark Sullivan noted, Cannon's tight control over the business of the House enabled members to dodge potentially embarrassing questions. They preferred to leave such an awkward responsibility in the hands of the presiding officer.[63] As for new members, their responses to the insurgents' overtures revealed a degree of unfamiliarity with the rules that militated against a decisive assertion of independence. "Under these circumstances," admitted William P. Sheffield, "I am inclined to follow the beaten path, until I am able to form an independent opinion in which I may have

---

[61] See, for example, A. S. Christenson to Tawney, 3 February 1909; H. O. Duncan to Tawney, 4 March 1909, Tawney MSS, MinHS; George W. Ira to George Norris, 24 February 1909; F. D. Donahue to Norris, 16 March 1909, Norris MSS, LC. On the *Success* poll, see Edward E. Higgins to James E. Tawney, 20 February, 2, 5, 20 March 1909 (the last of which included a tabulation of the results), Tawney MSS, MinHS; Higgins to Victor Murdock, 1, 8 March 1909, Murdock MSS, LC. See also Robert J. Collier to Murdock, 19 March 1909, Murdock MSS, LC; Atkinson, *Committee on Rules*, 75–92; Mowry, *Theodore Roosevelt and the Progressive Movement*, 88; Louis Filler, *The Muckrakers: Crusaders for American Liberalism* (State College: Pennsylvania State University Press, 1976), 344–6.

[62] Edward E. Higgins to James E. Tawney, 20 February 1909, Tawney MSS, MinHS; George Norris to F. M. Richards, 18 December 1909, Norris MSS, LC.

[63] James E. Tawney to J. B. Arp, 6 March 1909, MinHS; Mark Sullivan, "The People's One Hour in Two Years," *Collier's* 42 (13 March 1909): 10–11; Daniel R. Anthony, Jr. to William Allen White , 18 April 1908, White MSS, LC; La Forte, *Leaders of Reform*, 143–4.

confidence."[64] New and old members alike subscribed to a profound belief in the necessity and desirability of party responsibility and party discipline for effective legislation.

It is hard to avoid the conclusion that most Republicans, whatever their frustrations, did not go so far in their resentment of Cannon and "Cannonism" as the insurgents because, by and large, they did not disagree so strongly with the policies with which the Speaker was identified. Even more than in the previous Congresses, insurgency on the question of rules reform closely paralleled insurgency on a wide range of substantive issues.

Rules, Revision, Regulation

A sample of twenty-seven roll calls was selected on the same principles as before, with reference to substantive importance and the number of Republicans opposing the majority of the party. Cluster analysis of the Q-matrix this time produces one large grouping and no other of more than four items. The results are presented in Table 7.5.

The largest cluster, comprising fifteen items, includes the votes on rules revision taken in March 1909 and March 1910 (#1 and #12) and four others relating to the rules of the House. Norris's motion requiring the election of House members of the joint committee entrusted with the investigation of the Ballinger-Pinchot affair by the whole House, rather than their appointment by the Speaker in accordance with normal congressional practice, only in part reflected a desire to ensure a rigorous enquiry. It also constituted a slap in the face to the Speaker, whose capacity to select a balanced and effective investigating committee was blatantly impugned, as, indeed, by implication was his prerogative of appointing all committees of the House (#7).[65] Also included is the roll call on a decision of the Chair that census business could be brought up on Calendar Wednesday because it was "made privileged by the Constitution," which laid down the requirement for a decennial census (#11). The insurgents voted to defend the sanctity of Calendar Wednesday, but Norris fastened on the precedent to compel consideration of his own resolution for rules reform, which he insisted was similarly privileged.[66] Finally, two roll calls during the third session (#19 and #20) concerned the

---

[64] William P. Sheffield to Victor Murdock, 16 February 1909, Murdock MSS, LC. See also Charles A. Crow to Murdock, 19 February 1909; Hamilton Fish to Murdock, 14 February 1909; A. R. Johnson to Murdock, 15 February 1909, Murdock MSS, LC.

[65] *C.R.*, 61.2:390, 404–5; George Norris to G. L. Abbott, 31 December 1909; to W. H. Coleman, 10 February 1910, Norris MSS, LC. On the background, see Mowry, *Theodore Roosevelt and the Progressive Movement*, 73–87; Anderson, *Taft*, 72–8, Hechler, *Insurgency*, 154–8; Hays, *Conservation and the Gospel of Efficiency*, 147–74; Pinkett, *Pinchot*, 115–29.

[66] *C.R.*, 61.2:3240–51; Lowitt, *Norris*, 169–71; Hechler, *Insurgency*, 75–7.

TABLE 7.5. *Classification of House Roll Calls, 61st Congress*

Cluster	Roll Call No.	Roll Call Subject Matter	Cluster	Roll Call No.	Roll Call Subject Matter
I	1.	Rules of House	2	6.	Tariff, petroleum
	2.	Tariff, special order		13.	Battleships
	3.	Tariff, lumber		14.	Railroads, stock ownership
	7.	Ballinger-Pinchot inquiry		17.	Bureau of Mines
	9.	Immigration Commn.			
	11.	Census resolution	3	10.	D.C. playgrounds
	12.	Rules, Norris resolution		18.	Appalachian Forest
	15.	Railroad bill			
	16.	Labour prosecutions	4	23.	Canadian reciprocity
	19.	Discharge Calendar		24.	Canadian reciprocity
	20.	Discharge Calendar			
	21.	Transfer of cases to U.S. courts		4.	Tariff, barley
	22.	Judicial salaries		5.	Tariff, hides
	26.	Official salaries		8.	Unanimous consent
	27.	Official salaries		25.	Battleships

Note: The above classification was derived from the CLUSTER programme of SPSS-X using the group average method.

application of a controversial discharge rule adopted in the wake of the rules "revolution" of March 1910.[67]

The roll calls on substantive issues closely match those on the rules. The first (#2) is one of a number of procedural roll calls on the Payne tariff bill. It was taken on a special order from the Rules Committee setting the time for a final vote and allowing for record votes on the schedules covering hides, lumber, petroleum, barley, malt, tea and coffee. The rest of the bill would be considered in gross. Without some such arrangement, argued the veteran Washington Congressman Francis W. Cushman, the tariff debate would last all summer. Democratic spokesmen pleaded in vain for an opportunity to consider the bill item by item, arguing that the iron and steel, hosiery, glove and woolen schedules in particular needed greater attention than those enumerated. The twenty-one Republicans who voted, but did not speak, against the resolution presumably shared their disquiet. "It was evident that the machine desired a rule that would prohibit amendments," Norris told former Congressman John F. Boyd, but they were compelled to make some concessions in order to secure a majority. These did not embrace the schedules that

---

[67] C.R., 61.3:679–86, 964–75. On the discharge calendar, see Margulies, *Reconciliation and Revival,* 37–8; Hasbrouck, *Party Government,* 9–10.

Democratic and Republican opponents would have liked to vote on but did include those, like hides and barley, which would cause them the greatest embarrassment.[68]

All the insurgents voted for the Payne bill on final passage, regarding it, for all its deficiencies, as a significant improvement on the existing duties. The Senate bill they regarded as an abject betrayal of the party's manifesto. Yet even that had its merits, and the insurgents voted against a motion to reject the Senate amendments outright, preferring instead to give separate consideration to the few that actually did lower duties.[69] The conference report confirmed their fears. The protectionists appointed to the conference committee more often acquiesced in the higher duties imposed by the Senate than they insisted on the lower duties in their own bill. Despite the efforts of President Taft, whose last-ditch intervention obtained free hides and reductions in petroleum, coal, iron ore and lumber duties, the result was still too richly protectionist a mixture for the twenty Republicans who voted against the conference report.[70]

"Each of us," observed James Davidson of Wisconsin, "has demonstrated by our votes on the various paragraphs of this bill that we are largely influenced by our environment, by the wishes of the people we represent, by the interest of our district and our State."[71] In relation to specific duties the lines of division were markedly different from those appearing in the general tariff votes. Because the duties on which roll calls were permitted were on primary products, mostly of the West and Midwest, many of the insurgents voted alongside other members from their region in defense of protective duties. The proposal in the bill reported by the Ways and Means Committee to halve duties on barley met with a storm of criticism from the representatives of agricultural states, and an amendment restoring more than half of the reduction received overwhelming Republican support.[72] Confronted with the prospect of free hides, the result of a vigorous campaign by the boot and shoe industry, a succession of Western and Midwestern Congressmen stood up to demand protection for the farmer and the cattleman. "It is one of the few items in the tariff schedules which directly benefits the farmer," said Mondell. Seventy-one Republicans, including most of the insurgents,

[68] C.R., 61.1:1112–19; George Norris to John F. Boyd, 8 April 1909, Norris MSS, LC; *Outlook*, 91 (3 April 1909), 754–5; Detzer, "Payne-Aldrich Tariff," 46–54; Rager, "Fall of the House of Cannon," 152–8; Allen, *Poindexter*, 37.

[69] C.R., 61.1:4364–85; George Norris to Ernest M. Pollard, 13 July 1909; to Stein Bros., 13 July 1909, Norris MSS, LC; Lowitt, *Norris*, 150–1.

[70] C.R., 61.1:4688–75; Irvine Lenroot to Finly Gray, 13 August 1910, Lenroot MSS, LC; George Norris to W. C. Boldt, 29 January 1910, Norris MSS, LC; Margulies, *Senator Lenroot*, 80–3; Lowitt, *Norris*, 151–2; Allen, *Poindexter*, 41. Taft's efforts to improve the bill in conference are described in Anderson, *Taft*, 111–18; Detzer, "Payne-Aldrich Tariff," 172–89, 197–202.

[71] C.R., 61.1:4371.

[72] C.R., 61.1:1151–63.

voted in favor of a 10 percent duty on hides.[73] The committee's proposed reduction in duties on lumber were condemned by representatives of Northwestern lumbermen, who, said Cushman, "felt entitled to protection in a bill that claims to be a protection bill and framed by a protection party." Here too, predictable sectional divisions were in evidence, with a group of 56 Republicans, mostly from the less richly forested regions of the Midwest, holding out for the free admission of rough lumber.[74]

Standpatters pointedly contrasted the insurgents' eagerness to protect their constituents' interests in particular with their insistence on a downward revision in general. Miles Poindexter of Washington devotedly worked for cheaper coal, oil and jute bags but for higher duties on lumber and barley. Plains representatives like Norris and Gronna insisted on protection for barley and hides but complained of extortionate duties on timber and petroleum products.[75] In this respect they differed little from other Republican Congressmen from the same sections. Where they did differ was in their willingness to challenge the congressional leadership over the general management of the bill. Varying in their constituency interests, they came together in their insistence on a greater influence in the shaping of tariff legislation. To some degree they did so because they were more committed to downward revision than other Republicans and because they felt more keenly the disproportionate benefits that the protective system conferred upon the urban-industrial states of the Northeast, an imbalance which the present bill, with its radical move towards free raw materials and its modest adjustment of manufacturing duties, seemed to accentuate rather than alleviate. However, the identity of the tariff insurgents suggests that they were agitated also by procedural aspects of the bill's progress, which exemplified the very parliamentary practices that they sought to modify.

The same applies to House voting on the Mann-Elkins bill during the following session. Only four roll calls were taken, in one of which, on passage, no dissenting voice was heard. Twelve insurgents voted for a resolution to recommit the bill with instructions to remove the section creating a Commerce Court, the most objectionable feature in the eyes of supporters of rigorous regulation. A familiar muster of Midwestern insurgents assented, a few weeks later, to a motion to concur in the Senate amendments to the bill (#15). The roll call (#14) on an amendment revising the section covering stock ownership generated an unusual coalition of insurgent Midwesterners

---

[73] C.R., 61.1:659–60 (Mondell). For other examples of protest on behalf of the cattlemen, see ibid., 434–6, 1143 (Keifer), 686 (Haugen), 1139 (Scott), 918–23 (Kinkaid), 1149–50 (Martin). Pleas on behalf of the tanners and shoe manufacturers came from, among others, Gardner (421–6), McCall (760–1) and Roberts (1139–40) of Massachusetts. The shoe manufacturers' campaign is described in David W. Detzer, "Businessmen, Reform and Tariff Revision: The Payne-Aldrich Tariff of 1909," *Historian* 35 (1973): 196–204.

[74] C.R., 61.1:1134–5 (Cushman) and 1123–39 passim; Allen, *Poindexter*, 36–42.

[75] Ibid., 38–40; Margulies, *Senator Lenroot*, 80–3.

and conservative New Englanders – a classic case of the ends combining against the center.[76]

The other items in the cluster may be briefly identified. The thirty-nine Republicans who voted for the Hughes amendment to the 1910 Sundry Civil Appropriation bill refusing funds for the prosecution of labor organizations under the Sherman Act (#16) were mostly drawn from ranks of the insurgents.[77] Several insurgents voted for an amendment to the judicial code which would debar any corporation from removing a suit under state laws to the federal courts on the grounds of diversity of citizenship (#21), a practice which had long frustrated the efforts of state governments to attain a more effective control over the corporations operating within their borders.[78] Three other roll calls found the insurgents united with the Democrats against attempts to raise the salaries of circuit judges (#22), the Commissioners of the District of Columbia (#27), and the President's secretary (#26).[79]

None of the remaining clusters has more than four members; several satellites travel in wildly eccentric orbits around the main body. One incorporates two votes on Canadian reciprocity (#23 and #24). The reciprocity treaty presented by President Taft to the third session of the Sixty-first Congress, which offered to remove duties on several agricultural commodities, reduce those on selected manufactured products, and leave most industrial schedules intact, stirred up a hornet's nest of opposition within the Republican party. Not only Midwestern insurgents but Republicans from every section rose to condemn the treaty's betrayal of the cherished principles of Republican protection.[80] In the Naval Appropriation bills of 1910 and 1911 significant minorities voted for amendments to reduce from two to one the number of battleships to be laid down (#13 and #25).[81]

The Appalachian Forest bill (#18) closely resembled that of 1909. Once more the insurgent ranks were divided, with Gronna, Lenroot, Lindbergh, and Nelson among the fifty-eight Republicans voting against the scheme.[82] A roll call on the federal contribution to the maintenance of playgrounds in the District of Columbia (#10) also divided the party on lines quite different to those found elsewhere. A slight majority of the insurgents supported a more generous appropriation, but Western and Midwestern members generally

[76] C.R., 61.2:6030–1.

[77] C.R., 61.2:8656.

[78] C.R., 61.3:1060–6, 1070.

[79] C.R., 61.3:1449, 3592, 3611.

[80] C.R., 61.3:2375, 2428–59, 2506–64; Hechler, *Insurgency*, 178–80; Mowry, *Theodore Roosevelt and the Progressive Movement*, 168–73; Larson, *Lindbergh of Minnesota*, 99–104; Allen, *Poindexter*, 61–6; Sullivan, *Our Times*, 4:397–402.

[81] C.R., 61.2:4444; 61.3:3125.

[82] C.R., 61.2:8974–9, 8984–9028; *Outlook* 94 (5 March 1910): 507–8; Washburn, *Weeks*, 74–81.

showed themselves less sympathetic than those from the Northeast, especially those representing the urban areas more accustomed to such facilities.[83]
Although child welfare and conservation are commonly regarded as major
components of progressive reform, those who registered as "progressive" on
railroads and tariffs did not consistently vote for them. There is no strong
relationship between Republican voting on playgrounds or the Appalachian
Forest and the Norris resolution to revise the rules ($Q = .20$ and $-.03$, respectively). Each of the former drew substantial support from the East and the
urban Midwest, whereas the dominant form of insurgency was a mainly
Midwestern phenomenon. While Cary, Cooper, Hayes, Kopp, Murdock,
and Poindexter among the insurgents voted positively on both playgrounds and forest conservation, Davis, Gronna, Haugen, and Lindbergh
were unsympathetic to both, and a still larger number split their votes.

Insurgents and Progressives

Although the existence of a recognizable insurgent faction was evident, its
precise composition was not. The status of men like Lenroot, Norris, and
Poindexter, whom Norris described as "one of the truest of the entire Insurgent band," was beyond doubt, as was that of a standpatter like James
M. Miller of Kansas, who, as Bristow observed, "did not support a single
'insurgent' proposition." That of the newly elected Clarence L. Miller of
Minnesota, who had campaigned on the basis that the incumbent was "a
hide-bound Cannon man" but then withdrew from the insurgent group after
one meeting and proceeded to vote with the Speaker's friends on the organization of the House, only to rejoin the rules reformers at their moment
of victory in March 1910, or of Paul Howland of Ohio, who vaunted his
"progressive" credentials yet only occasionally voted with the insurgents,
was not. It was obvious also that some were more insurgent than others.
Bristow accepted that Edmond Madison was "all right" but considered him
"too conciliatory and compromising" to become a front-line insurgent.[84]

Although Howard W. Allen and Richard B. Lucas rely on party loyalty
scores to identify the insurgents, this method has the defect of using roll calls
indiscriminately, regardless of their substantive significance or the degree
of duplication between them.[85] Much more satisfactory is the use of scores

---

[83] C.R., 61.2:218–19, 225–9, 2918–31, 5964–71.

[84] George Norris to A. H. Curtis, 7 February 1910, Norris MSS, LC; Joseph L. Bristow to
William Allen White, 29 January, 3 February, 21 March; Victor Murdock to White, 28 December 1909, White MSS, LC; Paul Howland to Victor Murdock, 4 October 1910, Murdock
MSS, LC; Augustus P. Gardner to E. E. Gaylord, 11 January 1910, in Constance Gardner,
ed., *Some Letters of Augustus Peabody Gardner* (Boston: Houghton Mifflin, 1920), 58.

[85] Allen, *Poindexter*, 46–9; Lucas, *Lindbergh*, 77–80. The view taken here is that an element
of subjectivity is less dangerous than the distorting effect of using the whole population
indiscriminately.

derived from unidimensional scaling, which locates discrete areas of content. The fifteen votes in the dominant cluster are highly correlated with one another, and seven of them form a cumulative scale. The votes of Congressmen in these seven roll calls, arranged in order of "difficulty," are presented in Table 7.6. Shown also are their scores on the seven scale items and on all but two of the fifteen cluster items. In fact, these scores are closely correlated with one another (r = .96). There is no evidence here for the dichotomy between "progressive" and "non-progressive" insurgents drawn by Baker. What we have instead is a continuum ranging from the more radical insurgents like Nelson and Poindexter to confirmed standpatters like Dalzell and Tawney. Any cutting-point is more or less arbitrary. Insurgency, or "progressivism," was an ordinal, not a dichotomous, variable.

The Midwestern predominance in insurgent ranks was again pronounced. Of twenty-one leading insurgents only Poindexter did not represent a Midwestern constituency. The average scale score of all Republican Congressmen was 1.10, of Midwestern Republicans 3.18. The Pacific Coast came nearest with an average of 1.00, largely accounted for by the votes of Poindexter and Hayes.[86] "The centers of insurgent strength were overwhelmingly rural in character," observes Holt. It was by appealing particularly to the farm vote that Irvine Lenroot overcame John Jenkins in the Republican primaries of 1908 and Sydney Anderson dislodged Tawney from his Minnesota seat in 1910. However, Lenroot also appealed with some effect to labor, and both derived substantial support from the many Scandinavian voters in the region, as did other progressive candidates of Swedish or Norwegian antecedents, such as Lindbergh and Nelson. It is also clear that men like Norris and Poindexter drew support from small businessmen. Mostly inhabiting small towns themselves, they tended naturally to reflect the concerns of their leading citizens, sharing the ethos of "boosterism" which Sally F. Griffith has illuminated in small-town Kansas. That same "booster ethos" caused them first to welcome railroads and other "outside corporations" and then to seek curbs on their activities when they threatened to cramp the development of the local economy.[87]

We must look to political, as well as ecological, factors for an explanation of Midwestern insurgency. Positions on federal legislation were related to

[86] Cf. Holt, *Congressional Insurgents*, 3–5; Allen, *Poindexter*, 46–9; Lucas, *Lindbergh*, 12–15, 77–87. Average sectional scores for the full thirteen items are Midwest .59, West Coast .18, the remainder .08.

[87] Holt, *Congressional Insurgents*, 9; Sally F. Griffith, *Home Town News: William Allen White and the Emporia Gazette* (New York: Oxford University Press, 1989), 110–20, 132–5; Allen, *Poindexter*, 27–30; Lucas, *Lindbergh*, 80–3; Robert Griffith, "Prelude to Insurgency: Irvine L. Lenroot and the Republican Primary of 1908," *Wisconsin Magazine of History* 49 (Autumn 1965): 16–28; Roger E. Wyman, "Insurgency in Minnesota: The Defeat of James A. Tawney in 1910," *Minnesota History* 40 (Fall 1967): 317–29; Chrislock, *Progressive Era in Minnesota*, 32–4; La Forte, *Leaders of Reform*, 5–6.

TABLE 7.6. *Votes of Republican Congressmen on Scale Items, 61st Congress*

Name	11	12	19	1	7	15	2	Score	Cluster
Cooper (Wis.)	1	1	1	1	1	1	1	7	.86
Haugen (Iowa)	1	1	1	1	1	1	1	7	.86
Hinshaw (Neb.)	1	1	1	1	1	1	1	7	1.00
Kendall (Iowa)	1	1	1	1	1	1	1	7	.93
Kopp (Wis.)	1	1	1	1	1	1	1	7	.93
Lenroot (Wis.)	1	1	1	1	1	1	1	7	.93
Lindbergh (Minn.)	1	1	1	1	1	1	1	7	1.00
Morse (Wis.)	1	1	1	1	1	1	1	7	.79
Murdock (Kan.)	1	1	1	1	1	1	1	7	1.00
Nelson (Wis.)	1	1	1	1	1	1	1	7	1.00
Norris (Neb.)	1	1	1	1	1	1	1	7	1.00
Poindexter (Wash.)	1	1	1	1	1	1	1	7	1.00
Woods (Iowa)	1	1	1	1	1	1	1	7	1.00
Cary (Wis.)	1	1	1	1		1	1	7	1.00
Hubbard (Iowa)	1	1		1	1	1	1	7	.93
Good (Iowa)	1	1	1	1	1	0	1	6[a]	.79
Pickett (Iowa)	1	1		1	1	0	1	6[a]	.75
Davis (Minn.)	1	1	1	1	1	1	0	6	.93
Madison (Kan.)	1	1	1	1	1	1	0	6	.80
Gronna (N.D.)	1	1		1	1	1	0	6	.90
Kinkaid (Neb.)	1	1	1	1		1	0	6	.86
Davidson (Wis.)	1	1		1	0	1	0	5[a]	.58
Fish (N.Y.)	1	1	1	0	1	1	0	5[a]	.71
Hollingsworth (Ohio)	1	1	1	1	0	1	0	5[a]	.53
Hayes (Cal.)	1	1	1	1	1	0	0	5	.47
Volstead (Minn.)	1	1	1	1	1	0	0	5	.57
Miller (Minn.)	1	1	1	0	1	0	0	4[a]	.57
Steenerson (Minn.)	1	1	1	1	0	0	0	4	.67
Johnson (Ohio)	1	1		1	0		0	4	.27
Fowler (N.J.)	1	1		1			0	4	
Gardner (Mass.)	1	1		1		0	0	4	.33
Howland (Ohio)	1	1	1	0	0	0	0	3	.46
Dawson (Iowa)	1	1	0	0	0	0	1	3[a]	.54
Ames (Mass.)	1	1		0	1	0	0	3[a]	.44
Martin (S.D.)	1	1	0	0	0	1	0	3[a]	.43
McLaughlin (Mich.)	1	1	0	0	0	0	0	2	.15
Taylor (Ohio)		1	0	0	0	0	0	2	.07
Townsend (Mich.)	1	1	0		0		0	2	.17
Wilson (Ill.)	1	0	0	0	0	0	1	2[a]	.36
Foelker (N.Y.)	0	1		0			0	1[a]	
Plumley (Vt.)	0	1	0	0		0	0	1[a]	.17
Barnard (Ohio)	0	1	0	0	0	0	0	1[a]	.27
Stafford (Wis.)	1	0	0	0	0	0	0	1	.53

(continued)

TABLE 7.6 *(continued)*

Name	11	12	19	1	7	15	2	Score	Cluster
Stevens (Minn.)	1	0	0	0	0	0	0	1	.14
Fordney (Mich.)	1	0	0	0			0	1	.08
Higgins (Conn.)	1	0		0	0	0	0	1	.17
Langley (Ky.)	1	0	0	0			0	1	.20
Crow (Mo.)		0	0	0	0	1	0	1*	.10
Murphy (Mo.)	0	0		0	0	1	0	1*	.30
Austin (Tenn.)	0	0	0	0	0	0	1	1*	.21
Humphrey (Wash.)	0	0	0	0	1	0	0	1*	.23
159 Republicans	0	0	0	0	0	0	0	0	
Küstermann (Wis.)	0	1	1	1	0	1	0		.60
Parsons (N.Y.)	1	1	0	0	1	0	1		.29

Key: 11 Decision of Chair on status of Calendar Wednesday (61.2, 3251)
    12 Revision of rules, Norris resolution (61.2, 3438)
    19 Decision of Chair on whether motion to amend rules privileged (61.3, 686)
     1 Resolution to adopt rules of previous Congress (61.1, 20)
     7 Ballinger-Pinchot inquiry, election of committee members by House (61.2, 404)
    15 Do., motion to concur with Senate amendments (61.2, 7577)
     2 Tariff bill, special order (61.1, 1119)
     a Cases containing error responses

local factional struggles. Several Iowa insurgents had close ties to the dominant figure of Albert B. Cummins, while Lenroot and many of the newer members of the Wisconsin delegation were trusted lieutenants of La Follette.[88] In view of the political pressures acting upon Midwestern politicians to tread the insurgent path, those who did so laid themselves open to charges of "opportunism." After all, the insurgents of today were the regulars of yesterday. They had built up records of almost unimpeachable orthodoxy throughout their political careers, often converting to progressive positions quite late in life. Whether they underwent a genuine conversion or trimmed their sails to the prevailing winds of public opinion or state politics is in most cases impossible to determine. However strong the ideological roots of insurgency, it must be admitted that it was politically a prudent course for Midwestern members to take. Twenty-three of the twenty-seven Mid-western insurgents secured reelection in 1910, which was a disastrous year for Republican incumbents nationwide; three of the remainder did not seek renomination; and only one, Küstermann of Wisconsin, went down to electoral defeat. While nine of the region's sixteen non-insurgents were reelected, seven were defeated in their quest for renomination, including Calderhead, Miller, Reeder and Scott of Kansas, Stafford of Wisconsin, the veteran

---

[88] Margulies, *Senator Lenroot*; Hechler, *Insurgency*, 43; La Forte, *Leaders of Reform*, 137–45; Chrislock, *Progressive Era in Minnesota*, 42–3.

John A. T. Hull of Iowa, and, most significantly, Tawney of Minnesota. Whereas the regulars on average barely maintained their majorities, the insurgents boosted theirs by an average 10.6 percent.[89] Insurgency brought less obvious dividends in the older states of the Midwest, where progressive and conservative Republicans differed only slightly in their success rate in retaining their seats; further east the advantages of insurgency were more doubtful still.

The insurgent Republicans, according to Holt, focused on "two main areas of reform": regulation and control of corporate power and the extension of "popular government." Belief in the existence of a continuing struggle between the "people" and the "interests" forged a link between these themes. The destruction of "special privilege" required that the "interests" be stripped of their political power.[90] Progressive Republicans, said Poindexter, believed that the "special interests of vast accumulated wealth" exerted an improper influence on legislation:

> We have come to a point when some private interests vested with government franchises have become more of a menace to individual rights than the government ever was, and the peculiar spectacle is witnessed of a people, jealous of its liberty, seeking to enlarge the powers of the central government as a matter of self-protection. It is the only recourse, and unless that government, in all its branches, be kept perfectly free from the control of the great powers which it is sought to regulate and restrain, there is no redress at all.[91]

The destruction of "Cannonism" was part of this process, both as a move in itself to liberalize the parliamentary process and as a step toward necessary regulatory reforms.

During the course of the 1910 Republican primaries William Allen White pronounced in a letter to the conservative Congressman Charles F. Scott that "the difference between the insurgents and the Cannon Republicans is fundamental. They believe in the growing rights of men, you believe in the growing rights of property."[92] Not surprisingly, Scott, like other regular Republicans, resented being consigned to the ranks of defenders of corporate wealth and myrmidons of "special privilege." In a lengthy reply he contested the editor's right to draw so stark a moral distinction.

---

[89] Wyman, "Insurgency in Minnesota"; Mowry, *Theodore Roosevelt and the Progressive Movement*, 126–30; Harstad and Lindermann, *Haugen*, 112–15; Holt, *Congressional Insurgents*, 40–2.

[90] Ibid., 11–12.

[91] Miles Poindexter, "What Progressive Republicanism Stands for," enclosed in R. R. Wilson to Robert M. La Follette, 8 June 1910, La Follette MSS, LC.

[92] William Allen White to Charles F. Scott, 11 March 1910, in Walter Johnson, ed., *Selected Letters of William Allen White, 1889–1943* (New York: Henry Holt, 1947), 186–8. Poindexter agreed that the standpat leaders were "without exception . . . corporation and special interest men." Quoted in Hechler, *Insurgency*, 39.

What vote have I cast which indicates that I think more of the rights of property than I do of the rights of men? . . . You assume that in the fight to see who owns the Republican party, the people or the corporations, I am with the corporations. Here again I insist that you are wrong and that you have absolutely no facts on which to base your assumption. I haven't a particle of doubt in my own mind that I am just as anxious as you are that righteousness should prevail, that greed should be shackled, and the greatest good should come to the greatest number, and to the very utmost of my ability I have worked and shall continue to work to bring these things to pass. Why should you wish to drive me out of public life merely because for a moment you think I should go one way while I think I should go another?[93]

The difference between progressive and conservative Republicans was not simply one between defenders of the public interest and defenders of special privilege. Men like Scott sincerely believed that traditional Republican policies worked to the greatest good of the greatest number. Ernest H. Abbott, writing in the *Outlook*, put his finger firmly on the distinction between the two elements in the party. Conservative Republicans subscribed to the old idea that "the public interest is the sum total of all private interests. If each private interest gets all that it can, the public interest is served as fully as the public interest can be." On such a principle the new tariff bill, like all preceding tariff bills, was based. Against this he set the new idea that "the public interest is something else besides the sum total of all private interests." In the tariff, as in railroad regulation, this was represented by the "Ultimate Consumer." There was a similar contrast in attitudes toward legislative procedures. "The old idea was that each Representative represented his own particular constituents, and that the sum total of all good was accomplished by a method of trading and bargaining." To avoid confusion, "a clearing-house was created, with the Speaker at its head." This system worked as long as he succeeded in negotiating bargains and compromises. "Its effect, however, was to place almost insuperable obstacles in the way of legislation designed solely for the public welfare." It was a growing realization of the in-adequacies of the existing system that drove several members of Congress to demand reform, while others, conscious of mounting public dissatisfaction, moved in the same direction to protect their political futures.[94]

The "so-called regulars," argued Norris, even though many of them were acting "in the best of faith," did not "realize that the political methods of twenty-five years ago are absolutely unsatisfactory to the enlightenment of the present day." The contrast in political style was as striking as the contrast in ideas, which was never so stark as White and some of the more vehement progressives contended. Lenroot's primary victory in 1908 over the influential Congressman John J. Jenkins, a veteran of fourteen years standing who had fought in the Union Army and forged his career in the political arena

[93] Charles F. Scott to William Allen White, 14 March 1910, White MSS, LC.
[94] "The New Era in Congress," *Outlook*, 94 (5 February 1910), 289–92.

of the Gilded Age, illustrates the difference. Jenkins was a genial character who depended principally on his appeal to the soldier vote and his ability to win a generous share of patronage and pork for the people of the district, owing to his elevated position in the congressional power structure. Lenroot, on the other hand, was stiff and formal in his personal contacts but spoke with passion about the issues of progressive reform – about tariff reform, railroad regulation and popular control of the government, above all about "Cannonism" – and invited the voters to choose between the candidates on the basis of their publicly expressed views on the issues of the day. The object of politics, he insisted, was "to advance right principles." In La Follette's Wisconsin, as Robert Griffith points out, "right principles were also good politics," and Lenroot easily overcame the rather startled incumbent.[95] The congressional career of the still more eminent James A. Tawney was terminated in similar fashion two years later. Tawney, too, "worked assiduously," writes Roger Wyman, "to insure that the district received more than its share of federal buildings and other benefits from the pork barrel" and acted conspicuously to protect the interests of local dairymen and timber mills, practicing the kind of personalized, distributive politics that had operated effectively in Minnesota for generations. He succumbed to the unpopularity of the Payne-Aldrich tariff and "Cannonism" with Minnesota voters and the vigorous campaigning of his younger opponent. Trusting in his efficient campaign organization, Tawney responded too late to the danger.[96]

Another difference between regulars and insurgents, a difference which follows inevitably from the definition of the groups, lay in their attitudes to party loyalty. Lenroot deplored the political practices of the past "when good partisanship has been placed higher than good citizenship ... for I believe that the best service a man can render his party is to vote against men known to be lacking in principle, even though they be in his own party." The first question to be asked concerning "a measure of general importance" was not whether it was "a Democratic or Republican measure" but whether it was "in the public interest." Hence he refused to be bound by the party caucus "against my convictions and the interests of my constituents." Norris too, speaking with reference to the Ballinger-Pinchot investigation, insisted on "the principle that no man's partisanship ought to induce him to cover up anything rotten in his own party."[97]

[95] George Norris to A. R. Sauer, 31 May 1910, Norris MSS, LC; Griffith, "Prelude to Insurgency," 18 and passim; Lenroot, "Speech at Superior, Wisconsin"; Margulies, *Senator Lenroot*, 72–6.

[96] Wyman, "Insurgency in Minnesota," 319 and passim; Chrislock, *Progressive Era in Minnesota*, 40–2.

[97] Irvine R. Lenroot to S. Running, 25 May 1910; "Speech at Superior, Wisconsin," Lenroot MSS, LC; George Norris to Carl C. Engberg, 14 January 1910, Norris MSS, LC; Lucas, *Lindbergh of Minnesota*, 12–15.

Such attitudes brought them into conflict with the party's national leadership. The press was full of reports of a "purge" of dissident Congressmen. Many of the insurgents claimed to have been deprived of all patronage by the Administration. "I don't know of anything left to be done to us that has not been done except to call out the army and the navy," said Norris in a tone indicative of their embattled mood. Lenroot, Cary, and Miller of Minnesota also admitted to difficulties with patronage, but several "active Insurgents," including Murdock, Hayes, and Davis, reported "no trouble whatsoever." Gardner believed that Norris's and Lenroot's patronage problems had more to do with local factional struggles than with any systematic campaign on the part of the Administration to drive the insurgents out of public life.[98] However, there is no doubt that Taft was enraged by their behavior, especially in the Ballinger-Pinchot affair, and that he did intend to deny patronage to "opponents of the Administration and opponents of the declared objects of the Republican party." Like many senior congressional Republicans, he believed that the insurgents had distanced themselves so far from the center of the party as to warrant expulsion.[99]

The insurgents, of course, resisted attempts to read them out of the party. Norris insisted that, "with the exception of the Ship Subsidy proposition, they are nearly all lined up in favor of the so-called administration policies; in fact, they are very much more in favor of what the President wishes in the way of legislation than are Cannon or his followers."[100] Their distaste for party discipline limited the extent to which they were willing to align themselves with the Democrats, whom they also regarded as "slaves of the party caucus." As between Democrats and the most standpat of Republicans they almost invariably chose the latter. Therefore Norris would vote for Cannon in a contest with a Democratic candidate for the Chair, "who would have the same power as the present Speaker has and would carry out his ideas with the same power and of course, to the detriment of legislation and of the country generally."[101] At no point did they cease to think of themselves

---

[98] George Norris to F. M. Richard, 18, 23 December 1909; to J. J. McCarthy, 11 January 1910; to C. L Fahnestock, 11 January 1910; to A. F. Beurchler, 7 February 1910, Norris MSS, LC; Joseph L. Bristow to William Allen White, 26 January 1910, White MSS, LC; Augustus P. Gardner to E. E. Gaylord, 11 January 1910, in Gardner, *Some Letters*, 57–60; Hechler, *Insurgency*, 215–19; Lowitt, *Norris*, 161–4; Harstad and Lindermann, *Haugen*, 112–15; Mowry, *Theodore Roosevelt and the Progressive Movement*, 98–9.

[99] Anderson, *Taft*, 161–74; Archibald W. Butt, *Taft and Roosevelt: The Intimate Letters of Archie Butt, Military Aide* (2 vols., Garden City, N.Y.: Doubleday, Doran, 1930), 1:293; Holt, *Congressional Insurgents*, 36–40; Harlan Hahn, "President Taft and the Discipline of Patronage," *Journal of Politics* 28 (1966): 368–90.

[100] George Norris to J. J. McCarthy, 11 January 1910, LC; *Outlook* 94 (22 January 1910): 141–3.

[101] George Norris to W. L. Hilyard, 26 September 1910; to D. L. Crettin, 1 April 1910; to Carl C. Engberg, 14 January 1906, Norris MSS, LC; Lenroot, "Speech at Superior, Wisconsin"; Holt, *Congressional Insurgents*, 19–20; Margulies, *Senator Lenroot*, 112–15, 145–8.

as devoted Republicans. Their contest was for the soul of their party, not against it.

Conclusion

Studies of the Republican party in the Senate and the House of Representatives during the years between Roosevelt's second election and the Democrats' seizure of the House in 1911 reveal one dominant fissure, which deepened over time, relating to the promotion and regulation of business, tariff revision and banking reform. Voting on labor and social reform measures, and the conservation of natural resources, however, followed a very different pattern. In both chambers the social roots of Republican insurgency lay in the newer states of the Midwest and the Pacific littoral and its ideological roots in an older tradition of republican thought. In order to protect their constituents from the power of interstate corporations and to curb the political influence of the "interests," the insurgents supported, with greater consistency than other Republicans, the development of the regulatory state. At the same time, they questioned a system of distributive policies which appeared both inequitable and corrupt and, in doing so, challenged many of the operating assumptions that had held their party together for a generation or more. The insurgents' stance brought them into often acrimonious confrontation with the party leadership. The normative assumption of party unity – that individual Republican members, for all their personal and local preoccupations, could be expected to concur on major issues of legislation and shared an ideological commitment to distributive policies – no longer applied. Changes in the structure of congressional policy making followed directly from the intraparty divisions that emerged in the Progressive Era and manifested themselves in the form of Republican insurgency.

Insurgency was, by definition, a declaration of partial autonomy from the party leadership. Indeed, the insurgents made a habit of independent action. Out of a total of 265 roll calls taken in the Senate during the Sixty-first Congress, 154 saw six or more insurgents voting in opposition to the majority of the party; in only 63 did the Republican party attain unanimity. A similar, if less exaggerated, pattern of intraparty factionalism appeared in the House. "So pronounced is the difference of opinion between men such as Senator La Follette on the one hand, and Senator Aldrich on the other, that it presages, so some believe, a new alignment of parties," declared an *Outlook* editorial in 1910.[102] For all their disgruntlement with the Old Guard, progressive Republicans showed little inclination to form more than an alliance of convenience with the Democrats. Joseph Bristow made a point

---

[102] "The White House under Fire," *Outlook* 94 (29 January 1910): 241. Cf. Robert M. La Follette to Belle C. La Follette, 31 October 1909, La Follette MSS, LC; Albert J. Beveridge to Joseph L. Bristow, 16 July 1910, Beveridge MSS, LC.

of insisting "that the Democrats are no better than the Aldrich crowd." They, the insurgents, stood for "Republican ideals, Republican principles." In the last analysis, most were staunch Republicans who had more in common with their standpat colleagues than with the Democrats, including a continuing belief in the principle of tariff protection, a suspicion of organized labor, and a confidence in national power.[103]

Although the following years saw a deepening of the rift between the warring Republican factions, culminating in the Progressive campaign of 1912, they did not see a lasting realignment. Those who marched behind the banner of the Bull Moose in 1912 had mostly returned to the ranks of the Grand Old Party by 1916, while several of the insurgents, such as Bourne, Cummins, and Poindexter, abandoned their flirtation with progressivism shortly after America's entry into the First World War.[104] For many of their number, insurgency was a passing phase in a career that began and ended in the ranks of orthodox Republicanism. It reflected a particular conjunction of economic and political circumstances and a particular set of regional interests. Nevertheless, for all its limitations, Republican insurgency had a crucial impact on the legislative decisions that contributed to the formation of the modern American state, as well as on the procedures and practices of Congress itself.

---

[103] Bristow to Albert J. Beveridge, 27 August 1910, Beveridge MSS, LC; Sarasohn, "Insurgent Republicans," 252–3; Hechler, *Insurgency*, 205–11. Cf. John Gerring, *Party Ideologies in America, 1826–1996* (Cambridge: Cambridge University Press, 1998), 121–3.

[104] See Hechler, *Insurgency*, 220–6; James Oliver Robertson, *No Third Choice: Progressivism in Republican Politics, 1916–1921* (New York: Garland, 1983).

8

Progressivism, Democratic Style

"The chief difference between the Democratic and the Republican parties," declared Woodrow Wilson in 1910, "is that in the Republican party the reactionaries are in the minority, whereas in the Republican party they are in the majority." Senator Francis G. Newlands agreed that the Democratic party had for years been the chief repository of progressive sentiment. "Our propaganda embraced every feature of the contentions since so vigorously voiced by Roosevelt, La Follette and Cummins.... Every plank of every progressive Republican platform which... has been adopted is but a replica of previous Democratic platforms." Only the dramatic interjection of Theodore Roosevelt into the political arena had obscured the extent to which the Republican party remained, essentially, the party of reaction. His success in "forcing Democratic measures upon his reluctant and disgusted party... has tended to check the trend of events, which was rapidly creating a distinct cleavage between the two parties, along the lines of radicalism and conservatism." But it was a mistake to suppose that he had "radicalized the Republican party," whose leadership remained steadfastly conservative. What success he had achieved was due instead to the support of Democratic members of Congress.[1]

In view of their proven need for Democratic votes, insurgent Republicans were remarkably contemptuous of their occasional allies. George Norris dismissively remarked that "the progressive and independent members are confined almost entirely to the Republican party in the House of Representatives," forgetting the extent to which the passage of his own resolution for rules reform depended on Democratic votes. Joseph Bristow was similarly ungrateful, insisting that "the Democrats are no better than the Aldrich

---

[1] Wilson quoted in David A. Sarasohn, "The Democratic Surge, 1905–1912: Forging a Progressive Majority" (Ph.D. diss., University of California, Los Angeles, 1976), 4; Francis G. Newlands, "The Progressive Movement," notes on speech dated 15 October 1910; Newlands to [?] Williamson, 20 January 1908, Newlands MSS, SLYU.

crowd" and lamenting the absence of "a vigorous, compact, high-principled and clean-cut opposition party."² Even when Democrats manifestly supported reform policies, Republican progressives were profoundly mistrustful. Roosevelt admitted that the Democratic platform of 1908 was more radical than its Republican equivalent but saw in this no great virtue. "You have, indeed, advocated measures that sound more radical," he told William Jennings Bryan, "but they have the prime defect that in practice they would not work...and so far as they had any effect at all, would merely throw the entire business of the country into hopeless and utter confusion." The difference between the two, Taft agreed, was "that the Republican platform is progressive, while the Democratic platform is destructive."³

Those historians who did not simply regard the Democratic party as having no history before Wilson tended to draw their cues from the largely progressive Republican sources which they employed.⁴ Fortunately, a number of studies of the congressional Democrats have appeared in recent years to correct this stereotype. The investigations of Senate voting conducted by Howard Allen and Jerome Clubb clearly reveal the more consistent support for reform measures provided by Democratic, rather then Republican, members. David A. Sarasohn argues convincingly that, from 1905 at least, the Democrats were consistently the more progressive party, both in Congress and in their national candidates and platforms, and that the electoral victory of 1912 was not the result of a lucky windfall, in the shape of a Republican split, but the logical outcome of their growing identification with progressive policies over the preceding seven or eight years. Elizabeth Sanders's account of agrarian politics, *Roots of Reform*, which is essentially a congressional history of the Democratic party during the late nineteenth and early twentieth centuries, establishes its progressive credentials still more emphatically.⁵ Other scholars, like John B. Wiseman and Claude E. Barfield, present a

---

² Norris quoted in James Holt, *Congressional Insurgents and the Party System, 1909–1916* (Cambridge, Mass.: Harvard University Press, 1967), 20; Joseph L. Bristow to Albert J. Beveridge, 27 August 1910, Beveridge MSS, LC.

³ Roosevelt to William Jennings Bryan, 23 September 1908, Elting E. Morison et al., eds., *Letters of Theodore Roosevelt* (8 vols., Cambridge, Mass.: Harvard University Press, 1951–4), 6:1250–5; William Howard Taft to Theodore Roosevelt, 12 July 1908, METRP, Reel 85; "The Democratic Platform," *Outlook* 89 (18 July 1908): 597–9; "The Political Campaign: III-The Constitutional Issue," *Outlook* 90 (24 October 1908): 369–72.

⁴ For example, George E. Mowry, *The Era of Theodore Roosevelt, 1900–1912* (New York: Harper, 1958); Russel B. Nye, *Midwestern Progressive Politics, 1870–1950* (East Lansing, Mich.: Michigan State University Press, 1951).

⁵ Howard W. Allen, "Geography and Politics: Voting on Reform Issues in the United States Senate, 1911–1916," *Journal of Southern History* 27 (May 1961): 216–28; H. W. Allen and Jerome M. Clubb, "Progressive Reform and the Political System," *Pacific Northwest Quarterly* 65 (July 1975): 132–7; Jerome M. Clubb, "Congressional Opponents of Reform, 1901–1913" (Ph.D. diss., University of Washington, 1963); David A. Sarasohn, *Party of Reform: Democrats in the Progressive Era* (Oxford: University of Mississippi Press, 1988); Elizabeth Sanders, *Roots of Reform: Farmers, Workers, and the American State, 1877–1917* (Chicago: University of Chicago

more ambivalent picture of a party divided against itself, struggling to reconcile its adherence to an "antiquated Jeffersonian doctrine" with the need to come to terms with the governmental and electoral requirements of the twentieth century.[6] In the last analysis it does not matter which party can gain more marks for its contributions to progressive reform. More important than the allocation of credit is the task of defining precisely where the boundary between the two parties lay and locating it in relation to the various dimensions of reform and the broader process of state formation in the Progressive Era.

Strategies

John Sharp Williams had a very clear conception of what the strategy of the Democratic party in Congress should be: "Whenever anything comes from the other side of the Chamber that is right vote for it."[7] The lesson of the electoral debacle of 1904 seemed to be that the party's best hope was to establish its credentials as a viable progressive alternative by lending wholesale support to the "Roosevelt policies," a support that was not always forthcoming from the ranks of the President's own party, and, in some cases, by pressing for more radical alternatives.[8]

Though every inch the planter-statesman, an almost perfect exemplar of the ancient traditions of Southern statesmanship, and by no means an enthusiastic supporter of William Jennings Bryan, Williams was a longstanding advocate of stricter antitrust laws, railroad regulation and the income tax. Though a staunch defender of white supremacy, he insisted that Southern representatives must take on a wider role in national politics:

I do not believe...that it is wise for Southern statesmanship to narrow all its efforts and all of its play to a futile or dangerous attempt to reinject the race question into the arena of Congressional politics.... I think that the South ought to take its part in solving the great questions of the tariff, trusts, transportation, colonialism, et id

Press, 1999); J. J. Broesamle, "The Democrats from Bryan to Wilson," in Lewis L. Gould, ed., *The Progressive Era* (Syracuse, N.Y.: Syracuse University Press, 1974), 83–113.

[6] Claude E. Barfield, "The Democratic Party in Congress, 1909–13" (Ph.D. diss., Northwestern University, 1965); John B. Wiseman, "Dilemmas of a Party out of Power: The Democracy, 1904–1912," (Ph.D. diss., University of Maryland, 1967).

[7] *C.R.*, 59.1:965.

[8] On the lessons of 1904, see Wiseman, "Dilemmas of a Party out of Power," 5–51; Broesamle, "Democrats," 91–2; Paolo E. Coletta, *William Jennings Bryan: Political Evangelist, 1860–1908* (Lincoln: University of Nebraska Press, 1964), 351–89; Coletta, "The Democratic Party, 1884–1910," in Arthur M. Schlesinger, ed., *History of American Political Parties* (4 vols., New York: Bowker, 1973), 2:1007–14; J. Rogers Hollingsworth, *The Whirligig of Politics: The Democracy of Cleveland and Bryan* (Chicago: University of Chicago Press, 1964). On the ideology of the Bryan Democracy, see also John Gerring, *Party Ideologies in America, 1828–1996* (Cambridge: Cambridge University Press, 1998), 187–231.

omnum genus, and not occupy itself in "baying at the moon," or in a thing equally useless and much more dangerous.[9]

Instead of agitating the old issues, the party should formulate an attractive and constructive program to set before the nation. Its only hope, agreed Newlands, was "to convince the people that it stands for a progressive and constructive policy."[10]

The obstacle confronting them was, of course, Theodore Roosevelt, who was not only personally popular but had also succeeded in identifying himself, and by association his party, with the cause of reform – with what in his own, and to some extent the public, mind, were known as the "Roosevelt policies." Democratic leaders like Williams proposed that their party should adopt a strategy, not of outright opposition, but of persuading the electorate that it was more committed to the "Roosevelt policies" than the bulk of his own party. Hence in the Fifty-ninth Congress they endorsed the railroad legislation advocated by the President and lent their support to overcome the resistance of Old Guard Republicans in the Senate.[11] When the President placed a wide-ranging program of reform measures before Congress in 1908 it was the Democrats who applauded his messages and cried out for immediate action. Williams promised Democratic votes for a revised employers' liability law, restrictions on the power of the courts to issue labor injunctions, a campaign publicity law and the removal of duties on wood pulp and newsprint, should the House leadership ever assent to their consideration.[12]

Newlands, too, urged his colleagues in the Senate to commit themselves to elements of the Roosevelt program in order to drive a wedge between the President and his party. As he explained in a letter written in 1908 to members of the Democratic steering committee,

The Republican party in Congress is not disposed to put upon the statute book any of the reforms proposed by the President. But it will go into the next campaign upon the record made by Roosevelt and will claim the support of the people. By offering to consider these measures now we will, if the offer is accepted by the Republican party, succeed in putting upon the statute book desirable legislation; but if our offer is declined or evaded, as in all probability it will be, we will then be in a position to claim in the next campaign that the Republican party ... has refused to put upon the statute book the reforms for which the President stood, and that therefore its promises for the future should be regarded as hypocritical and insincere.

[9] John Sharp Williams to J. F. Gray, 10 January 1907, Williams MSS, LC.
[10] Francis G. Newlands to E. L. Bingham, 6 January 1906, Newlands MSS, SLYU.
[11] Sarasohn, "Democratic Surge," 28, 39–50; Charles G. Osborn, *John Sharp Williams: Planter Statesman of the Deep South* (Baton Rouge: Louisiana State University Press, 1943), 123–30.
[12] *New York Times*, 25 March, 3, 4 April 1908; C.R., 60.1:4354; Osborn, *Williams*, 130–5; Sarasohn, *Party of Reform*, 27–34.

To his letter he appended a list of Roosevelt's proposals and solicited comments.[13] The one extant reply consists largely of a list of negatives. Although the respondent, Hernando D. Money of Mississippi, approved of physical valuation of railroads, income and inheritance taxes, regulation of woman and child labor in the District of Columbia, protection of natural resources, and the free importation of lumber, he rejected almost everything else that the Chief Executive proposed: giving the Interstate Commerce Commission power over stock issues, extending federal control over interstate corporations, pure food legislation, restrictions on labor injunctions, compulsory investigation of strikes and lockouts, federal promotion of agriculture, construction of inland waterways, reclamation projects, federal acquisition of forest lands, postal savings banks, a parcels post, and the regulation of campaign expenditures. Some of these proposals were admittedly offensive to Democratic states rights principles, but, taken as a whole, they constituted precisely the kind of program that the party would have to adopt if it were to offer itself as a genuine progressive alternative.[14]

Some of Newlands's colleagues clearly resisted the conclusion that this was to be their destiny. Nor were they anxious to take the lead of a President of whom they heartily disapproved. "I cannot abandon mature conviction," the veteran Alabama Senator John Tyler Morgan told Newlands, "... to follow a man who has neither knowledge nor convictions on many constitutional questions" and whose attitude was one of "unmistakable hostility to free constitutional and just government." "Upon general principle," declared Money, "I am opposed to the Democratic party playing second fiddle [to] a Republican President or taking any formal *action* endorsing his recommendation." The party was "under no necessity of going to Mr. Roosevelt for suggestions." He, like other senior Democrats, was anxious to preserve both the independence of the party and the sanctity of its political traditions.[15]

The Democrats were far from united on the issues of progressive reform. In the House, while Champ Clark, Claud Kitchin, and Ollie James were spokesmen for the Bryan Democracy, other leading Democrats like Oscar Underwood, William Richardson, and Charles Bartlett held more conservative views. Whatever divisions existed among the House Democrats, though, were submerged in a common willingness to unite against the common enemy. Williams, by his insistence on a positive and coherent policy and by his

[13] Francis G. Newlands to Charles A. Culberson, 15 January 1908, Newlands MSS, SLYU.
[14] Hernando D. Money to Francis G. Newlands, 20 January 1908, Newlands MSS, SLYU.
[15] John T. Morgan to Francis G. Newlands, 18 March 1906; Money to Newlands, 20 January 1908, Newlands MSS, SLYU; Morgan to William Richardson, 3 August 1906, Morgan MSS, LC; Wiseman, "Dilemmas of a Party out of Power," 55–8; *New York Times*, 24 April 1908.

persuasiveness and charm, succeeded in welding his party into a disciplined political force.[16] In the Senate the egregious, but inconsistent, radicalism of Tillman and Bailey was offset by the traditional conservatism of Augustus Bacon, Thomas S. Martin, and the Alabama Senators Morgan and Pettus. This heterogeneous band lacked, or spurned, the firm hand of leadership. Democratic Senators reserved the right to act independently. In practice, however, they acted less independently than their opponents on the other side of the chamber. The median value of the Rice Index of Cohesion for the Senate Democrats during the Fifty-ninth Congress was 88, as against 83 for the Republicans. In other words, in half of all roll calls at least 94 percent of the Democrats voted together.[17] Whatever the ideological predilections of individual Democrats, the party was, in the eyes of the world at least, united upon a program of progressive reform. Even the most conservative Democrats compiled voting records more progressive than all but a few Republicans. The limits of their commitment to reform lay not in numbers or enthusiasm but in the range of progressive measures that they were willing to support.

What Divided Democrats from Republicans?

A preliminary step in the analysis of interparty differences is to identify those roll calls in which majorities of the respective parties opposed each other. In doing this, instead of the usual criterion for a "party vote," I have isolated those in which two-thirds of one party opposed two-thirds of the other. Most of the roll calls that meet this criterion can be placed in one or other of eight categories: matters of procedure, the level of federal expenditure, the tariff, subsidies, banking and currency, political reform, railroad regulation, and labor legislation.

The first of these follows automatically from the institutional nature of party conflict and the relationship between a Democratic minority and a Republican majority, covering such matters as the organization and rules of the House of Representatives, points of order, procedural questions, election disputes, and relations with the Executive. Over this territory the opposing parties engaged in a routine symbolic combat akin to medieval jousting. Appropriation bills, which were closely linked to the whole process of government housekeeping, also offered a field for conventional party warfare. The Democratic party maintained a commitment to "retrenchment" and a posture of vigilant opposition to extravagance in government spending

---

[16] Barfield, "Democratic Party," 1–11; Osborn, *Williams*, 108–14.
[17] *New York Times*, 4 March 1907; Barfield, "Democratic Party," 11–14; Allen and Clubb, "Progressive Reform and the Political System," 133; Wythe W. Holt, Jr., "The Senator from Virginia and the Democratic Floor Leadership: Thomas S. Martin and Conservatism in the Progressive Era," *Virginia Magazine of History and Biography* 83 (1975) 3–21.

that went back beyond former "watchdogs of the Treasury" like Samuel J. Randall and William Holman to the Jacksonian Era. This, indeed, was one of the hallmarks of the old Democracy: belief in a wise and frugal government.

For decades the tariff had provided the main staple of party warfare, the issue on which Republicans and Democrats most consistently agreed to differ. The attempted Republican revision of 1909 provided scope for a full-scale rehearsal of the issues. Congressional Democrats, effectively cut out of the crucial committee stages of the tariff-making process, criticized the tariff bill on the floor of both House and Senate and voted almost unanimously against it.[18] When it came to voting on specific duties, Democratic unity crumbled. Forty-one House Democrats resisted an attempt to place lumber on the free list, 29 voted for a ten percent duty on hides, as many as 92 for the same duty on skins and pelts, and 14 supported an amendment to raise the duty on barley.[19] In forty-six Senate roll calls from one to three Democrats voted in favor of higher duties. In twelve the defections were more serious. The most critical were on hides, where seven or eight Democrats voted for protection; lumber, which found ten, eleven, and on one occasion as many as seventeen, deserting to the enemy; iron ore and coal, where eighteen and ten respectively voted for protective duties.[20] Even after acknowledging the extent of Democratic disunity, it must be pointed out that their support for revision was more consistent than that of all but a few Republicans. Only the so-called "Aldrich Democrats," McEnery and Foster of Louisiana, voted for higher duties more regularly than the most determined of the tariff insurgents, La Follette, Clapp, Bristow and Cummins; no other Democrat broke ranks more than 18 times and only 14 in as many as 10 out of the 122 Senate roll calls on the bill (see Table 8.1).[21] Nevertheless, the defections on an issue so close to the party's definition of itself were embarrassing, as was the generally lackluster performance of its spokesmen in debate.[22]

The defectors, of course, claimed to be acting in defense of their constituents' interests. Several Southern members fought to preserve duties on

[18] See Claude E. Barfield, "'Our Share of the Booty': The Democratic Party, Cannonism, and the Payne–Aldrich Tariff," *Journal of American History* 57 (1970): 308–23; Barfield, "Democratic Party," 65–119; Wiseman, "Dilemmas of a Party out of Power," 141–56; Sarasohn, *Party of Reform*, 63–74; David W. Detzer, "The Politics of the Payne–Aldrich Tariff of 1909" (Ph.D. diss., University of Connecticut, 1970), 69–71.

[19] *C.R.*, 61.1:1293–8; Barfield, "Our Share of the Booty," 313.

[20] *C.R.*, 61.1:1995 (iron ore), 2337, 3680, 3681 (lumber), 3656, 3667 (hides), 3717 (coal).

[21] Cf. Sarasohn, "Insurgent Myth and Republican Reality," 253 and 247–52; Barfield, "Democratic Party," 113.

[22] Ibid., 87, 113–18; Barfield, "Our Share of the Booty," 312–15; Detzer, "Payne–Aldrich Tariff," 69–71; Albert J. Beveridge to Henry B. Needham, 2 October 1909, Beveridge MSS, LC.

TABLE 8.1. *Voting of Senate Democrats and Republican Insurgents on the Payne-Aldrich Tariff*

Members are ordered in descending order of support for tariff revision. The figures in parentheses are the percentages of revisionist votes cast.

Democrats	Republicans
21 other Democrats	
....	
Money, Miss. (89.2)	
Taliaferro, Fla. (87.6)	
Simmons, N.C. (87.5)	La Follette, Wis. (87.3)
Chamberlain, Ore. (87.2)	
Martin, Va. (86.9)	
Smith, Md. (86.8)	
Taylor, Tenn. (86.5)	
Daniel, Va. (85.7)	
Bailey, Tex. (85.3)	Clapp, Minn. (82.9)
	Bristow, Kan. (81.1)
	Cummins, Iowa (76.7)
Foster, La. (68.2)	Beveridge, Ind. (65.5)
	Dolliver, Iowa (60.9)
	Brown, Neb. (59.3)
	Nelson, Minn. (58.5)
	Burkett, Neb. (49.2)
	Crawford, S.D. (46.2)
	Gamble, S.D. (31.8)
McEnery, La. (27.3)	....
	49 other Republicans

lumber, several Western Democrats to preserve duties on hides, and smaller numbers in defense of other, more localized, interests. Though embarrassing to the leadership and contrary to the platform on which the party had contested the last election, such behavior had a certain logic to it. They lived under a protective system. Given the impossibility of changing it as long as the Republicans were in power, it seemed only right and proper that their constituents should enjoy some of the benefits, as well as the costs, of the system. "I am not willing," said Newlands, "that it should be revised entirely in the interests of Eastern manufacturers at the expense of Western products, and if there is to be a protective tariff, I shall endeavor to see that the West gets its fair share of protection." The crux of the matter was that the major reductions proposed in the Payne bill were on raw materials, some of the more important of which, coal, iron ore, and hides, were to be admitted free. Though the primary materials for industry, they constituted the principal products of large sections of the country, whose representatives naturally protested at the inequity of the proposed readjustment.[23]

Democrats rejected protection in principle. Not to do so would be to repudiate a major part of what their party stood for. Protective tariffs, they argued, levied an extortionate tax on the majority of Americans for the benefit of a favored few. "In the last analysis," claimed Oscar Underwood, "protective tariff bills are written to protect manufacturers' profits rather than to sustain wages or labor's standard of living."[24] In this they differed fundamentally from insurgent Republicans, who never ceased to declare their fealty to the doctrine. What a Democratic tariff policy should be in practice was less easily defined. Free trade was recognized by all but a few zealots to be wholly impractical in a nation so dependent on tariff duties for its government revenues. Democrats like Joseph W. Bailey accepted that a "tariff for revenue only," traditionally the Democratic doctrine, must inevitably confer "incidental protection" on those industries whose products were taxed, but this "incidental protection" should be equitably distributed. It was hard to see how this could be achieved without some of the "log-rolling" that characterized Republican tariff making. Oscar Underwood, on the other hand, advocated a system of "competitive duties" which would ensure "reasonable competition" between foreign and domestic producers. This formula was as problematic as the "equalization of cost of production" formula favored by Republican revisionists.[25] Thus the disarray shown by Democrats on the floor of the House and Senate reflected a more fundamental intellectual uncertainty in their approach to tariff reform.

The party displayed greater unanimity in opposition to Republican plans to subsidize merchant shipping. Like the tariff, with which it was often bracketed, the ship subsidy bill constituted "class legislation" conferring special privileges on the rich and powerful. "It is," said Williams, "the same old story of greasing the fat goose." It would, argued William Sulzer, act as an "entering wedge" for other such raids upon the Treasury. As Williams put it, "the whole essence of Democracy is in opposition to this bill and to this class of legislation."[26]

---

[23] Francis G. Newlands to John Henderson, 30 December 1908, Newlands MSS, SLYU; Barfield, " Democratic Party," 91–3,118–19; Barfield, "Our Share of the Booty," 319–23. See, for example, the arguments against free hides by Oscar Underwood (*C.R.*, 61.1:272–3), Edward W. Pou (340–1), and Albert S. Burleson (1140–1); against free lumber by Joseph E. Ransdell (1138) and Pou (4367–8).

[24] Oscar W. Underwood, *Drifting Sands of Party Politics* (New York: Century, 1928), 217; Geoffrey T. Morrison, "A Political Biography of Champ Clark" (Ph.D. diss., St. Louis University, 1971), 125–7.

[25] Morrison, "Champ Clark," 131–2; Underwood, *Drifting Sands of Party Politics*, 191–7; John D. Buenker, *The Income Tax and the Progressive Era* (New York: Garland, 1985), 88–90.

[26] *C.R.*, 59.2:3945, 4058; 60.1:3089–90; 60.2:3676–7; 61.3, 783. Analogies with the tariff are drawn by David E. Finley (60.1:3092–4) and Williams (59.2:3945).

The "money question" had since the 1890s separated the main bodies of the Democratic and Republican parties. So it was with the emergency currency legislation of 1908. The Aldrich bill proposed to deal with financial emergencies by issuing additional banknotes against specified state, municipal and railroad securities. Senate Democrats complained that, since the emergency currency would be too costly for banks outside the great financial centers, the measure would serve the needs of big-city bankers rather than those in the South and West.[27] A rather different bill was offered to the House in which the emergency currency was backed by selected commercial paper. The minority found this no more acceptable, since the assets required were those more commonly found in the vaults of Eastern city banks than of the smaller institutions which served most localities.[28] The conference report, according to Carter Glass, consisted of "fifty percent House infamy and fifty percent Senate infamy, thereby making the whole of it utterly bad." Democrats in both Houses voted against the Aldrich-Vreeland bill as they had voted against its respective progenitors.[29]

Certain themes stand out in the Democratic response to Republican currency bills, all of them logical extensions of earlier positions taken on the "money question." The Aldrich bill did nothing, claimed Isidor Rayner, to meet the underlying defect of the financial system, which was the way in which money was drawn away from the localities where it was most needed and into the coffers of banks in New York and other major financial centers, there to be used for stock market speculation. It would operate to the advantage of big-city bankers and the "predatory financiers" to whom they were allied. Several Democrats gave vent to a suspicion of the collective entity commonly known as "Wall Street" and earlier as the "money power," a privileged clique of financiers who enlisted the power of government to tighten their grip on the nation's financial system. Democrats generally desired to take the government out of banking and expressed some dislike for the national banking system. Ollie James touched upon a common pulse of Democratic concern when he warned against the wide discretion given to the Secretary of the Treasury in determining, first of all, whether a financial emergency existed and, secondly, which securities were eligible as backing for the additional currency. Such power in the hands of one man was an invitation to tyranny, not to mention the kind of favoritism exhibited by the Treasury Department during the 1907 panic. At the same time, Democrats

---

[27] *C.R.*, 60.1:3964, 4017, 4023, 7260–1. For a description of the bill and the Democratic response see *Outlook*, 88 (18 January 1908), 106–7; *New York Times*, 9, 26, 29 January 1908; Robert C. West, *Banking Reform and the Federal Reserve, 1863–1913* (Ithaca, N.Y.: Cornell University Press, 1977), 49–51.

[28] *C.R.*, 60.1:6246–7 and 6244–95 passim; *New York Times*, 14, 15 May 1908; Underwood, *Drifting Sands of Party Politics*, 292–4. On the Democrats' alternative proposal see *New York Times*, 5, 8 February 1908.

[29] *C.R.*, 60.1:7068–70, 7074–6.

favored the establishment of a United States currency to replace that issued by the national banks. Senate Democrats supported an amendment declaring the notes to be United States, not national bank, currency. It is notable that every Democrat voting on this amendment was in favor, every Republican against. In this respect conservative and progressive Republicans displayed their common heritage, even though some of the latter shared the Democrats' misgivings about other features of the bill.[30]

The bill creating a system of postal savings banks presented to the next Congress was compatible with the Democratic platform of 1908. But the platform had endorsed such a scheme only if it could "be constituted so as to keep the deposited money in the communities where it is established." Democrats in Congress united in condemning the Smoot amendment, which "changed the whole character of this legislation" by allowing the deposits to be invested in United States bonds. The effect, said Bacon, would be "to sponge up all the money all over the country at large and concentrate it in the money centers of the country, thus increasing and intensifying one of the radical and most objectionable features of the practical operations of our financial system." Like some Republican critics, they feared that the bill, with its bond-purchasing feature, was designed as a "Trojan horse" for a future central banking system. Democratic objections were wholly consistent, then, with their strictures on earlier Republican financial proposals.[31]

Also consistent with the traditions of their party was the support given by congressional Democrats to proposals to democratize the political system. Democrats voted regularly to liberalize the rules of the House of Representatives. It was, of course, Democratic votes that made possible the rules changes of 1910.[32] A majority of Democrats in the upper chamber voted for the direct election of Senators by popular vote, although several Southern members were deterred by the Republican insistence on national control of the election process.[33] It was in the name of democracy and local self-rule that Democrats opposed joint statehood for New Mexico and Arizona against the wishes of most of the citizens of Arizona, in what Edwin Webb of North Carolina hyperbolically dubbed "the most monstrous political crime" since Reconstruction. Five years later they continued to fight for self-determination for Arizona in opposition to Republican

[30] *New York Times*, 29 January, 13, 19, 25 February 1908; C.R., 60.1:4023, 6253–61, 6285–6.
[31] C.R., 61.2:2771–3, 8628–31. See also C.R., 61.2:2671–5, 2718–22, 2774, 2779–80.
[32] Sarasohn, *Party of Reform*, 62–3, 74–6; Barfield, "Democratic Party," 15–65.
[33] C.R., 60.2:6906; 61.3:3639. Every Democrat voted against the Sutherland amendment proposing federal control of senatorial elections, while nine voted against the resolution itself once amended. On the political calculations involved in Democratic support for direct election, see Ronald F. King and Susan Ellis, "Partisan Advantage and Constitutional Change: The Case of the Seventeenth Amendment," *Studies in American Political Development* 10 (1996): 69–102; Daniel Wirls, "Regionalism, Rotten Boroughs, Race, and Realignment: The Seventeenth Amendment and the Politics of Representation," ibid. 13 (1999): 18–20.

attempts to demand modification of the state constitution as the price of admission.[34]

With their deepest roots in the agrarian periphery of the South and West, the Democrats tended to be less sympathetic than Republicans to federal policies promoting industrial development. With their Jacksonian heritage, they were less hospitable, in principle if not always in practice, to the distributive policies that lay at the heart of the Republican program. "The question," says David Brady, referring to the 1890s, "was whether America was to be a major industrial-urban world power, or whether it was to be partly industrialized with large petit-bourgeois and agrarian sections. The Republican and Democratic parties were the primary vehicles for carrying into operation the two differing formulas."[35] This may be to map out the partisan battleground in greatly oversimplified terms, but it conveys a fundamental truth. The center of gravity of the Democratic party in Congress remained pretty much where it had lain for generations. Its opposition to tariffs, subsidies and other forms of "special privilege" constituted a restatement of ancient Jeffersonian and Jacksonian principles. So did its fear of the "money power," of powerful private banking interests occupying, through government favor, a privileged position in the financial system. A strong identification with the principle of popular democracy had been a key Democratic doctrine for just as long. In these respects the Bryan Democracy drew upon older traditions. It was from within these traditions that the party sought to come to terms with the new issues raised by corporate power in an integrated national economy and the status of labor in industrial society.[36]

"Democratic Doctrine"

We demand an enlargement of the powers of the Interstate Commerce Commission, to the end that the traveling public and shippers of the country may have prompt and adequate relief from the abuses to which they are subjected in the matter of transportation.[37]

With these words the Democratic National Convention of 1904 reiterated the pledges made, in almost identical language, in 1896 and 1900 to work for a more effective regulation of interstate railroads. No such words were included in the Republican platform. So, when a Republican president proceeded shortly after the election to call for railroad regulation Democrats

---

[34] C.R., 59.1:1559; 61.2:8237; 61.3:4319–20.

[35] David W. Brady, *Critical Elections and Congressional Policy Making* (Stanford, Cal.: Stanford University Press, 1988), 53.

[36] John Gerring, on the other hand, sees a major realignment in Democratic ideology from the 1890s. *Party Ideologies*, 161–231.

[37] Kirk H. Porter and Donald B. Johnson, eds., *National Party Platforms, 1840–1964* (Urbana: University of Illinois Press, 1966), 132.

were quick to accuse him of appropriating what for years had been a "Democratic doctrine." The bill presented to the House of Representatives by Hepburn in January 1906 contained elements not only of measures introduced by Republicans, like the earlier Esch-Townsend and Hepburn bills, but also of the Davey bill supported by the House Democrats during the previous session. Indeed, Williams pronounced that it contained such a strong infusion of Democratic ideas that it deserved to be called the Hepburn-Davey bill: "Several of its most indispensable – indeed its vital features – were engrafted on it by the insistence of the minority."[38] House Democrats, therefore, for all their misgivings, supported the Hepburn bill and, though critical of many of its features, voted unanimously for the bill on passage. Nearly every Republican also voted in favor of the bill, though not always, it seems, with good grace or enthusiasm.

The same pattern prevailed in the upper house. Most Senate Democrats fought strenuously against attempts to attach a broad review amendment to the bill and overwhelmingly supported attempts to strengthen it: by reinvigorating the long and short haul clause, by restoring imprisonment as a penalty for rebates, by requiring a physical valuation of railroad property as a basis for determining a "reasonable" rate, by imposing tight restrictions on the issue of free passes and by bringing pipelines under the supervision of the ICC. Not only did they, like all but five Republicans, vote for the commodity amendment, which barred railroads from engaging in the production and sale of goods that they carried, but a more elaborate clause offered by Tillman, which extended its provisions to companies connected to the railroads by stock ownership or interlocking directorates, was supported by most Democrats (19-4) and rejected by most Republicans (5-38). Many Democrats, however, worried about the constitutional viability of the commodity clause. It was Bailey's contention that "Congress has no power to control within a State the production of coal or any other commodity." The section had to be substantially rewritten to meet such objections. Most Democrats regarded the involvement of railroads in such activities as a grave evil that required correction, but they were anxious to ensure that in providing such corrective legislation Congress should not trespass beyond the boundaries imposed by the Constitution.[39]

Democratic backing for effective regulation was no less manifest four years later. Senate Democrats overwhelmingly opposed the proposal in the Mann-Elkins bill to create a Commerce Court and voted to expunge it. They took equal exception to the proposal to legalize traffic agreements between

---

[38] *New York Times*, 14 November, 4 December 1905, 31 January 1906; John Sharp Williams, "The Democratic Party and the Railroad Question," *Independent* 60 (1 March 1906): 485–8; Sarasohn, *Party of Reform*, 3–10; Sanders, *Roots of Reform*, 197–202.

[39] C.R., 59.1:6370, 6552, 6570, 7014. See also C.R., 59.1:6456, 6460, 6499–6500, 6504–5, 6562–8.

railroad companies. They voted almost unanimously to enlarge the powers of the ICC by, among other things, allowing it to suspend a rate increase for an extended period, inserting an effective long and short haul clause, providing for physical valuation, and bringing telephone and telegraph companies under ICC control. In three out of four roll calls a united, or nearly united, Democracy, alongside a dozen or so progressive Republicans, lined up against the bulk of the Republican party. "You will find that the great Republican leaders of the Senate furnished the oratory and the Democrats furnished the votes," suggested Newlands. That was indeed the case.[40] Only on one section were the Democrats reluctant to countenance an enlargement of federal regulatory power. That was the section authorizing the Commission to supervise the issues of stocks and bonds by railroad companies and prohibiting the purchase of stock in competing roads, a subject which Bailey regarded as "wholly beyond the jurisdiction of the General Government."[41] Here again, constitutional scruples proved a powerful inhibitor of Democratic support for regulation.

Although spokesmen for both parties were prone to discourse lyrically about the "horny-handed sons of toil" and loudly pronounce their friendship to the workingman, there was no doubt that, judging at least from their behavior in Congress, the Democrats could lay a stronger claim to that status. They proved consistently more sympathetic to labor legislation and to the demands of labor organizations.

One such demand, strongly pressed by the railroad brotherhoods, was for a limitation on the hours of work required of the employees of interstate railroads. Although anxious like Tillman to protect "necessitous employees" from the greed of the railroad companies, most Democrats, like most Republicans, supported the measure as much out of concern for the defenseless passenger as sympathy for the overworked railroad worker. "This is a very proper and sensible effort," said Bailey, "to preserve the public safety by requiring that overworked men shall not operate the trains upon which the public must ride."[42] Democrats supported an effective law more consistently than Republicans. Twenty-one Senate Democrats voted for La Follette's substitute bill and only four against; in his own party the figures were 16 and 28, respectively. Large majorities of Democrats joined La Follette to vote down amendments offered by Gallinger and Brandegee which expanded the

---

[40] Sarasohn, "Democratic Surge," 147–56; Francis G. Newlands, *Public Papers* (Arthur B. Darling, ed., 2 vols., New York, 1932), 1:352–62; *Outlook*, 94 (12 March 1910), 640–1, 816–19; William C. Adamson to Irvine Lenroot, 4 June 1910, Lenroot MSS, LC; Barfield, "Democratic Party," 141–95; Sanders, *Roots of Reform*, 203–7; Underwood, *Drifting Sands of Party Politics*, 394–8.

[41] C.R., 60.1:6972, 7135. See also C.R., 61.2:5900–1, 7573–4 (Adamson), 6965–6, 7132–3 (Bailey); Sanders, *Roots of Reform*, 207; Barfield, "Democratic Party," 185–9. For dissenting voices, see Newlands, *Public Papers*, 1:362–75; C.R., 61.2:6962–5, 7191–5.

[42] C.R., 59.1:9265 (Bailey), 9364–5 (Tillman); 59.2:763–4, 924–6 (Patterson).

range of mitigating circumstances under which railroads might evade the requirements of the law. On the Brandegee amendment Democrats and Republicans voted 6–17 and 16–28, respectively, on the Gallinger amendment 5–19 and 26–16. When Bacon, obsessive in his pursuit of constitutional rectitude, proposed the exclusion of railroads whose lines lay wholly within one state only two of his colleagues, Clark and Money, supported him, whereas thirteen Republicans did.[43] For the bill passed by the Senate the House Committee on Interstate and Foreign Commerce substituted a measure which the Democrats found thoroughly unsatisfactory – "a mockery and a delusion" according to William C. Adamson. Democratic members complained that the committee's bill was too hedged around with qualifications to be effective, and their united opposition denied the two-thirds majority necessary for passage under suspension of the rules. A few days later it reappeared in a form revised to meet most of their objections.[44]

Democratic leaders in both chambers proclaimed their support for anti-injunction and eight-hour laws and other measures requested by the American Federation of Labor. None of these came before either house. However, the Hughes amendment to the 1910 Sundry Civil Appropriation bill denying funds for the prosecution of labor unions under the Sherman Act, though opposed by most Republicans as "class legislation of the most pernicious and vicious character," received a solid Democratic vote in both houses.[45] Lacking further opportunities to vote for labor legislation, congressional Democrats took pains to go on record against measures which organized labor publicly opposed, such as the amendment abrogating the eight-hour law on the Panama Canal, the provision in the ship subsidy bill for the conscription of sailors in wartime, and the abolition of compulsory pilotage for coastal shipping.[46]

A growing sympathy for organized labor was evident also in the Democrats' responses to the Bill of Grievances presented by the American Federation of Labor in March 1906. The immediate outcome was a not altogether effective AFL endorsement of Democratic candidates in the congressional elections of that year and of Bryan in the presidential election of 1908. Despite the transparent reluctance of the AFL leadership to commit itself to any formal association, congressional Democrats continued to cultivate the working-class vote and did what they could to enact labor's legislative program. "This alliance," argues Sanders (although "alliance" is

[43] *C.R.*, 59.2:891–3. On the Bacon amendment see *C.R.*, 59.2:819–20, 883–4. See also *New York Times*, 11 January 1907.
[44] *C.R.*, 59.2:3235–52, 3755–60; *New York Times*, 17, 19, 24 February 1907.
[45] *C.R.*, 61.2:7325–7, 8654–6, 8847–50; Sarasohn, "Democratic Surge," 160–2.
[46] *C.R.*, 59.1:1603–11, 1629–30; *New York Times*, 30 December 1905, 26, 27 January 1906; *American Federationist* 13 (1906): 162–5, 880–2, 980–1; *C.R.*, 59.1:7030–1; 59.2:153, 3069, 4372–3.

perhaps too strong a word), "formed the basis for a revitalized Democratic party in the Progressive Era."[47]

The Limits of Democratic Progressivism

It is only by a considerable stretch of the imagination that one can see in the Democratic party of the early twentieth century a prototype of New Deal liberalism. Planter-statesmen of the stamp of John Sharp Williams were ill-suited to the role of spokesmen for the urban working class. Nor did Southern agrarians easily fit the part of precursors of modern social policy. The fact remains that, in Congress at least, the Democratic party was a predominately Southern party with, correspondingly, a pronounced agrarian bias and a continuing allegiance to states rights, both of which greatly restricted the range of reform measures which even the most progressive Democrats could gladly subscribe to.

The Senate Democrats furnished comparatively less support for child labor legislation than their Republican opponents. Democrats protested like Teller against government encroachment on the preserve of the family, defended like Money the right of children to engage in "lawful and wholesome" work to support their families, or proclaimed like Bacon the virtues of outdoor occupations.[48] The Nelson amendment allowing the employment of children under fourteen outside school hours in "mercantile establishments, stores, and business offices" attracted more Democratic than Republican votes, by a margin of 13–4 as against 19–26.[49] Constitutional considerations had no application to federal policy in the District; the preference of Southern Democrats for a less restrictive child labor law was, as much as anything, a reflection of the region's relative backwardness in social policy.[50]

Similar considerations influenced the response of Southern Congressmen to other aspects of social policy. As we have seen, they showed scant sympathy for proposals to establish a system of public playgrounds in the District of Columbia. They resented the cost of such newfangled experiments in child welfare, and they did not see the point of them. So when provision for public playgrounds came to a vote during consideration of the 1909 District Appropriation, and again in 1910, Southern Democrats were to be found almost unanimously in opposition to increasing the sum allocated. It is notable, on the other hand, that the growing number of Northern Democrats, many alluding directly to their experience of urban problems, provided more

---

[47] Sanders, *Roots of Reform*, 161.
[48] *C.R.*, 59.2:200, 202, 204; 60.1:5796–7. See also the remarks by Bacon and Rayner in *C.R.*, 59.2:1824–6.
[49] *C.R.*, 60.1:5792.
[50] *C.R.*, 59.2:1797; Samuel McCune Lindsay, "When Congress Acts as a State Legislature," *Charities and the Commons* 15 (3 March 1906): 756.

TABLE 8.2. *Democratic Voting on D.C. Playground Appropriations in the House of Representatives, 1909–1910*

Page in C.R.	North	South	Urban	Rural	Total
60.2, 819	18–10	14–64	17–14	13–57	32–74
61.2, 2930	13–16	12–63	18–16	7–65	25–79
61.2, 5970	15–20	17–54	20–18	12–56	32–74

Note: Urban representatives are here defined as those from districts in which over 30 percent of the population was urban.

support for such innovations. Roughly half of the Democrats who voted for increased playground facilities represented Northern constituencies; roughly half represented urban districts. Table 8.2 reveals a clear difference between the voting of Northern and Southern, urban and rural members on this issue.[51]

Democratic votes were frequently cast against the Administration's conservation policies. During the Fifty-ninth and Sixtieth Congresses Senators from the public land states launched a series of attacks upon the management of the forest reserves. Henry M. Teller and Thomas M. Patterson, themselves representatives of the Mountain West, joined gleefully in the attack, expressing the same outrage as their Republican neighbors at the overzealous intrusiveness of the Forest Service and the arbitrary behavior of the federal government in its unwonted role as landlord. "The men who cast their lot with a State and elect to live there are the proper persons to control the destiny of that State," declared Teller.[52] Only Newlands among Western Democrats defended Administration policies, arguing that, since the public lands belonged not just to the people of the states in which they lay but to "the entire people of the United States," the federal government must manage them in the general interest.[53] Southern Democrats like Clay, Tillman, and Bailey, whose constituents' interests were not directly affected, also expressed unease regarding the activity of the Forest Service, the wide discretion wielded by the Secretary of the Interior in managing the reserves, and the public propriety of government sales of timber.[54] On a number of occasions minority Senators voted to reduce the sum appropriated for the Forest Service.[55]

The only conservation measure to come to a vote in the House, the proposal to create a forest reserve in the Appalachian and White Mountains, naturally attracted support from Southern Democrats, since large areas in the Southern states were expected to benefit from reforestation of the watersheds

[51] *C.R.*, 59.2:1226–7, 1297–9; 60.1:4383–6; 60.2:859–75.
[52] *C.R.*, 59.2:3192–5, 3542–3 (Patterson), 3724–6 (Clark); 60.2:3223–9 (Teller).
[53] *C.R.*, 59.2:1959–62, 2207–14, 3194; Newlands, *Public Papers*, 1:108–11.
[54] *C.R.*, 59.2:3190, 3200, 3205; 60.2:3227.
[55] *C.R.*, 59.2:3197; 60.1:6076; 60.2:3252–3. Cf. Barfield, "Democratic Party," 199–215.

of the region's major rivers. For similar reasons, New England Democrats hoped that the measure would check the "criminal waste and destruction of the watershed forest growth." On the other hand, Democratic Congressmen from outside the affected area viewed the project as an unwarranted extravagance and an exercise in log rolling. John Fitzgerald of New York accused New England and Southern Congressmen of entering into a "community of plunder." Constitutional objections to the novel policy of federal acquisition of forest lands by purchase, which Democratic supporters of the bill were unmoved by, seemed of vital importance to Democratic opponents. William E. Cox of Indiana described the purchase by the Government of lands in the states and the establishment of an elaborate bureaucracy to manage them as "the worst case of an attempt at federal usurpation that I ever saw in my life." When the proposition came to a vote, while Democrats from states watered by streams flowing from the Appalachians and White Mountains voted almost as one in its favor, those from other sections of the country were divided, but mostly hostile.[56]

A Jeffersonian Democracy

It is all too easy, looking at the Bryan Democracy through the prism of the New Deal years, to forget how strong was its commitment to the traditional Democratic dogma of states rights and limited government. John Sharp Williams, while advocating a variety of progressive reforms, spoke jealously of the prerogatives of the states and the strict limits on federal power imposed by the Constitution. He did not, like, for example, Roosevelt, regard government as a beneficent instrument for the advancement of human welfare but as a "necessary evil growing out of the vices of human nature" and one whose excesses were earnestly to be guarded against. "My reading of history convinces me that most bad government has come out of too much government," he observed. Oscar Underwood spoke up for local self-government, declaring that "the prime purpose of government should be to protect the rights and the liberties of the people."[57] Even Bryan, the cynosure of the progressive Democracy, found it necessary to air his fears that centralization would result in a despotic government remote from the people and vulnerable to special interests. The 1908 Democratic platform contained, along with a clutch of reform demands, a ringing declaration in favor of states rights. Throughout the early part of

[56] C.R., 59.2:1909–12, 4481–9; 60.2:3532–40. In 1909 Democratic members from the Northeast and the states of Maryland, Virginia, North and South Carolina, Alabama, Tennessee, Mississippi, and Louisiana supported the bill by a margin of 50–15, the rest of the party by 28–47. C.R., 60.2:4489.

[57] Williams quoted in Osborn, *Williams*, 143–4; Underwood, *Drifting Sands*, 8, 38.

the century liberal Democrats wrestled with the implications of their party's traditions.[58]

Two recurrent themes were a defense of states rights and a distrust of bureaucracy. We have already seen how such considerations shaped Democrats' response to conservation and railroad regulation. A tenderness for states rights was evident in relation to other measures which they mostly favored. The pure food bill proposed to bar from interstate commerce fraudulent or deleterious articles of food or drink, since state regulation had failed to prevent the carriage of prohibited articles across state lines. This offended Democratic scruples. Money, believing that it infringed upon the "inherent and inalienable" police powers of the states, presented a substitute bill which made it clear that it was the shipper, and not the manufacturer, who was to be brought to account. The bill's sponsors viewed Money's substitute as an attempt to "nullify" effective legislation in the interest of the National Food Manufacturers' Association, whose officers had drafted it. According to McCumber, it "would no more prohibit the introduction of fraudulent and spurious goods in any State than a sieve would hold water."[59] If Money's opposition to the Heyburn-McCumber bill reflected more than a deep-rooted constitutionalism, his criticism of its constitutional underpinnings found support from other influential Democrats. In so far as the bill sought to protect the people against deleterious food and drugs, argued Bailey, it constituted a serious infringement on the police power of the states.

> If it were an attempt in good faith to regulate commerce, there could be no doubt as to the power of the Federal Government over it; but as it is intended, understood, and supported for the purpose of protecting the people of the several States against injurious articles of food and drink, it is purely and only an exercise of the police power, and therefore not within the power of the Federal Government. . . . I maintain that the Federal Government, under the guise of regulating interstate commerce, can not take charge of the health or morals of the people of a State.

Bailey heartily favored pure food legislation but insisted that responsibility lay with the states, "because with the States is left the right to control the health and morals of their people." If they were not to regulate public health and morals, what function had they left? "I am sincerely anxious," he went on, "that each State in the Union shall regulate its own domestic concerns without interference or suggestions from outside. . . ." The states must be relied upon to take action to preserve the health and morals of their citizens,

---

[58] Wiseman, "Dilemmas of a Party out of Power," 94–6.
[59] C.R., 59.1:2652–65. The bill's sponsors, Weldon Heyburn and Porter McCumber were highly critical of the Money substitute. See C.R.:59.1, 894–8, 1216–21. On Money's relationship to the National Food Manufacturers' Association see Oscar E. Anderson, Jr., *The Health of a Nation: Harvey W. Wiley and the Fight for Pure Food* (Chicago: Chicago University Press, 1958), 177; J. Harvey Young, *Pure Food: Securing the Federal Food and Drug Act of 1906* (Princeton: Princeton University Press, 1989), 206–7.

or else the "dual system of government" established by the Founding Fathers must be pronounced a failure.[60] Most Democrats, responding to the tide of public pressure, voted for the pure food bill. Only sixteen Democrats in the House took their constitutional scruples so far as to vote against it, but their number included men as prominent as Adamson, Bartlett, Burleson, and Williams. Four Southern Democrats registered the only votes cast against the bill in the Senate: Bailey, Bacon, Foster, and Tillman.[61]

Bailey had similar misgivings about federal meat inspection. Though "deeply anxious" for a "drastic inspection law," he was determined that Congress should regulate the entry of meat products into interstate commerce and not their manufacture. "The power to superintend the cleanliness of a manufacturing establishment...is a State and not a Federal power." Manufacturers could not be penalized for refusing inspection, but their goods might be barred from interstate commerce. Only if amended to remedy this "fatal defect" could the bill, in Bailey's view, pass the scrutiny of the courts.[62]

Although they supported regulation of the hours of work of railroad employees, Southerners like Bacon and Culberson were adamant that it should be explicitly confined to interstate transportation. So strong was this insistence on the part of Senate Democrats that La Follette, the bill's sponsor, found it necessary to incorporate an amendment drafted by Culberson making it applicable only to trains "carrying interstate or foreign freight or passengers." As he informed his wife, "unless I accepted Culberson's amendment I knew I would lose the *over sensitive states rights* votes among the Democrats." This did not satisfy Bacon, who pointed out that nearly all railroads carried some interstate freight and could be regarded as engaging in interstate commerce. This, therefore, would be a bill of "extremely wide scope." It would be "a tremendous stride, an almost immeasurable stride, in the direction of turning over to the Federal Government the management of all the internal affairs and business affairs and relations of people in the various States." Bacon offered a still more restrictive amendment which would have excluded altogether lines which lay wholly within the borders of one state, but this received few Democratic votes.[63]

Congressional Democrats regularly expressed unease regarding the role of the new regulatory agencies created during the Progressive Era. Their ambivalence towards the ratemaking powers of the ICC has already been noted. Similar concern was expressed about the Commission's role in administering the railroad hours law. An amendment giving it discretionary authority

---

[60] *C.R.*, 59.1:2757–62.
[61] *C.R.*, 59.1:2773, 9075.
[62] *C.R.*, 59.1:9017–18.
[63] *C.R.*, 59.1:9265 (Bailey); 59.2:765–7, 883–4 (Bacon, Culberson, and Tillman); Robert M. La Follette to Belle C. La Follette, 11 January 1907, La Follette MSS, LC.

to allow exemptions in "special circumstances" troubled Bacon, who was not convinced that an executive agency could be safely clothed with such powers. House Democrats were highly critical of a proviso in the final conference report which authorized the Commission to suspend the operation of the law until it was satisfied that the railroads were ready to carry out its provisions without an unacceptable level of disruption.[64]

Critical attention was similarly drawn to the role of the Chief Chemist in administering the pure food law. According to Money, he would become "the sole arbiter of the manufacturing interests of the United States, so far as food products, drinks and drugs are concerned." He could at will declare any food product to be "fraudulent" or "adulterated" and ruin its manufacturers. His own bill laid down precise standards to be followed. Tillman, too, felt the need to set standards "of what constitutes a wholesome, healthy article of commerce," rather than entrusting the establishment of rules and regulations to an administrative bureau. In a similar vein, Bailey inveighed against contemporary tendencies towards bureaucratic government. No longer content merely to pass a law, "we now feel that we must organize a bureau and subject everybody's business to its inquisitorial powers.... Thus it is that bureau after bureau is built up, and we vest them with such extraordinary power, until the American Republic will become a bureaucracy instead of a democracy." Instead of such elaborate mechanisms, Congress should pass clear, unequivocal laws and deal out condign punishment to transgressors. One adulterator in the penitentiary would achieve more than a bevy of bureaus.[65]

Along with "centralization" and federal encroachment, a recurrent theme in Democratic speeches, on the floor of Congress and on the stump, was that of "executive tyranny," a term which embraced the administrative excesses of Roosevelt and his more enthusiastic subordinates, as well as his energetic foreign policy. Conservatives like Morgan and Pettus frequently launched Ciceronian assaults upon Roosevelt's alleged abuses of power.[66] In an article in the *Independent* in 1906, Bacon complained that "the actual exercise of power by the executive branch of the Government in this day exceeds the bounds originally contemplated for it by the Constitution." In particular, the executive had encroached upon the legislative branch of the government, to such an extent that now "the controlling factor in national legislation is not in Congress... but in the President." The framers of the Constitution were careful to make of the presidency a purely executive office, in order to avoid

---

[64] *C.R.*, 59.2:821–4, 4619–26.

[65] *C.R.*, 59.2:2653–4 (Money), 2756 (Tillman), 2760 (Bailey). Note also the Democratic preference for imprisonment of business magnates responsible for violating the interstate commerce laws. See, for example, *C.R.*, 59.1:6620–8.

[66] John T. Morgan to Francis G. Newlands, 18 March 1906, Newlands MSS, SLYU; Edmund Pettus to John T. Morgan, 10 October 1906, Morgan MSS, LC.

the dangers that followed from the concentration of executive and legislative powers in one man's hands. They were well aware "that one so girt with power would grow great in his own conceit; that he would attempt to draw to himself all the authority of government, and ... might come to think of himself compassed by 'the divinity that doth hedge a king.'" Such overweening ambitions posed great dangers to the Republic.[67] Isidor Rayner was no less critical of the President's supposed usurpation of power. "The President is laboring under the honest impression that he is responsible to the country for the legislation of Congress." He made treaties with Santo Domingo and expected the Senate to ratify them; he neglected Congress in managing the Canal; he criticized the decisions of federal judges. In such fields as conservation policy he and his lieutenants undertook major policy initiatives without congressional authorization and, at times, directly contrary to congressional wishes.[68]

The Roosevelt antitrust policy was a case in point. As is well known, Roosevelt preferred to exercise a broad executive discretion in the control of large corporations than to rely on prosecution under so seemingly categorical a piece of legislation as the Sherman Act. It was not the prerogative of the Executive, insisted Williams, to choose whether to enforce the law or not. Only criminal prosecutions would make the antitrust laws effective. Bryan noted that the trusts had grown in size and number during Roosevelt's term, almost wholly unchecked by the enforcement of federal law.[69] Roosevelt's supposed dereliction of duty seemed clearest in his acquiescence in the acquisition by United States Steel of the Tennessee Coal and Iron Company, supposedly to mitigate the effects of the 1907 financial panic. In Culberson's view he had given his sanction to "a direct and deliberate violation of the law." The incident appeared to show how dangerous it was to allow the excecutive so much discretion in determining how and when the antitrust law should be enforced. During the final session of the Sixtieth Congresses the Senate Democrats, with the tacit encouragement of some of Roosevelt's own party, attempted to embarrass the President by ordering an investigation of the legality of his actions in that case.[70]

---

[67] Augustus O. Bacon, "The President and Congress," *Independent* 60 (22 March 1906): 546–9.
[68] *New York Times*, 1 February 1907, 24 April 1908.
[69] *New York Times*, 6 March 1906; *Outlook* 90 (5 September 1908): 3–5.
[70] C.R., 60.2:452, 574–6, 624; *New York Times*, 7–10 January 1909; *Outlook* 91 (16 January 1909): 88–9; James W. Madden, *Charles Allen Culberson* (Austin: University of Texas Press, 1929), 177. On the background to the TCIC merger, see Martin J. Sklar, *The Corporate Reconstruction of American Capitalism, 1880–1916: The Market, the Law, and Politics* (Cambridge: Cambridge University Press, 1988), 184–203; William Henry Harbaugh, *The Life and Times of Theodore Roosevelt* (New York, 1975), 295–301; Robert H. Wiebe, "The House of Morgan and the Executive, 1905–1913," *American Historical Review* 45 (1959): 49–60; Arthur M. Johnson, "Theodore Roosevelt and the Bureau of Corporations," *Mississippi Historical Review* 45 (1959): 571–90.

Such sallies were the normal currency of party conflict, with a Democratic minority calling a Republican president to account. But both the insistence of Democratic protests and the republican rhetoric in which they were couched testify to the continuing strength of the Jeffersonian tradition in the twentieth-century Democracy. They also betray a profound disquiet with regard to the statist implications of Roosevelt's presidential project. While broadly welcoming the objectives of progressive reform, especially in the field of economic policy, they were uneasy about the institutional mechanisms that were being put into place to carry them out and the broader processes of state building of which they formed a part. They were prepared to envisage a quite substantial enlargement of the powers of the federal government to check what they saw as abuses of corporate power and to correct what they saw as inequalities in the balance of sectional advantage, but they sought to do so, as far as was practicable, by laying down firm and unambiguous legal standards which would effectively enforce themselves, rather than by empowering administrative experts to make the necessary adjustments. As Sanders puts it, "Their goal was the broad expansion of the *statutory* state."[71] However, a "statutory state" could not address the complexities of a modern industrial society which kept throwing up disputes and problems which could not be covered by even the most exhaustively detailed legislation. Congressional Democrats were therefore compelled repeatedly to accede to administrative solutions to technical problems such as the determination of railroad rates, even if they did so reluctantly and inconsistently, because the alternative was in most cases the historically unwelcome one of arbitration by the federal courts.

Conservative and Progressive Democrats

"There is no Democratic party and Bryan is its leader," announced the New York *World* in December 1907. Such a remark was not only willfully paradoxical but blatantly untrue. Conservative Democrats in the Cleveland tradition were certainly extant, as were Southern Bourbons and doctrinaires to whom the propositions of Jacksonian Democracy possessed all the axiomatic verity of the theorems of Euclid. The repeated attempts to locate a conservative alternative to Bryan attest to their existence. However, the desperation that attended such efforts, the failure of which had become transparent long before the date of the Denver Convention in June 1908, attests equally to their relative fragility. Whatever views they might have harbored in the recesses of their being, where conscience and intellectual consistency wrestled with cravings for electoral success, most politically active Democrats had

---

[71] Sanders, *Roots of Reform*, 389 and 387–408 passim. See also Sidney Milkis, "Introduction: Progressivism, Then and Now," in Sidney Milkis and Jerome M. Mileur, *Progressivism and the New Democracy* (Amherst: University of Massachusetts Press, 1999), 17–22.

accepted, or recognized the inevitability of, Bryan's leadership and the progressive policies with which his name was linked.[72]

Whatever their antecedents, most congressional Democrats pledged their support to a progressive program of legislation. In both houses of Congress the party exhibited an unexpected degree of unanimity. Deviations from the party line were rare, consisting usually of isolated defections by small numbers of individuals, as against the broad factional division over a range of issues that characterized the Republican party.

In the House during the course of the Fifty-ninth Congress serious intra-party divisions, measured by a Rice Index falling below 67, occurred in only twenty roll calls. After the removal of one or two procedural motions, together with a number of questions remote from the central areas of political discourse, such as the erection of a whipping post in the District of Columbia for the chastisement of wife-beaters or the fortification of sweet wines, the bulk of the remainder reveal various sectional alignments. This applies to the Philippine tariff bill, approved by most Democrats as a step in the general direction of tariff reduction but opposed by those representing rice and sugar-growing districts in Florida, Louisiana and Texas; payments for "special facilities" in the transport of mail by the Southern Railroad, condemned as "graft" by most Democrats but defended by many of those whose constituencies lay along its route; the proposal to create an Appalachian forest reserve, regarded by many Democrats as a violation of Jeffersonian principles but supported by the substantial number whose territory was watered by streams flowing from those mountains; or the quarantine bill, an extension of federal power welcomed by representatives of Gulf states vulnerable to the scourge of yellow fever.[73]

The proliferation of roll calls generated by a Democratic filibuster rules out such an exercise for the following Congress, but a similar pattern emerges in the Sixty-first. Here twenty-eight out of a much larger number of roll calls meet the criterion. Once more sectional interests account for a sizeable proportion, including votes on the lumber and hides sections of the tariff bill and the Appalachian and White Mountain Forest bill, while sizeable minorities supported the expansion and reorganization of the Army and Navy. Of the remainder the most important involve the playground appropriation already referred to, the resolution for an investigation of the Ballinger-Pinchot affair, and the bill creating a Tariff Board. In each case the distribution of Democratic votes was more or less specific to that issue. It is impossible from the

[72] Barfield, "Democratic Party," 1 and 1–14 passim; Sarasohn, "Democratic Surge," 1–13, 71–94; Sanders, *Roots of Reform*, 154–60; Gould, *Reform and Regulation*, 121–34; Coletta, "The Democratic Party, 1884–1910." On the opposition to Bryan's nomination in 1908, see Wiseman, "Dilemmas of a Party out of Power," 89–106; Coletta, *Bryan*, 353–411; Coletta, "The Election of 1908," in Schlesinger and Israel, eds., *History of American Presidential Elections*, 2049–90.

[73] C.R., 59.1:1163, 5251, 4706; 59.2:4480, 4489.

roll call evidence to identify a consistently conservative faction among the House Democrats.[74]

Senators were more prone to independent action, but dissent took the form of scattered guerilla bands rather than organized factions. During consideration of the Hepburn bill small minorities of Democrats voted alongside the main body of Republicans, and in opposition to the main body of their own party, against amendments which would enhance the powers of the ICC. A similar configuration was evident with reference to other reform measures in the Fifty-ninth and Sixtieth Congresses. No consistent conservative bloc stands out, although the names of Bacon, Clark and McEnery feature more regularly than most in the lists of defectors, while Morgan and Pettus pursued so distinctly irregular a course as to "constitute practically," in the words of the *New York Times*, "a third party in the Senate." But even they voted more often than not with the rest of their party, compiling a record of support for reform that only a few Republicans could match.[75] In the Sixty-first Congress the most significant issues to divide the party were the tariff, railroad regulation, and postal savings banks. Once more a few names recur, notably those of the Louisiana Senators McEnery and Foster, along with Fletcher and Taliaferro of Florida, all of whom felt constrained by the need to cultivate influence among the majority members of the Finance Committee, Hughes of Colorado, whom Newlands described as a "corporation man," Bailey, Simmons, and Money.[76] The conservatives were drawn as often from the newer and younger as from the older and more established members, and there is no clear pattern of regional concentration.

Henry Watterson commented in 1906 that the Democratic party "meant one thing east and another west, discounted both ways in the south, where the Nigger, and nothing but the Nigger, tips the beam."[77] No such defined sectional groupings are discernible in Congress. How could they be at a time when the great majority of Democratic members were drawn from one section – the South? Of 135 Democrats elected to the House of Representatives in 1904, 112 came from former slave states, as did 26 out of 32 Democratic Senators, the other 6 representing the Rocky Mountain West – a living vestige of the free silver movement of the 1890s (three, in fact, were former silver Republicans). In the next Congress the number of non-Southern Representatives had risen to 50, with the greatest inroads being made in a band of densely populated states from Pennsylvania to Indiana, which elected 5 Democrats in 1904 and 21 in 1906. Two years later they numbered 57. However, in the upper house, Democratic representation from outside the South

---

[74] *C.R.*, 61.1:1293–8; 61.2:405, 4444, 5970, 9026–7; 61.3:1696, 1709, 3125.
[75] *New York Times*, 4 March 1907.
[76] Francis G. Newlands to Thomas M. Patterson, 20 November 1908; Samuel W. Belford to Newlands, 9 January 1909, Newlands MSS, SLYU.
[77] Quoted in Wiseman, "Dilemmas of a Party out of Power," 10.

did not rise beyond six. It was not until the appearance of much larger numbers of Northern Democrats after the elections of 1910 and 1912 that the force of what John Buenker and Joseph J. Huthmacher have called "urban liberalism" made itself felt.[78]

As it was, the congressional Democrats retained many of the ambivalent features of a party in transition. A party whose leaders were prepared to march behind the banner of a Cleveland Democrat in 1904 could not be expected to give itself over wholeheartedly to Bryan and progressive reform a few years later. Many older Democrats in particular resisted the apparent destiny of their party. A party whose congressional ranks were recruited almost exclusively from one section of the country could not be expected consistently to display a national breadth of vision. It was inevitably wedded to the interests and the point of view of the agrarian South. Finally, a party whose members were weaned on the principles of Jeffersonian Democracy felt more than a little inhibited in espousing progressive measures which entailed a substantial augmentation of federal power and an enhancement of bureaucratic discretion. When one considers all these constraints, products of its history and its electoral geography, it is remarkable just how far in support of progressive reform the Democratic party in Congress felt able to go.

According to Sarasohn, many Democrats "accepted the Populist concept of the positive state."[79] Their resentment at corporate power, their responsiveness to the needs of farmers and, more equivocally, urban workers, and their desire to redress the regional imbalance between the economic interests of the urban-industrial "core" and the agrarian "periphery" made early twentieth-century Democrats readier to contemplate an enhancement of the authority of the state than the traditions of their party would seem to allow. It was Democratic votes that most consistently supported the expansion of federal regulatory powers. Yet those same traditions preaching suspicion of tyrannical government authority and resentment at the untrammeled powers of an unaccountable bureaucracy – that potent antistatist legacy, in other words – left their mark on the institutions of the nascent American state. Their construction derived its impetus very largely from those elements which were congenitally least disposed to welcome the building of a powerful federal government. Some of the inconsistencies in the resulting state structure reflect this paradox.

---

[78] On "urban liberalism" see Joseph Huthmacher, "Urban Liberalism and the Age of Reform," *Mississippi Valley Historical Review* 49 (1962): 231–41; John Buenker, *Urban Liberalism and Progressive Reform* (New York: Scribner, 1973).

[79] Sarasohn, *Party of Reform*, 17–18. See also Sanders, *Roots of Reform*, 4.

9

Congress, Progressive Reform, and the New American State

In November 1905 Henry Adams affirmed that he would be present as usual to witness the opening of Congress. "If anyone were to come and take me by the ear, and lead me off to statesmen in the moon, I should go more readily, but, lunatic for lunatic, the Washington type has to me the merit that I have known him drunk and have known him sober, for fifty years, and drunk or sober there was never anything in him – but himself."[1] The statesmen on Capitol Hill responded in various ways to the demands of the new century, but, as Adams implied, for all the stresses and strains that they were subjected to, they remained largely true to type. Although Congress as an institution differed markedly from its nineteenth-century forbears, there remained significant elements of continuity. Although new legislative challenges and new problems of governance crowded in upon it at the start of the new century, its responses were shaped by habits of mind and structures of decision making inherited from an earlier epoch. And, although it was closely involved in the creation of a newly invigorated nation-state, Congress as an institution continued to transmit diverse constituency pressures and to give voice to the influence of "localism" in American political life.

Congressional action took very different forms in different areas of policy making. In the shape of the Hepburn and Mann-Elkins Acts Congress went a considerable way towards solving the political and legal, though less certainly the economic, problems of railroad regulation. Both the nature of progressive thinking on the "railroad problem" and the structure of congressional decision making militated against the attainment of an optimal pattern of regulation and control, illustrating many of the difficulties that attended the birth of the new American state. Chapter 4 traced the decisions, or more exactly the "non-decisions," taken by Congress in the field of labor relations. The demands of the American Federation of Labor, as enunciated in its Bill of Grievances of 1906, met with a stony refusal from a majority of

---

[1] Henry Adams to "My Adored Sister," 7 November 1905, Henry Cabot Lodge MSS, MasHS.

Republican Congressmen fearful of labor violence and fearful for property rights. Congress's failure to legislate on the subject had significant implications for the status of organized labor in American society, and therefore for the bargaining rights of working men and women. In the one locality, the District of Columbia, where it possessed plenary powers of government, untrammeled by any competing local jurisdiction, Congress was too preoccupied with other business, too divided on questions of social policy, and too influenced by narrow considerations of fiscal prudence to provide an exemplary progressive government for Washington and thereby to realize the reformers' dream of a "model city" on federal territory. The opportunity to use the governance of the federal domain as a template to guide the making of social policy in the several states was therefore not taken.

The preceding chapters explored the factional structure of the House and Senate. Analysis of the Republican party in both chambers revealed one dominant fissure, which deepened over time, over issues involving the promotion and regulation of business, tariff revision, banking, and political reform. Voting on labor and social reform measures and the conservation of natural resources, however, followed a very different pattern. The social roots of Republican insurgency lay in the newer states of the Midwest and the Pacific littoral and its ideological roots in older traditions of republican thought. Though small in number, the insurgents had a disproportionate impact on the tenor of congressional debate, on the formation of policy, and on the decision-making process, especially in the House of Representatives. Congressional Democrats were almost invariably more progressive than congressional Republicans on issues relating to economic regulation, taxation, and political reform but prone to defer to traditional states' rights principles, a traditional suspicion of bureaucracy and traditional views of social policy in their response to other aspects of progressive reform. They retained a deep-lying suspicion of the agencies of the nation-state.

It remains therefore to weave the various threads of the argument into the three main strands prefigured in the Introduction. First, we must reflect on what can be learned about progressivism by examining the ways in which it found expression in the national legislature. Second, we must consider what such an investigation can tell us about the dynamics of state making. Third, we must examine the changing nature of Congress itself as an institution in the context of the broader transformation of American political structures at the start of the twentieth century.

Progressivism in Congress

Does it make any sense to talk of a "progressive movement" in Congress? In a limited sense it clearly does. As David A. Sarasohn concludes, there certainly was a political progressivism in the sense of "an effort to limit the power of wealth in America and to give some protection to those who lacked it."[2] From the evidence of congressional debates and roll calls we can distinguish a fairly cohesive movement on the part of Congressmen from the South and Midwest to extend the regulatory powers of the federal government, in some cases to redress what appeared to be inequitable treatment of local business interests, particularly at the hands of the railroads, in others to protect the interests of consumers against abuses of corporate power. A rising "consumer consciousness," or more exactly a rising consciousness of consumers on the part of politicians and journalists, manifested itself in this period. It was around 1906, according to Richard Hofstadter, that the consumer first stepped forward as a serious factor in American politics.[3] The progressives in Congress, comprising Democrats and a smaller number of insurgent Republicans, supported stricter regulation of railroad rates and practices, a pure food and drug law, effective meat inspection, reform of the banking and currency system so as to make currency and credit more easily available outside the major financial centers, a system of postal savings banks, and a more vigorous prosecution of the antitrust laws. At the same time they protested against distributive policies which bestowed unwarranted largesse upon favored private interests, for example through ship subsidies and tariff protection.

There was a certain coherence in the positions held by congressional progressives. Feeling that the distributive policies of the past had brought disproportionate favors to certain groups in society and certain sections of the country and that the actions of "foreign" banking and railroad corporations jeopardized the economic interests of their constituents, Southern and Midwestern Congressmen supported an overall shift in the direction of federal economic policy from the distribution of economic benefits to the regulation of business. This flowed directly from the profound sense of regional disadvantage that past policies had engendered.[4] Their intention was not to replace the corporate system but to moderate its power over government, to check the perceived abuses arising from unregulated corporate power, and to redress perceived regional imbalances in economic advantage.

As Nelson Aldrich commented with reference to tariff revision, the progressives had their own sectional axes to grind. However, they garbed their

---

[2] David A. Sarasohn, *Party of Reform: Democrats in the Progressive Era* (Oxford: University of Mississippi Press, 1988), viii.

[3] Richard Hofstadter, *The Age of Reform: From Bryan to FDR* (New York: Random House, 1955), 170–1; David P. Thelen, *Robert M. La Follette and the Insurgent Spirit* (Boston: Little, Brown, 1976).

[4] Carl H. Chrislock, *The Progressive Era in Minnesota, 1897–1919* (St. Paul: University of Minnesota, 1971), 35–6. The strongest statement is by Elizabeth Sanders in *Roots of Reform: Farmers, Workers, and the American State, 1877–1917* (Chicago: Chicago University Press, 1999). Cf. Richard Franklin Bensel, *The Political Economy of American Industrialization, 1877–1900* (Cambridge: Cambridge University Press, 2001).

support for regulatory reform in a rhetoric that drew on elements of a long-standing republican tradition by drawing word-pictures of an enduring conflict between the "people" and the "interests." Historians are rightly wary of attempts to extend the intellectual domain of "classical republicanism" far beyond the Revolutionary era where its influence on American political thought is best attested (though by no means unquestioned). It is true that the conflict between "commerce" and "virtue," central to the classical republican world-view, had evaporated, for Americans, some time in the early nineteenth century, if not before, but fears regarding the implications of corporate ownership for good citizenship troubled many progressives. That thread of republican thought which saw liberty as perpetually endangered by private interest still shone brightly. In the form of an "obsession with the potentialities for corruption which lie in close relations between government and entrepreneurial capitalism," at least one element of the republican tradition was very much alive. In effect, the language of the "commonweal" was transmogrified into the all-encompassing language of "public interest."[5]

Progressives characteristically described themselves as devoted to the protection of an overall "public interest" against a variety of "special interests" which sought to exploit the powers of government to their own pecuniary advantage. The object, said Jonathan Bourne, was to substitute the "general welfare" for that of "special interests" as the objective of public policy, and this required political reforms to ensure that the public will was clearly expressed and the influence of favor-seeking minorities displaced.[6] The concept of the "public interest" was central to the progressive project. It served as a rhetorical device for handling social conflicts, and for negotiating the tensions between the democratic principle and the elitist implications of administrative decision-making. But it was highly problematic when applied to the politics of a pluralist society characterized by interest group competition and deep divisions along lines of region, ethnicity and class. It was highly problematic also when applied to political issues of great complexity the ethical dimensions of which were capable of being conceptualized in very different ways.[7]

---

[5] Robert Kelley, "Ideology and Political Culture from Jefferson to Nixon," *American Historical Review* 82 (1977): 536n., 549–50. For a contrary view, but one based on a rather rarefied sample of progressive intellectuals, see John L. Diggins, "Republicanism and Progressivism," *American Quarterly* 37 (1985): 572–98. For a review of recent literature on republicanism, see Daniel T. Rodgers, "Republicanism: The Career of a Concept," *Journal of American History* 79 (1992): 11–38; and the special number of *American Quarterly* 37 (1985): 461–598.

[6] Jonathan Bourne to William Allen White, 21 July 1910, White MSS, LC.

[7] Daniel T. Rodgers, *Contested Truths: Keywords in American Politics since Independence* (New York: Basic Books, 1987), 179–87; Elisabeth S. Clemens, *The People's Lobby: Organizational Innovation and the Rise of Interest-Group Politics in the United States, 1890–1925* (Chicago: Chicago University Press, 1998); Clayton A. Coppin and Jack High, *The Politics of Purity:*

In view of the social position of most progressive Congressmen and the trajectory of their political careers, it is easy, as many historians of progressivism have done, to dismiss such rhetoric as disingenuous, as a smoke-screen deliberately erected to cloak their support for policies which suited certain private interests and to deflect attention from the political opportunism that characterized their careers. "That there is a moral awakening is not true," commented a writer in the *Springfield Republican* in 1909, "and if there is a semblance of it, the appearance in fact is merely one class of property trying to get even with another class."[8] Such concepts as the "general welfare" and the "public interest" tend to induce ribald cynicism among contemporary scholars aware of their problematic nature and the ignoble uses to which they have been put. However, in the Progressive Era the serious contradictions embedded in such language were not yet wholly clear. The term "public interest" was employed more innocently, and therefore more ambiguously, than today. What it meant simply was the opposite of "special interests": a concern for the welfare of the community as a whole as against those elements which sought to derive undue advantage through government favor. This definition could embrace a wide variety of business groups as well as farmers, workers and consumers. "Legitimate" business interests were seen as in no sense antithetical to the "public interest."[9] Of course, all these concepts posed serious problems when embodied in specific legislation. Although the progressives were aware of some of these practical difficulties, they retained confidence in the general validity of this overarching conceptualization of reform. They remained convinced that, unless validated by some kind of commitment to the public good, the workings of government would become "simply an institutionalized scramble for private advantage."[10]

We cannot discount, Robert Crunden reminds us, the importance of sheer "moral indignation" in producing progressive legislation, as Crunden, like James Harvey Young, has shown most particularly with reference to pure food laws, where notions of "purity" had strong ethical connotations which shaded into broader concerns about the moral health of the nation. Business interests, Young concludes, were quite insufficient to secure passage of the

Harvey Washington Wiley and the Origins of Federal Food Policy (Ann Arbor, Mich., 1999); Thomas J. Pegram, *Partisans and Progressives: Private Interests and Public Policy in Illinois, 1870–1922* (Urbana: University of Illinois Press, 1992), 11–23, 213–23; James A. Morone, *The Democratic Wish: Popular Participation and the Limits of American Government* (New York: Basic Books, 1990), 97–115.

[8] Quoted in Richard M. Abrams, *Conservatism in a Progressive Era: Massachusetts Politics, 1900–1912* (Cambridge, Mass.: Harvard University Press, 1964), 161.

[9] Donna J. Wood, *The Strategic Uses of Public Policy: Business and Government in the Progressive Era* (Marshfield, Mass.: Pitnam, 1986), 195–6.

[10] James T. Kloppenberg, *Uncertain Victory: Social Democracy and Progressivism in European and American Thought, 1870–1920* (New York: Oxford University Press, 1986), 385.

Pure Food and Drug Act.[11] A purely economic interpretation of the politics of what Samuel P. Huntington calls a period of "creedal passion," when the discrepancy between American ideals and American institutions appeared to have grown distressingly wide, simply does not work. According to Daniel T. Rodgers, "no one looking back on the years before the First World War has failed to be struck by the vigor, the massive confidence of the era's appeal to ideals."[12]

We can thus identify a distinct "progressive movement" in Congress. But that movement did not embrace everything that we have been accustomed to classify as "progressive." The omissions – conservation, child welfare, trade union rights – are serious ones because they involve considerations that most historians would regard as essential ingredients of any complete representation of progressive reform. Midwestern Republicans of progressive leanings varied greatly in their response to the Administration's forestry policy and to those social reform measures that came before Congress; Democrats were still more ambivalent. On issues concerning the legal status of trade unions, especially the use of injunctions in labor disputes, although a few progressive Republicans, like Robert La Follette, were sympathetic to the pleas of organized labor and others, following Theodore Roosevelt, were willing to see some procedural modifications, the Republican party as a whole was much less favorable than the Democratic party as a whole. It is difficult to think of any issue, other than the tariff, which so clearly divided the parties during this period. These alternative strands of progressivism are hardly less closely correlated with one another than with the main strand described above.

On the other hand, although what emerges is a picture of several diverse streams moving in different directions, they were not equal in size and strength. The main "progressive" dimension, which embraced a very substantial portion of the business set before Congress, was central to the progressive tradition as it was understood by succeeding generations and, to a large extent, as we understand it today. Moreover, this strand of progressivism involved issues of great moment in redefining the place of the federal government in relation to the American economic order, that is, in the process of building a new American state. In many ways, the findings of this study go some way to restore older views of progressivism at a national level, ascribing to it a greater coherence than has commonly been allowed. It regards progressivism as rooted in a tradition of classical republicanism, expressing a clearly definable sense of sectional grievance and speaking to deeply-felt popular concerns about privilege and power.

---

[11] Robert M. Crunden, *Ministers of Reform: The Progressives' Achievement in American Civilization, 1889–1920* (New York: Basic Books, 1982); James Harvey Young, *Pure Food: Securing the Federal Food and Drug Act of 1906* (Princeton: Princeton University Press, 1989).

[12] Samuel P. Huntingdon, *American Politics: The Promise of Disharmony* (Cambridge, Mass.: Harvard University Press, 1983); Rodgers, *Contested Truths*, 179.

Progressivism and the New American State

Congressional progressives worked to create new institutions to correct what they saw as serious imbalances in economic advantage and political power. Although that is not in itself a sufficient explanation for the growth of the twentieth-century American state, recognition of their influence is a necessary starting point in any investigation of the forces which drove the state-building process and the specific historical circumstances under which it occurred.

That representatives from the South and West most consistently supported the legislation that chartered the institutions of the new regulatory state emerges very strongly from the evidence. Elizabeth Sanders's recent study demonstrates that "the agrarian periphery... furnished the 'foot soldiers' that saw reform through the legislature. It did so because [its] political economy... was innately antagonistic to the designs of core industrial and financial capitalism and had no effective means with which to fight it other than the capture and expansion of state power." [13] Although one might argue that Sanders's definition of the "periphery" lumps together very heterogeneous forms of economic activity and that she overstates the commitment of Southern and Western Congressmen to purely agrarian, rather than mercantile and manufacturing, interests in their constituencies, there is no denying the essential thrust of her argument. [14]

While it is true that congressional representatives from the "periphery" tended to vote together on issues of regulatory reform, further analysis is required to demonstrate that they did so because of shared economic rather than political interests. [15] Democratic Congressmen, despite their divergent political philosophies, constituency profiles, and political careers (which in many cases involved bitter hostility to Populism and later to Bryanism), had resolved after 1904 to place the Democratic party on a progressive platform because they believed that such a platform would attract votes and because they recognized that this was the only position from which they could hope to outflank the Republicans. It was the fact that the Grand Old Party was so firmly identified, on a national level, with conservative, "stand-pat" policies that, more than anything else, pushed their opponents, some of them kicking and screaming, towards a reformist stance. By the same token, the strength of Republican machines in what after 1896 had become virtual one-party states in the West and Midwest compelled many politicians who were

---

[13] Sanders, *Roots of Reform*, 1, 4.

[14] See the reviews of *Roots of Reform* by Gerald Friedman on H-Net (URL: *http://www.h-net.msu.edu/reviews/showrev.cgi?path=7980954878797*) and James D. Schmidt in *Labor History* 41 (2000): 364–5.

[15] Cf. Scott C. James, "Coalition-Building, the Democracy, and the Development of American Regulatory Institutions, 1884–1936: A Party System Perspective," (Ph.D. diss., University of California, Los Angeles, 1993), 63–97, 195–215.

unable to make headway within the state organization to build political coalitions outside it by exploiting the grievances of social groups whose interests had been ignored by the ruling regime.[16] In other words, the roots of reform politics have to be understood in terms of regional political, as well as economic, development.

Identification of Congressmen from the agrarian "periphery" as the principal authors of the regulatory state poses another interpretative problem that cannot readily be solved within the primarily materialist parameters in which Sanders operates. The "paradox of Progressive Era state expansion," she acknowledges, is that, "driven by social movements deeply hostile to bureaucracy, it produced a great bureaucratic expansion." "Agrarian" Democrats feared that autonomous regulators would sell their souls to political and economic elites. Yet their political demands gave rise to the creation of autonomous regulatory agencies.[17] This, she believes, was largely because they relied on the votes of Republican progressives, whose location on "the middle ground between two polarized positions" gave them a disproportionate influence in the shaping of regulatory legislation. Representing "diverse" constituencies in the Midwest, they shared the Democratic agrarians' resentment at the economic power of Northeastern corporations but feared that drastic regulatory measures might damage the developing industries within their own region. Regulation by commission presented itself as an ideal solution to their dilemma.[18]

That Midwestern progressives often held the congressional balance of power and that they were more amenable to regulation by commission than most Democrats is undeniable, but it does not follow that their position was primarily a function of the intermediate status of their regional economy. One reason they were readier to accept statist solutions to regulatory problems was because they were raised in the nationalist tradition of the Republican party rather than the Jeffersonian tradition of the Democracy.[19] However, the simplest explanation is a pragmatic one, and one which sometimes applies to Democratic as well as Republican progressives: those who sought effective regulation saw no practicable alternative, in view of the complex and shifting nature of the issues, to vesting discretionary powers in the hands of an administrative agency. Regulation by statute was not in most cases a viable option. For that reason Republican Congressmen preferred to leave the adjudication of labor disputes in the hands of the federal courts, rather than confront different and problematic decisions themselves. Republican

---

[16] Martin Shefter, "Regional Receptivity to Reform: The Legacy of the Progressive Era," *Political Science Quarterly* 98 (1983): 359–83.

[17] Sanders, *Roots of Reform*, 8–9, 387–9.

[18] Ibid., 280 and 389–97.

[19] See, for example, John Gerring, *Party Ideologies in America, 1828–1996* (Cambridge: Cambridge University Press, 1998), 78–86.

conservatives, like Foraker and Spooner, showed a pronounced desire to leave difficult issues of economic adjustment in the hands of the judiciary. This, not a "statutory state," was the realistic alternative to administrative regulation. The practical alternative was regulation by the courts, the detrimental repercussions of which were painfully apparent to anyone, for example, who was familiar with the early history of the Interstate Commerce Act. Thus progressive Republicans, and also progressive Democrats, fought tooth and nail to protect the Interstate Commerce Commission from close judicial scrutiny. If there was one thing that the Democrats abominated more than the "tyranny" of autonomous administrators it was the "tyranny" of unelected federal judges. Therefore, although they frequently gave voice to their disquiet, time and time again they were driven by necessity to acquiesce in the expansion of bureaucracy.

Progressive regulatory policy was designed, above all else, to cope with the sheer diversity of claims on the government, and regulatory agencies were established to resolve the numerous conflicts of interest that impinged so heavily on the working lives, and peace of mind, of legislators.[20] The universe of organized pressure groups, including "public interest" lobbies (of which the most interesting and innovative were women's groups like the General Confederation of Women's Clubs and the National Consumers League), professional associations, and labor federations, as well as trade associations and chambers of commerce, became both more densely populated and more diverse around the turn of the century.[21] The demand for railroad regulation arose out of a complex array of shippers' interests, the demand for pure food legislation out of a bewildering pattern of producers' rivalries. In the latter case, professional bodies, like the American Medical Association, also had a significant lobbying presence. These conflicts of interest were both troubling, in view of their divisive potential, and, in view of their technical complexity, exceedingly difficult to resolve. It was for that reason that members of Congress consented to yield up some of their power to executive agencies.

There is no doubt that the growth of government was inspired by the demands of various interest groups. A close examination of the history of almost every major piece of regulatory legislation will reveal the important role played by organized pressure groups, which worked tirelessly to turn to their advantage the authority of the state. But such influences were rarely determining. As Stephen Skowronek points out, interpretations that focus on the external pressures and interests that propelled state building "leave

[20] Cf. McCormick, *From Realignment to Reform.*
[21] See, for example, Clemens, *People's Lobby*; Theda Skocpol, *Protecting Soldiers and Mothers: The Political Origins of Social Policy in the United States* (Cambridge, Mass.: Harvard University Press, 1992); Lorine S. Goodwin, *The Pure Food, Drink, and Drug Crusaders, 1879–1914* (Jefferson, N.C.: MacFarland, 1999).

the emergence of the new state overdetermined but little understood."[22] The very complexity of interest-group pressures left space for autonomous action on the part of policymakers, who themselves acted to define the issues, generate solutions, and assemble coalitions in support of their enactment. Thus Harvey W. Wiley, the Chief Chemist of the Department of Agriculture, was responsible more than anyone else for constructing a coalition powerful enough to pass effective pure food legislation, and the resulting law bore the strong imprint of his idiosyncratic conception of "purity" in food supplies. Members of the Interstate Commerce Commission worked tirelessly to assemble support for ratemaking powers such as were finally conferred upon them by the Hepburn Act. President Theodore Roosevelt, in particular, played a significant role in pushing his party towards the acceptance of administrative solutions to regulatory problems, in railroad regulation, conservation, meat inspection, and the monitoring of food and drugs. The Mann-Elkins Act stemmed from the desire of President Taft to attain what he saw as an appropriate balance between administrative and judicial authority. Other significant "policy entrepreneurs" resided in Congress, like Albert Beveridge, in his successful campaign for effective meat inspection and his unsuccessful campaign for a tariff commission, or Francis G. Newlands, the author of the 1903 Reclamation Act and a longstanding advocate of an integrated waterways policy. Policy innovation requires the organization of ideas, which in most cases originate elsewhere, as much as the organization of political support, and such individuals were largely responsible for presenting plausible legislative formulas and for gathering support behind them.[23]

Obviously, to array a "state-centered" approach against one which gives priority to social forces is to set up a false dichotomy. Writers like Skowronek correctly draw attention to the freedom of maneuver that policymakers sometimes enjoy, but policy is not created in a vacuum. Legislators are continually aware of the social context in which they operate, of the state of public opinion, or at least of politically salient segments of it, and the power of organized interest groups. While the interplay of competing forces might leave space for substantial legislative discretion, such discretion is in turn constrained by social and economic forces. Congress was an arena in which a variety of interests and opinions competed for influence. It is crucial to determine what those interests and opinions were and to evaluate their relative impact on the legislative process. However, it is no less important to consider the institutional mechanisms by which external impulses were

---

[22] Skowronek, *Building a New American State*, 17–18.
[23] See, for example, Judith Goldstein, *Ideas, Interests, and American Trade Policy* (Ithaca, N.Y.: Cornell University Press, 1993); Dietrich Rueschemeyer and Theda Skocpol, eds., *States, Social Knowledge, and the Origins of Modern Social Policies* (Princeton: Princeton University Press, 1996).

converted into legislation, not only the wider constitutional structures within which American legislators worked but also the particular decision-making procedures that operated within the halls of Congress itself.

Beyond the "State of Courts and Parties"

The nineteenth-century United States, according to the historical sociologist Michael Mann, had "the weakest state in the Western world."[24] Certainly, the American nation-state acquired additional muscle in the early years of the twentieth century. Federal law and the regulatory power of federal agencies impinged upon a wider range of economic activities; interstate commerce became subject to a tighter federal control. During this period the national government established a much firmer regulatory grip on the railroads, monitoring freight rates, as well as bringing pipelines, express companies and telephone and telegraph companies under federal supervision; it made meat products subject to more rigorous federal inspection and set standards for drugs and food products crossing state lines; it created a national system of postal savings banks; it imposed restrictions on the use of timber and other natural resources on the public lands; and within its own federal District it made a few gestures towards the articulation of a more systematic social policy, reflecting, and in some cases encouraging, the efforts of the individual states. The Progressive Era saw the beginnings of a modern regulatory state. This was reflected in the dramatic growth of individual agencies. The staff of the Interstate Commerce Commission, for example, increased from 178 in 1905 to 527 in 1909 and 2370 in 1919, while the Bureau of Chemistry in the Department of Agriculture, which had 6 employees in 1883, had expanded to 600 by 1912 as a result of its responsibility for enforcing the pure food and drug law.[25] Thus the American state acquired new responsibilities and new administrative capacities to deal with them.

Nevertheless, despite the body-building exercises of the Progressive Era, the federal state had by no means attained a level of muscular efficiency that would have satisfied that apostle of the "strenuous life" Theodore Roosevelt. By the standards of other advanced Western societies, the United States Government remained puny. As a percentage of GNP, federal expenditure in 1910 was less than half that of the central governments of Britain, Germany or France. Even if all levels of government are taken into account, the American public sector, at 8.2 percent of GNP, was proportionally just over half of the French or German, two-thirds of the British.[26] A comparative perspective reveals the limitations of American regulatory policies. American railroad

[24] Michael Mann, *The Sources of Social Power: Volume II. The Rise of Classes and Nation–States, 1760–1914* (Cambridge: Cambridge University Press, 1993), 486.
[25] Hoogenboom, *Short History of the ICC*, 53; Sanders, *Roots of Reform*, 390–1.
[26] Mann, *Sources of Social Power*, 366–7.

policy before 1920, for example, was premised on the assumption of private ownership and control, leaving to the market the determination of rates and the allocation of services. Government intervened on a post hoc basis to resolve disputes and eliminate obstructions to the free flow of commerce, such as price fixing and discrimination. Other nations adopted more statist solutions involving larger components of government planning or even public ownership.[27] American labor market policies, too, were exceptional in the degree of latitude that they allowed to private employers. Responsibility for many areas of economic policy lay with the states, resulting in a patchwork quilt of dizzyingly variable laws and a general disincentive to regulate too strictly, for fear of driving business into the arms of less demanding jurisdictions. The same discouraging version of Gresham's Law applied still more forcefully in the field of social policy.[28]

Despite the patchy emergence of a bureaucratic state and increasing recourse to various forms of administrative process, one of the most striking features of American governance was its continuing dependence on the courts. The hand of the state lay heavily on the conduct of labor relations, but that hand wielded a judicial gavel rather than an administrative rulebook. In the absence of congressional legislation covering labor disputes (and, it might be said, even when, after 1914, congressional legislation was in place), the federal courts determined policy, reinterpreting traditional common law principles to justify an activist anti-union policy – with important consequences for the development of the American labor movement.[29] In view of the terse and ambiguous provisions of the Sherman Act, and in the absence until 1914 of more detailed declaratory legislation (and, it might also be said, to a substantial degree after its enactment), the Supreme Court set the parameters of federal antitrust policy – with equally important consequences for the developing pattern of industrial consolidation.[30] Some of

---

[27] Frank Dobbin, *Forging Industrial Policy: The United States, Britain, and France in the Railway Age* (Cambridge: Cambridge University Press, 1994). On different patterns of public ownership, see Daniel T. Rodgers, *Atlantic Crossings: Social Politics in a Progressive Age* (Cambridge, Mass.: Harvard University Press, 1998), ch. 4.

[28] David B. Robertson, *Capital, Labor, and State: The Battle for American Labor Markets from the Civil War to the New Deal* (Lanham, Md.: Rowan and Littlefield, 2000); David B. Robertson, "The Bias of American Federalism: The Limits of Welfare State Development in the Progressive Era," *Journal of Policy History* 1 (1989): 261–91; Clemens, *People's Lobby*, 67–73.

[29] Melvyn Dubofsky, *The State and Labor in Modern America* (Chapel Hill: University of North Carolina Press, 1994), 1–60; Christopher L. Tomlins, *The State and the Unions: Labor Relations, Law, and the Organized Labor Movement in America, 1880–1960* (Cambridge: Cambridge University Press, 1985), 44–52; William E. Forbath, *Law and the Shaping of the American Labor Movement* (Cambridge, Mass.: Harvard University Press, 1991); Herbert Hovenkamp, *Enterprise and American Law, 1836–1937* (Cambridge, Mass.: Harvard University Press, 1991), 207–38.

[30] Martin J. Sklar, *The Corporate Reconstruction of American Capitalism, 1890–1916: The Market, the Law and Politics* (Cambridge: Cambridge University Press, 1988); Tony Freyer, *Regulating*

the distinguishing features of American industrial society therefore flowed directly from the decisions of the courts.

In the case of insurance law the Supreme Court decided, first, that, since insurance contracts did not constitute "commerce," they did not come within the regulatory compass of Congress; second, that the federal courts had a responsibility to ensure that state regulation did not trespass beyond the limits set by the U.S. Constitution and to decide cases involving diversity of citizenship according to the "general common law"; and, third, that the federal courts (but not Congress) "could exert substantial lawmaking authority in the area." Proposals for federal regulation in the wake of the New York insurance scandals of 1905–1906 were shelved at an early stage because of the widespread assumption that the Court would find them unconstitutional. Such an assumption led Theodore Roosevelt, who had initially favored federal regulation, to abandon it, on the advice of Senator Philander Knox and Attorney-General William Moody, in favor of a more modest proposal for a model insurance code for the District of Columbia. In June 1906 the Senate Judiciary Committee concluded that such legislation lay outside the authority of Congress.[31] Rather than the courts losing authority in the face of an expanding modern bureaucracy, then, the period between the 1880s and the 1920s saw a massive expansion in their power.[32]

The phrase "state building as patchwork" which Skowronek applies to American political development in the period 1877–1900 could be applied with almost equal force to American political development in the early twentieth century. In the absence of an established administrative core, the enforcement of policy was entrusted to independent agencies, with wide discretionary powers and sometimes with discrepant and mutually inconsistent terms of reference. Constructed at different times and for different purposes, they differed widely in organizational structure and location. The new American state bore the mark, as Morton Keller reminds

Big Business: Antitrust in Great Britain and America, 1880–1990 (Cambridge: Cambridge University Press, 1992); William G. Roy, *Socializing Capital: The Rise of the Large Industrial Corporation in America* (Princeton: Princeton University Press, 1997).

[31] Theodore Roosevelt to Isaac W. MacVeagh, 23 September, 8 October 1905, in Elting E. Morison *et al.*, eds., *Letters of Theodore Roosevelt*, (8 vols., Cambridge, Mass.: Harvard University Press, 1951–4), 5:33–5, 50; *New York Times*, 19 December 1905, 18 April 1906, 26 June 1906, 25 January 1907; Edward Purcell Jr., *Brandeis and the Progressive Constitution* (New Haven: Yale University Press, 2000), 55–6; H. Rogers Grant, *Insurance Reform: Consumer Action in the Progressive Era* (Iowa City: Iowa State University Press, 1979), 157–66; Kolko, *Triumph of Conservatism*, 89–97.

[32] Purcell, *Brandeis and the Progressive Constitution*, Part I; Robert G. McCloskey, *The American Supreme Court* (2nd. edn., Chicago: University of Chicago Press, 1994), 91–105; Owen M. Fiss, *Troubled Beginnings of the Modern State, 1888–1910* (New York: Macmillan, 1993); Loren Beth, *The Development of the American Constitution, 1877–1917* (New York: Harper, 1971).

us, of "the massive, inertial persistence of existing interests, institutions and ideas."[33]

Some of the peculiarities of the American state follow naturally from the manner of its construction. A "progressive state," built by "progressives" for "progressive" purposes, it bore the stamp of its creation. Its chief legislative progenitors were the congressional progressives, namely the Democrats and insurgent Republicans who were its most consistent supporters. The Democrats, in particular, brought with them a longstanding suspicion of centralized government. Their acute sensitivity to states rights required careful drafting of regulatory measures like the railroad hours law and the commodity section of the Hepburn Act to ensure that they did not trespass on the prerogatives of the states, and it led to the elimination of federal supervision of railroad securities from the Mann-Elkins Act. The Democrats' longstanding distrust of bureaucracy emerged repeatedly in congressional debates on regulatory reform, for example in their ambivalent attitude to judicial review in the Hepburn Act and their desire to lay down detailed standards in the provisions of the Pure Food and Drug Act rather than leave discretion in the hands of the Chief Chemist. They frequently declared a preference for strongly worded and rigorously enforced statutory prohibitions over the exercise of administrative discretion. Progressive Democrats, observes Sidney Milkis, "wanted to expand the responsibilities of the national government but hoped to find nonbureaucratic and noncentralized solutions to the ills that plagued the political economy."[34] It is true that they repeatedly yielded in the face of practical necessity, but their ambivalence towards administrative regulation inevitably detracted from the momentum behind the state-building process in Progressive America.

Republican progressives were less uncomfortable with the exercise of federal power, but their commitment to regulatory reform was in some cases transitory and in most cases partial. Rooted almost exclusively in the newer states of the Midwest and the Pacific Coast at a certain stage in their economic and political development, Republican insurgency was above all else a sectional movement. Regionalism provided its motive force, accounting

[33] Morton Keller, "Social and Economic Regulation in the Progressive Era," in Milkis and Mileur, eds., *Progressivism and the New Democracy*, 128–9; Skowronek, *Building a New American State.* See also Morton Keller, *Regulating a New Economy: Public Policy and Economic Change in America, 1900–1933* (Cambridge, Mass.: Harvard University Press, 1990); Ellis W. Hawley, "Social Policy and the Liberal State in Twentieth–Century America," in Donald T. Critchlow and Edward Berkowitz, eds., *Federal Social Policy: The Historical Dimension* (University Park: Pennsylvania State University Press, 1988), 117–39; Barry D. Karl, *The Uneasy State, The United States from 1915 to 1945* (Chicago: Chicago University Press, 1983).

[34] Sidney M. Milkis, *Political Parties and Constitutional Government: Remaking American Democracy* (Baltimore: Johns Hopkins University Press, 1999), 49.

for both its intensity and its restricted focus. It reflected a particular set of economic interests and a particular conjunction of political forces that obtained between the realignment of the 1890s and American intervention in the First World War. On issues of social reform, conservation, and labor relations the insurgents, as a group, were no more and no less progressive than other Republicans. Focusing on a limited range of economic policies, Republican insurgency descended all too readily into the narrow-gauged interest-group politics that characterized the farm bloc of the 1920s. Hence congressional progressivism, in either its Democratic or its Republican manifestation, formed a narrow and uncertain basis for the construction of the new American state.

Partisanship remained a potent factor in congressional politics, especially when the insurgents are taken out of the equation. Levels of party voting were high throughout the period. Partisanship, combined with divergent sectional interests and a continuing devotion to an older style of "distributive" politics, ensured that only a minority of congressional Republicans joined the insurgents. As a result, John Gerring concludes, on the basis of a detailed analysis of national party platforms and campaign documents, "the mainstream of the Republican party looked very similar before, during, and after the Progressive era."[35]

For much of the period under consideration the reins of power were held by a coterie of conservative Republicans in both houses who used their influence to block progressive reform, yielding only under overwhelming pressure from the Executive, from outside pressure groups, and from public opinion. Not until after 1911 was their grip to some degree loosened. Speaker Cannon enjoyed the support of a majority of Republican Congressmen, chiefly because, for all their qualms about his sometimes vulgar obduracy, they agreed in essence with the policies that he stood for, that is, for a continuation of the distributive economic program with which the Republican party had been identified since the Civil War era. Likewise, a majority of Republican Senators supported the Aldrich-Hale axis, for all the criticism from the press, reform groups, and senatorial opponents that it was subjected to. As in the House, the majority of members shared a common set of ideas and values, a common set of priorities, and a common adherence to established ways of doing things – in short, a common political culture.

We must look to the legislative process in Congress for at least a partial explanation of the stunted development of the American state. Congress, by virtue of its constitutional function, voiced particularistic concerns. Its members were drawn from "parochial elites" with different priorities and perceptions from the "cosmopolitan elites" of policy intellectuals and professionals who worked to achieve their ends through bureaucratic channels. They kept closely in touch with, and expressed the interests of, their diverse

[35] Gerring, *Party Ideologies*, 121.

constituencies. As Senator Thomas Bayard observed some years earlier, "The members of the Senate and the House are the advocates and representatives of different local interests all of which naturally seek to influence the transactions of the government on their own behalf."[36] Thus Congress was diffused with the spirit of localism. The institution provided several points of access to those who sought to influence its deliberations. The complex machinery of congressional decision making, with its numerous "veto points" and its many opportunities for covert consultation in committee or in conference, offered considerable scope for negative interventions, but it was less easily turned in a positive direction. The only agencies that mitigated this dispersion of power and diversity of purpose were the party organizations, but in this period the uses to which their coordinating authority was put were predominately conservative. Thus policymaking in Congress was characterized much of the time by "continuity, stability, and policy incrementalism."[37]

Most frequently we find Congress reacting to impulses emanating from outside. As we have seen, the major railroad legislation of 1906 and 1910 was introduced at the instance of the Executive and drafted substantially by officials of the Interstate Commerce Commission and the Department of Justice. Likewise, responsibility for drafting and marshaling support for the Pure Food and Drug Act fell principally upon the government's Chief Chemist, Harvey Wiley. Such a process was characteristic of the complex economic legislation of the new century. Congress, itself possessing neither the inclination nor the resources to engage in detailed planning and systematic policymaking, its role was more often reactive than innovative. The legislation that resulted was piecemeal, haphazard and uneven, a product of compromises and concessions reluctantly made to outside pressures, in each case reflecting the peculiar conjunction of ideas and interests that had formed around that issue. For example, the solutions that Congress found to the "railroad question" offered no effective way of tackling the problems of the system as a whole, while tariff duties were calculated on a "case-by-case basis."[38] Legislation for the District of Columbia was produced in ways which left no real possibility for the construction of a systematic and progressive social policy. More contentious matters like the "labor question" were, as far as possible, avoided altogether, leaving policymaking effectively in the hands of the federal courts.

[36] Shefter, *Political Parties and the State*, 75–81; Bayard, quoted in David J. Rothman, *Politics and Power: The United States Senate, 1869–1901* (Cambridge, Mass.: Harvard University Press, 1966), 81.

[37] David W. Brady, *Critical Elections and Congressional Policy-Making* (Stanford, Cal.: Stanford University Press, 1988), 1.

[38] Louis Galambos and Joseph Pratt, *The Rise of the Corporate Commonwealth* (New York: Basic Books, 1988), 47–53, 64.

Congress and Political Change

Political scientists surveying the history of the U.S. Congress since its creation have discerned a persistent and progressive, though irregular, pattern of longitudinal development, variously described as "institutionalization" or "professionalization," whose end-product is the modern Congress. The elements of "institutionalization" include a clearer demarcation of the institution's boundaries, as members enjoy longer terms and as structures of authority are built up internally instead of being imposed from without; a greater complexity, exemplified by the elaboration of the committee system and the expansion of party leadership roles; and the replacement of informal and arbitrary practices by universal rules, such as the growing dominance of seniority as a criterion for preferment and the proliferation of rules governing procedures on the floor.[39] Congress in the Progressive Era derived some of its special character from these developments. However, a detailed examination of institutional changes in the early twentieth-century Congress reveals that they were both more complex and more ambiguous in their results than the more sweeping longitudinal studies would suggest. Though parallel in some ways to the development of federal administrative capacity described by Skowronek, the "institutionalization" of Congress had very different consequences: confirming Representatives and Senators in their often self-regarding habits; insulating Congress from outside pressures, and thereby strengthening, rather than weakening, its resistance to political change; dispersing authority among quasi-autonomous committee chairmen, each dominant in his own legislative fiefdom, and thereby severely constraining the possibilities of responsible party government and of systematic legislative policymaking.

House membership, though volatile by contemporary standards, was rapidly receding from the high turnover rates of the mid-nineteenth century. In the Senate the transition from an early nineteenth-century pattern of shifting membership to a twentieth-century pattern of greater persistence and longer terms had begun in the 1870s and was nearly complete by 1905.[40] However, Congressmen were hardly less obsessed with the distribution of patronage and "pork" among their constituents than were their nineteenth-century predecessors. If the supply of patronage had been curtailed by civil service reform (though not reduced in aggregate), the supply of "pork," in

---

[39] See, for example, Nelson Polsby, "The Institutionalization of the U.S. House of Representatives," *American Political Science Review* 62 (1968): 144–68; Randall B. Ripley, *Congress: Process and Policy* (4th edn., New York: Norton, 1988), 48–67; H. Douglas Price, "Congress and the Evolution of Legislative 'Professionalism,'" in Norman W. Ornstein, ed., *Congress in Change* (New York: Praeger, 1975), 2–23; H. Douglas Price, "Careers and Committees in the American Congress: The Problem of Structural Change," in William O. Aydelotte, ed., *The History of Parliamentary Behavior* (Princeton: Princeton University Press, 1977), 28–62.
[40] Ripley, *Congress*, 54.

the shape of federal expenditure on public buildings and the improvement of rivers and harbors, had greatly expanded. Indeed, the most important lessons that legislative experience afforded were those which concerned getting reelected; a significant component of legislative "professionalism" was the careful nourishing of constituency support. Therefore localism remained a potent force in the twentieth-century Congress.[41]

The membership of both chambers had stabilized enough to permit the development of a durable leadership cadre, a greater continuity in committee membership and higher standards of legislative "professionalism," which may or may not have been conducive to greater efficiency in the transaction of business. They were not especially conducive to political innovation. As David Brady suggests, it is new members that have commonly provided the impetus for major policy changes, and new members were becoming rarer. Congressional committees, their membership increasingly secure against the shifting winds of electoral fortune and held in place by the tightening grip of seniority, able to cultivate longstanding relationships with bureaucratic agencies and private interest groups, were less open to new ideas. Party leaders, drawn from the ranks of senior members, which by 1910 would mean that they had enjoyed fifteen to twenty years of uninterrupted service, internalized the values and working practices that prevailed on the Hill. Insulated by large and stable majorities, they were relatively immune to outside pressures.[42]

The most important structural transformation during this period was the reform of the House rules in 1909–1911. This was itself a product of major changes in the agenda of national politics. The new political issues, which by their very nature were highly contentious and divisive, created a context in which the wide discretionary power of the Speaker began to appear arbitrary and autocratic to a growing number, eventually a majority, of the members. The result was an attempt to develop decision-making procedures which reflected the growing diversity of interests in a pluralist society. Viewed in these terms, "congressional modernization" was an integral part of that broader transformation of the issues and practices of American politics known as "progressivism."[43]

The campaign against the rules went some way towards weakening the influence of party. That the reconstitution of the Committee on Rules and the removal during the following Congress of the prerogative of appointing committees substantially reduced the Speaker's power is incontestable. As

---

[41] Richard F. Fenno Jr., *Home Style: House Members and Their Districts* (Boston: Little, Brown, 1978); Roger H. Davidson and Walter J. Oleszek, *Congress and Its Members* (Washington, D.C.: Congressional Quarterly, 1981).

[42] Brady, *Critical Elections*, 1.

[43] David W. Brady and David Epstein, "Intraparty Preferences, Heterogeneity, and the Origins of the Modern Congress: Progressive Reformers in the House and Senate, 1890–1920," *Journal of Law, Economics, & Organization* 13 (1997): 26–49.

George Norris informed a constituent, the inflexibility of the Cannon regime was to some degree mitigated, and there was "a different atmosphere in the House. . . . There is a freedom of action that has never existed before since I have been a member of Congress." When Cannon stepped down in 1911, his successor James Robert Mann adopted a more conciliatory approach in allocating committee places and formulating strategy. Political scientists like Randall B. Ripley, Joseph Cooper, David W. Brady, and Ronald M. Peters Jr. see the rules changes of 1910–1911 as marking a fundamental shift in the nature of the House leadership, replacing what Peters calls a "partisan speakership" with a "feudal speakership" in which the Chair shared its power with a number of leading committee chairmen and other party chieftains. The new system, says Peters, "most resembled a set of feudal baronies." To some extent that had always been true. Nicholas Longworth, who later filled the Chair himself, commented on the similarity between a congressional Republican party led by Mann with the assistance of Cannon, Mondell, Moore of Pennsylvania and Fordney and that led earlier by Cannon with the assistance of Dalzell, Tawney and Payne: "As I gaze upon these two pictures, I find it impossible to differentiate between them." Though the changes reinforced the collegial aspects of party leadership, they did little to enhance the autonomy and influence of the ordinary member. As under the ancien régime, a small coterie of senior members dominated proceedings.[44]

In the long term, however, we can see the rules revolt as marking an epochal change in the way in which the House of Representatives organized its business. Under the "feudal" system that emerged under the revised rules power was to a substantial degree decentralized. The number of leadership roles increased. Committee chairmen, their position fortified by seniority, became largely impervious to the commands of party leaders, whether located in the White House or the Speaker's Chair, and carrying out a coordinated party program became possible only under exceptional conditions. Party organizations, while still critically important, were less tightly disciplined; party no longer had such a determining influence on voting. Their formal authority diminished by the rules changes of 1910–1911, party leaders were compelled to resort to negotiation and bargaining where once they could virtually command consent.

A similar, though less pronounced, transition is discernible after 1918 in the upper chamber, where, in order to accommodate the insurgent

---

[44] George Norris to William Owen Jones, 8 May 1910; to C. H. Aldrich, 8 May 1910, Norris MSS, LC; Ronald M. Peters Jr., *The American Speakership: The Office in Historical Perspective* (Baltimore: Johns Hopkins University Press, 1990), 91, 5–12; Joseph Cooper and David W. Brady, "Institutional Context and Leadership Style: The House from Cannon to Rayburn," *American Political Science Review* 75 (1981): 411–26; Herbert F. Margulies, *Reconciliation and Revival: James R. Mann and the House Republicans in the Wilson Era* (Westport, Conn.: Greenwood, 1996); Randall B. Ripley, *Party Leaders in the House of Representatives* (Washington, D.C.: Brookings Institution, 1967), 81–6.

Republicans' demands for a voice on key policymaking committees, a rule was adopted which debarred a member from serving on more than two major committees, thereby substantially diminishing the pluralism that had contributed so greatly to the concentration of power. Here, too, the divisive impact of Republican insurgency led to an at least partial decentralization of authority.[45]

What, however, was to take its place? The "partisan speakership" had been established during the last quarter of the nineteenth century to achieve a greater degree of efficiency and coordination in managing the business of a large and diverse legislative body. It permitted a kind of "responsible" party government, albeit for conservative ends, that has rarely been attained since. In the absence of strong party leadership, Congress was all too liable to give way to the centrifugal tendencies that were implicit in its composition and structure. In the absence of a strong internal leadership, programmatic direction could only come from outside, and most obviously from the White House. Theodore Roosevelt set a compelling model for presidential leadership in the legislative arena, but it was a model that Congressmen, except for short periods of grace, were constitutionally disposed to resist.

The dilemmas of early twentieth-century state building were firmly embedded in the dynamics of progressive reform and the structures of congressional decision making. "In all settings," concludes Martin Shefter, "... the central thrust of Progressivism was an attack upon the political party ... and an effort to create an executive establishment to supplant the party in this pivotal position in the American political system." Progressivism entailed an assault on at least some of the procedures of party politics, while regulatory reform was predicated on an acknowledgement of "the inefficiency of the party state" and its replacement by newer forms of bureaucratic authority.[46] In Congress, too, the passing of the progressive tide left the structures of party government significantly weakened. Yet party organization was the principal agency of coherence and uniformity in congressional decision-making. Its weakening left the legislature less able to play a constructive part in the process of institutional rebuilding that produced the modern American state.[47]

It is impossible, then, to appreciate the character of the new American state without giving due consideration to its origins in the Progressive Era. However it manifested itself in other political contexts, progressivism in Congress was primarily a movement of Southern and Western representatives who sought to employ the regulatory power of the federal government to correct

---

[45] Brady and Epstein, "Intraparty Preferences," 44–8.

[46] Shefter, *Political Parties and the State*, 71 and 72–81 passim; Morone, *Democratic Wish*, 107; Milkis, *Political Parties and Constitutional Government*, 42–71; Eisenach, *Lost Promise of Progressivism*, 111–22.

[47] Skowronek, *Building a New American State*, 285–8.

perceived imbalances in economic advantage. Although many of the finishing touches were applied by executive officials and even business lobbyists, the principal impetus for regulatory reform came from this sectional movement. However, the unevenness of state making in early twentieth-century America follows from the very nature of that reforming impulse. Those progressives who were Democrats, who in Congress constituted the majority, had serious reservations about the creation of powerful, partially autonomous administrative agencies, and at key points their misgivings weakened the reforming impetus. Those progressives who were Republicans sometimes exhibited a transitory and contingent commitment to regulatory reform. In rebelling against the disciplines of party government, the progressives themselves damaged the major source of central direction in congressional policymaking. Progressive reform undermined the system of party government without displacing it, ensuring that the modern American state would be a hybrid structure in which newer forms of governance coexisted with elements drawn from the older "state of courts and parties."

Appendix

The Analysis of Roll Calls

Roll call analysis offers considerable advantages in this type of study: it uses information about all the members of a legislative body, not just a few prominent or especially vociferous individuals, enabling a more complete and accurate reconstruction of the distribution of opinion; it facilitates comparison of voting on two or more issues; and it permits analysis of parties and factional groupings. There is a compelling "hardness" about roll call data. Legislators have been set a specific question and have responded yea or nay, not, one hopes, out of whim or fancy, but with due appreciation of the substantive importance and political implications of the subject matter. The interpretation of their responses can proceed without much further reclassification or recoding. This makes them invaluable as a source of evidence about political attitudes, particularly for historical periods when survey and interview data are not available.

A word of caution is in order. In the first place, the questions on which votes were recorded were not selected for the convenience of the historian but often for purely fortuitous reasons, perhaps to drive home a partisan advantage on a point of limited substantive interest. They emerged from a lengthy process of filtration during the course of which many important alternative possibilities were ruled out and others compromised. On many important issues members either avoided having their votes recorded or else doggedly adhered to an agreed party line. Important differences of opinion might be tested by amendments or procedural motions which addressed the main issues obliquely and therefore do not provide straightforward tests of members' views. Second, the motives behind the votes of individual members must remain obscure. Their decisions might be influenced by indifference, ignorance or error, obscure personal obsessions, or elaborate tactical maneuvers to which we are not privy. Hence, while it is not unreasonable to draw inferences about the perceived relationship between issues on the basis of roll call evidence, it is much more dangerous to employ it to categorize individuals. We cannot with confidence infer a particular ideological stance from a particular set of legislative votes.

Guttman scaling has been widely employed in legislative roll call analysis. It was first developed in the analysis of survey data as a means of testing whether a group of propositions belong, in Guttman's words, to a common "universe of content." Take, for example, the votes of Republican Senators on amendments to the Hepburn bill listed in Table 3.3. Senators voted by margins ranging from 56–10 to 23–54 in favor of strengthening the interstate commerce law. If the eight propositions do indeed correspond to points along a one-dimensional continuum of attitudes, then Senators who respond positively to the last and most demanding question should also respond positively to the remainder, while those who reject the first should not give positive consideration to any of the others. As the propositions become more radical, or "difficult," support should drop away. The fact that the data largely correspond to this pattern tends to confirm our hypothesis that the questions are related, that they form a single one-dimensional scale. Arrangement of the data in this fashion not only provides evidence regarding the relationship between roll calls but also ranks individuals with reference to the underlying issue revealed.[1]

This method is especially appropriate to the analysis of attitudes to progressive reform in that the question that we began with can be rephrased as a hypothesis that all, or some, of the votes on reform measures will, when suitably arranged, form a cumulative scale – in other words, that the issues of progressive reform belong to a common "universe of content." In the ideal case, we would find Senators arrayed along a continuum between progressive and conservative poles. Not surprisingly, the behavior of legislators in the real world falls considerably short of that ideal. The vagaries of individual behavior make deviations inevitable. Too many would probably convince us that a one-dimensional scale is not a satisfactory way of describing the underlying structure of our data.[2]

Such techniques may be used to ascertain whether a given set of roll calls corresponds to the unidimensional scale model. How do we determine which out of a larger sample of roll calls might form a scale? The first step was to calculate for each pair of roll calls the value of Yule's Q, a unidimensional measure of association which has been employed extensively in

[1] For a description of Guttman scaling, see Duncan MacRae Jr., *Issues and Parties in Legislative Voting: Methods of Statistical Analysis* (New York: Harper, 1970), 15–38; John P. McIver and Edward G. Carmine, *Unidimensional Scaling* (Sage University Paper series on Quantitative Applications in the Social Sciences, 07–024, Beverly Hills, Cal., 1981), 40–71. The SPSS-X suite of programs was employed for all computations.

[2] The treatment of absences and errors follows McIver and Carmine, *Unidimensional Scaling*, 41–4, 51–3. So do the procedures for determining scalarity. See ibid., 47–51.

roll call analysis.[3] The resulting matrix of associations was then subjected to cluster analysis, which has the advantage of presenting results in a form which remains closer to the original data and may well have made sense to the legislators themselves The technique employed here was the group average method, which generally produces well-rounded clusters and avoids "chaining."[4] The clusters were in turn inspected to identify sets of roll calls which form cumulative scales. However, the clusters themselves may be regarded as describing broader policy dimensions which incorporate a larger number of related roll calls and subjects of legislation. Criteria for defining such policy dimensions have been developed by Aage Clausen and Barbara Sinclair. The individual scores produced in this fashion turn out, in fact, to be closely correlated with those derived from the smaller unidimensional scales. In either case we are dealing with a classification "inferred from voting behavior" which is "based on the legislators'" *own* sorting and labeling of roll calls according to *their* categories of policy content, or policy concepts."[5]

[3] For the formula and properties of Yule's Q, see MacRae, *Issues and Parties*, 41–51.
[4] For a discussion of cluster analysis, see Mark S. Aldenderfer and Roger K. Blashfield, *Cluster Analysis* (Sage University Paper series on Quantitative Applications in the Social Sciences, 07–044, Beverly Hills, Cal., 1984); Brian Everitt, *Cluster Analysis* (London: Heinemann, 1974). The group average method is described in ibid., 15; Alexander and Blashfield, *Cluster Analysis*, 40–3.
[5] Aage Clausen, *How Congressmen Decide* (New York: S. Martin's Press, 1973), 22. See also Barbara Sinclair, "Party Realignment and the Transformation of the Political Agenda: The House of Representatives, 1925–1939," *American Political Science Review* 71 (1977): 940–53.

Index

Abbott, Ernest H., 224
Adams, Henry Brooks, 255
Adams, Henry Carter, 53.n.8
Adams, Henry Cullen, 21, 22, 47, 59, 195
Adams, Samuel Hopkins, 165, 167
Adamson, William C., 105, 243
AFL. *See* American Federation of Labor
Aldrich, Nelson W., 227, 257
  personal characteristics, 30, 31, 36
  and pure food, 166
  and railroad regulation, 58, 63, 67, 68, 69, 86
  and tariff, 174–175
Alger, Russell A., 31
Allen, Howard W., 219, 230
Allison, William Boyd, 32, 34, 35, 36, 62, 68, 69, 71, 161, 171
American Federation of Labor (AFL)
  "blacklist," 106
  in campaign of 1906, 106–108
  in campaign of 1908, 116
  Congress unresponsive to, 98–99, 119, 270
  endorsement of Democratic candidates, 99, 104, 105–107, 115, 243
  and labor injunctions, 109–110, 113, 114, 116
  Labor Representation Committee, 106
  legislative demands, 98, 117, 243
  political strategy, 97–99, 100–101
  Protest to Congress, 113, 118
  reasons for political action, 98–99
  voluntarism, 124

  See also Bill of Grievances; Gompers, Samuel
American Federationist, 98, 101, 104, 106
American Medical Association, 166, 263
American state
  administrative agencies in, 5, 46, 248–249
  in comparative terms, 265–266
  Congress, role in formation, 3, 9–10, 269–275
  courts, role of, 266–267
  development of, 2–3, 6, 265–266
  expenditures, 265
  and labor relations, 99–100, 123–124
  limitations of, 6, 265–268
  and political parties, 4, 5–6, 274
  policymakers, role in formation, 9, 51, 263–264
  progressive reform and, 3, 7, 261–265
  reasons for expansion, 6–9, 156, 261–265
  reasons for weakness, 268–270
  and sectionalism, 8, 261–262
  See also regulation, federal
Anderson, Sydney, 220
Anthony, Daniel R., Jr., 22
Appalachian and White Mountains Forest.
  See under conservation
Arizona, admission of, 239
Ashbrook, William A., 106
Atlantic Monthly, 144

Babcock, Joseph W., 133, 151
Bacon, Augustus O., 74, 84, 243, 244, 248, 249–250, 253